WORLD YEARBOOK OF EDUCATION 1993

World Yearbook of Education 1982/83
Computers and Education
Edited by Jacquetta Megarry, David R F Walker,
Stanley Nisbet and Eric Hoyle

World Yearbook of Education 1984
Women and Education
Edited by Sandra Acker, Jacquetta Megarry,
Stanley Nisbet and Eric Hoyle

World Yearbook of Education 1985
Research, Policy and Practice
Edited by John Nisbet, Jacquetta Megarry and Stanley Nisbet

World Yearbook of Education 1986
The Management of Schools
Edited by Eric Hoyle and Agnes McMahon

World Yearbook of Education 1987
Vocational Education
Edited by John Twining, Stanley Nisbet and Jacquetta Megarry

World Yearbook of Education 1988
Education for the New Technologies
Edited by Duncan Harris (Series Editor)

World Yearbook of Education 1989
Health Education
Edited by Chris James, John Balding and Duncan Harris (Series Editor)

World Yearbook of Education 1990
Assessment and Evaluation
Edited by Chris Bell and Duncan Harris (Series Editor)

World Yearbook of Education 1991
International Schools and International Education
Edited by Patricia L Jonietz (Guest Editor) and Duncan Harris (Series Editor)

World Yearbook of Education 1992
Urban Education
Edited by David Coulby, Crispin Jones and Duncan Harris (Series Editor)

WORLD YEARBOOK
OF EDUCATION 1993

SPECIAL
NEEDS
EDUCATION

Edited by Peter Mittler, Ron Brouillette and Duncan Harris (Series Editor)

KOGAN
PAGE

London • Philadelphia

First published in 1993

Kogan Page Limited
120 Pentonville Road
London N1 9JN

© 1993 Kogan Page Limited and contributors

British Library Cataloguing in Publication Data

A CIP record for this book is available from the British Library.

ISBN 0 7494 0854 5

Typeset by DP Photosetting, Aylesbury, Bucks
Printed and bound in Great Britain by
Biddles Ltd, Guildford

Contents

List of contributors

Foreword

With the end of 1992, the world concluded the United Nations Decade of Disabled Persons. One of the objectives of the Decade was to expand educational opportunities for half a billion people worldwide who have a physical, mental and/or sensory impairment. Disabled people share the right of 'Education for All' with their fellow citizens. However, most of the disabled people are denied this right.

In spite of the proclamation of 1992 as the International Year of Literacy, the global problem of mass illiteracy requires considerable imaginative efforts to resolve. For the approximately one billion illiterate people in the world, the right to education guaranteed in the Universal Declaration of Human Rights is not yet a reality.

Illiteracy is particularly prevalent among disabled people and constitutes for them a double disadvantage. In addition to being disabled, they are isolated by illiteracy. The international community needs to pay special attention to the educational needs of disabled people and, where needed, to take measures to enable them to enjoy equal access to all levels of education.

Education moulds and builds a new and better society, a society that can face the challenges of life with courage and conscience. Disabled people need to be liberated socially and economically, and to have self-confidence, self-reliance and the ability to work towards their own development.

To achieve these educational needs, we need to develop the capacity to change our own attitudes and the attitudes and behaviours of society; negative attitudes have in many ways isolated disabled people from education, social and cultural life.

Education and literacy are the responsibility of all. A literate society results from collective efforts by governments, non-governmental organizations and international agencies through formal education carried out in schools and non-formal education taking place in the community. Education is not a matter of financial resources as much as it is a question of commitment and political will. The political relationship between education and disability has been one of disorder rather than of harmony and understanding. While the world claims to be striving to wipe out illiteracy, people with disabilities seem to be ignored and neglected as if they were not part of the same society.

Education must be geared towards empowering marginalized populations in their liberation struggle for equalization of opportunities. To be educated is to become liberated from the constraints of dependency. To be educated is to maintain a voice and to participate meaningfully and assertively in decisions that affect one's life. To be educated is to become politically conscious and critically aware and to demystify social reality. Education provides access to written knowledge, and knowledge is power.

This 1993 *World Yearbook of Education*'s focus on 'Perspectives on Special Education' is timely and highly important. The publication will offer its readers current thinking and practices that can lead to the liberation of disabled people through education and literacy.

Khalfan H Khalfan

Editors' Preface

The goal of Education For All, set by the United Nations at the 1990 Jomtien (Thailand) Conference and adopted by heads of state at the *World Summit for Children* in the same year, confronts all of us with the fundamental challenge of including children with disabilities in the education system of all nations. Such children are still too often excluded from schooling or offered only inferior forms of education. There is no country where they are afforded the priority or the resources which their needs and their families demand.

The aim of this book is to record, analyse and celebrate positive signs of growth and development in the field of special needs education but with particular reference to children with significant disabilities. The special education theme was selected for the 1993 edition of *The World Yearbook of Education* in synchrony with the ending of the UN Decade of Disabled Persons, 1983 to 1992. The Decade carries the theme 'Full participation and Equality'; the same one that steered the successful 1981 UN International Year of Disabled Persons. The Decade has been guided by the World Programme for Action Concerning Disabled Persons, a set of objectives leading to 'Full participation and Equality'. Ways to implement these objectives as highlighted in Khalfan's foreword run central throughout many of the chapters in this volume.

Writing with an international readership in mind, the focus is largely on children and young people with disabilities causing various degrees of difficulty in learning or in benefiting from the ordinary school curriculum without additional support. These difficulties may be related to physical, sensory or intellectual impairments, or to social and emotional difficulties which may make adjustment to school problematic. But difficulties can also arise from the failure of the school to provide an appropriate learning environment for the individual pupil.

In some countries, particularly the United Kingdom and the United States, the terms 'special educational needs' and 'exceptional' have been used for over a decade to describe an average of around 17 to 20 per cent of pupils who may at any time or at some time experience difficulties in learning and who may need additional help either from the school or from outside agencies. Current thinking emphasizes that the definition of special educational needs is both relative and interactive. In other words, the same child can have special educational needs in one school but not in another, if the first school is able to meet the child's needs and the second is not. Furthermore, it is increasingly accepted that schools, too, can create and complicate special educational needs – by the inaccessibility of the curriculum and physical environment to the whole range of its pupils; by failing to communicate the nature of learning tasks to pupils; by individual lessons which do not reach all the pupils in a class because the concepts or the language of the teacher are simply not understood (Ainscow, Chapter 19, this volume). The origins of learning difficulties thus lie in complex interactions between the child and the environments in which he or she is living and learning. Clearly, these include the home and community as well as the school.

Surveys of current developments by UNESCO's Special Education Unit and other agencies suggest that some progress is being made, though the number of children whose needs are being met is still extremely low (less than 2 per cent) in many countries. At the international level, United Nations agencies such as UNESCO, UNICEF and WHO have done what they can with limited resources to provide guidance materials and examples of good practice and have used their influence to help governments to reconsider their priorities. At national level, governments are increasingly taking over from voluntary agencies responsibility for the education of children with disabilities, with the result that more children are being given access to education either in special or ordinary schools. Parents and family members are forming voluntary organizations and lobbying for better educational facilities, occasionally providing such facilities themselves. More attention is also being given to the preparation and training of teachers and to the development of closer working links with families. In most countries, there is now greater awareness of the needs of such children and a commitment to provide access to whatever educational resources are available, however limited these may be.

The aim of this book is to highlight these and other developments and to subject them to critical scrutiny from a variety of conceptual backgrounds. Each of the four chapters in Part 1 (International perspectives) and Miles and Miles in Part 2 provide an overview of current issues, largely from an international stance, though inevitably coloured by the authors' experience in their own countries. The opening chapter (Mittler) seeks to place educational issues in a wider perspective by considering available information on the causes of disability and the extent to which they could be and are being prevented, as well as reviewing recent estimates on prevalence. It also broaches the problematic nature of providing and resourcing education for disabled children in ordinary schools. The complex issues of development of services are further elaborated by Hegarty and by Brouillette and are set in a wider context by Herr's contribution concerning the translation of human rights declarations into national legislation.

Part 2 focuses more sharply on specific disabilities and needs, beginning with a chapter by Christine and Mike Miles on the education of children with moderate and severe learning difficulties which draws on their knowledge of cultural traditions, philosophies and practice in developing countries, particularly northwest Pakistan. This is followed by accounts of progress in the education of children with visual impairments (Best and McCall) and hearing impairments (Joutselainen).

Part 3 summarizes key developments at regional level for Western and

Eastern Europe (New Democracies) (Daunt), Asia (Kohli), Africa (Kisanji) and Ibero-America (Malbrán and Mac Donagh). It also provides country studies from the USA and Canada (Martin) and Australia and New Zealand (Ward).

Part 4 is concerned with key transitional stages of education, specifically early childhood (J Brouillette, Thorburn and Yamaguchi) and transition from school to work in developed countries belonging to the Organization for Economic Cooperation and Development (Evans).

Finally, Part 5 looks in greater depth at a variety of issues and problems concerned with access to education for children with disabilities and difficulties. First, O'Toole provides a critical survey of the world-wide movement towards community-based rehabilitation as a background to schooling at local level. This is followed by Baine's analysis of questions of access to schooling and the appropriateness of school curricula to the needs of disabled children. Wedell analyses a range of strategies for school integration which have been developed in various countries and re-examines themes concerned with education in ordinary schools outlined in the first section by Hegarty. Ainscow introduces implications for teacher education of the new dimension of 'inclusive' education which reconceptualizes the issue of integration in a wider framework, involving the radical reform of the school and of the curriculum in such a way as to make them fully accessible to all pupils in the school, including those with disabilities and difficulties, however caused. Finally, Brouillette speculates on the future of special education planning and provision in the light both of positive future trends lead by the UN World Programme of Action Concerning Disabled Persons such as information technology as well as barriers arising from low priorities and lack of resources at a time of world recession.

Our conclusion is one of cautious optimism about the future, based on our knowledge and first-hand experience of trends in a number of developing and developed countries, our continuing contacts with professionals, parents and students from many regions of the world and above all on what we have learned from disabled persons themselves about their right to education, their ability to learn and develop like anyone else and their determination to have a say in the running of their own lives. They are more determined than anyone to achieve 'Full participation and Equality': the international goal of a Society for All.

Peter Mittler and Ron Brouillette

Part 1: International perspectives

1. Childhood disability: a global challenge

Peter Mittler

A global village?

It has become a truism to say that we live in a global village. Television pictures penetrate instantly to remote parts of the world. Most rural areas have access to a transistor radio; telephones, telefax and electronic mail can bring us into instant communication with people tens of thousands of miles away.

It is ironic that we live in a world capable of such technological achievements, a world which can put people into space and thinks nothing of spending billions on means of destruction but which fails to provide for the education of its children and for the prevention of avoidable illness and disability.

Is it idealistic to suggest that we must insist on greater priority being given to meeting the needs of all children in all countries and that this vision must include children who are disadvantaged by lack of schooling, poverty, ill health, malnutrition and disability? Is it realistic to ask for a world movement to secure a better future for our children in the 21st than in the 20th century?

A vision of excellence for the world's disabled children would include·

- greater priority for prevention of avoidable disability;
- early identification and intervention to help children and support families;
- closer partnership with parents;
- the integration of children into their local school and the development of a learning environment suited to their needs;
- relevant preparation for adult life and participation in all community services;
- learning to listen to children with disabilities and giving them more opportunities for exercising choice and decision-making so that they can gradually exercise more control over their own lives and over their environment.

We know very little about children with disabilities in other countries, their day-to-day lives and aspirations, the attitudes, beliefs and values of their local communities towards disabled children and their families. What are their chances of attending their local schools (if there is one)? Are they accepted by other children, by teachers and by other parents? How relevant are the experiences provided by the school to their individual needs?

Prevalence and types of disability

Global totals and national variations

The original United Nations estimates prepared for the 1981 International Year of Disabled Persons suggested that one in ten of the world's population was disabled and that the total number of disabled people in the world would rise from 400 million in 1980 to well over 600 million by the end of the century.

More recent evidence suggests that these figures were an over-estimate and that national figures vary dramatically. After studying disability statistics collected by the World Health Organization and other United Nations agencies, Helander (1993) concluded that the global average for the prevalence of moderate and severe disability is around 5.2 per cent, made up of 7.7 per cent for developed countries and 4.5 per cent for less developed regions. On these figures, the total number of disabled people in the early 1990s is probably nearer 93 million for the former and 183 million for the latter – ie, a total of 276 million, rather than the 500 million projected in earlier forecasts. Prevalence estimates from 55 countries varied from 0.2 to 21 per cent for all age groups.

Clearly, such variations reflect different definitions of disability, as well as 'true' differences in prevalence. Current estimates provided by 13 countries in the Arab region as part of a United Nations regional review of the World Programme of Action in Favour of Disabled Persons, ranged between 0.17 and 2.20 per cent of the population (Brouillette and Mittler, 1992).

The projected rapid growth in population, particularly in the less developed regions of the world, will inevitably be paralleled by an increase in numbers as people live longer and as health services improve in the poorer regions of the world. Helander (1993) forecasts an increase from 183 million to 435 million disabled people by the year 2025 in less developed regions and a corresponding increase from 93 to 138 million in more developed regions in the same period. These figures reflect percentage increases from 4.5 to 6.1 and 7.7 to 10.2 respectively.

Table 1.1 summarizes currently available information on the prevalence of moderate and severe disabilities of adults and children in developing countries.

Table 1.1 *Global estimates of prevalence of observed ranges of moderate and severe disability in developing countries (Helander 1993)*

Type of limitation	Prevalence in %
Moving difficulty	2.5–3.0
Seeing difficulty	0.5–1.0
Hearing/speech difficulty	0.5–1.0
Learning difficulty	0.2–0.4
Chronic fits	0.3–0.6
Strange behaviour	0.1–0.3
Feeling difficulty (hands/feet)	0.1–0.2
Combinations of above	0.2–0.3
TOTAL	4%–5%

Children

At one time, UNICEF publicity suggested that one in ten of the world's children was disabled and that one family in four was in some way affected by disability. It is now thought that the true figures are considerably lower than this. If we include only children with moderate and severe levels of disability, Helander (1993) suggests that numbers in developing countries will rise from 31 to 40 million between 1990 and 2025 and will remain fairly static at around six million in developed countries.

But the *proportion* of the world's disabled children in developing countries will actually increase, as advances in health care and primary prevention lead to the survival of children who would previously have died at birth or in the first few months of life. Many of the surviving children will have profound and multiple impairments; meeting the needs of these children presents new challenges for the family, the local community and for service planners and providers.

It is not only the scale but also the pattern of disabilities found among children in developing countries which is different from that familiar to Westerners. Sensory impairments are much more common. Many more children become disabled as a result of infections such as meningitis and encephalitis, as well as from severe and persistent malnutrition, iodine deficiency, head injuries and as a direct result of armed conflict and civil disturbances.

Significant degrees of disability are directly caused by conditions of gross deprivation and neglect. No one will forget the pictures of abandoned children in the orphanages of Eastern Europe whose physical and mental growth has been stunted by such lack of basic human care and stimulation. There are countries where children in institutions are still lying in cots without contact with another human being for most of the day. Others are tied to the furniture while their parents work in the fields. There are children in all societies who are disabled as a direct result of drug or alcohol abuse even before they are born and we are now becoming aware of children who are victims of HIV infection.

But it should not be assumed that nothing is being done to help such children in developing countries (Brouillette, Chapter 3, this volume). The majority are being looked after by their families to the best of their abilities, though with varying degrees of support from their local community. Furthermore, there is more 'casual' school integration than is commonly believed. A survey carried out in rural areas of Pakistan showed that many disabled children are attending their neighbourhood or village school, simply because they are local children and because their parents took them there (Miles, 1985; Miles and Miles, Chapter 5, this volume).

Preventing disability

The World Summit for Children (1990) estimated that each day 40,000 children die from malnutrition and disease, including AIDS, from the lack of clean water and inadequate sanitation and from the effects of drug problems. Half a million mothers die each year from causes related to childbirth. Current UNICEF estimates provide the chilling statistic that each year 35 million children die and another 35 million become disabled.

Half of these deaths and disabilities are preventable by the use of knowledge already in our possession. Applying the knowledge we already have to the prevention of disability is not expensive. Much has been achieved already. The World Summit of leaders which met to discuss a comprehensive programme of targets for the world's children estimated that the five billion dollars needed to fund the whole of a comprehensive 22-target programme for children to the year 2000 amounted to what the world chooses to spend on armaments in ten days. The President of Ecuador has said that the cost of a single nuclear submarine would finance the entire educational budgets of 23 developing countries for a year. It is all a matter of priorities.

A great deal could be achieved through improvements in the basic health of communities, in the supply of clean water, sanitation and uncontaminated food. The means to reduce the impact of malnutrition are in our grasp. Immunization against common childhood diseases, oral rehydration therapy to combat the wasting effects of constant diarrhoea, the judicious use of vitamin A supplementation, antibiotics and even aspirin, the addition of iodine to salt where necessary, just keeping children with measles out of bright sunlight – these are all examples of measures within our grasp. Ensuring the health and nutrition of expectant mothers, training of traditional birth attendants to deal with neonatal asphyxia and to support mothers in breastfeeding and in basic hygiene would all contribute to the prevention of disability (Helander, 1993; Werner, 1982, 1987).

United Nations' estimates suggest that there are at least 70 million people in developing countries whose sight, movement or hearing could be restored at a unit cost of $15–40 (UNDP, 1991). Half a million children go blind every year, of whom 60 per cent die in childhood, leaving a total of about 1.5 million, of whom four-fifths live in the developing world (Wilson, 1992).

We must celebrate such progress as has been made. For example, the World Health Organization reports that immunization coverage among infants has reached 85 per cent for polio, and over 80 per cent for diphtheria, pertussis, tetanus, measles and tuberculosis. Some half a million cases of polio and 84 million cases of measles are being prevented every year. Eye camps in Africa and Asia have already enabled millions to have their sight restored by means of a simple cataract operation (WHO, 1991).

Early intervention and community-based rehabilitation

Where childhood disability cannot be prevented, our efforts must be focused on early identification and on family support and empowerment, beginning as soon as a child is born or suspected of having a disability. Early intervention projects such as the Portage programme represent an innovative approach to home-based support of the whole family which has now been adapted and used in many developing countries (J. Brouillette *et al.*, this volume). Similarly, the World Health Organization's development of community-based rehabilitation (CBR) has also been highly influential in developing low cost methods of rehabilitation and family support (Helander, 1993; Helander *et al.*, 1989). The work of David Werner (1982; 1987) pioneered a community-based approach both to primary health care and to community-based rehabilitation (O'Toole, this volume).

For educationalists, a major target must be that CBR workers, who are generally health trained, should join forces with local teachers. They need to plan together to consider how a disabled child can be prepared to attend the local school, what adaptations may have to be made and what obstacles may need to be overcome.

Empowering parents and families

What we have learned from the early intervention projects throughout the world is that programmes that have involved parents and families have consistently achieved better outcomes for children. The lessons learned from the early intervention programmes such as Portage and from the community-based rehabilitation reports throughout the world is that we might all rethink the nature of our relationship with families and learn to form new bonds of partnership. However good we think our relationships with parents, there is always scope for development; at any rate, that would be the view of most parents.

In the past, we talked about collaboration or involvement of parents; then we realized that we needed to aim for a partnership of equals. Perhaps the vision for the future should be one of empowering parents to insist on an education which is suited to their childrens' needs, an education to which their children have a right and an entitlement.

There is a universal commitment to the principles of partnership with parents but practice frequently lags behind. A UNESCO survey of partnership between parents and professionals which we carried out with the help of parent societies in 70 countries highlighted some examples of good practice but also revealed many examples of parents feeling that they were not receiving basic information about their child, not being involved in discussion and decision-making and not sharing in the teaching of their child with the teachers and other professionals involved (Mittler *et al.*, 1986).

We need to reappraise the whole basis of our relationships with parents; to see them as equals and as partners, to listen to them and consult them from the outset, not only about their child but about the nature of our programmes and what we have to offer. This applies equally to all countries but particularly to societies where few or no resources are available to disabled children.

Towards education for all

Today, over 100 million children are without basic education; two-thirds of these children are girls. One in four adults in the world cannot read or write; again, two-thirds are women. Around half the world's children fail to complete four years of primary education. Boys have twice as much chance of becoming literate as girls, despite the evidence that 'female literacy is probably the best investment that any nation can make in its future health and well being' (Grant, 1991).

We might think that slow but definite progress is being made in providing education for the world's children. But Federico Mayor, Director-General of UNESCO is quoted by Grant (1991) as saying that:

> we have witnessed an unprecedented halt in the growth of basic educational services and a stagnation and deterioration of educational quality. In nearly half of the developing countries, the goal of universal primary education is now receding rather than drawing nearer.

Contrast this with the sheer scale of need for all children. Given the rise in the world's population of children, the number of school places will need to rise from 300 million in 1980 to between 500 and 600 million by the end of the century.

Against this sombre background affecting all children, how can we hope to gain access to quality education for the worlds's disabled children 'who are the most in need of education but are the least likely to receive it, wherever they live?' (Hegarty this volume).

In many developing countries, only a minority of non-disabled children attend any form of school (Thorburn and Marfo, 1990); classes may have up to 100 children and be staffed by teachers who have only just left school themselves. In such circumstances, it is not surprising that some schools may be unwilling to take disabled children or that some parents prefer to keep their children at home, working in the fields or looking after younger children. This is especially so in the case of girls.

In countries where a significant number of children do not attend any form of school, or drop out after three or four years, the issue of integrated education for disabled children has to be seen in a wider perspective. Various official estimates suggest that perhaps one disabled child out of a hundred attends any form of school in most African and Asian countries. Such provision as exists is generally in towns and cities, often organized by parent groups or voluntary organizations and is restricted to those that can pay for it. Reaching the unreached is therefore the major challenge for the rest of the decade and for the 21st century.

Although countries are at vastly different starting points, there is evidence of some degree of consensus on long-term goals and some encouraging signs for the future. Whether or not these opportunities are realized depends on positive public and community attitudes, based on continued and forceful advocacy and disseminated examples of good practice showing what can be done (ILSMH, 1990a).

Positive signs

Despite the chasm which exists between the rhetoric and the reality, we can note a number of positive indications which may bring us closer to the vision and which certainly deserve support at all levels.

International support

International agencies such as the United Nations, UNESCO and UNICEF all have a strong commitment to encouraging governments to meet the needs of disabled children and adults and to increase their activities in this field (Mittler,

1992a). The International Year of Disabled Persons in 1981 helped not only to increase public awareness in many countries but also led to significant developments in provision for disabled people. This was followed by the World Programme of Action and the Decade of Disabled Persons which finished in 1992. The UN has recently adopted a Convention on the Rights of Children (1989). This Convention is binding on the 130 governments that have already ratified it. Article 23 refers to the rights of disabled children to have access to ordinary schools and to the health and welfare resources of the country.

UNESCO and UNICEF have done a great deal with limited budgets to stimulate national and regional projects for disabled children in developing countries. UNESCO has issued low-cost publications on aspects of education and also provides small sums in support of educational equipment, books and materials to schools and parent groups by Co-Action, a scheme which avoids the usual bureaucracy of going through governments.

Another strand of activities and support comes from international non-governmental organizations such as the International League of Societies for Persons with Mental Handicap, Rehabilitation International, Cerebral Palsy International, the Word Blind Union and the World Federation of the Deaf. For example, ILSMH has organized a number of regional training workshops for parents and professionals in pre-school, school and vocational education. These have been funded by UN agencies and other international donors. Disabled Peoples International has gone from strength to strength since its establishment in 1981 and has exerted a major positive influence both on UN agencies and on national governments in promoting equal opportunities and the rights of disabled persons to participate in policy-making and implementation at all levels.

Mainstreaming for all?

Ease of international communication carries a certain risk of a new kind of colonialism which takes the form of exporting philosophies and practices which have been developed in one region but which will not necessarily be appropriate to others.

For example, 'experts' sometimes tell developing countries that they have a golden opportunity to avoid the mistakes made by industrialized countries in setting up special schools by planning for an integrated education system from the outset. These experts are by no means all from industrialized countries. Some of them come from developing countries but have been so impressed by what they have seen and read about special education practice during anything ranging from a brief visit to a four-year doctoral programme in an industrialized country, that they wish for nothing more than to export the local school system to their own settings.

But how relevant to children in developing countries are the issues which preoccupy us in North America and Europe – mainstreaming, education in the least restrictive environment, individual educational plans, targeted funding, the use of the courts to enforce rights of access, quality training programmes for teachers and a host of other imperatives? To some, such issues may seem an irrelevant luxury when the day-to-day concerns of families with a disabled child are with the basic necessities of food and drink, the beliefs and superstitions of neighbours about disability and their inability to secure a school place for their child. As Sir John Wilson (1992) has argued, 'Integration can seem a bleak prospect to a blind boy in a Calcutta beggars' guild or in a river blindness community'.

The proliferation of aid and support programmes forces us to confront issues about the advice which is being given to developing countries. Is such advice always based on experience of living there, knowing something of its social systems and values, its attitudes to disabled people and the nature of its school system?

Transplants from other cultures and societies, even when cemented with money, may not last beyond the last cheque or the departure of the last volunteer. There are a number of examples of aid programmes which have led to model services in some developing countries, with the donor agency agreeing a timetable for their phased withdrawal, in parallel with increasing local involvement. But all too often, such programmes do not prove to be sustainable, resulting in disappointment and frustration.

In countries where the majority of non-disabled children are not attending school, it is not surprising that parents are likely to press for special schools, run either by themselves or with the support of public or private funds. They may well argue that such schools will be under their own overall control, the classes may be smaller and their children are more likely to receive more specialist attention suited to their individual needs.

Even countries committed to integration have argued the need for a small number of well-resourced special schools, to provide specialist services, a place where teachers can be trained and perhaps a base from which children can be individually integrated into ordinary schools wherever this is possible. Such schools can also form a convenient focus for local, national or international fund-raising.

Government responsibility

UNESCO (1988) has reported that in 48 out of 58 countries which they surveyed, responsibility for the education of all disabled children now rests with education departments both at national and state levels, rather than with health or social welfare agencies or with non-governmental organizations (NGOs) or with no one at all. More ministries of education now have divisions concerned with special education and try to ensure that special education issues are included in policy development for all other divisions, such as pre-school, primary, secondary, tertiary and adult education, as well as in the appropriate curriculum development sections and in all branches of teacher education. But some of these countries are still unable to provide for children with severe mental retardation, with the result that such children remain at home without the stimulus of learning opportunities and contact with other children which can be provided by schools.

In other countries, the government prefers to fund private and independent schools to provide a service, either by paying teachers' salaries or by means of a direct grant per pupil. Such an arrangement is better than nothing but is a long way from providing education in the same setting as other children. Not only is this contrary to principles of normalization but it also makes it difficult to negotiate the return of such children into mainstream schools, all the more so if they have been following a different curriculum.

Commitment to integrated education

Most countries, however limited their services, express a commitment in principle to the education of disabled children in ordinary schools; but putting such principles into practice is problematic. Indeed, there are few countries, whether developing or developed, where high quality, properly planned and resourced integrated education can be said to be in place. We have slogans, rhetoric and fine principles in plenty but we are still lamentably short on practice.

In Europe, Italy legislated for a radical approach to mainstreaming by ordering the closure of special schools and insisting that all children, including those with profound and multiple disabilities, were placed in the ordinary class. Although doubts have been expressed about the quality of the education which they receive, there is wholehearted support for the social benefits of school integration for all children.

In Spain, there is a large pilot scheme with a 25 per cent reduction in class size when two disabled children are integrated, together with a guaranteed support team of teachers, psychologists or therapists.

In many countries, including Britain, large numbers of mobile support teachers are supporting children in mainstream schools who were previously in special schools. They work with teachers as well as with children, suggesting ways in which the curriculum can be modified to make it more accessible to all children. The focus is on curriculum reform and adaptation as much as on learning support for the individual child.

In developing countries, there are many encouraging examples of disabled children attending ordinary schools. Even though they tend to be in separate classes, these can provide a springboard for fuller social and educational integration.

Children with disabilities can be supported in a variety of ways in the ordinary class. There are reports of buddy systems, peer tutoring, the use of volunteers, including parents and family members (Baine, this volume). The number of children involved in such programmes is still very small but the fact that it can be done for a few suggests that it could be done for many others as well.

Preparation for adult life

One way of thinking about the relevance of the curriculum is to take as our starting point the day-to-day life of a disabled adult and ask ourselves what schools can contribute to enable their pupils to realize the vision of being accepted as valued citizens in their local communities.

Such a vision is no different for disabled people than for all of us – a place to live; a job that brings economic independence from others or, failing that, access to a fair welfare system; access to the whole range of community resources and services and the chance to enter into satisfying relationships with others. The

United Nations Declaration on Human Rights applies to disabled people as much as to anyone else.

In reality, the lives of adults with disabilities are generally bleak throughout the world. In some countries, disabled people are seen only as vagrants and beggars. In others, they lead a marginal existence on the edge of villages and towns and are treated as outcasts. Many disabled people in Western countries are living below the poverty line and very few are in full-time paid employment. Even in the few countries where they are in receipt of social welfare payments, most still lack the means to follow leisure pursuits such as sport and recreation and can barely afford to use public transport (where there is any).

To what extent, then, can schools prepare a disabled child to make a valued contribution to the community? In many countries this means looking after young children, herding animals, drawing water from a well, selling goods in the market place (Baine, 1988, and this volume). Some disabled children will learn these skills from their parents simply by watching and participating. Children with a significant degree of intellectual impairment may need more systematic and structured teaching (Miles and Miles, this volume).

Most special schools and classes give priority to ensuring that pupils become competent in the basic living skills, such as dressing, eating, washing and toileting. Many also concentrate on social independence skills, such as using money, shopping, budgeting and 'survival cooking' and also in the use of language and communication skills. But relatively few schools seem to spend very much time on helping their students to anticipate and cope with some of the harassment and discrimination which they will encounter. Assertiveness training of the kind that is given to other groups experiencing discrimination and victimization can be based on real experiences in the lives of these young people or be carried out through simulation and role play. For example, how might a wheelchair user respond to being asked to leave a sports ground, cinema or place of entertainment on the grounds that other people would be upset by the presence of a disabled person? Similarly, how many schools try to help their older students understand welfare entitlements or at least to learn where and from whom they can obtain assistance in making applications for welfare support?

Employment is the key to participation and integration into the community. At a time of world recession, we need to rethink our school and pre-vocational programmes to provide more effective preparation and direct training for employment (Evans, this volume). Many of the activities found in so-called pre-vocational programmes throughout the world are basically art and craft rather than vocational.

Traditional rehabilitation practice emphasizes step-by-step increases in competence and exposure to real life demands. More recently, this approach has been stood on its head. The disabled person is placed directly into a normal work or housing environment but is given a great deal of support in adapting to that environment. In the field of housing, for example, some countries are abandoning the notion of hostels and halfway houses between institutions and ordinary houses and placing people in ordinary housing from the outset but with maximum living-in support. This is then gradually reduced as the individual becomes more competent. Similarly, individuals with mental retardation are placed directly into work but with a high level of support to help them to learn what they have to do in the work setting but also to learn to adapt to the social demands of work (ILSMH, 1990b).

Empowering staff

The visions of excellence which have been outlined here have all been achieved, at least in part, in some areas of the world, not always the richest or most advanced. If they are to come within the reach of the majority, a new approach is needed to the development, training and empowerment of staff who work with special needs populations of all ages.

All countries, whatever the stage of development they have reached, need to reappraise their manpower development strategy. Without adequate professional training and continuous updating of knowledge, we are in danger of abandoning tomorrow's children to yesterday's ideas and methods. No matter how clear our vision of what we want to achieve and how schools and services should develop, progress depends on the attitudes, knowledge, skills and understanding of all those who are in day-to-day contact with children with disabilities (Mittler, 1991).

Each country and each locality needs a clearly defined strategy for manpower development. This starts with those who are in day-to-day contact with special needs populations – not only teachers but parents, family members and volunteers. Such training should be provided mainly in the work place. Community-based rehabilitation and Portage programmes are examples of low-cost, low-technology, locally-based and locally-supported training. Most of these people have previously been unreached by training opportunities. Instead, advanced training has been provided for senior and supervisory staff, often far away from the work place and sometimes in another country with entirely different systems of education and service provision. Some staff are then promoted out of special education and are never seen again; others are frustrated by their inability to put into practice what they have learned from their course or from fellow practitioners, even when these lessons are relevant to their own practice.

We also have to ensure – if necessary, by legislation – that an element concerned with special education is included in the training of teachers and other professionals, such as doctors, nurses, therapists, psychologists, social workers and administrators (Mittler, 1992b). There may be time to provide only a degree of awareness of the main issues and possibly how to obtain help for a child with special needs. But experience of such training for new teachers suggests that students are highly interested and keen to learn; indeed a surprisingly large number have worked with disabled or disadvantaged children before training to become teachers.

Similarly, all serving teachers, as well as other professionals, need to be exposed to short but relevant in-service training to bring them up to date with new developments, to provide examples of good practice in such areas as mainstreaming, curriculum adaptation, the use of computer technology and microelectronics to help disabled children control their environment and express choice and decision-making.

The UNESCO surveys indicated that very few countries provided opportunities for special education awareness in either initial or in-service training. Such limited training as was available was based on the model of a segregated special school. Although it is still important to train specialist teachers, the time has surely come when training courses need to provide preparation for teachers who will be working in ordinary schools. In response to this situation, UNESCO has launched a major in-service training initiative involving eight countries (Ainscow, 1991, and this volume). The project is underpinned by a clear philosophy which emphasizes that learning difficulties do not always lie in the child but can be caused or complicated by the school – for example, by the inaccessibility of its curriculum or of a particular lesson or by textbooks or teacher language that are out of reach of the child. Meeting special educational needs is therefore not only a matter of working with the child but may call for a reform of the curriculum and of the policy and organization of the whole school.

Conclusions

If we look beyond our own country and our own immediate neighbourhood, we may be appalled by the sheer size of the task that faces families and professionals as they try to meet the needs of children with disabilities. At the same time, there are some encouraging signs of innovation which reflect a determination to make progress despite the obstacles. As we near the end of the century we should be working and thinking more internationally to achieve a vision of the kind of future which we would like to see for disabled children, a future to which they are entitled as a matter of right.

Eduard Shevardnadze, the former foreign minister of the former Soviet Union has said that 'a new political intellect is prevailing over the dark legacy of the past'. James Grant (1991) Executive Director of UNICEF, echoes this in saying:

Amid so many other pressing concerns, it is difficult to find time on the world's agenda for problems which, it may be argued, have always been with us and cannot be regarded as exceptional or urgent. But for the children who will unnecessarily fall to malnutrition, disease, disability and an early death in the decade ahead, and for the families of those children, such an argument carries very little weight. If the 21st century is to be a better one for mankind than the twentieth has been, then it is essential that the principle of first call for children becomes part of the new political intellect.

References

Ainscow, M (1991) 'Towards effective schools for all', in Upton, G (ed) *Staff Training and Special Educational Needs*, London: David Fulton.
Baine, D (1988) *Handicapped Children in Developing Countries: assessment, curriculum and instruction*, Edmonton: University of Alberta.
Brouillette, R and Mittler, P (1992) 'Implementation of the World Programme of Action Concerning Disabled Persons in Countries of the ECSWA Region', United Nations, Amman: Economic and Social Commission for Western Asia (unpublished report).

Grant, J (1991) *State of the World's Children 1991*, Oxford: UNICEF and Oxford University Press.

Helander, E (1993) *Prejudice and Dignity: an introduction to community based rehabilitation*, Geneva: United Nations Development Programme (in press).

Helander, E, Mendis, P, Nelson, G and Goerdt, A (1989) *Training Disabled Persons in the Community*, Geneva: WHO.

International League of Societies for Persons with Mental Handicap (1990a) *Education for All: helping people with learning difficulties to be full members of their communities*, Brussels: ILSMH.

International League of Societies for Persons with Mental Handicap (1990b) *Work Opportunities for People with Mental Handicap*, Brussels: ILSMH.

Miles, M (1985) *Action Study on Integration of Handicapped Children in Pakistan*, Peshawar: NW Frontier Province Mission Hospital.

Mittler, P (1991) 'Manpower development: a priority for the '90s', paper to conference of Asian Federation for Mental Retardation, Karachi, Pakistan, November.

Mittler, P (1992a) *Making the Most of the United Nations*, Brussels: International League of Societies for Persons with Mental Handicap.

Mittler, P (1992b) 'Preparing all initial teacher training students to teach children with special educational needs: a case study from England', *European Journal of Special Needs Education*, 7, 1–10.

Mittler, P, Mittler, H and McConachie, H (1986) *Working Together: guidelines on collaboration between professionals and parents of children and young people with disabilities*, Guides for Special Education No. 2, Paris: UNESCO.

Thorburn, M and Marfo, K (1990) *Approaches to Childhood Disability*, St John's: Project SEREDEC, Memorial University of Newfoundland.

UNESCO (1988) *Review of the Present Situation in Special Education*, Paris: UNESCO.

United Nations Development Programme/IMPACT (1991) *Disability Prevention: A Priority for the '90s*, UN Vienna: International Centre.

Werner, D (1982) *Where There is No Doctor*, Palo Alto, CA: Hesperian Foundation.

Werner, D (1987) *Disabled Village Children*, Palo Alto, CA: Hesperian Foundation.

Wilson, J (1992) 'Towards equality', keynote speech to 9th Quinquennial Conference of the International Council for Education of the Visually Handicapped, Bangkok, Thailand, July.

World Health Organization (1991) 'WHO's role in disability prevention', paper presented to UN Inter-agency meeting, Vienna, Austria.

World Summit for Children (1990) *World Declaration and Plan of Action on the Survival, Protection and Development of Children in the 1990s*, New York: United Nations.

2. Education of children with disabilities

Seamus Hegarty

Introduction

All children have the right to be educated. One of the tragedies of our time is that very many children are not educated – and have no opportunity to go to school. This is compounded by the scarcity of educational opportunities in adult life.

The failure to provide education for all children ranks alongside famine and war as a major indictment of the current political order. It is also a significant challenge to it. A world with the technological and economic resources to achieve instantaneous global communication and put people into space can hardly say that educating all its children is impossible.

This challenge has all the more force where children and young people with disabilities are concerned. Those with disabilities, who ironically have the greatest need of education, are the least likely to receive it. This is true of developed and developing countries alike. In developed countries many children with disabilities are formally excluded from the education system or receive less favourable treatment within it than other children, whereas in many developing countries the struggle to develop compulsory education for a majority of children takes precedence over meeting the special educational needs of those with disabilities.

Details of provision are given by Mittler (this volume). The stark reality underlying these figures is that the great majority of children and young people with disabilities do not receive an appropriate education – if indeed they are offered any education at all.

Basic principles

The basic principles underlying special education are very simple. Translating them into practice may be far from easy, but there is broad agreement on what they should be. The principles can be formulated in various ways; here they will be set out in terms of three rights:

1. the right to education;
2. the right to equality of opportunity;
3. the right to participate in society.

1. The right to education

The right of all children to education is enshrined in the United Nations Declaration of Human Rights and reiterated in many national policy statements. Regrettably, millions of children are not accorded this right. This fact does not weaken the right or reduce its relevance; indeed, it makes action to secure its universal implementation all the more urgent. Children with disabilities are a major group for whom this right has still to be won in effective terms. Many countries – and educational policy-makers – simultaneously accept the UN Declaration guaranteeing education for all and exclude children with disabilities from education. That is, to say the least, illogical. Either the UN Declaration is accepted in its sweeping simplicity and children with disabilities of whatever kind are brought into education, or the Declaration should be modified and tinkered with so that it fits the exigencies of current practice.

It is important to bear in mind that the right to education is a fundamental human right, something which each person has by virtue of the fact that they are human beings. In other words, it is not dependent on vocational or economic considerations. Education does of course make people more employable in a general way and can enhance their capacity to contribute to the economic well-being of the community, but neither of these is the reason why they are *entitled* to education. At a time when public expenditure is increasingly governed by market forces and instrumental views of education prevail, it is easy to lose sight of the inherent nature of the right to education. This is particularly significant where people with disabilities are concerned. Education may not succeed in making some people employable or economically self-sufficient, but that in no way reduces their entitlement to the resources that their education requires.

2. The right to equality of opportunity

Equality of opportunity raises very difficult questions. Like the right to education, the right to equality of educational opportunity is routinely accepted as a general principle and widely ignored in practice. The problem here is more than the customary gap between rhetoric and reality that is imposed by scarce resources and limited vision. Even where there is a commitment to implementing this right, it can be difficult to establish what is required in practice.

Equality of opportunity does not mean treating everybody in the same way. Thus, in education, equal educational treatment is not the answer. Children are not the same and should not be treated as if they were. Indeed, the principle of justice requires that they be treated unequally. As a simple example, consider the education of blind people: if equal treatment means being exposed, along with peers, to teaching with a high visual content, this is manifestly not giving them equality of educational opportunity. What is required is a means of translating the general principle of equal opportunity into concrete rights that are meaningful at the level of actual educational provision. Since children are different from each other, they must be treated in different ways in order to reach common goals. This brings the general principle down to the domain of practical decisions about pedagogy and resource allocation. These decisions can be extremely difficult in practice, particularly when teaching expertise and resources are in short supply. Some such framework, however, is essential both to moving advocacy for special education beyond placid generalities and to ensuring a meaningful place for special education at the level of actual educational provision.

3. The right to participate in society

This right is often expressed in negative terms – people should not be discriminated against or suffer restrictions on their lives over and above those common to other people. In education it has become commonplace to speak of educating children in the 'least restrictive environment'. These negative formulations abound because barriers and obstacles to participation are more evident and easier to pinpoint than actual participation.

As far as education is concerned, the right to participate means that children must not suffer needless restrictions – in their access to education, in the range of curriculum on offer or in the quality of teaching they receive. They should not, without good reason, be educated separately from their age peers. Expressed positively, this means that children have the right to attend ordinary schools and to participate in the normal activities of the school alongside age peers unless there are specific reasons to the contrary. Where it is judged necessary to educate children in a segregated special school, care must be taken to ensure that the nature of the education on offer matches the mainstream curriculum as much as possible and that the quality of teaching is at least as good as it would be if they went to an ordinary school.

Strategies to improve the provision of special education

This section sets out a number of strategies which policy-makers can adopt to improve the provision of special education in their countries. Much of the information on current practice at national level is drawn from a UNESCO survey conducted in 1986/7 (UNESCO, 1988); this will be referred to as the UNESCO Review.

Legislation

It may seem odd to start with legislation as a key strategy for improving special educational provision. Legislation is couched in generic terms and can be very distant from the point of implementation. There are several reasons, however, why appropriate legislation is of paramount importance. First, it can articulate and reinforce a country's policy on special education. Educational and social policies are usually more detailed and flexible than the legislation that underpins them. A legal framework can, however, hold the different elements of policy together, clarify ambiguities and resolve tensions between them. Second, legislation can help to secure resources, or the appropriate channelling of resources. Thus, legislation can be used to target expenditure on certain groups of children, it can require that provision be supported by certain administrative structures, it can insist on certain levels of teacher training and it can require that special educational provision be made in ordinary schools.

Passing laws of itself achieves nothing, and legislating for these desirable outcomes is in no way to guarantee that they will be realized. This brings in two further functions of legislation – to draw attention to any discrepancies between policy and practice, and to give ammunition to those who seek change. Take parental involvement in decision-making, for example. There is a lot of rhetoric about taking account of parents' views but in practice they are often ignored. Legislation that guarantees their right to be consulted on their child's assessment and any decisions taken as a consequence can help to narrow the gap between rhetoric and practice by ensuring that parents have redress in the event of disagreement.

Third, legislation can help to change attitudes. What is required by statute has more status than what is optional. A country that legislates for special educational provision confers legitimacy on that provision and makes it more likely that professionals, parents and the public will view it in a positive way.

It is worth noting that most countries in the UNESCO Review had legislation of some kind concerning the education of those with disabilities. (In a few cases pupils with disabilities were deemed to be included in the general legislation on education for all pupils.) Two-thirds of the countries referred to had new legislation under discussion or about to be introduced. This ranged from loosely formulated discussion of the need for various legislative developments, to definite plans to introduce regulations governing specific aspects of educational provision. A wide range of topics was covered – early intervention, family support, new curricula, developments in general education to facilitate integration, teacher training and administrative responsibility for mentally retarded children.

The Review noted the different legislative baselines of the different countries but identified two tentative trends none the less: a general acknowledgement of the need to underpin developments in provision with appropriate legislative action; and a tendency for the frameworks for special education and general education to move toward each other, albeit slowly.

The key elements of appropriate legislation have been implied above – clear statement of policy, coherent framework for provision, conduit of resources and guarantee of consumers' rights. In addition, special education legislation should be based on a correct understanding of disabilities and their educational implications. There is a great deal of outmoded thinking on disability and special education, and it is very unfortunate when these defective understandings are built into legislation. National legislation must take account of a country's stage of development, but limited resources do not justify adopting laws that will lead down blind alleys and foster inappropriate forms of provision.

Finally, legislation must be enforced. Instruments are mere ornaments unless they are used. Legislative instruments likewise must feed into practice. Thus, provision must be made for implementation and monitoring if legislative action is to have its intended effect.

Administrative support

The administration and organization of special education raise particular problems. These stem from the multiplicity of tasks to be carried out, the dispersion of responsibility for them and, in many countries, the diversity of funding sources. Special education extends beyond education into health, social welfare and rehabilitation. As well as teachers, it involves psychologists, health workers and therapists.

The most common administrative arrangement (see Chapter 1, this volume) was to have within the ministry of education a separate department dealing with special education. Generally, the special education system ran parallel to the mainstream system, with modifications as judged necessary, and the function of the special education department was to provide the administrative structure for this parallel system. In some cases, the age range was divided up differently in the two systems, or the special education system extended over a longer period of time. There were other organizational models. In some cases, special education was subsumed under the department dealing with primary education, reflecting the main thrust of provision. In other cases, special education was administered as part of the general system, without any separate administrative structure.

About one-third of countries had a special education coordinating body at national level. These bodies had representatives from various government departments and non-governmental agencies concerned with special educational provision. They were charged with maintaining an overview of developments relating to children and young people (and sometimes adults as well) with disabilities.

The importance of appropriate administrative support for special education is twofold: it shapes the nature of the provision made; and it provides the coordination that is necessary. The impact of the administrative arrangements on the nature of provision can be seen clearly in relation to integration. When special education is administered quite separately from the general education system, it is difficult to achieve much integration at the level of practice. Even if the policy is in favour of integration, the separation of funding, teacher supply and curriculum that is entailed by separate administrative arrangements places major obstacles in the way of implementing the policy.

This example shows that administrative structures are not neutral in their effect. They create the framework within which educational provision is made but also determine the nature of that provision to an extent. This framework can facilitate or obstruct setting up certain types of provision, and so can determine whether or not policy objectives are met.

The coordinating functions of administration are wide-ranging where special education is concerned. They can encompass planning, resource allocation, the supply and training of personnel, buildings, materials and transport in addition to coordinating the different service elements. In many countries these functions entail activity, and corresponding administrative structures, at national, regional and local levels.

Financial arrangements impose another layer of complexity. While state funding is the predominant source of financing for special education, funding is also supplied by voluntary bodies, parents and, in some developing countries, aid programmes and international organizations. In many countries voluntary bodies, while no longer providing substantial funding have, through their legacy of past initiatives, a central role in organizing educational and other provision for those with disabilities.

These various factors combine to underline the importance of having a strong and coherent administrative structure. When basic educational services are missing or inadequate, it can be tempting to disregard the need for administrative support. Expenditure on administration must be kept in proportion of course, and subject to regular review, but it would be shortsighted to scrimp on it unduly. An effective and appropriately resourced administrative service is essential to getting best value from the resources that are available and ensuring that they are expended in accordance with policy objectives.

Educational provision

The whole point of special educational provision is to ensure that children and young people with disabilities receive an appropriate education, and everything within the underlying system must be directed to achieving that. Currently the predominant form of provision is segregated special schooling. This is evident from Table 2.1 which presents the summary of provision reported in the UNESCO Review.

When this is set alongside the figures in Chapter 1, this volume, showing how few children with disabilities receive an appropriate education, the limitations of existing schooling structures become very plain. It is difficult to see how they can meet the enormous shortfall in provision. This conclusion has major implications for special schools and ordinary schools alike. Special schooling is not the answer to the shortfall in special educational provision. Moreover, the resources currently devoted to special schools which serve a relatively small number of children need to be examined in the context of the widespread failure to make any special educational provision for large numbers of children. Ordinary schools too must come under scrutiny. The reason special schools are established is to cater for children that ordinary schools fail. Ordinary schools that continue to be inadequate can hardly be offered as a serious alternative to special schools.

The way ahead has to be by bringing about change in both special schools and ordinary schools. Ordinary schools have to develop their teaching and curricula so that they cater for a greater diversity of pupil need than at present, while special schools must develop an outward-looking stance and take on new roles.

In an ideal world there would be no special schools since every child would receive an appropriate education in a local community school. No country is near achieving that goal – apart, perhaps, from Italy – and it has to be assumed that special schools will feature on the map of special education for some time to come. But that does not mean they can continue unchanged.

Good special schools have many advantages – concentration of expertise in teaching pupils with various disabilities, modified curricula and programmes of work, adapted buildings and equipment, training opportunities for staff, links

Table 2.1 *Number of countries using different forms of provision*

Day special schools	54
Boarding special schools	53
Special classes in regular schools	44
Support teaching in regular classes	37
Schools in hospitals	31
Schools in other institutions	28

with local employers and post-school training agencies. These are the very things whose absence in ordinary schools makes them ineffectual in educating pupils with disabilities. The challenge to special schools then is to find ways of sharing their expertise and resources and embedding them in a wider educational context.

Some special schools have already begun to develop outreach programmes. This can entail setting up working links with neighbourhood ordinary schools where staff and pupils are shared. Some special schools act as resource centres, providing information and consultancy to local schools, organizing support services for families and contributing to in-service training activities. Discharging these functions successfully requires considerable changes within special school staff. New skills must be developed and attitudes fostered. Transmitting a skill to others is not the same as exercising it oneself, and operating across several schools or in the community is very different from working in the closed confines of a single special school. The most important changes required are attitudinal: staff who are jealous of their autonomy and intent on maintaining lines of professional demarcation will not set up effective collaboration. There must be a willingness to move beyond existing institutional bases and any status that may go with them and to work cooperatively in whatever new structures may be advised.

The upshot of all this is that special schools of the future could be very different from now. The emphasis would move away from educating limited numbers of pupils in relative isolation and toward acting as resource centres. The latter could encompass curriculum development, in-service training, the collection and evaluation of equipment and computer software, specialist assessment, as well as advice and consultation on all matters relating to the education of pupils with disabilities.

If special schools have to make changes, ordinary schools need to undergo a revolution. Ordinary schools have generally failed pupils with disabilities, and major school reform is necessary before they can make adequate provision for them. This reform must operate at two levels: the academic organization and curriculum provision of the school; and the professional development of staff. The former requires rethinking the ways in which pupils are grouped for teaching purposes, the arrangements that schools can make for supplementary teaching, and the modifications to the mainstream curriculum that teachers can make so as to give pupils with disabilities access to it. All of these necessitates major change in teacher behaviour. Attitudes, knowledge and skills must all be developed to create and sustain a new kind of school where those previously disenfranchised are given an equal say and differentiated provision becomes the norm for all pupils.

Early childhood education

Experience in a wide variety of settings has shown the importance of early childhood education. The absence of appropriate stimulation in infancy and early childhood ranks alongside malnutrition and poverty as a major source of disadvantage and retarded development. This is true of all children but is especially so for children with disabilities. If sensory perception is impaired, for instance, enhanced stimulation is required to compensate, but frequently what is offered is even less stimulation, not more. Indeed, the interruption of normal patterns of development arising from a disability is often more handicapping for the child than the direct consequences of the disability itself.

Despite this, the provision of early childhood education is very restricted. Half of the countries in the UNESCO Review acknowledged that they had limited or no pre-school provision for children with disabilities. Where provision was available, it tended to be focused on those with overt physical or sensory impairments. It was also concentrated on urban areas, so that those living in the countryside had very little access to provision. The forms of provision most commonly reported were early intervention programmes allied to home teaching, pre-school groups attached to special schools, and placements in nursery schools and classes for normal children.

Given the dearth of provision, almost any form of placement or support for early childhood education must be welcomed. There are two principles which should be given paramount importance, however: normalization; and parental/community involvement. Even when children's development is very retarded, the developmental gap between them and age peers at this stage is relatively small – certainly in comparison with later – and every effort should be made to provide for them alongside peers and within a common organizational framework. As to involving parents and the community, this can hardly be over-stressed. Parents and the extended family are the principal, and in some cases the only, source of structured stimulation these children receive. Whatever little can be achieved by formal intervention, it can only be enhanced by being tied into and made to reinforce family activities and community relationships.

A particular challenge arises from the fact that much early intervention is not statutory. Where state support is provided, there is an additional problem of coordination because of the multiplicity of agencies concerned. Given these circumstances, it is important that all concerned – voluntary bodies, staff, parents and state officials – develop a common policy and approach. Overcoming the disadvantages resulting from disability must be the paramount concern of all so that the limited resources commanded by early childhood education have maximum beneficial effect.

Preparation for adult life

Schooling is for all young people a form of preparation for adult life. The knowledge and skills acquired at school help them make their way when they leave it. For many young people the normal school curriculum is not sufficient preparation, whether it be for the world of work or for independent adult living, and specific preparation provided during the later years of school and subsequently is extremely beneficial.

All of this holds true in far greater measure for those who have disabilities. Many of these learn more slowly than their peers and may have limited academic achievements at the time of normal school-leaving age. More significantly, a great many will not yet be ready for independent adult living. The conclusion to be drawn from this is not the traditional one that little can be done since independent living is a remote target, but rather that far more needs to be done precisely because existing support efforts have left this target so remote.

Regrettably, the amount of provision available to assist people with disabilities toward independent adult living is far too little. This holds true of developed and developing countries alike. More attention has been given in recent years in some countries and there have been a number of widely documented initiatives, but provision generally is sporadic at best and frequently non-existent. The UNESCO Review found that a majority of countries responding had limited or no post-school provision for those with disabilities.

The twin goals of action in this area are to help young people become economically active and to lead lives that are as full and independent as possible. Where special educational provision is well developed at school level, steps should be taken to ensure adequate preparation for life after school. This should cover both work and daily living. Preparation for work can include careers education and guidance, pre-vocational training and work experience. In some cases, schools will provide direct vocational training, though substantial programmes in this area would normally be the responsibility of post-school agencies. The primary task for schools is to give young people, regardless of whether or not they have disabilities, a broad range of appropriate life skills, rather than to train them for specific jobs.

Technical and vocational training must take account of the local labour market and industrial infrastructure. It must, however, be forward-looking in respect of technological developments, which can significantly expand opportunities for people with disabilities. Training can be provided in specialist training colleges or training centres catering exclusively for people with disabilities, and many such establishments have been set up. There is a growing realization that those with disabilities can benefit from the training opportunities available to the general population. This is leading to initiatives to incorporate training provision for people with disabilities into the general system for technical and vocational education. This entails substantial alterations in the latter as well as major changes in attitude, but it is a step toward the normalization of experience for people with disabilities.

Parental involvement

Parents of children with disabilities can play a major role in their education – if facilitated and allowed. This can include assisting in school activities, contributing to assessment and curriculum planning, implementing programmes at home and monitoring progress.

This role is first and foremost a matter of principle: parents have the right to be involved in their children's education. It is also, particularly in developing countries, a matter of securing the best interests of children with disabilities. An account of a family support programme in Kenya opens with the claim that 'the greatest resource in a developing country for helping the disabled lead lives which are as fulfilling and productive as possible is a well-advised and supported family' (Arnold, 1988). Parents are the child's first and natural teachers and it makes sense to help them discharge this role to the best of their ability.

The UNESCO Review gathered information on parental involvement in assessment procedures and placement decision-making. Practice generally fell short of the ideal of parents as partners. In some countries, assessment procedures included asking parents for details on the child's early development, but in the majority of cases no role was reported for them. As for participating in decision-making, the best they could generally hope for was the reactive role of agreeing to, or taking issue with, the educational placement proposed for their child by the professionals.

There is little argument about the desirability of involving parents as partners in their children's education. The challenge now is to translate the rhetoric into practical action. The strategies to be adopted will vary from country to country and must be articulated with local conditions and resouces in mind. There are three fundamental conditions that must be borne in mind in all instances.

1. Empowering parents

If parents are to play an effective part in their children's education – after having been excluded for so long – they must be enabled to do so. This entails sharing information with them – on their child's condition and programme and on the facilities available. Teachers and other professionals must value what parents do and take steps to build up their confidence. They must give parents appropriate programmes and other ways of structuring their children's experience. They must give them access to schools and their own professional sanctums. Above all, they must acknowledge their right to contribute to decisions that affect their children.

2. Changing the roles of professionals

None of the above can happen without major changes in the role perceptions of professionals. If parents are to be truly empowered, professionals have to be convinced of the need to demystify their professional domains. They must be willing to give their skills away, or at least to deploy their skills through less expert hands. This in turn calls for new skills on their part – skills of dialogue, collaboration, team building and review. Above all, it requires on the part of many professionals a different concept of their professional domain and a different attitude to the exercise of their professional skills.

3. Working toward community participation

Community-based approaches to health, social welfare and rehabilitation have attracted much attention in recent years. They are seen to have particular relevance to developing countries where there is a vast pool of untapped human resources. Community-based approaches have not been developed extensively in special education but the model is likely to be just as appropriate to it as to other aspects of provision. It provides a natural context for parental involvement in special educational provision. Parents and family are part of a community, and a holistic involvement of the former also enrols the wider community in support and responsibility.

Training

Developments in special educational provision are critically dependent upon the quality of teaching available. This in turn depends on the opportunities for training and professional development open to teachers. Teacher training, particularly in-service training, takes on extra significance at a time of change. When conceptualizations of handicap are being revised and integration means that teachers in ordinary schools are expected to teach pupils with disabilities, training that was previously adequate may now need to be supplemented or restructured. This fact is a particular challenge in countries where basic teacher training is limited anyway.

The UNESCO Review painted a gloomy picture on training. Only a minority of the 58 countries reported coverage of disability issues in the teacher training available to all teachers. In-service training opportunities for teachers in ordinary schools were similarly limited. A wide range of training opportunities were reported for teachers in specializing in special education – a five-year course in a training college at one extreme to one-the-job instruction offered on an *ad hoc* basis at the other. A further UNESCO study, specifically on teacher training, provided more detailed information on training arrangements in 14 countries (Bowman, 1986; Bowman *et al.*, 1985). This showed the diversity of arrangements made, ranging from extended full-time courses in specialist training institutions to distance learning offered on a modular basis to serving teachers.

While it is difficult to generalize across so many contries at different stages of development, it seems clear that the main thrust of training at present is directed at the specialist who will be working in segregated special schools. It is important to have such specialists and any training blueprint for the future should allow for a continuing supply of appropriate specialists. But there is also a major need of less highly trained workers. A very great number of children with disabilities could be helped in ordinary schools by relatively minor adjustments to the teaching provided in ordinary schools. Thus, a modest investment in low-level training could bring about major improvements in the special educational provision offered by schools.

A national plan for teacher training has to start with initial training. A major objective for all countries should be to ensure that all trainee teachers should learn something about disabilities and be aware of some of their educational implications. They would not become experts in teaching pupils with disabilities but they would learn how to modify the curriculum content and teaching approach of the ordinary classroom so as to give access to substantial numbers of pupils with disabilities. They would acquire some skills in identifying and assessing pupils with disabilities. They would appreciate the importance of working with parents and develop appropriate skills. They would also know where their own competence stopped and how they could benefit from collaborating with specialists.

A national plan should also make provision for in-service training for classroom teachers and headteachers on matters relating to disabililty. Even if substantial improvements were made in initial training, this is at the edge of the problem and is best seen as an investment in the future. Most serving teachers for many years to come will not be affected by innovations in initial training. It is, moreover, those teachers who are long-serving and experienced who occupy the positions of leadership in schools.

Relevant in-service training can be provided in a great variety of ways. At the most basic level, general awareness courses can be provided for individual teachers or, more usefully, for all the staff in a school. The latter can be arranged quite economically by occasional training days when staff come together without pupils. The training input for such school-based training can come from a member of the school's own staff who has been on a training course, from special school staff or from some other disability specialist in the neighbourhood. More substantial training can be provided by arranging for individual staff members to go on appropriate courses.

Training arrangements must also ensure a supply of specialists in disability. Some countries have separate training routes for ordinary teachers and for teachers specializing in disability. This may be compatible with a high level of expertise on the part of the latter, but it is not conducive to integrated education. Many countries incorporate training for specialists within the framework of training for all teachers, and some require those intending to specialize in pupils with disability to first spend some time teaching in ordinary schools. However the initial training of specialist teachers is organized, it is important that regular opportunities for in-service training and professional renewal be offered to these teachers.

Research and development

Educating pupils with disabilities is a complex matter. It is likely to be significantly improved if based on good information about the nature of these children's learning needs and how best to meet them.

The UNESCO Review found that one-third of countries responding allocated separate national funds for research and development in special education, though the size of the allocations was not recorded. The research topics cited with greatest frequency were integration, early intervention, the organization of special education, the transition from school to adult life and incidence surveys.

The priority given to research and development is worth noting, and it is to be hoped that the very modest expenditure on it will not be seen as an expendable luxury in the face of the inexorable pressure on service budgets. This is related to the major need for better information exchange. The UNESCO Review pointed out that 'much can be learned from others' research and curriculum development, from their legislative practices and from the ways in which they organise and deliver services'. No less important than maintaining a research and development capacity to service local needs is an efficient means of exchanging information with other countries and capitalizing on their information bases.

Conclusion

While estimates of disability and access to education are imprecise, particularly in developing countries, it is clear that the shortfall in appropriate educational provision for children and young people with disabilities is immense. There are some hopeful signs. Governments, inter-governmental agencies and non-governmental organizations are more aware of the challenge and many positive initiatives are in train, but a great deal still needs to be done.

This chapter has set out underlying principles and strategies to assist in building up appropriate educational provision. These are necessarily at a general level and need to be translated into the specific cultural and economic context of given countries. That does not detract from their value, however. To the extent that many children and young people with disabilities have limited or no access to education, or experience services based on outmoded concepts of disability, it is important that the principles underlying provision be subject to critical scrutiny from time to time. In order to be meaningful, this must be done in relation to the different aspects of provision. Likewise, the effort to build up provision benefits from systematic attention to the strategies that can be used and how they relate to each other and to underlying system variables.

References

Arnold, C (1988) 'Family and parent support programmes: the community-based approach', in Ross, D H (ed.) *Educating Handicapped Young People in Eastern and Southern Africa*, Paris: UNESCO.

Bowman, I (1986) 'Teacher training and the integration of handicapped pupils: some findings from a 14 nation UNESCO study', *European Journal of Special Needs Education*, **1**, 1, 29–38.

Bowman, I, Wedell, N and Wedell, K (1985) *Helping Handicapped Pupils in Ordinary Schools: strategies for teacher training*, Paris: UNESCO.

UNESCO (1988) *Review of the Present Situation in Special Education*, Paris: UNESCO.

3. Theories to explain the development of special education

Ron Brouillette

Introduction

Special education development throughout the world progresses through predictable stages as a result of social, political and economic forces from within and outside a nation. As discussed by Mittler (this volume), despite admirable, mostly voluntary, efforts in developing nations, approximately 2 per cent of the estimated 112 million children with special needs receive an education (UNESCO, 1988).

This chapter describes the global state of special education and those gradually evolving social, political and economic influences that affect the education of individuals with disabilities. The cross-national information in this chapter provides a global context from which one might view the contents found in other chapters in this volume. The topics discussed in this chapter include cross-national comparisons of disability categories served; patterns of service establishment; and selected hypotheses to explain special education development.

Cross-national comparisons of disability categories served

Table 3.1 presents the known categories of disability served in 152 nations for which information exists. The data are derived, in part, from the international documents of disability organizations found in the annotated bibliography at the end of this volume. These documents include ILSMH directories; reports from Gallaudet University's Center for International Research in Deaf Education and the World Federation of the Deaf; a survey of least developed nations (Cavanagh, 1991); proceedings from international conferences; personal communications with individuals from these nations; UN reports; UNESCO surveys and national case studies; other national publications on special education and the author's personal knowledge. The full table of 152 nations is found in Brouillette (1992).

The information in Table 3.1 is not exhaustive. There are most probably services in nations that have not been reported or have not been discovered by the author. The categories served by the 152 nations found in the table may be considered, at best, the beginning of a baseline for reported services in the early

Table 3.1 *Summary of disability categories served in 152 nations*

Disability served	Number of countries N = 152	Percentage of countries N = 152
Visually impaired	121	80%
Hearing impaired	116	76%
Mentally retarded	120	79%
Physically impaired	106	70%
Emotionally disturbed	74	49%
Speech impaired	46	30%
Learning disabled	26	17%
Gifted and talented	06	04%

1990s. Unfortunately, there are no standard criteria for what constitutes existing educational services. A range of service delivery approaches from non-governmental and governmental agencies are reflected within the table.

The results of the original table reveal a positive relationship between the Human Development Index (a mix of economic and social indicators), GNP per capita and the number of disability categories served. There is a negative correlation between the under-five mortality rate and the number of categories served (these correlations are shown in Table 3.3). There is also a tacit relationship between the major religion practised in a nation and the number of categories served (Miles and Miles, this volume).

Patterns of services' establishment by categories

The order in which disability categories are served in a nation follows a predictable pattern. The developmental pattern is revealed in an analysis of Table 3.1 and through surveys of national histories of social development. In nearly all nations, services for children with visual impairments start first, followed by services to hearing impaired children and then to children with mental retardation (learning difficulties). Slightly later, services for children with physical impairments begin, followed by services for children with emotional and behavioural difficulties and then for children with speech and communication disorders. As seen in Table 3.2, services to children with learning disabilities or specific learning difficulties such as dyslexia are provided in only 26 educationally rich nations. Children who are considered gifted or talented are included in the area of special education by some nations due to the special needs for accelerated learning which they require.

Table 3.2 illustrates this pattern. The first column of statistics contains information on categories served in 110 nations reported by UNESCO in 1970. These figures run parallel to the more up-to-date statistics (Brouillette, 1992) on the 152 nations reported in Table 3.1. Services for individuals with intellectual impairment (mental retardation) appear to be accelerating at a faster pace than for individuals with hearing impairments. This may partially be explained by the vigorous promotion by the International League of Societies for Persons with Mental Handicap (ILSMH) and its national members, for services. In addition

Table 3.2 *Disability categories served in 1970 and 1991*

Disability served	Number of countries (1970 N = 110; 1991 N = 152)	Percentage of countries (1970 N = 110; 1991 N = 152)
Visually impaired	(82)	(75%)
	121	80%
Hearing impaired	(79)	(71%)
	116	76%
Mentally retarded	(72)	(66%)
	120	79%
Physically impaired	(68)	(62%)
	106	70%
Emotionally disturbed	(49)	(45%)
	74	49%
Speech impaired	(18)	(16%)
	46	30%
Learning disabled	(03)	(03%)
	26	17%
Gifted and talented	(04)	(04%)
	06	04%

to stimulating national development, the ILSMH is fastidious in its data collection in order to assess development. The World Federation of the Deaf is the corresponding organization in deaf education (see Joutselainen, this volume).

Historical perspectives

The history of special education development in nearly every nation follows a similar pattern. Briefly, the evolution of services is begun by missionaries, typically from the Catholic faith in the mid- to late-19th century, who sought ways to provide religious instruction to blind adults and children. Residential institutions were built for this purpose. Instruction to the less obviously disabled deaf children follows soon after.

Following World War II, charitable, non-governmental organizations (NGOs) emerged and established parallel services for children with sensory impairment, intellectual impairment and physical disabilities. The voluntary bodies associated with intellectual impairment were typically organized by parents and friends. It was not uncommon to find competing voluntary societies in the same capital cities where services initially began. In developing nations, especially those that were under colonial rule, expatriate wives were among the most active in early development. Many special schools were started by foreign volunteers such as the US Peace Corps and Volunteer Service Overseas. From 1961 to 1981, for example, as many as 2,000 Peace Corps Volunteers had served in special education programmes in over 60 nations (Dixon, 1981).

The UN International Year of Disabled Persons (IYDP) in 1981 fuelled activities aimed at sensitizing the community to the needs and rights of disabled people. Many governments increased their annual grants and funding of teachers in special schools and established special education departments in their Ministries. Thompson's (1982) assessment of the impact of IYDP on the Commonwealth nations was positive. He reports that 'IYDP aroused the expectations of the voluntary societies . . . and has challenged governments to decide on national policy' (p. 51). During the past decade, governments have assumed greater responsibility in special education, though non-governmental organizations have viewed their government's actions with mixed feelings. It can be said with some certainty that fewer than 20 per cent of individuals with special needs can be provided with adequate services through the private resources of NGOs alone, but only when governments are sufficiently sensitized and have adequate resources will they be able to respond in any meaningful way. Some supporting evidence for this follows.

Selected hypotheses to explain special education development

Six hypotheses are briefly presented in an attempt to explain some of the cross-national differences affecting the numbers and types of children with disabilities served and the quality of those services provided. Four of these hypotheses have been postulated by Putnam (1979): (1) the need hypothesis (2) the demand hypothesis (3) the educational effort hypothesis, and (4) the resource hypothesis. Additional hypotheses include (5) 'keeping up with the Joneses' (Dybwad, 1982) and (6) the developmental stages hypothesis.

1. The need hypothesis

The need hypothesis attempts to pair epidemiological measures to the development of special education, suggesting that the number of children in need of special services will influence the numbers that receive these services (see Mittler, and Hegarty, this volume).

As shown in Table 3.3, the need hypothesis appears to be supported by the significant positive correlation between health expenditure of a nation and 'the special education index' (Putnam, 1979). The special education index is the proportion of all school-aged children who are enrolled in special education. The need hypothesis, however, appears to lose support by the appearance of a negative correlation between infant mortality and the provision of special education. Children who survive episodes of diseases and malnutrition may be at greater risk for a handicapping condition and may need special education.

2. The demand hypothesis

The demand hypothesis in special education development predicts that it is not merely the presence of large numbers of children with special needs (the need hypothesis) that leads to their education, but moreover the public demand for such actions that will result in their education. UNESCO (1974) states: 'Special education is a sector which is heavily dependent on public opinion' (p. 192); it not

Table 3.3 *Correlations between the Special Education Index (SEI) and selected measures of socio-economic and educational development in selected nations (N)*

Predictor variable	Pearsonian Correlation with SEI	(N)
Per capita educational expenditure (1965)	0.81	96
Per capita gross national product (1965)	0.79	96
Per capita health expenditures (1965)	0.76	91
Literacy rate (1965)	0.64	81
Enrolment in primary and secondary education as percentage of school aged population (1965)	0.58	96
National pupil-teacher ratio	−0.49	77
Infant mortality rate	−0.33	77

All correlations significant at the 0.01 level confidence level. Adapted from Putnam (1979).

only exposes the need, but also demands priorities be established for speedy solutions. UNICEF Executive Director, Grant (1981) remarks:

> We have had a remarkable amount of structural change in the past 30 years . . . . Most of this change has been brought about by public pressure, with people ahead of governments . . . (p. 1).

The demand theory appears to be supported when one analyses the universally effective agents in the form of family members and their friends, persons with disabilities and international promotion (Dybwad, 1982).

A startling example of parental support in Japan, in the 1950s, concerns a mother driven by desperation due to a lack of support services who attempted to suffocate her severely disabled son and herself. Only her son died. At the mother's trial, a parent's support group persuaded the jury that Japanese society (rather than the mother) was guilty for not providing needed services. This decision caused a shift in public opinion which resulted in increased government contributions to special education. Since that time, citizen advocacy groups in Japan have served as the 'yeast in community consciousness raising . . . to exert strong pressure on political parties and government agencies' (Ogamo, 1978, p. 65).

The demands articulated during the past decade by persons who have a disability on the development of services is paramount. Bowe (1981) stated that people with disabilities, often referred to as 'consumer groups', are gaining in influence throughout the world. These organizations are acting as lobby groups to bring about changes in the equity of service provision and new opportunities for disabled persons.

Miles (1982) describes the urgency for the promotion of self-advocacy:

> The image of the disabled has so far been in the hands of able-bodied persons. The future must see a new set of images controlled by disabled

persons . . . . People en masse do not change their thinking very rapidly on social or moral issues, which is why development cannot run very far ahead of public opinion. Minority groups . . . can shift their position forward with remarkable speed . . . (p. 9).

3. The educational effort hypothesis

The educational effort hypothesis suggests that a nation's financial expenditure on all education will be directly proportional to the expenditures on special education (Putnam, 1979). The hypothesis stresses governmental initiatives in the provision of special services, suggesting that as a country devotes a greater share of its resources to education, it will allocate a higher proportion of those resources to providing education to its disabled population. The result, presumably, will be greater numbers of students enrolled in special education. This hypothesis appears to be supported by the data presented in Table 3.3. Educational expenditure per capita, primary and secondary enrolment ratios and literacy rates all correlate in the expected direction with the index of special education.

Support for the educational effort hypothesis is provided by Mehta (1981) who reports that the per capita expenditure on education is highest in the Indian state of Maharashtra where, perhaps, the best special education services in that nation are located.

Ade-Williams (1972) from Sierra Leone suggested that so long as a significant proportion of a country's population is illiterate, its main concern must be the education of the masses of normal children. However, 'it is evident that provision to handicapped children must, at present, come forward from the end of a long list of priorities' (p. 13).

4. The resource hypothesis

The resource hypothesis suggests that wealthier nations will spend more on education, including costlier special education. However, when Putnam (1979) further analysed the 1970 UNESCO data from which she made her initial correlations, she realized that the independent variables that inter-correlated with the special education index were inter-correlated with the wealth of the nation. By applying a multivariate analysis that controlled for per capita GNP, nearly all of the statistical relationships shown in Table 3.3 diminish. The correlations between the special education index and literacy, infant mortality, urbanization and enrolment and pupil-teacher ratios are essentially low or spurious:

> The underlying correlational pattern is remarkably simple: wealthier nations provide more special education for their children. Once this central fact is taken into account, few of our other variables add any explanatory power (p. 93).

Putnam's conclusion was that the higher a nation's GNP per capita, the more its per capita educational expenditure (an inter-correlation of $r = 0.94$) and the more special education will be provided (see Chapter 20, this volume).

In spite of the above arguments supporting the importance of the resources hypothesis in special education development, some contradictory evidence, from wealthy Arab states for example, discounts the influence of resources alone; social and political factors can be equally important.

5. The 'keeping up with the Joneses' hypothesis

The 'keeping up with the Joneses' imitation hypothesis suggests that cross-national diffusion or transfer of ideas, finances, materials, personnel and techniques related to disability services is the greatest influence for accelerated development of special education. Dybwad (1982) termed the acculturation process, 'keeping up with the Joneses'. Dybwad's theory implies that popular special education methods will become a catalyst for implementation in other nations seeking improved services. Often, this model replication or imitation of methods is effected with little or no modification to fit cultural patterns, and without vision for future implications. This kind of 'blind cross-fertilization', according to Juul (1981) has, since World War II, resulted in an uncritical and not always wise adaptation in Europe of America's (and others') 'glamorous' special education system.

The field of special education has been one in which information most easily crosses frontiers, according to UNESCO (1974). A cross-fertilization for special education development has been immeasurably accelerated by the actions surrounding the International Year of Disabled Persons (IYDP). The successes are, however, tempered through a critical analysis of the extent to which concomitant Western cultural transference dominated the Year (see Mittler, this volume).

6. The developmental stages hypothesis

The developmental stages hypothesis suggests that the dynamic evolution of society creates structural stages conducive to the progression of special education development. The hypothesis states that an interactive combination of social, economic and political factors must exist in order for a nation to reach the 'take off' point in its development of comprehensive education that is the right of all disabled children and others living on the fringes of society.

Jorgensen (1980) suggested that the development of special education is characterized by the levels of resources, interdisciplinary cooperation, teacher training, individualization, and integration made possible by increased staffing ratios and level of tolerance displayed at the school and in the community toward children who are different.

It appears that all five of the other hypotheses could be accommodated under the developmental stages hypothesis. UNESCO (1974) suggests that a nation's acknowledgement of the developmental stages and their understanding of their place along the development continuum can serve as a practical tool for special education development. Implicit in this awareness is the possibility to '. . . find a short-cut to development by passing directly from a simple to a much more sophisticated model, without introducing intermediate ones' (p. 173). Finding inexpensive but valued alternatives is the first call for the special education community in the next decade or two.

Conclusion

Education for children with special needs has evolved slowly but consistently with other areas of social development. For the parents and friends of the estimated 117 million children in developing nations with special needs who have yet to receive any appropriate education, there is a growing impatience. At least 30 nations have yet to provide any special education to the three largest categories of disability. While it is true that most of these nations are among the least developed nations, it is also true that something can be started with very few resources. If the developmental stages hypothesis is accepted, nations that are under-providing need only to encourage concerned local individuals to start non-governmental, voluntary associations and request some of the international disability-specific agencies to assist in any ways they can. Increased demand and resources will surely follow.

For nations that have only basic services for a few categories, a redistribution of very few resources to the regular education sector can result in many times more places for children with special needs who can learn in the ordinary classroom. The hard part of this process is sensitizing and preparing teachers, pupils and parents for the move towards integrated, functional education starting at the pre-school level.

A synergism seems to exist between all social and economic sectors linked to social development. If these components are teased apart, one might find, however, that the greatest factor in special education development is the human one.

References

Ade-Williams, V (1972) *Proceedings of the Seminar on Deafness*, Accra, Ghana: Commonwealth Society for the Welfare of the Deaf.

Bowe, F (1981) *Who represents the disabled people? Participation of People with Disabilities: An International Perspective*, E Lansing, MI: University Center for International Rehabilitation.

Brouillette, R (1992) *The Development of Special Education in Mauritius: a case study*, Ann Arbor, MI: University of Michigan Microfilms.

Cavanagh, I (1991) '*A review of the aetiology of disability and the equational provision for children with disabilities in low-income countries*', MSc report, London: Institute of Education University of London.

Dixon, G (1981) *Peace Corps in Special Education and Rehabilitation*, Washington, DC: Peace Corps Information Office.

Dybwad, G (1982) personal communication, November, Nairobi, Kenya.

Jorgensen, I S (1980) *Studies: Special Education in the European Community*, Brussels: ECSC.

Juul, K (1981) 'Special education in Europe', in Kaufmann, J Hannahan, D (eds) *Handbook of Special Education*, New Jersey: Prentice Hall.

Grant, J (1981) 'Achieving social and economic goals for the year 2000', *Compass*, 8, January-April.

Grant, J (1991) *The State of the World's Children: 1990*, New York: Oxford University Press.

Mehta, V (1981) 'Services for disabled children and youth: the challenge for developing countries', paper presented at Project Hope Conference, Development of Programs for Disabled Children and Their Families, Millwood, VA, November.

Miles, M (1982) 'Why Asia rejects Western disability advice', *International Rehabilitation Review*, **33**, 1, 5.

Ogamo, H (1978) 'The impact of the Japanese culture on special education programming', in Fink, A (ed.) *International Perspectives on the Future of Special Education*, Reston VA: CEC.

Putnam, R (1979) 'Special education: some cross-national comparisons', *Comparative Education*, **15**, 1.
Thompson, R (1982) *Programs for Disabled People in the Commonwealth*, London: Commonwealth Press.
UNESCO (1974) *Case Studies In Special Education*, Paris: UNESCO.
UNESCO (1988) *Review of the Present Situations of Special Education*, Paris: UNESCO.

4. Special education as a human and legal right

Stanley S Herr

Introduction

International bodies have long recognized the rights of children with disabilities to receive suitable education. Over the last 40 years, this right has been firmly enunciated in a series of UN declarations and covenants. From the Universal Declaration of Human Rights (1948) to the Convention on the Rights of the Child (1990), formulations of the right to special education have become more specific and binding in character.

Legislative developments in many parts of the world now regard access to education for the child with a disability as a right, not a privilege. In developed nations, statutory frameworks often carefully prescribe such a child's right to a free and appropriate education. To varying degrees of detail, those laws require due consideration of the educational environment least restrictive to the particular child's needs, as well as safeguards in identifying, assessing and placing the child recognized as having special educational needs.

In developing nations, such legal provisions are often rudimentary or non-existent. Countries at different stages of economic and political development may seek or adopt laws designed to be inclusive of all children with disabilities, while acknowledging that the implementation of such laws is inevitably gradual and incomplete. Israel and Czechoslovakia are but two of many such examples.

This chapter offers an overview of a complex and rapidly evolving field of social legislation. The first part identifies the main sources of international human rights addressing educational and special educational requirements of the child with a mental or physical disability. The second part illustrates the incorporation of such rights in national laws by looking at selected case studies. The conclusion notes some of the implications of these international and national experiences for countries around the world.

International standards

General human rights

The UN adopted the Universal Declaration of Human Rights (1948) as a common measure of 'achievement for all people and all nations', with prescribed rights to be protected by the rule of law and by progressive steps of implementation. Article 26 proclaims that 'everyone has the right to education' and that, at least in its elementary stages, it should be free and compulsory. This guarantee was cited by a US court in support of the educational rights of a teenager (described as 'borderline retarded' and emotionally disturbed) who was denied schooling while waiting trial under adult criminal laws (*Commonwealth v Sadler*, 1979). In addition to this pledge of universal education, the article is significant for its insistence that parents have a right to choose the kind of education given to their child. Other articles affirm rights to equal protection and freedom from discrimination (7) and to a fair hearing by an impartial tribunal when basic rights are at issue (10).

International covenants as treaties can give legal force to the rights agreed to by the signatory parties. An example of this standard-setting and implementation process is the International Covenant on Economic, Social, and Cultural Rights (UN, 1966). Article 10 recognizes that families should receive the 'widest possible protection and assistance', especially when responsible for the education and care of dependent children. State parties affirmed 'the right of everyone to education' and the obligation to make primary education compulsory, available and free to all (Article 13). The liberty interests of parents and legal guardians to make educational choices for their children is also recognized. Although the Covenant's rights are subject to the caveat of 'available resources', treaty nations accept the duty to achieve the full realization of these rights on a progressive basis and to adopt legislative measures consistent with these human rights objectives (Article 2).

Disability rights

Parents and other advocates for persons with mental retardation led the way for the specific inclusion of persons with special needs in human rights charters. The International League of Societies for Persons with Mental Handicap, promulgated a declaration in Jerusalem in 1968 that became the basis for the United Nations Declaration on the Rights of Mentally Retarded Persons (1971). Article 2 of the UN Declaration expressly listed education as one of the essential rights and services to enable the person with mental retardation to develop his or her 'ability and maximum potential'.

Educational and equality rights were then extended to persons with all types of disabilities. The UN Declaration on the Rights of Disabled Persons (1975) enumerated education, training, rehabilitation and other services as rights to enable not only maximum development of capabilities and skills, but of the person's 'social integration or reintegration' (Article 6). Furthering integration goals, the Declaration called for measures to foster self-reliance, normalization, and fundamental rights equal to their 'fellow-citizens of the same age'. If school-aged children without disabilities enjoyed entitlements to public education, it would follow that their peers with disabilities should have similar access rights.

Children's rights

The UN Declaration on the Rights of the Child (1959) was adopted unanimously by the General Assembly. Principle 7 states, without exception, that 'the child is entitled to receive education, which shall be free and compulsory, at least in the elementary stages'. The child's best interests constitute the 'guiding principle' for determining that education, as a matter of equal opportunity, should enable the child to become a useful member of society and to develop his or her abilities, judgement and sense of responsibility. Principle 2 promises, 'by law and other means', that the child shall have the opportunities for mental, physical, moral, spiritual and social development, while Principle 5 makes clear that the child with a disability is also entitled to 'the special treatment, education and care required by his (sic) particular condition'.

These rights have now been strengthened and made more concrete by a United Nations treaty. The UN Convention on the Rights of the Child (1990) requires ratifying nations to recognize the child's right to education and the right to habilitative and rehabilitative services, including education for the child with a disability. Article 23 incorporates these services under the rubric of the 'right to special care'. Such services shall be provided free of charge, 'whenever possible', and,

> shall be designed to ensure that the disabled child has effective access to and receives *education*, training, health care services, rehabilitation services, preparation for employment and recreational opportunities in a manner conducive to the child's achieving the fullest possible social integration and individual development . . . (Article 23, 3, emphasis added).

The right to education is also spelt out under Article 28, not only in terms of the familiar guarantees about primary education but in encouraging the different forms of secondary education, regular school attendance and vocational information and guidance for *all* children. In framing educational programmes, ratifying states agree to recognize the diversity of abilities that children present (including development of the child's talents and abilities to the child's fullest potential), and to respect the values of the child's parents. These 119 states must report periodically to the UN Committee on the Rights of the Child on the realization of their convention obligations (Article 44). The initial reports were due in September 1992 for the first group of ratifying states and the Committee (formed in February 1991 and chaired by Ms Hoda Badan) will review the reports to ascertain national progress in adopting and implementing children's rights. Even though its fulfilment will take years of progressive implementation, the convention represents an extraordinary consensus of UN members on the standards and values which ratifying states accept as legally binding.

National case studies

United States of America

The United States has a strong tradition of using litigation, legislation and child advocacy to secure and defend the rights of children with disabilities. The right to a free appropriate education for such children offers an excellent case study of this interplay of forces.

Judicial decisions in the early 1970s revealed school practices that often excluded, misclassified or inappropriately educated children with disabilities or suspected disabilities. *Mills v Board of Education of the District of Columbia* (1972), a class-action precedent based on equal protection, due process and statutory grounds, ruled that children with physical or mental disabilities were entitled to a suitable publicly-supported education. As a matter of constitutional law, the federal district court in *Mills* held that lack of funds was not an adequate defence and that if sufficient additional funds could not be obtained, public officials would be obligated to spend available funds 'equitably in such a manner that no child is entirely excluded from a publicly supported education . . .' (p. 876). Another federal class action, *Pennsylvania Association for Retarded Children v Pennsylvania* (1972), produced a statewide consent decree requiring a free programme of education and training appropriate to 'every retarded child'. This decree was also noteworthy for its finding that the state could no longer deny or postpone a child's education on the basis of presumed ability to profit from instruction.

The two landmark cases sparked similar right-to-education cases across the country. This advocacy led to a substantial body of case law upholding the so-called 'zero reject policy' of universal education for all children, regardless of the nature or severity of their handicaps (Turnbull, 1986). Beside inclusion, court decisions also focused on fairness in identifying and placing children in special education classes, ensuring 'mainstream' and other least restrictive educational environments appropriate for a particular child, and setting minimum standards for the habilitation of children housed in institutions that had previously offered inadequate programmes of instruction (Herr, 1983).

Mills and related cases helped to persuade Congress that a national legislative solution was needed. The Education for All Handicapped Children Act (EAHCA), 1975, produced that solution: a federal grant programme to the states, conditional upon assurances that the state educational agency would guarantee 'free appropriate public education' at pre-school, elementary and secondary school levels. The law required an 'individualized education program' that included both special instruction to meet the child's unique needs and 'related services' such as transportation, developmental services and other supportive services needed to assist the child to benefit from special education.

The 1975 Act was also notable for its procedural safeguards and individually enforceable rights. Due process considerations were emphasized at every stage of a child's identification, evaluation and placement as a student with a disability. The Act mandated that parents receive prior written notice whenever the educational agency proposes to initiate or change the child's identification, evaluation or placement, as well as the provision of a free appropriate public education. These requirements also apply when the agency refuses to take such action requested by the parent, guardian or parent surrogate. No child is to lack a representative since the state education agency must assign a parent surrogate to a child whose parents are unknown or unavailable or if the child is a ward of the state. The written notice must describe, in language understandable to a member of the general public, the proposed action, the reasons for it, the evaluation procedure or report relied upon by the agency, and the procedural safeguards available to the parents.

Procedural safeguards in contested special education matters are extensive. The child's parents have an opportunity to examine all relevant school records.

They are entitled to an independent educational evaluation by a qualified examiner not employed by the educational agency responsible for their child. If aggrieved by an agency decision, they have the opportunity to have a due process hearing before an impartial hearing officer. At such a hearing, the parents may be accompanied by a lawyer, experts or other advocates. They have the right to present evidence; compel the attendance of witnesses and cross-examine them; to make oral and written arguments; and to receive a written decision and findings of fact. If still dissatisfied, the child's representatives can obtain an administrative appeal on the state level. After exhausting these administrative remedies, representatives can bring a civil action in state or federal court. The court will then receive the administrative record, hear any additional evidence that is offered and grant appropriate relief. If the parents or guardians are the prevailing parties, that relief can include the payment of their attorney's fees, a possibility which acts as a strong incentive for educational agencies not to contest weak cases.

Other hallmarks of American law are its emphasis on the least restrictive educational alternatives and non-discrimination in the provision of services to persons with disabilities. Under the EAHCA, states must, 'to the maximum extent appropriate', ensure placement practices that only remove the child from the regular educational environment when the severity or nature of the child's disability precludes the satisfactory use of regular classes with supplementary aids and services.

Federal anti-discrimination law incorporates a similar requirement. The Rehabilitation Act (1973) and its accompanying regulations bar discrimination by recipients of federal assistance – which includes virtually every public school in the country. Its equality and integration goals require that children with disabilities receive non-academic services such as meals and recess periods in as integrated a setting as possible; that their facilities and services are comparable to those for non-disabled students; and that their education is provided as close to home as possible. The Americans with Disabilities Act (1990) extends these non-discrimination norms to governmental services as well as to public accommodation in the private sector, such as day-care centres, private schools, adult education centres and other places of education. With strenuous efforts and full implementation over time, this Act is expected to lower barriers to the mainstreams of American life.

Although the US Supreme Court has tended to interpret disability rights in a conservative fashion, the lower courts and Congress continue to be vigorous protectors of children with disabilities. This continuing activism is due to the strength and sophistication of the disability rights movement and the wide array of class and individual advocacy techniques available to child advocates in the field of special education (Herr, 1991).

In *Hendrick Hudson Central School District v Rowley* (1982), the US Supreme Court held that where a deaf child was achieving success in a mainstream classroom, a sign-language interpreter would not be required since the Individualized Educational Program (IEP) was properly determined, provided some benefit, and the child was reasonably expected to make progress toward the programme's educational objectives.

Post-*Rowley* decisions of the lower courts show, however, that judges have used a variety of interpretive techniques to read these standards expansively to the advantage of child litigants and their parents (Weber, 1990). Furthermore, after the Court weakened the enforcement of disability rights in a decision on state sovereign immunity and a decision barring attorneys' fees in special education cases, Congress struck back in 1986 with two laws lifting the state immunity defence and restoring the rights of prevailing parents to recover attorneys' fees and other litigation costs. In recent years, the Court has seemed more accepting of lower court activism, for instance, letting stand an award of attorneys' fees to parents who prevail in EAHCA administrative proceedings (*Moore v District of Columbia*, 1990) and letting stand an order for compensatory education, in which the trial court awarded a 12-year-old child with a disability 30 months of appropriate education at public expense beyond age 21 (the upper age limit of eligibility under the Act) because the school district had unreasonably delayed the placement (*Lester H v Gilhool*, 1991).

In summary, the US has witnessed substantial progress over the last two decades through implementation of a legislative framework that generally exceeds international human rights standards. As a result of coordinated legal, parental and professional association advocacy (eg, Council for Exceptional Children, American Association on Mental Retardation), that framework has survived economic recession and conservative Presidential administrations. Although the ambitious goals of the 1975 Act were sometimes undermined by bureaucratic resistance and underfunding, the law contributed to transforming special education in America (Weber, 1990). On a local level, child advocacy techniques of fact-finding, negotiation, mediation and litigation continue to assure that special education's rights are taken seriously, thus narrowing the gap between rhetoric and reality.

England and Wales

The UK Parliament has mandated 'special educational provision' for children with 'special educational needs'. The Education Act (EA) 1981, is the main, but not exclusive source of duties imposed on local education authorities (LEAs) 'for securing that special educational provision is made for pupils who have special educational needs' (§2[1]). The 1981 Act modifies the Education Act, 1944, which had imposed duties on LEAs to 'ascertain' the local children requiring special educational treatment under a medical model of examination by a medical officer, with the option of an LEA requiring a medical certificate for the 'purpose of securing the attendance of the child at a special school.' (§34[5]). The 1981 Act repealed those procedures, and substituted a statutory framework of LEA discretion to determine which children with 'a learning difficulty which calls for special educational provision' are to receive an assessment and statement of educational needs, and which are to have their special educational needs met more informally. The core provision embodying this discretion – Section 7(1) of the EA, 1981 – states that where an assessment has been made, the LEA,

> shall, if they are of the opinion that they should determine the special educational provision that should be made for [the child], make a statement of his (sic) special educational needs and maintain that statement. . . .

This two-tier system of special education has provoked critical commentary and litigation. Buss (1985) noted that the vague statutory definitions and lack of statutory standards for classifying children with statements from those without statements produced the possibility that a 'wider group' of children with milder handicaps might be excluded from the statutory protections of the statement-recording and implementing processes, while still imposing on them a special label and a different form of education. Hannon (1982) has criticized the 1981 Act for its 'omissions and generalities' and for its failure to embody the Warnock Report's (the 1978 policy review of the Committee of Inquiry into the Education of Handicapped Children) call for clear entitlements for the wider group of children who would not have statements of their special educational needs.

Appellate decisions have confirmed the interpretation that LEAs have substantial discretion to trigger the statutory safeguards of assessment and statement making. In *R v Secretary of State for Education and Science Ex Parte Lashford* (1988), the Court of Appeal observed that it appeared to be educational policy that a statutory statement was not needed if the child's special educational needs could be provided in the child's ordinary school. In upholding the LEA's refusal to provide a statement and residential schooling for a teenage girl with 'learning difficulty' and 'low average ability' who was receiving 'a remedial class' in an ordinary school, Dillon L J questioned the two-tier structure of special education in these terms:

> It is difficult to see why the Act, in making provision with respect to children with special educational needs, has not simply imposed on the local education authorities a general duty to assess the special educational needs of all children who have such needs, and to make whatever special educational provision should be made for the child's needs so assessed, if the child's parents were not making suitable arrangements.

This statutory scheme may be designed to avoid the perceived burden of requiring special education plans for the less severely disabled students who could receive education in ordinary schools. As noted in *R v Secretary of State for Education and Science Ex Parte Edwards* (1991), only 2 per cent of the school population receives the statutory statement under EA §7 while a wider group – an estimated 18 per cent – are presumed to have their special educational needs met by ordinary schools without the Act's formalities.

For the child with special educational needs that call for a statement, the authority must observe certain procedural rights. Before an assessment can be made, the parent must be notified of the procedure to be followed in making the assessment and the right to make representations and submit written evidence. If the LEA on the basis of that assessment determines special education provision is required, the LEA shall specify that service and arrange for it to be made available to the student.

The duty to mainstream or integrate the student is imposed on ordinary schools (ie, children with special needs in such schools should engage, as far as is 'reasonably practicable', in school activities together with children who do not have special educational needs, §2[7]) and on LEAs. This latter duty is qualified by the views of the child's parents, and is conditional on the compatibility of integration with the child's receiving the required special education, the 'efficient education' of the child's classmates, and the 'efficient use of resources'. The breadth of these conditions and the lack of additional resources have led some commentators to describe integration as a weak duty under the Act (Hannon,

1982; Kirp, 1982). Although some progress towards education in ordinary schools has been achieved (at present about 40 per cent of children with statements attend such schools), new education laws may reduce integration as schools seek to attract higher achieving students and as educational policies favour the most able students over those with special education needs or social disadvantages (Mittler, 1992).

Parents can participate in the statement-making process and challenge statements in several ways. They can submit their views and written evidence at the assessment and statement-making stages. If they disagree with any part of a proposed statement, they may arrange one or more meetings with an LEA representative 'to discuss the relevant advice'. If the LEA then determines to modify, leave unchanged or make no statement, the parents will receive notice of their right to appeal to an appeal committee which has only advisory powers, or to the Secretary of State if appealing from a decision to make no statement. If still dissatisfied after an appeals committee's opinion, the parents may turn to the Secretary of State. Parents of children without statements can request an assessment, which will be granted unless the LEA deems it unreasonable. In general, the process is one of extended consultation, with some possibility that the Secretary will, after consulting with the LEA, amend the statement regarding special educational provisions.

Although judicial review is not specifically mentioned in the Act, a line of cases reveal the possibilities of limited court intervention. For example, *R v. Lancashire County Council Ex Parte M* (1988) held that intensive speech therapy was a special educational provision that could be required under the EA, 1981. The court concluded that teaching a child with a congenital speech deformity to communicate by speech was clearly educational, and rejected the LEA's attempts to evade as an 'oversight' its own statement acknowledging access to individual speech therapy as a special educational provision. The LEA had sought to reclassify such therapy as a non-educational provision, which under the Education Reform Act 1988 it would not have had a mandatory duty to arrange. *R v Secretary of State for Education and Science Ex Parte Edwards* (1991) also resulted in an order in favour of a child with a disability, specifically dyslexia and discalcula. The Court of Appeal ruled that the Secretary reconsider his affirmance of a statement that identified a special educational need (ie, numeracy), but failed to specify the special provision to meet that need.

Other cases reveal uncertainties about integration or the production of up-to-date statements, but yield no remedy. In *R v London Borough of Newham Ex Parte D* (1991), the court discovered that the child's assessment was done eight years before and that it was 'high time' that her needs were reassessed, but ruled that no judicial relief could be granted in view of her mother's failure to make a timely request for reassessment. *Re D (a minor)* (1988) is remarkable for the evident judicial disapproval of parents who sought to assert their rights and oppose their child's residential school placement when they felt the child could attend a nearby special day school and thus remain, in the court's words, in a loving home as 'a member of a united and boisterous family'. In this wardship proceeding, the court was unwilling to entertain 'legalistic arguments based on an enforced compliance by the local education authority with its statutory duties', and the appellate court echoed these sentiments, urging the father to cooperate with the plans for segregated education and to drop litigation that under the EA, 1981 might have offered an alternative solution to his son's special educational needs.

In summary, the English system relies on professional discretion with only limited legal interventions. It is a system that promises participation for parents, yet results in relatively few parents who will contest educational placement decisions and less parental involvement than the 1981 Act contemplated. Law reform may be part of the remedy, particularly if parents of children with special education needs are accorded the legal right to opt for ordinary or special school placement. Such a proposal is advanced in a recent authoritative report that criticizes implementation of the 1981 Act for the long delays in issuing statements, lack of definitional clarity, lack of national guidelines on assessment, and other deficiencies (Audit Commission, 1992). Better laws, policies and practices may ultimately depend upon a change in political climate. To realize that change for children with special needs, 'determined advocacy will be needed by teachers and other professionals, working in partnership with families and with the local community' (Mittler, 1992, para. 35).

Canada

Canada is a federal state in which laws on special education vary considerably from province to province. Commentators have criticized these laws for their lack of precision in defining entitlements to special education, let alone appropriate education and enforceable rights (MacKay, 1984; Smith, 1981). Furthermore, the legal right to a free appropriate education is not adequately protected or subsidized on a national level, with one legal commentator observing that '[m]uch needs to be changed in our laws if Canada is to be true to the ideals to which she has put her name in several international undertakings' (Smith, 1980). The Canadian Charter of Rights and Freedoms (1982), effective in 1985, has roused expectations that constitutionally entrenched guarantees of equal protection and due process would lead to judicial enforcement of special education rights. To date, court interpretation of statutory or constitutional provisions have not yielded that result.

The law in Ontario has been described as 'Canada's boldest education initiative' and the 'one serious effort to copy the landmark U.S. legislation' (MacKay, 1984, p. 49). The following discussion will, therefore, focus on the Ontario Education Act, 1980 (as revised 1990) and its judicial interpretation.

The Act defines 'exceptional pupil' as a pupil whose 'behavioral, communicational, intellectual, physical or multiple exceptionalities' are considered by a committee to require the pupil's placement in a special education programme. Under the Act, the Minister must ensure that 'all exceptional children in Ontario have available to them . . . appropriate special education programs and special education services' that are free, as well as provide an appeal process permitting parents to challenge the appropriateness of their child's special education services.

The problematic features of the Act are their classifications of some children as 'trainable retarded' (as distinguished from 'educable retarded pupils'), and of other children as 'hard to serve' pupils determined by a school board to be 'unable to profit by instruction' offered by a board due to mental or multiple handicaps. For the latter category of children, the school board need only assist the parent to locate a suitable placement, with the actual cost of such placement paid by the province.

The Act and accompanying regulations also set up two systems of appeal, one from special education decisions made by the Identification, Placement and Review Committee, and one from 'hard to serve' determinations made by a school committee to a Special Education Tribunal.

Courts have struggled to make sense of the wide obligations imposed on the Minister and the procedural complexities of classifying children as eligible for special education. In *Thompson v Ontario* (1988), the court characterized the Act as 'far from clear' and upheld the school board's power to overturn a 'hard to serve' committee's decision that the pupil was not hard to serve. In *Re Dolmage and Muskoka Board of Education* (1985), the court adopted a 'hands-off' approach to the issue of the appropriateness of special education and the parent's appeal that their son receive a 'total communication programme'. While commending the parents for their zeal on their child's behalf, the court declined to order a change in the broad programme of special education that the Minister had approved in the Act's early years of phased-in implementation. During this period, the court opined that the 'most appropriate placement . . . may not only be less than ideal, but may be far less than ideal' (p. 555). Other cases have denied parents the right to appeal 'hard to serve' determinations on the basis that the child was not then enrolled in a local school as a 'resident pupil' (*Re Maw and Scarborough Bd of Education*, 1983; *Re Townsend and Bd of Education for Etobicoke*, 1986). One commentator has noted that this appeal process is inaccessible to working-class families who lack advocacy resources, and that to date even those families with lawyers or the support of lobby groups who do appeal have not been successful (Crux, 1989).

The Canadian Charter of Rights and Freedoms (1982) has been hailed as a means of vindicating the rights of persons with disabilities. Section 15(1) guarantees equality before and under the law and the 'right to the equal protection and equal benefit of the law without discrimination' to persons with mental or physical disabilities. MacKay (1984) concluded that, along with human rights statutes, the Charter could lead to US-style judicial intervention to ensure rights to appropriate education and equal educational opportunities for children with disabilities. Cruickshank (1986) also speculated on the use of §7 (procedural fairness) and §15 (equal protection) to challenge procedural flaws in statutes or the exclusion of pupils from schools. Although the possibilities of stricter scrutiny of ministerial discretion under the Charter are significant, to date the one reported case addressing the application of the Canadian Charter to special education law declined, with little discussion, to find a §7 violation in the denial of hearing rights to a non-enrolled student under the Ontario Education Amendment Act, 1980 (*Maw*, 1983). However, parents seeking integrated education and relying on the Charter's equality rights have succeeded in obtaining two favourable settlements (negotiated on the verge of trial) that permit their child to attend a regular classroom with non-disabled peers. These victories suggest that the Charter, advocacy and educational innvovation can be forces for inclusion (Porter and Richler, 1991).

Under the impetus of the Charter, the Canadian Human Rights Act, 1977 (which proscribes discriminatory practices based on disability or other grounds), and international conventions, Canadian provinces can review special education laws to make them fairer, clearer and more comprehensive. Such a review would need to be assisted by a concerted campaign of advocacy and law reform analysis.

Other countries

In many other regions of the world, legislation on special education has been enacted or is under consideration. Unfortunately, considerations of space preclude lengthy discussion. For example, the World Health Organization's (1990) survey of European countries noted that Sweden, France, Germany, Finland, Austria, Portugal, Spain and others reported a trend toward integration of children with disabilities in normal schools. Several Eastern European countries emphasized laws and provisions on special boarding or day schools, including Bulgaria, Hungary, Poland, Romania and Turkey. Although Czechoslovakia was not included in that survey, its specialists in this field have expressed the desire to move from an institution-based to a more integrated and legally-based system of special education.

In Israel, the Special Education Law of 1988 is designed to require free, appropriate education in the least restrictive environment for children in need of special education. The law stipulates that a multidisciplinary placement committee shall determine the services required by eligible children aged 3 to 21. Due to budgetary restraints, the law is to be implemented in phases.

Like Israel's law, Korea's special education law (the 1977 Act for the Promotion of Special Education for the Handicapped) is also reported as modelled after the 1975 US EAHCA law (Seo *et al*, 1992). Although Korea's law mandates free public education with related services such as physical and speech therapies, the law does not contain due process or least-restrictive alternative provisions.

In contrast, Australia lacks detailed national legislation, and its special education arrangements stress autonomy by individual school principals (Levin, 1985). Although the laws of Western Australia confer rights on parents in the special education planning process, the traditions of strong states' rights and deference to educational professionals tend to favour decentralized states and informal approaches. While one state, Victoria, pioneered an integration plan, its implementation depended more on ministerial discretion, good faith and professional judgement, than any legal foundation (Safran, 1989).

In Denmark and Sweden, laws and policies stress integration, normalization and decentralization. They bear many similarities to the United States, except that Scandinavian 'child-find procedures' are more advanced and the laws are less detailed and more closely linked to general education laws (Walton *et al.*, 1989).

Conclusions

The international community has made commitments to secure education for children with disabilities as a human and legal right. UNESCO's Sundberg Declaration, for instance, categorically states that every person with a disability 'must be able to exercise his (sic) fundamental right to have full access to education, training, culture and information' (UNESCO, 1981, Article 1).

However, laws reflect the cultural, economic, professional and political traditions of a particular country, so it is hardly surprising that special education laws
range from the highly detailed and legalistic US model to the general laws of
developing countries which have not even begun to address this topic. The
challenge to law-makers in those latter countries will be to balance realistic
aspirations with low-cost, largely non-institutional special education models
that respect human rights and the values, beliefs and practices of their own
cultures. Laws which fail these tests will be irrelevant or little more than pious
wishes.

In the developed nations, the main issue which must be addressed concerns
the clarity and usefulness of legal frameworks to do justice for children without
undue stigma. Specifically, laws, regulations and policies must be able to identify
children in need of special education, to assure non-discriminatory assessment,
to deliver appropriate services, to foster integration, to secure periodic review of
individualized educational plans and to guard against arbitrary or unreasonable
decision-making. In every country, these tasks remain a work in progress. In
every family with a child with a disability, the quest for a realized right to an
appropriate education is a decisive experience on which so many other rights and
possibilities for the child hinge.

References

Americans with Disabilities Act of 1990, 42 USCA §§12131–65 (West, 1991).
Audit Commission and Her Majesty's Inspectorate (1992) *Getting in on the Act: Provision for pupils with special educational needs – the national picture*, London: HMSO.
Buss, W G (1985) 'Special education in England and Wales', *Law and Contemporary Problems*, **48**, 119–68.
Canadian Constitution (Constitution Act, 1982) pt. I (Canadian Charter of Rights and Freedom), §15(1).
Canadian Human Rights Act, Revised Statutes of Canada, ch. H-6 (1977).
Commonwealth v. Sadler, 3 Phila. 316, 1979 Phila. Cty. Rptr., Lexis 92 (Pa. Common Pleas Ct, Phila. Co., December 10, 1979).
Copeland, I (1991) 'Special educational needs and the Education Reform Act, 1988', *British Journal of Educational Studies*, **39**, 190–206.
Cruickshank, D (1986) 'Charter equality rights: The challenge to education, law and policy', in Manley-Casmir, M E and Sussell, TA (eds) *Courts in the Classroom: Education and the Charter of Rights and Freedoms 51*, Calgary, Canada: Detselig Enterprises.
Crux, S C (1989) 'Special education legislation: Humanitarianism or legalized deviance and control?', *Education Canada*, 24–31 (Spring).
Education Act, 1944, 7 and 8 Geo. 6 (Eng.).
Education Act, 1981, ch. 60 (Eng.).
Education for All Handicapped Children Act of 1975, Pub. L. 94–142, codified as amended at 20 USC §§1400–1485 (1988).
Education Reform Act, 1988, ch. 40 (Eng.).
Hannon, V (1982) 'The Education Act 1981: New rights and duties in special education', *Journal of Social Welfare Law*, 275–84.
Hendrick Hudson Central School District v Rowley, 458 US 176 (1982).
Herr, S S (1983) *Rights and Advocacy for Retarded People*, Lexington, MA: Lexington Press.
Herr, S S (1991) 'Child advocacy in special education', in Westman, J C (ed) *Who Speaks for the Children? The Handbook of Individual and Class Advocacy 147*, Sarasota, FL: Professional Resource Exchange.
Israel Special Education Law of 1988, Statutes of the State of Israel (No. 1256).
Kirp, D L (1982) 'Professionalization as a policy choice: British special education in comparative perspective', *World Politics*, **34**, 137–74.
Lester H v Gilhool, 916 F.2d 865 (3rd Cir. 1990, *cert. denied* 111 S. Ct 1317 (1991).

Levin, B (1985) 'Equal educational opportunity for children with special needs: The federal role in Australia', *Law and Contemporary Problems*, **48**, 213–73.

MacKay, A W (1984) *Education Law in Canada*, Toronto, Canada: Emond-Montgomery Publications.

Mills v Board of Education of the District of Columbia, 348 F. Supp. 866 (DDC 1972).

Mittler, P (1992) 'School integration in England and Wales', invited paper given to international convention on school integration of disabled children, Cosenza, Italy.

Moore v. District of Columbia, 907 F.2d 165 (DC Cir. 1990, *cert. denied* 111 S. Ct 556 (1990).

Ontario Education Act, 1980, Revised Statutes of Ontario, ch. E.2 (1990)(Can.).

Pennsylvania Association for Retarded Children v Pennsylvania, 343 F. Supp. 279 (ED Pa. 1972).

Poirier, D, Goguen, L and Leslie, P (1988) *Educational Rights of Exceptional Children in Canada: A national study of multi-level commitments*, Toronto, Canada: Carswell.

Porter, G and Richler, D (1991) 'Changing special education practice: Law, advocacy and innovation', in Porter, G and Richler, D (eds) *Changing Canadian Schools: Perspectives on Disability and Inclusion*, North York, Ontario, Canada: Roeher Institute.

R v Lancashire County Council Ex Parte M (1988) 2 Family Law Reports 279 and 395 (CA).

R v London Borough of Newham Ex Parte D (QB), *The Times*, May 27, 1991.

R v Secretary of State for Education and Science Ex Parte Lashford (1988) 1 Family Law Reports 72 (CA).

R v. Secretary of State for Education and Science Ex Parte Edwards, (CA) *The Times*, May 9, 1991.

Re D (a minor) (1988) 1 Family Law Reports 131 (CA).

Re Dolmage and Muskoka Board of Education, 49 Ontario Reports 2d 546 (1985).

Re Maw and Scarborough Board of Education, 43 Ontario Reports 2d 694 (1983).

Re Townsend and Board of Education for the Borough of Etobicoke, 54 Ontario Reports 2d 449 (1986).

Rehabilitation Act of 1973, 29 USC §794 (1988).

Safran, S P (1989) 'Special education in Australia and the United States: A cross-cultural analysis', *Journal of Special Education*, **23**, 330–41.

Seo, G H, Oakland, T, Han, H S and Hu, S (1992) 'Special education in South Korea', *Exceptional Children*, **58**, 213–18.

Smith, J A C (1980) 'The right to an appropriate education: A comparative study', *Ottawa Law Review*, **12**, 367–91.

Smith, J A C (1981) 'The Education Amendment Act, 1980', *Ottawa Law Review*, **13**, 199–209.

Thompson v Ontario, 63 Ontario Reports 489 (1988).

Turnbull, H R (1986) *Free Appropriate Public Education: The Law and Children with Disabilities*, London: Love Publishing Co.

UN Convention on the Rights of the Child (1990), 28 ILM 1456 (1989) (entered into force September 2, 1990).

UN Declaration on the Rights of Disabled Persons (1975) GA Res. 3447, UN Doc. A/10034.

UN Declaration on the Rights of Mentally Retarded Persons (1971) GA Res. 2856, UN Doc. A/8429.

UN Declaration on the Rights of the Child (1959) (adopted unanimously by the UN General Assembly on November 20, 1959).

UN International Covenant on Economic, Social, and Cultural Rights (1966) (entered into force January 3, 1976).

UN Universal Declaration of Human Rights, UN Doc. A/811 (December 10, 1948).

UNESCO Sundberg Declaration (1981) Declaration of the the World Conference on Actions and Strategies for Education, Prevention and Integration (affirmed by representatives of 103 nations and 15 NGOs, Torremolinos, Malaga, Spain, November 2–7, 1981).

Walton, W T, Rosenqvist, J and Sandling, I (1989) 'A comparative study of special education contrasting Denmark, Sweden, and the United States of America', *Scandinavian Journal of Educational Research*, **33**, 283–98.

Weber, M C (1990) 'The transformation of the Education of the Handicapped Act: A study in the interpretation of a radical statute', *University of California Davis Law Review*, **24**, 349–436.

World Health Organization (1990) *Is the Law Fair to the Disabled? A European Survey*, European Series, No. 29, Copenhagen, Denmark: WHO Regional Publications.

Part 2: Meeting specific disability needs

5. Children with learning difficulties

Christine Miles and Mike Miles

Development of attitudes and information

Throughout history, most of what was to be learnt, by most people, was learnt in everyday life. Children watched and imitated adults, negotiating what was acceptable or desirable. Younger copied older siblings, peer groups mutually tried out actions and behaviour. Some children have been noticeably quicker than average in reproducing adult skills, and some noticeably slower. A few have not acquired the normal skills and behaviour, long past the expected time, regardless of rewards and sanctions.

Those acquiring skills very slowly, or not at all, but who had no evident physical impairment, commonly were categorized by pejorative terms indicating abnormality. The assessment might be lightened by an imputation of religious or spiritual benefit, for example as a 'holy fool' or person who is 'innocent' of the normal human drives. An early judgement of mental abilities occurs in the *Brhad-aranyaka* and *Chandogya Upanisads*, where Speech, Hearing, Sight, Mind and Breath debate their relative merits. Each ability in turn takes a year's leave. When Mind returns, and asks what effect its absence had, the others (in Radhakrishnan's version, 1953) report that they were 'as the stupid not knowing' (p. 307), 'like the children mindless' (or 'undeveloped minds') (p. 423). Despite 2,500 years' interval, the story communicates readily to our century.

This century, however, has begun to challenge negative terminology. Convergence has occurred, across cultures and nations, toward an ideal of human societies in which, regardless of genetic endowment, children should have learning environments that enable them to develop a wide range of abilities, overcoming any obstacles they may encounter; societies that both value them individually and find valued roles for them. No society yet claims to have achieved this. Indeed, its very 'idealism' causes some to dismiss the vision as unrealistic. Yet there has been an impressive growth of empirical information, of concepts, knowledge, skills and design, towards achieving the ideal.

Earlier experience arose mostly in religious or medical domains. Where a religious or medical 'explanation' was accepted for a given child's failure to do the things or play the roles expected, the matter might be closed. If God had made a child so, or a trauma had damaged the brain, or a demon had snatched the child and substituted a changeling, educational remedies would hardly be considered.

Where help was sought, it would be in medical or religious terms, by herbal drugs or visits to miracle-working shrines. Such views, common in information-poor countries, have not disappeared even in countries where an abundance of informed experience suggests alternative explanations.

Formal experience of teaching children who learnt slowly or little accrued in Europe in the 18th and 19th centuries, but reporting and replication were limited. Some local, informal experience of teaching such children has probably been gained at many times and places, but not so recorded as to enlarge the public stock. An exception is the Indian *Panchatantra*, a book of animal fables compiled over 1,500 years ago to instruct slow-learning princes whom their father deemed 'utter fools' (Edgerton, 1924, p. 271). Perhaps the earliest extant teaching material for children with learning difficulties, it influenced Middle Eastern and European folk tales through multiple translations; illustrating, as does Maria Montessori's work, that the gains from investing in special needs education may enrich mainstream culture.

Special needs information began accumulating seriously with the growth of literacy, the mass media and the internationalization of knowledge through global communications technology. Recent decades have also seen growing inter-disciplinary exchange between medical and educational fields, and also among psychologists, sociologists, families whose children have special needs and other advocates. Information formally communicated and exchanged about children with learning difficulties since 1960 exceeds the total of previous human exchange on the topic. Most of the recent flow has been in English, originating from only a dozen Western countries, reaching a largely professional audience. There is a glut of over-specialized production, but a dearth of local-language information for front-line teachers, parents and carers for the vast majority of the estimated 50 million children in the world with learning difficulties. Only a very modest start has been made by some Open Universities and by community radio stations for wider dissemination of ideas and materials for meeting special educational needs.

The meaning of 'learning difficulties'

The phrase 'children with learning difficulties' is now used by some European educators to describe, in an educational context, some of the above phenomena. Since 'learning' and 'difficulty' are common words, anglophones tend to construe the phrase as they please. There are few children who have never had difficulty learning something, yet a 'child with learning difficulties' must be one in whom difficulties are normal rather than exceptional. Again, there are children who have no difficulty learning when sufficiently motivated, but without special encouragement will do no more than other children who have difficulties learning; or the problem may be not so much learning a new skill, as using it in a different context; or not so much learning once, as repeating later.

The term 'learning difficulties' was intended to focus more accurately than, for example, 'educational subnormality', 'mental retardation' or 'intellectual impairment', which suggest deviation from a norm, hindrance of mental process or deficient capacity. The Warnock Committee (1978, p. 43–4) recommended its use, stating that difficulties would be 'significant' (p. 48) and hoping that the term would be used descriptively rather than for categorization. This hope was confused by the Committee's suggestion or supposition that learning difficulties could be described as 'specific', 'mild', 'moderate' or 'severe' (p. 43).

Nations with compulsory schooling and where enrolment exceeds 95 per cent, usually have a country-wide system to register births and so to know children's age. Age-linked achievement norms become known, and most children move up school grouped by 12-month age bands. In such systems, children with learning difficulties perceived as 'mild' or 'moderate' far outweigh those counted 'severe', 'profound' or 'complex'. At least half of all children, however, live in countries with below 90 per cent school attendance and where birth registration and age-grouping are lax. There may still be perceived age-linked achievement norms, but it is less clear how many children do reach these within a given time range. Meanings of the word 'learning' also differ substantially, in many countries, from the discovery-based, incremental construction of reality that has become the accepted idea among the culturally dominant classes of Europe and North America during this century. Learning more often means memorizing or obeying the words of a master or mistress, or copying desired behaviour, activities often done simultaneously by classes of 40 or more children. Here, 'learning difficulties' would also mean something else; but in fact the term is little used.

Some children have difficulties only in a specific context, for example, at school. Elsewhere, they learn enough, and quickly enough, to avoid being noticeably different. Their problem in the specific context may be one of motivation or compliance, rather than a deficit of innate capacity, or it may result from the inability of teachers to recognize and remediate specific problems before the child's learning becomes generally more delayed. Sometimes the label 'children whose teachers have teaching difficulties' could be appropriate. In many cases, particularly where poor nutrition and chronic minor ailments are common, attention to these physiological problems would remove much of the learning difficulty. Many Western studies have suggested this, but local work such as that of Agarwal *et al* (1991) may have greater impact in India.

What is being done

As has been identified in Chapters 1 and 2, a minority of all children with learning difficulties have some special schooling. Most other children with learning difficulties either attend their local primary school, or never start school.

In the Indo-Pak subcontinent and China, supporting half the world's school-age children, the situation differs appreciably from that in Europe now. In Bangladesh, Zaman (1990, p.20) suggests that 'the mildly retarded' may pass unidentified in the community and be accommodated in school, where attainment standards are comparatively low. 'Casual integration' has been studied in Sri Lanka (Gunewardena, 1987, pp. 24–6) and in Pakistan, where at least 2 per cent of pupils in ordinary school have noticeable impairments without any special measures being taken (Miles, M, 1985). An Indian report (Policies, 1975) states that nearly 5 per cent of pupils in ordinary classes could be considered mentally retarded. Narasimhan and Mukherjee (1986, p. 61) note that, for lack of identification, many 'mildly retarded' Indian children are casually integrated. They find little merit in this, as teachers adapt neither method nor curriculum to the pupils' special needs. However, though these children may gain little by way of cognitive and literacy skills, some at least may gain in social and communicative skills by spending time in the company of age peers.

Education planners in developing countries seldom realize how many British pupils with learning difficulties have been casually integrated in ordinary schools for decades past. Pringle et al. (1966, pp. 38–9) found, among 11,000 English 7-year-olds born in one week of 1958, that more than 5 per cent received special help within ordinary schools, for educational or mental backwardness; another 8 per cent would benefit from such help. HM Inspectors reported on slow learners in 158 English secondary schools in 1967–8 (DES, 1971, p. 1): 14 per cent of pupils were deemed to need special help; only half were said by head teachers to be getting it. The level of casual integration looks similar to that found later by Narasimhan and Mukherjee in India, but there is a difference of resources to meet the needs.

Development of educational facilities specifically for children with learning difficulties in India began in the 1940s, but there was little growth until the 1960s (Vohra, 1987). In Pakistan, the start was in the 1960s and a surge came in the 1980s when the Federal Government entered the field (Miles, M, 1991). In both countries, the past 20 years have seen hectic efforts to assimilate Western ideas and methods, on a local experience base not fully adequate for evaluating these imports, some elements of which have been spread with crusading zeal by Western specialists.

Ideological factors in China may work more positively for casually integrated children with learning difficulties. Robinson (1978) found a reticence about 'mental retardation' as such. Her sources admitted individual differences in school readiness and in learning speed, but not fundamental differences of intelligence, which would be inconsistent with socialist doctrine. Robinson noted that many school activities were of a practical nature that easily accommodated the mildly retarded child, who were observably present in primary schools. There was also an emphasis on mutual help, on smoothing out differences of individual performance and on the needs of the group rather than the individual. During the 1970s, official recognition of mental retardation grew, spurred by various surveys (Kuo-Tai, 1988). Yongxin (1986) suggests there are some two million school-aged children with learning disabilities. The first formal special classes for mentally retarded children began in Shanghai in 1979, catering mainly for mildly retarded children. By 1986, education of these children was said to be a widely identified priority need among Chinese educators (Stevens et al., 1990).

The early special needs work in Shanghai emphasized the building of a friendly teacher-pupil relationship, growth of pupils' self-respect through positive reinforcement, flexible curriculum and timetable, close school-family cooperation, and some mother-tongue teaching for children of linguistic minorities (Shih, 1979). Such emphases match the politically correct picture of 'Wenhsing Street Primary School' (Anon, 1973), where a somewhat idealized teacher does not merely impart knowledge to the pupils but cares for them and is their wise, older comrade, showing them how to think and solve problems. It contrasts with the competitive atmosphere of the later primary school portrayed by Juemin (1987). Here, entrants are swept on to a tread-mill of achieving high marks, aiming by colossal feats of memorization to gain entry to one of the 'fast-track' high schools, with great loss of self-esteem for those who fail in the rat-race.

Contrasts are not surprising. In China, as in many smaller countries, there are great variations between the ambience and achievements of schools in any one area, between urban and rural schools, between schools with more or less children from ethnic minorities or backward classes, between schools with more or less funding and resources, between schools as they appear in official reports and as they might be found by unnotified visit, plus variation across the time span from 1970 to 1990. Undoubtedly, appeals for an early, liberal, child-centred education, in which children with learning difficulties can blossom in their own good time, have been heard since the 1920s (Hsing-chih, 1928) or earlier, and continue to the present. Weber (1979), Potts (1989), and Stevens *et al.* (1990) report features of such an approach. However, Unger (1977) notes the ease with which schools shown to foreign visitors can give a false impression. The more typical rural school has very modest facilities. There, education remains traditional, with an emphasis on direct instruction and unison chanting to assist memorization. Students are not expected to work at their own individual pace.

There is evidence of this vast nation mobilizing resources towards goals which are impressive in scope. Plans for children with learning difficulties extend to remote and 'culturally impoverished' areas, with practical research on socio-cultural cognitive delay (Menglan, 1983), and some use of minority mother-tongue teaching to ease entry to the normal curriculum. Education of the children of scattered, nomadic tribes herding sheep in mountain areas is being tackled by putting teachers on horseback and organizing peer tutoring between the visits of these peripatetic teachers (Joint Investigation, 1975). The cultural and geographical 'learning difficulties' of such children appear substantial. The efforts to reach them, even if described in politicized jargon, suggest an admirable spirit among the teachers and local organizers.

Progress in these Asian nations is important both for the numbers involved and because experience painfully won over two centuries in Europe is here telescoped into a few decades. Worldwide, provision tends to be made first for children with physical, visual or aural impairment. In numbers, however, provision for those with learning difficulties may rapidly outstrip facilities for other special needs. In 1986, over half of South Korea's 100 special schools and 93 per cent of all special classes were for students with mental retardation (Seo *et al.*, 1992). In Japan in 1990, comparable figures were 51 per cent and 71 per cent (Rehabilitation, 1991, pp. 16–19). On the other hand, when provisions are limited by socio-economic and attitudinal factors, pupils with severe or complex learning difficulties are among those least likely to receive education. They may even be excluded from the state system (UNESCO, 1988, p. 11).

A 'modern' approach

Development of special needs education is believed by some writers to involve several successive stages through which all systems must pass (Labregere, 1974; Tuunainen, 1988). Miles, M (1989) suggests an incremental development of attitudes that may underlie such stages. Yet exceptions and anomalies abound. For example, Hrnjica (1990) reported three parallel systems for educating disabled pupils in different parts of Yugoslavia (before the political divisions of 1992). Singapore, by vigorous exam-and-IQ streaming, stops its children with learning difficulties from dropping out of normal schools, despite the unfashionable nature of these policies (Quah, 1990). Pakistan also has at least three parallel systems, in one of which responsibility for special education was transferred from the Department of Education to that of Social Welfare. There are no infallible rules.

To children whose current learning performance, not always an accurate guide to their ability, falls substantially below the normal range, education systems typically respond with one of five measures:

a. Expulsion
b. Compensation/Remediation
c. Alternative/Special Provision
d. Integration/Equalization
e. Individualization.

Some systems test would-be entrants and reject those who, for example, cannot or will not recite numbers and the alphabet at the age of 5. Some expel children on their first or second exam failure, maybe at 6 years old or after they have repeated a year. Others, more positively, make efforts somewhere between adjusting the child to fit the system and adjusting the system to manage the child. A further, radical, possibility is that education systems should act 'in reverse', changing society so as to create space and appreciation for children and young adults having substantially different abilities; alternatively, a rapidly-changing society should not sustain schools that make inappropriate and pointless demands on children, accentuating the lack of capacities among some, when such capacities will not be required of them by the time they are adult.

Generally, the milder the child's difficulties, the more effort is made to adjust him or her to fit the system; the more severe his or her problems, the more likely the system is to make some special provision. Between the latter alternatives, the possible range of practice and philosophy is so vast that there can seldom be two practitioners, even in the same system, who have exactly the same idea of what they are trying to do and why. Nevertheless, some common observations and practices have emerged in European and North American schools, that are regarded as broadly-agreed Western foundations:

1. All children can learn and can make measurable progress (apart from a very small number with active degenerative conditions).
2. The teacher's work is to devise and implement means by which each child does learn and make progress (rather than to appear before pupils and issue statements of knowledge).
3. The process is likely to be facilitated by a collaboration of mutual respect with children's families and homes.
4. Close observation of the individual child in a variety of situations, over weeks or months, is a major key to assessing the child's abilities and potential, identifying motivational factors and finding ways to overcome difficulties in learning.

5. Learning proceeds best by starting from the child's existing knowledge and abilities, including the child's normal home and neighbourhood environment.
6. Teachers' step-wise analysis of tasks or behaviours to be learnt, their timely use of appropriate motivators, and their detailed recording of results, are methods of known effectiveness.
7. The teacher's relationship with the child is usually a major key to motivation. A fruitful relationship will often extend to activities outside the school routine.
8. Development of the child's general communication skills is vital to facilitating the interaction between child, teacher and curriculum.
9. For children who have appreciable difficulties, a carefully modified curriculum is usually required, for progress to be made in the earlier years. This may lead on to a curriculum similar to that for children of normal abilities, including literacy and numeracy skills and opportunities for creativity and sport, while the child's abilities may suggest additional, more practical, curriculum goals.
10. Learning problems arising from, or exacerbated by, nutritional deficiency or imbalance, chronic infestation, mild sensory impairment and similar physiological causes, are commonly overlooked in every country, while physical or psychological abuse may be overlooked or ignored. Prevention and early attention to such causes is more effective and less costly than later remedial measures.

Whether this pedagogical decalogue is globally relevant and practicable, remains uncertain. In no country are all teachers guided by it. There has been no controlled study of its effectiveness in the many countries where very few teachers practise it. A mere 30 years ago in Britain it was thought 'innovative, experimental' to study the use of kindergarten-style organized free play with mentally retarded pupils, as against formal, teacher-directed activity (Brandon and Stern, 1962). Similar ideas were in fact tried in Europe more than a century earlier, but their influence on formal systems of mass education was small.

Imported foreign know-how, then as now, met many problems. Froebel's kindergarten approach, for example, needed rethinking when first shifted from its origins in open-air, rural Germany with 15 pupils per teacher, to the English city school with classes of up 70 children and a curriculum enforced by a Board of Education (Marsden, 1990). Similar obstacles are apparent in the 1990s to educationists in developing countries, faced with Western advocacy of child-centred education (Miles, C, 1991). Unease is growing over current attempts to transfer programmes that assume modern Western concepts of 'the child' to countries where substantially different concepts are held (Boyden, 1990; Miles and Miles, in press).

Integration, curriculum and community involvement

The idea that adults of different gender, race, caste, creed and taste would co-exist more cordially had they been schooled together, has attracted social engineers in many countries. A further category, 'people of different abilities', is now to be added to the pot, or noticed as having casually been there all along. A broad spectrum exists of arguments for 'integrated schooling' of children with learning difficulties. Some find integration self-evidently right and so to be tried regardless of difficulties and without wasting time defining exactly what it is. Others argue that some sort of integration works better for all children, and may be cheaper, than the alternatives. The debate is reviewed elsewhere in this volume.

Whatever their ideal of integration, very few believe it will be easily done on the macro-scale. Mass schooling is an increasingly modest part of mass culture. In a diminishing number of countries, mass culture is purposefully directed by religious exhortations or political slogans. In many more, the inspirational mode has ceded to a demotic approach, mirroring the common denominators of the disparate groups and individuals who comprise 'the masses'. In the former cases, such as China and some Islamic states, schools may still decisively shape children's thoughts and behaviour. In many countries, however, there is little central control over what happens in schools. Schooling may appear feeble and dated beside the latest 'realities' purveyed powerfully to children by the mass media.

Increasing numbers of countries have a mix of separate and integrated provisions. This at least provides some degree of choice and a basis for comparing strengths and weaknesses. Ideally, in such a situation, the decision between alternatives will be made according to the needs of the child and wishes of the parents. Most children benefit from having peers who are a little more advanced than they are themselves, but personality factors are important too – a cheerful, extrovert child will learn more readily from her peers than would a shy, fearful child; the latter might gain more from a period in a more protective environment with more attention from friendly adults. Some children need to learn behaviour patterns less distressing to others before they are acceptable in an ordinary school. Parents may have personal reasons for preferring one school to another. More countries are beginning to facilitate this choice.

In deciding whether separate provision should be made, another important factor is the degree to which the normal curriculum is adaptable to children's special needs. Where there is sufficient flexibility, the education of children with learning difficulties can be seen as appropriately placed within the continuum provided in the normal education system. Where there is little flexibility for the individual's needs, a separate special system can give opportunities for innovation, which will in turn influence the mainstream.

Both Gaylord-Ross (1987) and Mittler and Farrell (1987) observe that when existing segregated schools produce publicly acceptable results, there is little incentive to substitute for them a system, the merits of which are not clearly proven. Local planned classroom and social integration has been piloted successfully by highly motivated innovators; but macro-planners inevitably seek policies that are visibly practicable, in terms of prevailing social attitudes, when operated in the average school by run-of-the-mill teachers, while both giving scope for the most able and limiting the damage potential of the moderately subnormal professional.

Debate about integration inevitably embraces issues of curriculum, family and community involvement. Mittler (1983) identified an educational trend towards seeing the child, as an integral part of several linked communities – family, peers, local community and society as a whole . . . . We are learning to teach not only in the classroom and in the home but in the community, in shops, on buses, in the market, in the field.

Some pre-industrial or newly industrializing societies in fact have yet to divorce the child from his or her community environment or treat them as a numbered peg to fit into a factory slot. Also, a few wealthy societies with populations thinly scattered in rural areas have developed home-based schooling for children with or without special needs, in which educational material in printed or broadcast form is supervised by adult relatives, aided by itinerant teachers or counsellors.

Some families and local communities are no doubt only too willing to tell special educators what they should do, yet a more demanding participation may not be so attractive. Among front-line teachers too, even among those who see the merit in a whole-life curriculum, cumulative everyday pressures may reinforce a tendency, noted by senior Soviet pedagogues, merely to adjust the content and methods of teaching special children to the content and methods customary in ordinary schools (Working Group, 1990, p. 26). Further, 'the community', while being an attractive, often romanticized term, is not invariably benign. Even when planners and educationists agree on the need for integration, some parents may still feel that the community, whether urban or rural, is not a safe place for their child to move about in freely. Many societies would need to change fundamentally, if fears of abuse and exploitation were to become groundless. Some parents feel that their children must take some risks in order to live fuller lives, but the level of permissible risk is variably perceived.

A forward move

Despite some scepticism over the pace, direction and quality of progress, the next decade will presumably see more countries developing services for children with learning difficulties similar to those now found in some Western nations. More efforts will be made in normal classrooms, for children with mild learning difficulties and for children whose difficulties would be severe if action were not taken to remedy physiological causes such as malnutrition, impaired hearing or sight. For children with severe or complex difficulties, flexibility of method, curriculum and environment is likely to grow. It will increasingly be understood that most children can achieve much more than at first appears, if they are given suitable facilitation as well as direct teaching.

It has already become clear that effective special needs education demands more than merely a pale version of 'chalk, talk and stick'. Modern approaches demand multiple and rapidly evolving combinations of the skills of many professionals with the informal resources of local communities and a positive national political will. Planners may reconceptualize these many factors as an 'information system', in which concepts, knowledge, skills and design are input and fed back from many sources, via many media, with impact also on normal education and on the place of disabled adults in society. Such a reconceptualiza-tion may help to overcome some of the professional and psychological barriers that at present reduce the needed flexibility of curriculum, location and personnel.

With 'information' understood as concepts, knowledge, skills and design, education will be seen increasingly in terms of developing children's abilities to access, manipulate and create information. These processes, the wealth of the 21st century, depend on language input and output. The 1980s saw a growing recognition of the importance of language and communication for empowering children with learning difficulties to appropriate the education their community offers, and increased knowledge of how children acquire such skills. Research on language and communication, in both person-person and person-computer interfaces, will grow in the 1990s.

In information terms, much of what is currently done in special needs education is multiply inefficient. It uses antiquated technology, poorly suited to communicating, to maintaining attention and to producing rapid, attractive results. This is not to say that the child sitting in a wheelchair in front of a computer would necessarily be doing anything more relevant to his or her needs than the child in the village street, helping his or her brothers build a dam of rubbish across the waste water outflow. Either situation has learning potential. Either could be used merely as a way of passing the time. Rather few teachers utilize the instructional potential of dam building. Prospects for the imaginative use of modern information technology, which has much greater potential but makes heavier demands on teacher competence, are not therefore immediately bright.

Doubtless this situation will prevail until planning and teacher education begins to be done by people who grew up in information societies, and who think in information terms. For many economically backward countries, the delay may last several decades. However, this is not inevitable. Very few countries are economically too weak to afford modern information technology in schools. For most, it is a question of vision and motivation. In countries lacking the political will to use modern information technology in more than a tiny proportion of schools, even so very modest an input, if skilfully handled, could serve to change beliefs about how much and how fast children can learn, and how some learning difficulties may be overcome.

References

Agarwal, K N, Agarwal, D K, Upadhyay, S K and Singh, M (1991) 'Learning disability in rural primary school children', *Indian Journal of Medical Research, Section B*, **94**, 89–95.

Anon (1973) 'A model elementary school', *China Reconstructs*, June, 7–12.

Ballard, K (1990) 'Special education in New Zealand: disability, politics and empowerment', *International Journal of Disability, Development and Education*, **37**, 2, 109–24.

Boyden, J (1990) 'Childhood and the policy makers: a comparative perspective on the globalisation of childhood', in James, A and Prout, A (eds) *Constructing and Reconstructing Childhood*, pp. 184–215, London: Falmer Press.

Brandon, M and Stern, D (1962) 'An experiment comparing two educational methods with young imbecile children', *Proceedings of the London Conference on the Scientific Study of Mental Deficiency, 1960*, pp. 357–60, Dagenham: May and Baker.

Department of Education and Science (1971) *Slow Learners in Secondary Schools*, Education Survey No. 15, London: HMSO.

Edgerton, F (1924) *The Panchatantra Reconstructed*, New Haven, CN: American Oriental Society.

Gaylord-Ross, R (1987) 'School integration for students with mental handicaps: a cross-cultural perspective', *European Journal of Special Needs Education*, **2**, 2, 117–29.

Gunewardena, M (1987) *Prevention of Childhood Disability and Community-Based Rehabilitation of Disabled Children. Anuradhapuda District*, Colombo: UNICEF.

Hrnjica, S (1990) 'Special education in Yugoslavia', *International Journal of Disability, Development and Education*, **37**, 2, 169–78.

Hsing-Chih, T (original 1928) 'How is kindergarten education to be made available to all?', *Chinese Education*, 1974/75, **7**, 77–80, trans. Harris, L.

Joint Investigation Group of the Education and Health Division, Ma-to Hsien (1975) 'Strongly popularise pastoral-area primary school education', *Chinese Education*, **8**, 44–52, trans. by Brainin, P, from *Hung-ch'i*, **5**, 83–6 (1974).

Juemin, Z (1987) Thought-provoking and worrisome aspects of our primary and secondary education, *Chinese Education*, **20**, 40–47.

Kuo-Tai, T (1988) 'Mentally retarded persons in the People's Republic of China: review of epidemiological studies and services', *American Journal on Mental Retardation*, **93**, 193–9.

Labregere, A (1974) 'Introduction', *Case Studies in Special Education*, pp. 11–30, Paris: UNESCO.

Marsden, B (1990) '"Mrs Walker's merry games for little people": locating Froebel in an alien environment', *British Journal of Educational Studies*, **38**, 1, 15–32.

Menglan, Z (1983) 'The effect of cultural education on children's cognitive development: a study of conservation development with six- to eleven-year-old Jinuo tribe children', *Chinese Education*, **16**, 124–39.

Miles, C (1991) 'Mobilising skills for special education in Pakistan. A personal cross-cultural experience', *International Journal of Special Education*, **6**, 2, 201–12.

Miles, M (1985) *Children with Disabilities in Normal Schools*, Peshawar: Mental Health Centre.

Miles, M (1989) 'Rehabilitation development in South West Asia: conflicts and potentials', in Barton, L (ed) *Disability and Dependency*, pp. 110–26, London: Falmer Press.

Miles, M (1991) *Mental Handicap Services: Development Trends in Pakistan*, Peshawar: Mental Health Centre.

Miles, M and Miles, C (in press) Education and disability in cross-cultural perspective: Pakistan', in Peters, S (ed) *Education and Disability in Cross-Cultural Perspective*, New York: Garland.

Mittler, P (1983) 'New trends in community special education', *Assignment Children*, **63/4**, 45–57.

Mittler, P and Farrell, P (1987) 'Can children with severe learning difficulties be educated in ordinary schools?', *European Journal of Special Needs Education*, **2**, 4, 221–36.

Mittler, P and Serpell, R (1985) 'Services: an international perspective', in Clarke, A M, Clarke, A D and Berg, J (eds) *Mental Deficiency: The Changing Outlook*, pp. 715–87, London: Methuen.

Narasimhan, M C and Mukherjee, A K (1986) *Disability. A Continuing Challenge*, New Delhi: Wiley Eastern.

Policies for the Mentally Retarded in Asia. Report Presented to the 2nd Asian Conference on Mental Retardation, Tokyo 1975, Tokyo: Japan League for the Mentally Retarded.

Potts, P (1989) 'Working report: educating children and young people with disabilities or difficulties in learning in the People's Republic of China', in Barton, L (ed) *Integration: Myth or Reality*, pp. 168–81, London: Falmer Press.

Pringle, M, Butler, N and Davie, R (1966) *11,000 Seven Year-Olds*, London: Longman.

Quah, M M (1990) 'Special education in Singapore', *International Journal of Disability, Development and Education*, **37**, 2, 137–48.

Radhakrishnan, S (1953) *The Principal Upanishads. Edited with introduction, text, translation and notes*, London: Allen and Unwin.

Rehabilitation Services for People with Mental Retardation in Japan (1991) Tokyo: Japan League for the Mentally Retarded.

Robinson, N M (1978) 'Mild mental retardation: does it exist in the People's Republic of China?', *Mental Retardation*, **16**, 295–8.

Seo, G-H, Oakland, T, Han, H-S and Hu, S (1992) 'Special education in South Korea', *Exceptional Children*, **58**, 3, 213–18.

Shih, C (1979) 'Helping mentally handicapped children to learn', *International Child Welfare Review*, **42**, 31–4.

Stevens, R, Bowen, J, Dila, K and O'Shaughnessy, R (1990) 'Chinese priorities in special education', *International Journal of Special Education*, **5**, 3, 324–34.

Tuunainen, K (1988) 'Future trends in Scandinavian special education', *International Journal of Special Education*, **3**, 1, 51–60.

UNESCO (1988) *Review of the Present Situation of Special Education*, (ED-88/WS/38), Paris: UNESCO.

Unger, J (ed. and trans.) (1977) 'Post-cultural revolution primary-school education: selected texts', *Chinese Education*, **10**, 2, 4–29.

Vohra, R (1987) 'Institutional services for the mental retardates', *Disabilities and Impairments*, **1**, 1/2, 91–117.

Warnock, H M (1978) *Report of the Committee of Enquiry into the Education of Handicapped Children and Young People*, London: HMSO.

Weber, L (1979) 'Early childhood education', *Chinese Education*, **11**, 86–96.

Working Group of the USSR Academy of Pedagogical Sciences Scientific Research Institute of Defectology (1990) 'A conception of special education and upbringing of children with impaired mental and physical development', *Soviet Education*, **32**, 10, 5–30.

Yongxin, P (1986) 'Special ed comes of age', *Women of China*, December, 2–7.

Zaman, S S (1990) *Research on Mental Retardation in Bangladesh*, Dhaka: Bangladesh Protibondhi Foundation.

6. Planning mainstream education services for children with visual impairments in developing countries

Tony Best and Steve McCall

Introduction

In many parts of the developing world, only a tiny minority – probably about 5 per cent (Carey, 1985) and perhaps as few as 1 per cent (Kristensen, 1989) – of children with visual impairments (VI) receive education. A lack of school places, together with low expectations of the abilities of these children, effectively mean that for the vast majority schooling is inaccessible. Parents may even be unaware that blind children can benefit from education and the child may only be taken to school late in childhood, to receive some basic education before entering adult life and the search for a job.

In most countries, the education which is available to these children is provided in residential special schools, but it is unlikely that residential schools for the blind will ever be able to accommodate all the children needing education. For the majority of these children, a system which utilizes existing local mainstream provision offers the only realistic prospect of attending school.

In Western Europe and North America, the educational integration of children with disabilities developed as part of a general acknowledgement by society of the needs of people with disabilities and their rights to social equality and consequently to equal access in employment and education. It was argued that children could remain an integral part of their families, attend school with brothers and sisters, and be accepted as part of the school and the community. They would be seen to receive a regular education and learn to compete with, and learn from, other children in the 'real' world. A variety of models evolved to support children with visual impairments in mainstream schools. The main models are summarized below.

Special school partnership

Here the special school takes the initiative in developing integration. The scale of the integration varies, but is likely to take two main forms:

a. the special school sets up links with a local mainstream school and some of the children from the residential school receive their education in mainstream, supported by staff and resources from the special school;

b. the special school becomes the resource base for an 'area' support service.

Itinerant teachers based at the school support children with visual impairments in ordinary schools and use the equipment and resources housed in the special school to support their work throughout the region. The residential special school then takes only children whose needs are complex and cannot be adequately met in mainstream.

The unit/resource room model

Here the education authority nominates a mainstream school to meet the needs of children with visual impairments, and then commissions a special classroom within the school for the use of these children who may be recruited locally or regionally. A residential hostel may be built nearby to house the children with visual impairments in cases where children are drawn from areas beyond daily travel.

Unit provision

In this system children with visual impairments receive most of their lessons in the special classroom and are the responsibility of the specialist teacher. They share facilities with the sighted children and attend mainstream classes for some lessons.

Resource room provision

Here children with visual impairments receive most of their lessons in mainstream classes and are generally the responsibility of the mainstream class/subject teacher. They attend the resource room for initial training in basic skills such as Braille and mobility, and once these skills are developed, visit the resource room only to collect materials and equipment prepared by the specialist resource room teacher. The resource room teacher liaises with the class teacher to provide appropriate materials for the children and appropriate advice to the teacher. In some cases the resource room teacher may also have an outreach/itinerant responsibility.

Itinerant services

Children with visual impairments usually attend their local mainstream school and are supported by a specialist visiting teacher of the visually impaired. The specialist itinerant teacher may have a teaching role or an advisory/consultant role.

Itinerant services may be *child-based*, ie, primarily responsible for supporting and teaching children, or *teacher-based*, ie, seeing their priority as advising and supporting teachers to enable them to meet the special educational needs of the children. Typically, services will have some elements of both child-based and teacher-based work.

The itinerant teacher may be responsible for education of school-age children or may have a role in the identification and pre-school education of VI children and sometimes vocational/post-school provision. The teacher may support all children with visual impairments in an area across the age and ability range, or may be given responsibility for supporting a particular group of these children, eg, those who are partially sighted and can use print, or blind children who are in primary school.

In many developing countries, the majority of children with visual impairments are thinly distributed over vast rural areas. Traditionally, the solution adopted has been to gather together these children in a residential special school, often based in an urban centre. This solution, while allowing for efficient use of resources, has inherent weaknesses. The arguments described above in respect of the social and educational benefits of receiving education in a local mainstream school apply even more convincingly to children in developing countries with a diversity of cultural traditions and local languages, where out-of-area residential schooling may mean that some children may receive education hundreds of miles from their home in a a strange language and an unfamiliar cultural setting. In these circumstances a system which allows the child to receive education in local village schools and utilizes existing resources would seem to be a logical solution. But how can such integrated systems be organized to afford equal opportunities in education?

In East Africa and parts of Asia, the resource room model was the basis of the first moves towards the integration of children with visual impairments However, except in a few urban areas where children could travel to school daily, these resource rooms attached to mainstream schools were residential, the children being housed in hostels near to the receiving school. While these children gained some of the benefits of mainstream placement, they still received their education away from their immediate community. In the last ten years, particularly in parts of Africa, South East Asia and India, services in which itinerant specialist teachers support VI children placed in the local village school have been introduced.

But how can that placement be supported? An itinerant teaching service is a sophisticated model of service delivery which requires careful planning. How can such support services be organized? What are the decisions that have to be reached in setting up an itinerant teaching service? This chapter seeks to define the considerations that administrators planning such a service need to have in mind.

The decisions

In order to decide which options should be adopted, we have identified five elements in a decision-making process. These encompass a consideration of principles, location, children, organization and roles. Each one of these elements requires the planner to consider several questions and the answer to these questions will help establish the best way forward. We will now examine each of these five elements and discuss the issues raised.

Principles

The decisions reached in this section will have implications for the number of teachers required and and the range of skills they need. Planners will obviously need to take into account the resources available and the prevailing educational policies.

Planners need to decide whether itinerant teachers should be deployed at primary or secondary schools, or at both levels. At primary level, itinerant teachers will need to be familiar with the skills of teaching literacy and basic subjects. In addition, children with visual impairments may need to be taught the foundations of mobility, daily living skills and personal organization. Some specialist equipment (such as the abacus, Braille writing frame, etc) is essential to allow these children access to the curriculum, and teaching young children with visual impairments requires a thorough knowledge of the effects of visual impairment. These effects should be understood by all specialist teachers who serve any of these children at this stage in their education.

At secondary level, the subject work is more specialized. Itinerant teachers may lack the expertise to help directly with some subjects and will be primarily concerned with making available to the subject teacher and the child the Braille materials required for access to ther curriculum. However, children at secondary school should be more independent in their learning and, if adapted materials can be prepared for them, may be able to cope with fewer visits from the teacher. The role of the teacher may move from child teacher to counsellor for teachers and head teachers.

In deciding where itinerant services should operate, planners should be aware that in large urban areas, integration is probably much easier to support than in rural areas, since the geographical concentration of children results in working practice which is more efficient. Teachers spend a smaller proportion of their time travelling and a greater amount actually working with children and their teachers. In rural areas, careful planning is necessary to avoid the situation where case load sizes become very inefficient, with perhaps only two or three children being served by one teacher. In rural areas, visits to the children are likely to be less frequent and the schools will have a greater responsibility for providing the child's education. The itinerant teacher may need to teach the ordinary class teacher skills such as the ability to communicate in Grade 1 Braille or the use of the abacus so that the child continues to receive education during the itinerant teacher's absence.

In most countries, neither the telephone nor short-wave radio is used currently to maintain contact between support teacher and the school, although there may be some potential in using these methods in selected areas.

Decisions about who has the responsibility for the child supported by an itinerant teacher need to be resolved from the outset. After early experiences in integration of children with special needs, most services now firmly give the school and class teacher the primary responsibility for a child with a visual impairment. The support teacher visits to help the school with the child, but should not be seen as the child's teacher. The danger is that class teachers might leave the child out of class activities on the basis that the support teacher has responsibility for teaching the child during visits. If for some administrative reason the children do have to be part of a 'special education' service, then the responsibilities of the school should be clearly defined when the service is set up. In addition to a sound understanding of the needs of children with visual impairments, the itinerant teacher needs to be able to communicate those needs to enable the class teacher to understand and help the child.

The decision about whether itinerant teachers should have a responsibility for children before they start school needs consideration. There is a widely accepted belief that time spent with children with visual impairments at the pre-school stage produces rewards in establishing the basis of learning, literacy, daily living skills, personal organization and mobility. This might reduce the amount of support likely to be needed later in the child's education. It may also help the parents and family to see the child in a positive light and develop the supportive attitudes which will help with schooling and independence.

If support services are concerned with the pre-school child, then more teachers will be required who will need additional skills in understanding and promoting early development and in understanding how to help families change attitudes and develop their parenting skills. A wider age range increases the size of the case load but can also allow for more efficient working practice, particularly in areas where children are widespread.

Similar arguments apply to the post-school issues. The pool of 'clients' in any one area becomes larger and more efficient use can be made of the teacher if young people who have left school are included in the case load. But teachers will need additional skills such as counselling and familiarity with social welfare and employment opportunities and will need to liaise with those who provide vocational training or employment. A region, district or country setting up a service will have to decide how many teachers it can afford to employ and what level of knowledge and responsibility the teachers can be given, so that it can determine the range of clients served by one teacher. Some countries are experimenting with teachers dealing with rehabilitation of adults but it is not yet possible to say whether this requires too broad a range of skills for one person.

These are the primary decisions that need to be made about the design of the service. We now turn to some of the practical arrangements for the organization of a service.

Location

In deciding on where itinerant services should be based, the elements of accessibility, supervision and professional support all need to be considered. Ideally, the base should afford the itinerant teacher easy access to schools and opportunities for support and supervision from a senior experienced colleague. There are arguments for and against the variety of possible bases. In Kenya, Kristensen (1989), after summing up the arguments, favoured the Educational Assessment Resource Services (EARS) Centres as the bases for itinerant services. The EARS are multi-disciplinary and their centres are often attached to schools. Each main regional centre has a network of sub-centres to which itinerant teachers may be attached. Kristensen maintained that the range of professionals and the carefully planned geographical distribution of the centres met the requirements of an itinerant service well. Using such a system, one can envisage that the centre could house a senior experienced itinerant teacher who would have overall responsibility for itinerant teachers based in the sub-centres and who would be responsible for the organization and administration of the service.

In general, services which are based at a resource centre (whether it be a regional assessment centre for children with special needs or a centre for secondary services for the visually impaired) can keep the itinerant teacher in contact with fellow professionals who are involved in broadly the same type of work. They may be able to share some support services, such as typists or a telephone, and give advice to each other.

An alternative is to use existing special schools for the visually impaired as bases for itinerant services. Special schools can offer a wide range of specialist equipment and colleagues with expertise in all aspects of education. It may even be possible for children supported by the itinerant teacher in mainstream classes to visit the school for some special purpose such as a complex visual assessment, or to learn a special skill. Members of the school staff may be able to support the itinerant teacher by visiting a child in the mainstream school to help in a complex subject area where the itinerant teacher may have no expertise. The coordination of all services for children with visual impairments may result from such an arrangement, making the best use of the equipment, knowledge and people. Of course, this is only possible if the school is located within reasonable travelling distance of all the itinerant teachers. Although the itinerant teachers need not visit the special school every day, they should be close enough to be able to attend meetings and submit travel reports regularly to the base.

Services may also be housed away from schools. An itinerant teacher might be based in buildings used by the educational administration. A district education office provides a location which ensures the itinerant teacher is seen as an integral part of the school services in that district, accountable to a supervisor in that office. The itinerant teacher would make frequent visits to the office where it should be possible to discuss problems with the relevant administrative officers responsible for the school or service. The weakness of this kind of base is the lack of any support for the teacher from a person knowledgeable about visual impairment and the fact that itinerant teachers may be seen by the classroom teachers they are trying to support as having a position among the élite and therefore as someone to be treated with caution and anxiety.

The teacher's home is sometimes used as the base, but usually only when the travelling required makes any other base inconvenient. In this case there must be a clear system of supervision to ensure the teacher is actually doing the job and opportunities for professional support for the teacher should be made available. The teacher's home is probably the least satifactory choice for a base.

The children

Some children with visual impairments may have partial sight and some will be blind, so planners need to decide whether services should be available to print users or Braillists or both. Behind this question is the fact that integrating partially sighted children who use print is generally found to be much easier than providing for the needs of children who use Braille. Much of this difference is in the need to transcribe printed material into Braille, although blind children will probably also need more support in understanding regular lessons and more help with the 'additional' curriculum such as mobility and activities of daily living. The Braille reader is likely to require more frequent visits than the print user (particularly in the early stages of primary education) and the differing needs of these children need to be taken into account when the teacher's case load is being planned.

Provided there is adequate support, there is no reason at all why blind children should not attend local schools; indeed their need to stay in the family and to grow up with local children is at least as great as it is for children with partial sight. The use of uncontracted Grade 1 Braille (as opposed to the traditional use of the complex Grade 2 form) might make the integration of blind children very much easier.

The most usual criterion for accepting a child within services for the visually impaired is a measured vision loss. This may be a satisfactory basis for the referral of a child, but the decision to take on the child should be based on educational need. There is unlikely to be any dispute about this in the case of a blind child, but some other children with moderately poor vision may be referred simply because of lack of progress or bad behaviour and these children, although no doubt benefiting from extra teaching or support, may be taking scarce resources away from the children for whom the service was designed. It is therefore often important, from the outset, to define exactly for whom the service is intended and to establish criteria for adding a child to the case load.

The organization of the case load, which will cover decisions about the frequency of visits and type of support offered is a separate issue. Once children are accepted on to a case load, consideration needs to be given to the type of service each child requires. General guidelines need to be established for the service, clarifying policy with regard to central questions such as how often children should be visited, what weighting should be given to children's age and visual status, what kind of teaching they may need and what the focus is likely to be for support of the class teacher.

There should also be a system for removing a child if they are no longer eligible for services, perhaps through age or a change in their visual status and educational needs. Classification of children within the case load should help ensure that the service is not spread too thinly because of the continued inclusion of children who no longer need support.

Organization

The itinerant teachers need to be supervised. The supervision required takes two forms: administrative and academic. Administrative supervision ensures that teachers make the visits that are required; balance their use of time between visiting, travelling, meetings and administrative tasks; submit the necessary reports. Academic supervision is primarily concerned with monitoring the quality of the teacher's work and helping teachers when they require advice about problems concerning individual children or working practice.

Administrative supervision can be carried out by a local senior person who sees the teacher every week or so. The itinerant teacher might be required to present a record book recording each visit, its duration and a brief description of the work completed, countersigned by the headteacher of each receiving school. Academic supervision is best provided by a senior fellow professional knowledgeable about visual impairment. This may be needed only occasionally and could perhaps be provided by a colleague who is primarily available through the telephone. A service definitely needs both types of supervision built into the design – it is very easy for integration to go badly wrong.

In deciding upon whether services need ancillary support, it is necessary to keep sight of the fact that specialist itinerant teachers of the visually impaired are scarce and expensive to train. It is important, therefore, that a system uses their expertise in the most efficient way. There are aspects of the work that do not need a highly qualified person, for example the transcription of passages into Braille. A service should examine the activities that are carried out and establish what can only be done by the itinerant teacher and what could be done by someone with less training working under the supervision of the teacher.

It could be argued that an itinerant service cannot succeed unless the bulk of the Braille material required (text books, etc) is available in advance from a Braille printing press. The ABCD project based in Nairobi, for example, provides Braille materials for blind children in East and Central African countries. The fact that many developing countries have standard prescribed key texts does make it possible to predict children's requirements more precisely in terms of Braille text books than is the case in some Western industrialized nations.

The optimum size of a case load for an itinerant teacher is very difficult to establish but it is possible to identify three elements which ought to be considered. The time needed to travel to a school (rather than the distance) is one factor. The visual status (Braille or print reader) of the children and their ages are two other factors which will determine the frequency of visits needed. If a general guide were needed, then a target ratio of ten children to one teacher, working within a 35km radius could be suggested, but this would vary with local conditions.

The status of the itinerant teacher will vary with individual systems, but it is usual for this role to be graded as similar to, or slightly senior to, a class teacher. It is not common for itinerant teachers to be able to direct or supervise class teachers, although their job requires them to give advice and support to the class teacher. The success of the system ultimately rests on the itinerant teacher's ability to develop good relations and professional trust with the headteacher and staff in each school and interpersonal and consultancy skills are an essential part of their training needs.

The regional supervisor or head of service certainly does need to have sufficient seniority to work with inspectors and school principals.

Roles

This section examines several potential roles, each of which requires a different set of skills and knowledge. Underlying each decision about roles is the principle that teachers must serve a sufficient number of clients to make the system efficient and economically viable, but care needs to be taken to avoid a situation which makes unrealistic and excessive demands on teachers. The availability of teachers, the quality of their training, their status, experience and work expectations, the degree of supervision and support available, all help determine their ability to undertake specific roles.

The answer to the question of whether the visiting teacher should teach the child within the classroom or withdraw the child from lessons for tuition is likely to be that each of these options will be used, depending on the topic that is being taught. Where withdrawal is favoured, the school will need to be prepared to allow the child to miss some of the regular lessons and to provide a working area outside the classroom. Where support is provided within the classroom, teachers must be prepared to have the itinerant teacher working alongside them in the classroom and perhaps even taking the regular class while the class teacher concentrates on giving extra help to the child with visual impairments.

When considering whether the service should be child-based or teacher-based, it is often argued that the most effective role for the itinerant teacher may be as consultant to the class teacher passing on skills and information so that they become less needed as the class teacher becomes more familiar with the child and visual handicap. There will, though, always be some direct teaching that the specialist teacher will need to undertake, such as Braille skills, mobility, living skills and use of residual vision.

We referred above to the need to make efficient use of the itinerant teacher's specific skills. It is a waste to use a highly trained teacher as an itinerant Braille transcriber. Inevitably, working with blind children will involve some Braille transcription, but the use of volunteers, 'minimally' trained workers or computers could meet most of the need for Braille, with the teacher becoming directly involved only when a difficult task is presented.

The job of screening children is generally carried out by primary health care teams but medical teams are unlikely to have more than a hazy idea about the educational implications of visual impairment, so there are certainly strong arguments for liaison between the health care teams in a region and the local itinerant teaching service. In this way, children identified as visually impaired can be referred directly to the itinerant service for help. In remote areas, the itinerant teacher may be the only person available to identify children but in these circumstances follow-up referral to a medical specialist should be available to confirm the diagnosis and provide medical treatment where necessary.

Every itinerant teacher will have a role in training class teachers to understand and meet the child's special needs. There is also a need for more formal training involving the whole school so that all the teachers understand the implications of visual impairment and the best way to help the child. This formal training might be best provided by an outside training team, perhaps from a teacher training college. They would be specialists in teacher training and their presence could support the itinerant teacher both by reinforcing the suggestions being made to the school staff and by giving advice to the itinerant teacher on ways of working within the particular school.

Conclusion

In this chapter we have outlined a process designed to identify the critical elements in a successful itinerant teaching service. Throughout, we have emphasized the need to take into account local conditions. There is no global 'blueprint' that fits every region.

In countries which are beginning to develop universal education for children with visual impairments, the system must make the maximum use of the few trained personnel who are available. This has critical implications for the nature of the training that teachers receive and also for the number of teachers that need to receive training – or re-training. Both the content of the courses and the nature of delivery will need to be examined to enable teachers to receive the training they must have in order to make the system work. One possibility is that some form of distance education would enable large numbers of teachers to receive training without the difficulties of long-distance travel.

We believe that children with visual impairments should have the same opportunities for education as sighted children. We have tried to specify for planners the knowledge that is required, to identify the decisions that have to be made, to present the options and their implications. These children need the most efficient service that circumstances allow so that their childhood prepares them for a full life as an adult. We hope this chapter has contributed in a small way to that process by clarifying a way forward for the design of educational services.

References

Carey, K (1985) 'Who needs literacy?', *British Journal of Visual Impairment*, **III**, 1, 14–16.
Kristensen, K (1989) *KISE Bulletin*, 3, Nairobi.

Additional reading

General

Best, A B (1992) *Teaching Children With Visual Impairments*, Milton Keynes: Open University Press.
    A recent publication which covers all aspects of education of children with visual impairments including services, implications of visual defects, access to the curriculum and services.
Scholl, G (ed.) (1986) *Foundations of Education for Blind and Visually Handicapped Children and Youth*, New York: American Foundation for the Blind.
    The most comprehensive textbook available. Contributions cover many specific aspects of subject teaching as well as assessment, multiple handicaps and technology.
Sandford-Smith, J (1986) *Eye Diseases in Hot Climates*, Bristol: Wright.
    Designed for the non-specialist medic working in developing countries, it provides clear, illustrated information on the nature, causes and treatment of tropical eye diseases.

Services

Dawkins, J (1991) *Models of Mainstreaming for VI Pupils*, London: RNIB/HMSO.
    A guide to the establishment of integrated services. Some of the details and examples are specific to the UK but many of the principles and options are relevant to other countries.
Hegarty, S, Pocklington, K and Lucas, D (1981) *Educating Pupils with Special Needs in the Ordinary School*, Windsor: NFER-Nelson.
    An overview of service options within special education; some reference to services for children with visual impairments.

Curriculum and teaching

Abang, T B (1986) *Teaching the Visually Handicapped*, Ibadan: University Press.
    One of the few books written from an African perspective. The contents describe current Nigerian approaches to services and teaching for children who are totally blind.
Chapman, E K C and Stone, J M (1988) *The Visually Handicapped Child in your Classroom*, London: Cassell.
    A modern textbook which will be particularly helpful for the non-specialist teacher needing to learn how to adapt their classroom and teaching to meet the needs of a child with visual impairments.
Torres, I and Corn, A L (1990) *When you have a VH Child in your Classroom: suggestions for teachers*, New York: American Foundation for the Blind.

A best-selling, accessible booklet full of practical advice for the mainstream class teachers, parents and administrators.

Willoughby, D M and Duffy, S M (1989) *Handbook for Itinerant and Resource Teachers of Blind and VI Students*, Baltimore: National Federation of the Blind.

Contains many practical tips for those providing itinerant services.

Olmstead, J E (1990) *Itinerant Teaching: tricks of the trade for teachers of blind visually impaired students*, New York: American Foundation for the Blind.

Insider's information on becoming an effective itinerant teacher, a lively and informative handbook.

Additional handicaps

Ellis, D (ed.) (1986) *Sensory Impairment in Mentally Handicapped People*, London: Croom Helm.

Despite its publication date, this volume contains relevant information on population, needs and approaches to management.

Fullwood, D, Harvey, L and White, G (1983) *Living and Learning*, Melbourne: Royal Victorian Institute for the Blind.

Designed for teachers and parents, this book has practical suggestions for the management of young children.

McInnes, J M and Treffry, J A (1982) *Deaf-Blind Infants and Children*, Milton Keynes: Open University Press.

Gives a theoretical basis for work with deaf-blind children and includes many practical ideas to help teachers.

7. Deaf people in the developing world

Marjo Joutselainen

Introduction

The great majority of deaf people live in the developing world where malnutrition, infectious diseases and accidents are common causes of hearing loss. Deaf persons, regardless of whether born deaf or deafened at a later stage of their life, are frequently considered a marginal, neglected and socially discriminated group with a limited share of even the very elementary human and civil rights within their communities. Deaf persons are commonly labelled with disparaging and superstitious qualities that push them outside human communication and social life, and deny them access to education, work and other equal opportunities that would make them self-supportive and full members of their respective societies.

Discovering this, the World Federation of the Deaf (WFD), an international organization of nearly 100 deaf associations all over the world, made a decisive policy statement in the Federation's World Congress in 1987 to design strategies to strengthen deaf communities in the developing countries to advocate their participation and equalization of opportunities through representative organizations. In order to support this, the WFD first had to conduct a census regarding the life of deaf people in the target countries in Asia, Africa and Latin America. This was a unique effort to systematically collect data of various vital concerns of deaf people in the developing world, as earlier information available was based on usually informal documentation of individual counties' circumstances only.

Despite the challenges in the diversity and magnitude of the information needs, including sometimes only occasional contacts to national deaf communities in the target countries, the WFD launched in 1988 a project entitled *Deaf People in the Developing World*. The project focused on compiling data of the human and language rights of the deaf, access to education, job opportunities, and national deaf associations. The data were compiled by conducting a survey which was targeted at over 200 organizations of the deaf, government agencies and other institutions in nearly 100 developing nations. The survey was financed by the Finnish International Development Agency and the Nordic Deaf Associations.

The outcome of the project is an international database, *The WFD Developing*

Database, which includes data of 68 developing countries and is updated with current information of the countries included and those which were not in the initial survey. Apart from the computerized database which is available for universities, researchers, libraries and organizations of the deaf, a report of the survey was published in 1991. The results highlighted in this chapter are mostly based on the report concerned.

Research setting

Target countries of the survey

The research task used a comprehensive and yet uncomplicated and efficient data-compiling method that would meet the practical and widespread information needs of the implementing organization *and* meet the criteria of reliability and validity, notwithstanding the great geographical, cultural, social and linguistic variation of the countries surveyed. The method employed had also not to exceed the limited resources available for the exercise. The only feasible approach available was the survey method, which was expected to produce a relatively successful outcome, as no type of field study could be considered due to the great number of countries to be covered. The survey was carried out by sending a questionnaire to the target groups in respective countries.

The selection of target countries was made according to the United Nations and OECD classifications of developing countries, with the exceptions of the People's Republic of China and Mongolia, which were included, while all European nations were omitted. This classification was considered as good as any more sophisticated one, bearing in mind that at the time of launching the project, a wider introduction of more advanced development indicators than the traditional economic equivalents had just been launched.

The survey was aimed at national deaf organizations, associated groups related to the deaf community such as charity societies and deaf schools, and government agencies in the field of education and social welfare. A direct contact to representatives of the deaf community was prioritized whenever possible. In a few cases the questionnaire had to be addressed to a ministry, as it was the only contact that could be identified in the country concerned.

The network of 210 target organizations or institutions in 97 countries was completed with the assistance of UNESCO, the Disabled Peoples International and Gallaudet University. A few countries in South Asia and sub-Saharan Africa could not be included. This network has also proved very useful for information-sharing purposes after completing the actual survey.

Conducting the survey

Designing the survey questionnaire form was indeed a challenge. Because the same form would be used for all respondents, it had to be simple, comprehensive and yet informative. Several essential items had to be left out, given too little emphasis, or formulated in a standard reply option, simply to avoid discouraging the respondents with a massive form.

After several drafts and a pilot phase in three of the target countries, the final version of the form in English, French and Spanish, along with a covering letter, was ready to be mailed in early 1989, followed by a reminder to non-respondents and an extension of the mailing in Central America where new target groups were identified during the process.

After three major mailings and questionnaires distributed individually, the number of forms returned to the WFD amounted to 96, with replies from 68 of the 97 countries included in the survey. Considering the severe limitations of carrying out an international survey with little if any sensitivity to national characteristics, the 46 per cent response rate achieved is surprisingly high. Of all respondents, deaf associations replied almost without exception. The distribution of respondents according to the organization he or she represents is a secondary outcome of the survey. Relatively speaking, nearly half of the respondents were charities ('societies *for* the deaf'), local deaf schools, other service institutions and few local deaf clubs. One third (31 per cent) of the replies came from deaf associations which met the criteria of a national representative organization *of* the deaf. The remaining 20 per cent were government agencies (mostly a ministry of education) and individual professionals working with the deaf.

Geographically, the most enthusiastic outcome came from English-speaking African countries, Asia and the Caribbean region, while the Latin American and in particular the French-speaking African countries did not respond very eagerly. Among the non-respondents were several densely populated countries with a large deaf community: Mexico, Senegal, Bangladesh and Egypt. Despite the 14 letters sent to various organizations in China, no replies were received until the questionnaire form was filled in with a representative of the national deaf association attending a UN expert meeting in Finland.

Establishing a database

The data gathered from the replies were computerized on a database specially established for this survey. *The WFD Developing World Database* was designed with the Paradox relational database management program to fit ordinary PC use. The database comprises eight tables that are equivalent to the categories of the initial questionnaire form as follows:

1. respondent data
2. national deaf association (NAD)
3. support groups for the NAD
4. other organization or institution in the field of deafness
5. deaf education
6. human rights
7. services available
8. deaf culture.

Number three or four was chosen, depending on whether a national deaf association was established or not (charities were included in this class). Sometimes it was difficult to identify if the responding organization was indeed a national deaf association in cases when there were several deaf organizations (not exceptional in Latin America), or the organization was operating in the capital area only. All information available was then used to decide upon the actual national representative organization of the deaf community.

Another advantage of the program running the database is its capacity to make queries of the inserted data. This allows sorting out data on individual countries, items (such as deaf education in selected countries), and combining variables with various criteria (picking countries where the number of deaf schools is below ten; there is no indigenous sign language; and no deaf association established).

Additional data on countries included in the 1989–90 survey and an increasing number of new ones are inserted into the database to make it a useful and comprehensive source of information for all those organizations, institutions and professionals in need of this type of data.

Results

The status of sign language

Language rights, calling for the recognition of indigenous sign languages of deaf people as their primary and natural language, is one of the fundamental demands of deaf communities worldwide (see, for example, the WFD Commission of Sign Language Recommendations of 1991). Accordingly, a deaf child should have the right to learn the natural sign language of the local deaf community at an early age through the normal language acquisition process. This is critical in view of the cognitive, linguistic, social, emotional and cultural development of the child, including later access to educational content.

Deaf people in most countries have established organizations and developed a natural sign language. Recently, systematic work to develop the national sign language has begun by gathering signs deaf people use to compile dictionaries and start research on the language and teaching of it to parents of deaf children, teachers, etc. Countries undertaking this work include several East African nations, five Central and Latin American nations, Nepal and Thailand. Altogether, 22 countries reported having a more or less standardized national sign language.

Access to information

Deaf people are a most disadvantaged group in terms of access to information. In spite of those few lucky ones who ever get to school, the deaf do not have access to even the occasional means of public communication available in developing countries, in rural areas particularly. Radio broadcasts reach most rural and urban communities for spreading information and, increasingly, educational programmes. Not deaf people, however. The television is uncommon too; of 53 countries with a TV broadcasting network, six countries (Belize, Brazil, Cuba, Ghana, India and Pakistan) report they have specially-produced programmes, mainly news and documentaries, while in 12 countries (eg, China, Colombia and El Salvador) there are news, religious and entertainment programmes with sign language interpretation. In five countries some of the TV programmes are subtitled.

Interpretation services

An issue closely linked to deaf people's access to information, participation and, finally, their civil rights, is the availability of sign language interpretation. According to the WFD survey, there were sign language interpreters in 29 of the 65 countries who responded to the question concerned. Sadly, 28 countries, mostly in Asia and Africa, reported they have no sign language interpreters at all.

The professional level of the interpreters was not asked about, but the general rule is that any systematized training of sign language interpreters is unusual in any developing country. The persons interpreting for the deaf are usually family members or professionals such as teachers, social workers, priests or missionaries. The number of interpreters is small; Barbados, Colombia, Kenya and Thailand report that there are just one or two interpreters available for deaf people in the whole country.

Sign language interpreters usually have a connection with the national deaf association: although rarely directly employed by the association, interpreters in some countries have their fees paid by the organization. In many cases, however, the associations have no funds for training or paying the interpreters. Government agencies repay sign language interpretation services in China, Colombia, Ghana, Malaysia, Uruguay and Zambia, although it is only in official cases, such as in court.

Primary education opportunities

Education is a privilege of very few deaf children and young people. Deaf schools are few and of varying quality, and the number of children that are ever enrolled in them is minimal. Apart from adverse attitudes towards educating children with disabilities anyway, this is a result of the overall decrease of educational opportunities for children in most developing areas in the world. According to the United Nations Development Programme (1991), allocations made to education are directed inappropriately, too: although basic schooling should be given a priority in education, the primary level presently accounts for less than half the total education expenditure. Over 100 million children receive no primary education, and a further 200 million receive no education beyond the age of 12. Reduced allocations for the educational sector also affect the quality of education, resulting in repeating classes, high dropout, lack of trained teachers and materials and declining results of the educational services (UNICEF, 1990; World Bank, 1989, 1990).

With this overall background in mind, it is easier to understand why education of deaf children is declining, too: children with special learning needs are not given priority in allocating scarce resources for education of the rapidly increasing new generations. It may be suggested that this may lead to deaf children's education becoming increasingly dependent on schools run by private charities and international aid agencies.

According to the WFD survey, elementary education of deaf children is organized in 64 of the 69 countries that responded to this subject. The five countries that do not have an established public education system for the deaf are Bolivia, Madagascar, Mali, Morocco and Papua New Guinea. (The situation in Bolivia is uncertain because of contradictory replies.)

The number of deaf schools is usually very small. In 57 countries there were less than 20 schools, which is very few in regard to the estimated number of deaf people. It should also be noted that some countries did not differentiate between deaf schools or any other education unit for deaf children. In replies from the same country, the number of deaf schools varied sometimes drastically; in Peru, for example, between four to 114. The largest number of deaf schools were found in Brazil, China, India, Colombia and Peru.

Twenty two countries have established, in addition to specialized deaf schools or instead of them, what could be called educational programmes for deaf children. A few of these countries integrate deaf children into regular classrooms without any special arrangements such as a sign language interpreter or a specialized teacher. The majority of countries, including Chile, Ghana, Nigeria, Panama and Zambia, have established special units within regular schools, whereas Indonesia has a unit for deaf children in a specialized school for children with disabilities. Some countries have organized deaf education in a combined model. In Colombia, for example, deaf children go to a specialized school during the first five years and are then integrated into regular schools with individual pedagogical support, or sometimes without any special support services at all.

Education enrolment

The percentage of deaf children enroled in primary education was discovered to be very low: deaf children are definitely among the last to become literate and numerate – if ever. In one-fifth of the 66 replies, the number of deaf children in the country's elementary schools was reported below 1 per cent. The percentage of deaf children in primary education was below 20 per cent in seven African countries, six Asian countries and four countries in the Caribbean and Central America. Deaf children seem to have almost equal access to education compared to the general school-going age group in nine countries, four of which are in Central America.

Opportunities for vocational and academic education

Vocational training was available to deaf school-leavers in 59 countries, and was the only way to post-primary education in 30 of them. In 16 countries there were neither vocational schools nor any other opportunities for post-primary training. This is not surprising in the light of the very low educational enrolment of deaf children, which was almost nil in 16 these countries. It should be noted, however, that vocational training in many developing nations is not organized institutionally; rather, school-leavers learn their professional skills within the traditional apprenticeship, or a retrained in-service just like anyone of their non-deaf age group.

The trades deaf people are trained in are mostly traditional: carpentry, joinery, masonry, shoemaking and tailoring for the boys; sewing, dressmaking and handicrafts for the girls. Deaf people accordingly mostly hold manual, often low-paid jobs in the labour market. Deaf carpenters, masons, dressmakers and tailors are common in 40 per cent of the countries surveyed, while deaf women do domestic work and handicrafts.

The distribution of the vocational training programmes in regions seemed rather non-variable in the light of the general economic and technological development of the region. It was encouraging to notice that in several Latin American and Asian countries the deaf, including deaf girls, are trained for modern non-manual jobs, such as librarians, accountants and computer programmers and operators.

Entering a college or university is rare for a deaf person: 33 countries report that it is possible, but hardly realistic due to the very limited primary and secondary education opportunities and lack of qualified sign language interpreters. Adverse attitudes and the high costs also block the road of many talented deaf young persons. To overcome these obstacles, a number of them seek funds to continue their studies overseas.

Government policy on deaf education

The administration of special education in the countries responding to the WFD survey is usually run by the ministry of education either alone (43 countries) or jointly with another government agency, such as the ministry of health and social affairs who are responsible for deaf education in nine countries. In six countries (Guatemala, Haiti, Madagascar, Panama, Papua New Guinea and Singapore) mission or charity societies and other private institutions organized all deaf education, and also played a major role in educating deaf children in Bolivia, Colombia and El Salvador.

Mode of instruction in deaf schools

The mode of instruction in deaf schools reveals much of the prevailing situation in deaf education. Instruction was classified as oral, manual (signs, sign language), both of these (simultaneous oral and manual), and total communication. Looking at individual replies, the high percentage of 'total communication' implies that the alternative 'oral and manual modes simultaneously' did not work out very well. All in all, the variation in the items was substantial as respondents of each organization within one country seemed to have differing opinions on the mode of instruction used in deaf schools. Taking all 89 replies from 64 countries with most respondents naming more than one approach, the distribution of replies appears as follows:

oral method	63
manual method	44
both methods simultaneously	3
total communication	42

The oral method, implying the use of spoken and written language, was mentioned as the only approach in deaf education in seven African nations and six nations of Latin and Central American and the Caribbean. Oralism in its traditional form is gradually giving way to the use of signs and sign language in classrooms. A few countries, namely Argentina, Uruguay, Brazil, Guatemala and Cameroon, are promoting sign language in education, although the steps taken are small, mainly because teachers' mastery of sign language is inadequate.

Signs and sign language were reported as the only mode in deaf education in Pakistan and Western Samoa. In China, deaf children are widely taught in sign language in the majority of the 500 plus schools. However, the official educational policy encourages integrating deaf children in regular schools (and taught, therefore, orally) with the help of 'proper training and hearing aids'.

Total communication is an approach to deaf education which encourages the use of a wide range of communication methods, including sign language. It does, not however, imply the simultaneous use of signs and fingerspelling along with spoken language or any other sign-supported speech. Simultaneous use of signs and speech simply exceeds a hearing person's psychological and physical capacities, (Johnson *et al.*, 1989): one or both parts of the signal will deteriorate as the hearing person omits signs randomly or deletes those signs that do not fit the rhythmic pattern of the speech, while the spoken signal is slowed down and altered phonologically. Moreover, because natural sign languages have different grammatical, morphological, phonological and lexical structures from a spoken language, it is virtually impossible to speak full sentences and sign complete sentences in sign language simultaneously.

In this survey, the total communication approach was introduced (without a specific definition) in deaf education in 14 countries, including such nations as Dominica, Gabon and Jamaica. Interestingly, total communication was not mentioned as an educational approach in any country's national curriculum for deaf education, but was found in half the replies concerning the methods used in classrooms.

Training of the teachers of the deaf

Professional training of teachers of deaf children seems relatively well organized in the majority of the 64 countries which responded to the question. A total of 41 nations have specialized training for teachers, while no systematized training was established in 13 countries: five of these were African, five Latin American, and one Asian; two were small insular states. The extent of the teacher training programmes varies from half-year in-service training to Bachelor's degrees. Several countries have traditionally sent teachers for specialized training overseas.

Whether teacher training is available to the deaf is unknown. However, in 28 countries there are deaf teachers in deaf education. They are very few in number, however, and the data suggest that they often work as assistant teachers or, as in the case of Brazil, teach mainly vocational subjects.

The majority of countries surveyed organize sign language training for the teachers in deaf education. The extent and type of the training was not investigated, but the following examples may well illustrate the situation: in Argentina, there is no systematized training but individual sign language courses are available; in Cameroon, only deaf teachers are trained; and in Malaysia, instead of the native Malay sign language, teachers are trained in 'manually coded Malay'.

Eighteen countries have no training for teachers of deaf children in their natural first language: sign language. Most of these countries also encourage speech-dependent means of communication in deaf education.

Understanding and recognition of sign language as the first language of deaf children is critical for successful teaching of deaf children. The WFD Commissions on Sign Language and Pedagogy have underlined in their recommendations (1991) that teachers of the deaf must be expected to use the natural sign language as the primary mode of instruction in most academic subjects, while instruction of the national spoken and written language should occur separately but in parallel to sign language, as is common in bi- and multilingual education programmes for other languages. As further discussed in Johnson *et al.* (1989), anyone attempting to teach curricular content to deaf children must be a fluent signer, and spoken language should be taught according to the principles of teaching it as a second language in order to achieve what should be the ultimate goal of deaf education: well-educated, bilingual children.

Deaf advocacy organizations

The development of independent advocacy organizations of deaf people in the countries surveyed has been fast: already 40 nations have their own national deaf associations. The majority of these organizations are recently established: while the national associations in Chile, Uruguay and the Philippines date back to the late 1920s, over 20 associations were established during the International Decade of Disabled Persons, the majority in Africa.

At the time of the survey in 1989, there were deaf associations in 38 countries; in 18 countries there was no advocacy organization of the deaf. The members of the associations varied from deaf-only to deaf, deafened, and the hard of hearing; over one-third of the organizations limited the membership to deaf and deafened persons only. All associations have deaf leadership. The role of hearing persons in the organizations was not enquired.

According to the survey, more than a third of the national deaf associations receive financial support from their government. The support is, however, often irregular or is limited to specific purposes, such as office rent or for projects. Foreign aid, either in terms of direct funding or long-term development cooperation between the national association and an overseas agency, is contributing to the development of deaf associations in countries such as Burkina Faso, Cuba, Ethiopia, Kenya and Nepal. Cooperative relations are usually established with United Nations specialized agencies such as UNICEF and UNESCO (Ethiopia, Nepal), as well as sister societies in the Nordic countries (Kenya, Tanzania, Thailand and Zambia).

Scope of activities

Working as a pressure group was the most frequently mentioned task of the national deaf associations. Apart from that, the associations facilitate a number of other activities and services. One third of the associations have had to assume the responsibility of arranging educational programmes so as to compensate deaf persons' limited educational attainments. Several deaf associations run literacy and other courses for adults. Vocational training and job placement are also among the most important services provided by the associations. While it is still a minority of deaf people who ever can have access to elementary education and vocational or any such type of training, the status of deaf job-applicants and employees remains weak in the competition for jobs. Therefore, advocacy organizations are doing what they can to help the deaf make a decent living. Vocational training and employment exchange were mentioned among the services provided by the associations in ten countries. It is not unusual for associations to employ members of the deaf community for the small enterprises run for fund-raising purposes. Sometimes, as in Ecuador, deaf people are also supported in establishing small businesses themselves.

Apart from advocacy, deaf associations the world over are encouraging the unity of the deaf community, culture and sign language through a variety of social, cultural and sports activities. In 78 per cent of the replies, deaf people were reported to meet in local deaf clubs, churches and the like. On the other hand, there were 17 countries where the replies suggested the deaf community would not get together at all, at least not in terms of any organized events. This seems to be partly a result of the small number of deaf schools in the countries concerned.

While it is the schools that have traditionally contributed much to the establishing of deaf communities, sign language and deaf culture, the limited and often non-existent access of children to deaf schools discourages a sense of community. There are four countries, Bolivia (information not confirmed), Mali, Morocco and Papua New Guinea where there are no deaf schools, as reported, nor any representative organization of deaf people. Sadly enough, one of these countries is known to forbid deaf people to get together for meetings and social events.

Cultural events are arranged in 30 countries. There are cultural festivals and competitions within the deaf community (ten countries), or in cooperation with other organizations of persons with disabilities (four countries). These festivals often take place in conjunction with annual celebrations of the national deaf association. The International Deaf Awareness Day/Week in autumn brings these festivals to the attention of wider audiences. Interest in theatre, mime and folk dance is shared by deaf communities everywhere.

Deaf people are frequently talented painters, and are often brought into the tourist business in their countries. In Ethiopia, for example, several deaf artists have been employed in a workshop producing traditional handicrafts and paintings for export. In addition to this commercial production, deaf artists and artisans hold exhibition in Ecuador, Syria and Bolivia.

Discussion

The data compiled for the WFD Survey of Deaf People in the Developing World in 1989–90 reflects the disadvantaged condition of deaf people in Asia, Africa and Latin America. The survey raises a number of concerns on the basic human rights of deaf individuals and communities. Thirteen countries, five of them in Latin America and the Caribbean, six in Africa, and one in Asia, report that deaf people do not have equal citizenship rights with the hearing majority. In some cases, deaf people do not have the right to vote; their freedom of assembly or to establish representative bodies is restricted; deaf persons marrying each other is forbidden. Apart from these legislative violations to equal rights in society, the lack of recognition of sign language as the natural language of the deaf and very limited access to educational programmes make deaf persons disadvantaged in their desire for full participation in society and overall equalization of opportunities.

Discovering the grave concerns of deaf communities in the developing world, the World Federation of the Deaf, in its capacity as the international specialized organization for the promotion of the rights of deaf persons worldwide, encourages deaf associations and deaf communities to take active measures in deaf advocacy. In all its work for the abolition of discrimination against deaf persons and sign languages, equalization of opportunities and support for representative bodies of the deaf, priority is given to developing countries where the vast majority of deaf people live. Working towards this goal, the WFD collaborates with the United Nations specialized agencies and other international organizations, national deaf associations, and with experts specializing in education, communication and other disciplines. The aim is to include deaf persons' concerns in UN programmes and projects in the developing areas of the world, and through the national deaf associations and other relevant agencies, promote the language, education and other rights of the deaf.

Decisive actions which have taken place in recent years to unite deaf communities both nationally and internationally have contributed to increasing the north-south and south-south cooperation of national deaf associations. Initiatives taken mostly by national bodies of deaf people in the Nordic countries to support structural development, human resource building and sign language promotion of the sister organizations in various Asian and African countries have shown an encouraging outcome. The strengthening of deaf associations and other communities in the developing world are, along with international advocacy, prerequisites for deaf persons' improved status as a cultural and linguistic minority with legitimate rights to equal opportunities and full participation in their respective societies.

References

Johnson, R E, Liddell, S K and Erting, C J (1989) *Unlocking the Curriculum: Principles for Achieving Access in Deaf Education* (Working Paper 98–3), Washington, DC: Gallaudet University, Department of Linguistics and Interpreting and the Gallaudet Research Institute.

United Nations Children's Fund (1990) *The State of the World's Children 1990*, New York: Oxford University Press.

United Nations Development Programme (1990) *Human Development Report*, New York: Oxford University Press.

United Nations Development Programme (1991) *Human Development Report 1991*, New York: Oxford University Press.

UNESCO (1986) *Directory of Special Education*, Geneva: Steffen.

World Bank (1989) *Sub-Saharan Africa: From Crisis to Sustainable Development*, New York: Oxford University Press.

World Bank (1990) *World Development Report 1990*, New York: Oxford University Press.

The World Federation of the Deaf (1991) *Recommendations of the Commission on Pedagogy. Proceedings of the XI World Congress of the World Federation of the Deaf*, Tokyo, Japan.

Part 3:   Regional reports and national case studies

8a. Western Europe

Patrick Daunt

Introduction

Policies for special needs education in all the countries constituting what is generally known as Western Europe share as a common prominent factor the intention to integrate children with special needs into ordinary schools. Integration has a solid theoretical base, expressed notably in the concept of democratic psychiatry developed by Franco Basaglia in Italy (Brabant, 1981) and in that of normalization first propounded as early as the 1940s by Niels Erik Bank-Mikkelsen in Denmark (Bank-Mikkelsen, 1981). It is significant that both these notions extend beyond the domain of formal education to embrace also the social and economic integration of adults with disabilities in the open community. It is no matter of chance that the relevant programmes of both the Organization for Economic Cooperation and Development (OECD) and the European Community have focused on integration, not on special education in general.

In parallel with these movements, rather than as a direct result of them, the official report on special educational needs published in the United Kingdom (DES, 1978) has been influential in insisting on the need to consider the realities of individual children rather than of categories and to explore how far problems are caused by the system rather than by the personal deficits of children. The responsibility to respond to all those who experience significant difficulty in school (the 'twenty per cent', not only the 'two per cent') was also stressed, as was the appropriateness of speaking of 'children with special needs' rather than 'handicapped children' or the like.

These 'Warnock ideas' are compatible with the World Health Organization's definitions of impairment, disability and handicap, and also with much of what is promoted by the militant independent living movement of disabled people. It is no surprise, therefore, that they have become common currency in Western Europe and helped to establish a shared language and common agendas among researchers, policy-makers and practitioners. This has happened in spite of the differences between the national education systems and of such facts as that, for example, 1.8 per cent of all children are regarded as in need of special education in Italy, 7 per cent in The Netherlands and 13 per cent in Denmark, whereas in

Sweden no official figure is given since special education is no longer recognized as a distinct function (Pijl and Meijer, 1991).

This chapter will deal first with policies and progress concerning integration in the countries of the European Community and the European Free Trade Area, since this is the thrust of policy which more than anything else gives it its purpose and character, and will then consider some of the principal specific means whereby these countries have tried to improve special needs education, whether in its integrated or its segregated form. The chapter will end with a brief prospective conclusion.

Integration in the West – policies and progress

In the light of what has been said about the theoretical base, it is natural that integration is most advanced in Italy and Scandinavia. Legislation in Italy in 1971 established mainstreaming as a right, and four years later severity of disability was legally eliminated as an exception (Ferro, 1985; Posternak, 1979; Vianello, 1992). The method for introduction has been the progressive opening of integrated classes in ordinary schools, each of these being limited to a total of 20 pupils (the normal limit being 25), and each being afforded with a part-time support teacher; no more than two children with special needs have been permitted in a class and this is now reduced to one. Some schools are specially equipped to receive children with physical disabilities.

In a situation where only children with severe disabilities are recognized as in need of special provision, over 95 per cent are said to be individually integrated. About 20 per cent of all classes (some 90,000) include a child with special needs. There are about 36,000 support teachers all of whom, at least at primary level, are said to have had some special training. Whereas the special needs children are thought to be well received by their peers, the motivation of teachers is more variable. Instances of successful coordination of local services of health, social welfare and education are a striking feature.

In the Scandinavian countries (Hansen, 1984, 1992; Helgeland, 1992; Ministry of Education, 1989; Soder, 1981; Stangvik, 1989; Vislie, 1981, 1985; Walton et al., 1990) the rights of children with special needs are included in general educational legislation. Great stress is laid on the right of children to live in their own family and on the diversion of resources from long-stay institutions to family support; the bringing out of children with mental disabilities from such establishments has been facilitated by devolution of responsibiities and resources to local communities. Of mentally retarded children in Sweden, for example, only 0.5 per cent are in long-stay residential institutions.

Individual integration has been achieved in the great majority of cases, the proportion being particularly high at the nursery level (90 per cent in Sweden, priority of places being guaranteed to children with special needs). Yet there are some special classes in ordinary schools too: in Denmark, of the 80,000 children considered to need special support at some time in their school careers, about 87.5 per cent are individually integrated, 7.5 per cent (mostly children with more severe mental disabilities) are in small special classes in ordinary schools and 5 per cent are in special schools. In Sweden a considerable proportion of children with mental handicaps are in special classes; all physically and visually impaired pupils are in ordinary schools, only 12 per cent of the former and 3 per cent of the latter being in special groups rather than individually integrated. The motivation of teachers is recognized as one of the key issues; Soder (1981) observed the importance of the positive role of special teachers in the integrating process.

An important exception to the strongly integrationist trend derives from the attitudes of parents and the deaf community to the education of profoundly and pre-lingually deaf children. There is a tendency in Norway and Denmark for such parents to prefer segregated education, and provision for them in special schools is official policy in Sweden, where 30 per cent of deaf children are so accommodated.

In France (Labregere, 1981; Ministere de l'Education Nationale, 1990, 1991) while the official commitment to integration is unambiguous, less progress has been made in achieving it. There are several reasons for this: effective policy is not so long established, and the regime of French schools is typically more severe and competitive. It must be recognized too that in France a significant number of children with more serious impairments are still the responsibility of the ministry of social affairs, so that much of the effort of the ministry of education is concerned with children who in Italy would not be recognized as needing special provision.

None the less, recent official figures give over 16,000 children with physical, sensory or mental disabilites as integrated at primary level, and over 8,000 in secondary schools. Essential to individual integration is the development of personal learning programmes ('projets pedagogiques'). There is a considerable stress on flexibility, time in either special schools or special classes being seen as quite possibly a stage of development or respite rather than a permanent placement. Important too has been the evolution of the role of special schools as resource centres in support of group or individual integration. A more recent development of special interest has been the creation in ordinary schools of 'classes d'integration scolaire' (CLIS) of a maximum of 12 children with special needs; these represent a more positive, flexible and individual approach than the special classes in ordinary schools previously established. There is therefore considerable encouragement for innovation, but in a national context in which an ongoing significant role for special schools is also foreseen.

In two countries, Germany and The Netherlands, progress towards full integration has been limited less by a lack of resources than by the complexity of the educational system and the existence of a highly developed and separate special provision. In Germany (Haasen, 1990; Muller, 1989; Schindele, 1986) there is also the restraining effect of a highly developed separate system of special schools, heightened by the fact that educational responsibility is delegated to the various Laender; as with comprehensive education, policy for or against integration tends to follow conventional lines according to the political leaning of each Land. In a competitive climate, there is a fear that children with special needs may lower the level of performance of the class; in conservative Laender it might be difficult to find a single child with learning difficulties integrated at any level, and what links exist between special and ordinary schools may have little functional content. None the less, there are pressures from parent groups to make integration possible and available in the local school.

The most significant progress has been in the nursery schools, many of which are wholly or partially integrated in the less conservative Laender. Real progress has been made in primary schools in Bonn, and there are plans to extend this to secondary level; an ambitious plan in Hamburg, following the the Italian development model, aims to have established 50 integrated primary schools by 1996. Schindele (1986) describes the elaborate and impressive enhancement of the role of a special school for visually impaired children in Schleswig-Holstein which offers a comprehensive range of services in support of integration.

In The Netherlands (Brandsma, 1991; den Boer, 1990; Rodbard, 1990) there are about 1,000 special schools in 15 different categories providing education for about 100,000 children. This provision consumes some 20 per cent of the education budget; since a majority of the special schools are under private auspices yet funded 100 per cent by the state, the motivation for radical reform is not likely to be strong. Indeed while the total school population is falling, that of special schools is rising, and there are considerable waiting lists; an endeavour to 'freeze' this population in 1987 had to be abandoned. It is interesting that a large proportion of children in separate provision (39 per cent) are in the establishments for children with learning and behaviour difficulties (LOM); the greatest growth is also to be found here. Yet, as in Germany, there are parental pressures for change, to which the authorities have responded cautiously by means of an Interim Act establishing a period of ten years research and experiment due to end in 1995. A chief strategy has been the setting up of six regional cooperative groups or clusters; the four options for collaboration between the special and ordinary schools comprise peripatetic supervision, split placements, part-time attendance and the setting up of liaison committees. A curious feature is the use of apparently outmoded vocabulary: the new conception of the role of the ordinary school is called a 'broadening of care' and there is mention of 'individual treatment programmes'.

A number of countries, while not having achieved radical integration, are committed to gradual progress in that direction which can be seen to be continuing. In Portugal (da Costa, 1989; Department of Special Education, 1991) where commitment is strong, well over 50 per cent of children assessed as having special needs are being educated in ordinary schools; further progress is limited by the effects of decentralization, and by difficulty in transferring resources from special to integrated settings. Belgium (Detraux and Dens, 1992; de Vriendt and Marco, 1986; de Vriendt et al., 1988) has also seen strong commitment, hindered, however, by a complex general system. As in France, flexibility is stressed, and the development of cooperative clusters and the resource centre role of special schools are favoured; the creation of special classes in ordinary schools is, on the other hand, contrary to policy owing to negative experience in the past.

In Austria (Gruber, 1989) the legal basis for pilot projects to promote 'joint instruction' was extended from the primary to the secondary school in 1988; the latest detailed figures available indicate 50 integrated and 52 partly integrated classes in operation. The cantons of Switzerland (Buerli, 1987) show considerable variation, the percentage of children in separate provision ranging from 1.3 to 7.5 per cent; the overall number of children segregated is, however, diminishing. In Finland (Ihatsu, 1987; Maki, 1989) while the great majority of those with mild learning or behaviour difficulties are integrated with part-time support, this is not the case for children described as having visual, hearing, physical or mental impairments; of these, over 70 per cent are in special schools and 15 per cent in special classes.

For parents in Ireland (McGee, 1990) the relatively good resources available to private special schools is a disincentive to integration; where it has been achieved it most usually takes the form of special classes in ordinary schools. Thirty-two per cent of children with mild mental handicaps are reported as being educated in this way. This 'half-way' solution is also the usual method of integration in Greece (Bardis, 1991; Nicodemos, 1990) where it can take various forms according to the assessed level of learning difficulty; experiments in Attica and Thessalonika are enabling special schools to develop new supportive roles.

There remain two countries, the United Kingdom and Spain, which present very different features of particular interest. In Great Britain (Bowman, 1986; Centre for Studies on Integration in Education, 1992; Conway, 1985; Fish, 1985; Hegarty and Pocklington, 1981; Jowett, 1989; Jowett et al., 1988; Mittler, 1992) the tradition, only recently diminished, of delegating responsibility for education to local authorities has tended to impede the even dissemination of national policies; this limitation has, however, been compensated for by considerable freedom and propensity to innovate, together with the development of the 'child-centred' approach to learning, first in the primary schools and later (through the comprehensive movement) at secondary level as well. The establishment of functional links between special and ordinary schools has often been used as a basis for further evolution: it has been calculated that 85 per cent of all special schools are, have been, or are planning to be, involved in such cooperation.

Of particular importance has been the location in ordinary schools of special units (rather than simply classes, with their somewhat static connotations), recalling the French CLIS but appearing to go further than these. While these may be above all appropriate for chldren who are profoundly deaf or who have severe learning difficulties, they can and are available to, meet all manner of needs. Their two greatest advantages are that they can take on the role of centres of excellence, advice, resources and training from special schools, and that they can offer to children with special needs authentically individual learning programmes which provide the best of special and ordinary facilities.

The 1981 Education Act which appeared in the light of the Warnock Report encourages placement in the ordinary school but recognizes that some special schools will survive. An offical survey (OPCS, 1989) calculates that 66 per cent of children with special needs are in ordinary schools. This could have been perceived as a reasonable basis of achievement from which a concerted effort could have been launched to aspire to Italian and Scandinavian levels of mainstreaming by the end of the century, had not the Education Reform Act of 1988 and subsequent measures put the whole future of integration in question. It is impossible to see how such developments as the stress on competition between schools, the encouragement of schools to opt out of local authority control and the priority given to summative testing are compatible in principle or practice with further progress in the direction of integration.

Very different from this is the scene in Spain (Gortazar, 1991; Marchesi, 1986; Marchesi et al., 1991) where national government has exploited all the advantages of learning from the experience of others – an option open to those who are relatively late in joining an innovative movement. This has enabled the

Spanish authorities not only to identify specific effective measures but to perceive the need for a master plan which brings gradualist means to the service of radical ends. Over an eight-year period (1985–93) major progress is assured by the designation each year of one new integrating primary school for every 100,000 to 150,000 inhabitants; provision of support teachers and limitation of class sizes broadly follow the Italian model, but the pace of developement is designed to ensure that 50 per cent of all primary schools will be fully integrated by the end of the period. Choice of schools to enter the scheme each year is designed for a more or less even development over all the regions of the country.

The results of a three-year evaluation study are available and show that the programme is generally succeeding in reaching its objectives. There is substantial individual integration and the effectiveness of individual support is improving; the majority of children with mental disabilities are, however, in special classes. The children with special needs benefit, particularly in social ways; the other children do not perform less well. The programme is popular with parents. Of vital importance has been the quality of each school's 'integration project' on which new procedures of coordination and communication among teachers depend. The role of the head teacher has emerged as more important than was expected. Although teacher training has been built into the programme, the need for it remains a leading problem.

Summary

The European experience can be said to have shown that the individual integration of almost all children with special needs can be successful, provided the values of the school and of the system of which it forms a part are congenial to this, and provided adequate resources (especially of personnel) are made available. There are numerous means for ensuring flexibility and enabling progress to be made gradually by stages; these include: the forming of links between special and ordinary schools; the creation of new advisory and supportive roles for specialized teachers; the development of advisory, resource and training functions for special schools; the arrangement of temporary or part-time placements; and the establishment of special classes in ordinary schools. Special classes or units may perform a most valuable function, either as stages in a child's progress or even as a permanent base – provided there is individual programming. Special classes as a permanent full-time setting may, on the other hand, achieve virtually nothing in the way of integration, and could even result in the worst of both worlds.

The future for integration could be good, but this is by no means certain. Most obviously in Germany, The Netherlands and the United Kingdom, but quite possibly elsewhere too, there is the danger that integration will fall victim to conventional politics, with detrimental consequences for many thousands of children with special needs.

Improving the quality of service overall

Extension of the range of special education

When, in the United Kingdom, the Education (Handicapped Children) Act of

1970 tranferred responsiblity for the training of all children with moderate, severe or profound mental handicaps from health to education authorities, some 25,000 children were entitled to special provision within the normal education system for the first time. The positive results were dramatic (Segal and Varma, 1992). This change was not, however, extended to Northern Ireland until 1987, nor was the equivalent legislation carried through even in Denmark until 1980, in Finland, seven years later. In France, official figures for 1990 give over 85,000 children with impairments as under the responsibility of the ministry for solidarity and social protection as against 190,000 within the domain of the education authority. The Greek ministry of health, welfare and social security has similar responsibilities. Similar situations can be found in a number of countries, including The Netherlands and Finland; the problems in Greece are rather well known.

It is clear that progress in this direction in the Western European countries has been noticeably slower than might have been expected; there is evidently an issue of children's rights here which needs to be addressed. There is a reminder here, too, that in some countries figures which present the proportion of children with special needs who are integrated in the ordinary system should be treated with a certain caution.

Early intervention and assessment

This is a vast and complex topic and a brief account cannot do more than indicate some of the priorities identified and lines of development at work. Universal recognition of the importance of early intervention in favour of children who experience impairments from birth or early infancy has evolved into a growing recognition that this involves not only professional action but also support for an active role which only parents can perform.

In the United Kingdom, 1981 legislation regularizing and strengthening assessment procedures has been complemented by many specific initiatives such as the introduction of Portage (home-visiting) schemes and the comprehensive service operated by the 'KIDS Centres' in London; participation in pre-school education for all children is, on the other hand, at a far lower level than, for example, in France or Belgium. In Sweden, as in other Scandinavian countries, high priority has been given to early intervention and assessment, and the problem of large, sparsely populated areas has been met by a system of weekly visits by pre-school teachers where no nursery school is available. Early intervention also is a priority in the innovatory programmes in Germany and Spain participating in the European Community's network of model projects. The role of the psycho-socio-medical centres in Belgium has been seminal; in Greece, too, Guidance Centres operated by the ministry of health, welfare and social security have been set up in the cities, while rural areas are served by multidisciplinary mobile diagnostic teams. Yet in Belgium the importance of educational (as well as medical, psychological and social) input into assessment is now stressed. This view is also observed in Sweden.

Adapting the ordinary school

The Warnock Report highlighted a phenomenon which was becoming increasingly evident throughout the region: that there was a need to reform the education system if it were to counter the persistent school failure of large numbers of children not assessed as having any specific learning difficulty or other disability. The notion that the ordinary school must become more sensitive to individual needs (more 'child-centred') has not, therefore, originated solely or even principally from the perception that the integration of more than a few talented individuals with disabilities makes demands on the mainstream provision which go far beyond personally-targeted support services. Rather, this perception has encountered a system already endeavouring to change in the same direction for its own large-scale purposes. These policy trends are commonly accompanied by a determination to use a more sensitive terminology than in the past, above all by avoiding descriptions of children which carry with them stereotypes or stigma.

That the integration of children with special needs, if conceived as a serious policy objective, entailed more in terms of adaptation of the schools than of the children, and that there were radical implications, not only for teaching methods and class organization but for teachers' roles and school values, was made widely known through the programme of the Centre for Educational Research and Innovation (CERI) of the OECD more than a decade ago (Labregere, 1981; Vislie, 1981); more recently it has been taken up as a main theme of the current disability programme of the European Community – 'Helios'.

The notion of individualized learning ('pedagogie differenciée') underlies the whole approach of the French authorities to mainstreaming; the need for more diversity of teaching methods is officially recognized in Switzerland. New technology has proved a useful ally for teachers pursuing these objectives, to the benefit of children with many different kinds of disability. It has been suggested (Ministry of Education, 1989) that integration has been easier in Scandinavia partly because the values and styles of the folkschool were already much closer to what was required than those generally found in other countries. The Austrian provision of a personal counselling service for all school children will favour integration. In Italy the substitution in 1977 of profiles for the traditional 'giudizi' (precise marks, requiring an overall annual 60 per cent if the child was to be promoted to the next year group) established an essential precedent for subjecting a tradition of 'doubling' the year to the realities of integration. Recently, the University of Padua has prepared, for use throughout the Veneto, a scheme for the articulation of whole-class, group and individual learning in integrated settings. New legislation in Portugal is also designed to make the ordinary school more receptive of children with special needs. These initiatives are in stark contrast to the current reactionary trend in the United Kingdom, with its insistence on precise assessments and whole-class teaching.

Transition from the primary to the secondary, and especially the upper secondary, level in the ordinary school constitutes for chidren with special needs a problem which has not been satisfactorily solved even in Italy or Scandinavia, and greater flexibility in this has been recognized as a need in Switzerland. In Italy exclusion from secondary education on the grounds of disability was ruled unconstitutional by a court judgment in 1987; yet while 'doubling' the year has been virtually eliminated for children with special needs in the primary school, it still affects some 11–13 per cent at secondary level. The difficulty is recognized in Norway; in Denmark, while there are about 3,000 young people needing special support in the secondary vocational schools, the figure for the gymnasium is 200, which looks low. In Belgium, it is recorded that young people with physical disabilities often have to go to residential institutions for secondary education, and Ireland records the difficulties experienced by children with mild mental handicaps in making the transition to the secondary system from special classes integrated in ordinary primary schools. Though the opportunities in vocational education may generally be better, the end of the period of compulsory education remains a time of risk for very many young people with special needs.

Support systems

Official advisory centres and services have played an important part in the improvement of the quality of education available to children with special needs, whether in separate or integrated settings. This function has formed part of the normal responsibilites of local education authorities in the United Kingdom, for example, and of the departmental inspectorates and special education commissions in France. In The Netherlands, regional advisory centres offer support to individual pupils as well as to teachers, and a similar function is performed by School and Guidance Centres in Spain; the importance of the medico-socio-psychological centres in Belgium has already been mentioned. In Sweden, a national institute has been established to advise local municipalities in view of their enhanced role in special needs education; the Swiss Institute of Special Education is broadly representative and has wide-ranging responsibilities.

The evolution of the function of special schools within an integrating process is also a widespread feature. The French national Centre for Training and Research in Special Education at Suresnes is coordinating a European Community (Helios programme) project to develop this role in the areas of Paris, Lille, Toulouse and Lyon. In Belgium, special schools are supporting the integration of children with specific learning difficulties. In Denmark, special schools have developed as Knowledge Centres, offering advice, resources, in-service training courses and research and development activities. These functions are similar to those offered by the school for visually disabled children in Schleswig-Holstein; the new legislation in Portugal also provides for this kind of development.

Finally, the supportive role of individual professionals working in direct contact with the schools is an essential element in a good service. The educational psychology service is regarded as a keystone of the provision in Denmark; in France the educational psycholgists advise in the development of a school's 'educational project' as well as in the running and evaluation of in-service training. Itinerant specialized teachers play an important part in the support of integration in Ireland, Portugal and Germany (for example, in Bonn), as do mobile multidisciplinary teams in Hamburg and Sweden. The relative shortage of educational psychologists in Ireland and Greece has been seen as a constraint on innovation in special education and on integration in particular.

The participation of parents

A growing insistence on the part of parents and other family members to be involved actively in the making and carrying out of decisions directly affecting children with special needs has been a prominent feature throughout the region; the response of authorities and professionals to this pressure has been sometimes reluctant and generally variable. In some systems real progress has been made: in Norway, no new action can be undertaken without the written consent of parents, and the same applies to decisions on placement in special education in Greece. In the United Kingdom, participation at all stages of assessment, 'statementing' and placement are provided for under the 1981 Act, yet this is a domain where there can be gaps between what is provided by law and what actually happens.

Of very great importance has been the increasing influence and effectiveness of voluntary organizations, including those – typically concerned with congenital impairments, such as cerebral palsy, spina bifida, autism and various kinds of mental handicap – in which parents are predominant or prominent members. As well as affording advice and support to their membership, these associations are often engaged in raising funds for research, directly providing services and influencing national policy. The impact of parental pressures in favour of integration, for example, has been observed in many countries, including Germany and The Netherlands.

Conclusions

For whatever kind or level of special need, there exists in Europe a wealth of knowledge and understanding, based on experience and study, of how the quality and range of education can be promoted. It is possible to speak too of a significant degree of convergence of views among professionals and families on the values which should underlie the aims of policy and the priorities which should be observed in its implementation; this convergence extends to a general (though certainly not unanimous) recognition both of the value of integration and of the need for a strategic approach to its development, implying the pursuit of radical objectives by flexible and gradualist means.

All this would suggest that the future for special needs education in Europe is a promising and exciting one, and this would indeed be the case if it were not for two powerful countervailing forces. The first of these is one which affects disability in all policy sectors and is a matter of *economic fragility*; in many if not most cultures within Europe provision for special needs is likely to remain vulnerable to neglect or retrenchment whenever times are hard. Second, *political trends* which may loosely be called élitist or anti-egalitarian, in so far as they are prevalent, will unquestionably militate against the interests of all but a few children with special needs; this danger need not be exaggerated but should not be ignored either.

In this situation, activity at European level should not be viewed as a luxury, offering by means of exchange programmes an extra layer of inspiration or sophisticated learning to top up the quality of solid national effort. Rather, the aim should be to develop an authentic European policy for special needs education, expressed in terms both of funds aimed at promoting research and innovation as well as at the support of regions or countries with exceptional development problems, and of legislation guaranteeing unequivocally the rights of every child with special needs to all levels of education to which he or she can aspire and chooses to undertake.

References

Bank-Mikkelsen, N E (1981) 'The principle of normalization', in Grunewald, K and Jonsson, T (eds) *Handicappade barn i u-lander*, Natur och Kultur: Stockholm.

Bardis, P (1991) *The Integration of Children with Special Needs in Rural Greece*, Athens: Karditsa.

Brabant, M (1981) *Entrance of Disabled Persons into the Open Environment: operation Trieste*, Mulhouse: Centre de Readaptation.

Bowman, I (1986) 'Teacher training and the integration of handicapped pupils', *European Journal of Special Needs Education*, 1, 1, 29–38.

Brandsma, J (1991) *Teacher Training for Special Education in the Nineties*, Utrecht: Seminarium voor Orthopedagogik.

Buerli, A (1987) 'A propos de l'integration des enfants handicapes en Suisse', *Aspects*, 19, Lucerne: Secretariat Suisse de Pedagogie Curative.

Centre for Studies on Integration in Education (1992) *Segregation Statistics*, London: CSIE.

Conway, J (1985) 'Integration at secondary level in England', *Integration of handicapped in secondary schools: five case studies*, Paris: OECD (CERI).

da Costa, A M Benard (1989) 'Educational integration programmes in Portugal', paper presented at a European Community conference on 'Special systems and integrated situations', Rotterdam, October.

Daniels, H and Hogg, B (1992) 'Report on the European exchange of experiences in school integration (Aarhus, Arezzo, Greenwich, Reutlingen)', *European Journal on Special Needs Education*, 7, 2, 104–16.

Daunt, P (1991) *Meeting Disability: a European response*, London: Cassell.

den Boer, K (1990) 'Special education in the Netherlands', *European Journal of Special Needs Education*, 5, 2, 136–50.

DES (1978) *Special Educational Needs (The Warnock Report)*, London: HMSO.

Detraux, J-J and Dens, A (1992) 'Special education in Belgium', *European Journal of Special Needs Education*, 7, 1, 63–79.

de Vriendt, M-J and Marco, C (1986) *Des Etudiants a Audition ou Vision Deficiente en l'Enseignement Superieur*, Universite de Mons-Hainaut.

de Vriendt, M-J, Eyckerman, A and Pankowski, D (1988) 'Des deficients visuels, etudiants a l'universite', *European Journal of Special Needs Education*, 3, 2, 113–18.

Ferro, N (1985) 'Scuola di Rienzo: integration in a secondary school in Rome', *Integration of Handicapped in Secondary Schools: Five case studies*, Paris: OECD (CERI).

Fish, J (1985) *Educational Opportunities For All?*, London: Inner London Education Authority.

Ministere de l'Education Nationale (1990, 1991) *Circulaires No. 90–082 (Mise en place et organisation des reseaux d'aides specialisées aux éleves en difficulté); No. 90–083 (Missions des psychologues scolaires); No. 91–302 (Integration scolaire des enfants et adolescents handicapés); No 91–304 (Scolarisation des enfants handicapes a l'école primaire: classes d'integration scolaire – CLIS)*, Paris: MEN.

Gortazar, A (1991) 'Special education in Spain'. *European Journal of Special Needs Education*, 6, 1, 56–70.

Gruber, H (1989) 'Integration behinderter Kinder', *Erziehung und Unterricht, Oesterreichische Paedagogische Zeitschrift*, 5, 263–9.

Haasen, K (1990) *The Unification of Germany: implications for the integration of individuals with development disabilities*, Chicago, IL: University of Illinois.

Hansen, J (1984) *Teaching and Training the Handicapped through the New Information Technology*, Brussels: Commission of the European Communities.

Hansen, J (1992) 'The development of the Danish folkeskole towards a School for All', *European Journal of Special Needs Education*, 7, 1, 38–46.

Hegarty, S (1991) 'Towards an agenda for research in special education', *European Journal of Special Needs Education*, 6, 2, 87–99.

Hegarty, S and Pocklington, K with Lucas, D (1981) *Educating Pupils with Special Needs in Ordinary Schools*, Windsor: NFER-Nelson.

Helgeland, I (1992) 'Special education in Norway', *European Journal of Special Needs Education*, 7, 2, 169–83.

Ihatsu, M (1987) 'The social integration of disabled pupils in the lower levels of the comprehensive school', *Publications on Education*, University of Joenssu.

Jorgensen, I (1980) *Special Education in the European Community*, Brussels: Commission of the European Communities.

Jowett, S (1989) 'Links between special and ordinary schools – a study of their prevalence and purpose', *European Journal of Special Needs Education*, **4**, 1, 23–34.

Jowett S, Hegarty, S and Moses, D (1988) *Joining Forces*, Windsor: NFER-Nelson.

Labregere, A (1981) 'Changes in the educational system favouring integration', in *Integration in the School*, Paris: OECD (CERI).

McGee, P (1990) 'Special education in Ireland', *European Journal of Special Needs Education*, **5**, 1, 48–64.

Maki, O M (1989) 'Hearing impaired children in primary schools in Finland', *European Journal of Special Needs Education*, **4**, 3, 199–202.

Marchesi, A (1986) 'Project for the integration of pupils with special needs in Spain', *European Journal of Special Needs Education*, **1**, 2, 125–33.

Marchesi, A *et al.* (1991) 'Assessment of the integration project in Spain', *European Journal of Special Needs Education*, **6**, 3, 185–200.

Ministry of Education (1989) *Handicapped Students in the Danish Educational System*, Copenhagen: Ministry of Education.

Mittler, P (1992) 'Preparing all initial teacher training students to teach children with special educational needs: a case study from England', *European Journal of Special Needs Education*, **7**, 1, 1–10.

Mittler, P and Farrell, P (1987) 'Can children with severe learning difficulties be educated in ordinary schools?', *European Journal of Special Needs Education*, **2**, 4, 221–36.

Muller, H (1989) 'Integrating the handicapped in primary schools in Hamburg', paper presented at a European Community conference on 'Special systems and integrated situations', Rotterdam, October.

Nicodemos, S (1990) *Special Education in Greece*, Athens: Ministry of Education.

Office of Population Census and Surveys (1989) *Statistics of Disabilities*, London: HMSO.

Pijl, S J and Meijer, C J W (1991) 'Does integration count for much? An analysis of the practices of integration in eight countries', *European Journal of Special Needs Education*, **6**, 2, 100–111.

Department of Special Education (1991) *Children and Young People with Special Educational Needs in the Portuguese Educational System*, Lisbon: DSE.

Posternak, Y (1979) *Integration of Handicapped Children and Adolescents in Italy*, Paris: OECD (CERI).

Rodbard, G (1990) 'Going Dutch! A perspective on the Dutch system of special education', *European Journal of Special Needs Education*, **5**, 3, 221–30.

Schindele, R A (1986) 'Educational support for visually handicapped students in regular schools', *European Journal of Special Needs Education*, **1**, 1, 39–57.

Segal, S and Varma, V (eds) (1992) *Prospects for People with Learning Difficulties*, London: David Fulton.

Soder, M (1981) 'Integration of the mentally retarded', in *Integration in the School*, Paris: OECD (CERI).

Stangvik, G (1989) 'Special education and social context', *European Journal of Special Needs Education*, **4**, 2, 91–101.

Vianello, R (1992) 'Post-professional training; training for innovation', Paper presented at a conference 'Across disciplines: innovation in training for those working with people who have severe learning difficulties', British Institute for Mental Handicap, London, January.

Vislie, L (1981) 'Policies for basic education in Norway and the concept of integration', in *Integration in the School*, Paris: OECD (CERI).

Vislie, L (1985) *The Forsoksgymnas, Oslo: a case study of integration in a Norwegian school. Integration on handicapped in secondary schools: five case studies*, Paris: OECD (CERI).

Walton, W T, Emanuelsson, I and Rosenqvist, J (1990) 'Normalization and integration of handicapped students into the regular education system; contrasts between Sweden and the USA', *European Journal of Special Needs Education*, **5**, 2, 111–25.

World Health Organization (1980) *International Classification of Impairments, Disabilities and Handicaps*, Geneva: WHO.

8b. The 'new democracies' of Central and Eastern Europe

Patrick Daunt

Some common problems

Some, albeit tentative, generalizations can be made about special needs education in the new democracies of Central and Eastern Europe which distinguish them from the countries in the previous chapter. There are, of course, no characteristic difficulties or constraints which are not also familiar in the West; none the less, it can fairly be said that progress in the new democracies has been relatively limited, certainly in respect of integration, but also in a number of other ways which affect improvement in the range and quality of services.

Underlying this difference is the persistence of a sense of shame in response to disability and a tendency to associate it with stigma. The continuing practice of segregating children with physical or mental impairments both influences and is influenced by the general lack of accessibility to public transport and other facilities and the consequent infrequency with which adult disabled people are visible on the streets. Not only are very large numbers of disabled children more or less isolated from society in specialized institutions; the majority of these establishments – schools as well as homes and hospitals – are residential. Moreover, they are often large: official figures from Romania give an average of 279 children in each of 499 residential institutions of various kinds. In Czechoslovakia, residential establishments for 'young people' cover the age range three to 25; there are 129 of these for the mentally handicapped, the average number of residents being about 110, one for the multi-handicapped (438 residents), and three for the physically handicapped (averaging 515 residents).

It can also be said that a predominantly 'medical model' of disability has been subject to less dilution through other influences than has happened further west. In particular, the impact of the theory and practice of defectology propounded by Professor Luria has been strong in Russia and its neighbours. The terminology of 'recuperation' is prevalent, and the preoccupation with cure – and its concomitant, incurability – would seem to Western eyes to leave little room for the promotion of positive, 'coping', attitudes to stabilized but persistent disability. From this can follow limitations to the aims and content of professional training, of high quality though this may be in many other respects.

Another implication of this thinking has consequences which are ambiguous.

Typically, children in the new democracies with problems deemed to be temporary or 'curable' have not been assessed as in need of special education. Among these are included the very large groups of children with what are sometimes called 'specific learning difficulties' (such as dyslexia), and children who present difficult behaviour. In at least some Western European countries the latter are especially important because they are subject to a greater rate of numerical growth than any other; in all countries which use a wide definition of children with special needs, the two groups together form a large percentage, perhaps the majority, of those so defined. The question is therefore one that cannot be overlooked. The exclusion of these categories of children from special education can have the positive effect that any school failures among such children may be thought to be the 'fault' of the teacher, not of the 'defect' in the child. However, unless there is evidence of a well developed capacity within the ordinary schools to cater for individual needs, the much more likely general consequence is that an education appropriate to the needs of these children is simply not available.

In this context, it is not surprising that policies favouring integration have been either tenuous or non-existent. Indeed, governments planning future progress may need to give priority to the number of children still regarded as ineducable, and to the need to extend the range of authority of education ministries. In 1969, responsibility for many children with mental handicaps in what are now the New Laender of Germany was moved from special schools to the ministry of health. In Czechoslovakia, the 16,000 children and young people reported in residential institutions are under the responsibility of the ministry of social care. In Romania at present, many children are in institutions run by the ministry of health or even the ministry of labour. There are examples, too, of apparently undifferentiated treatment of children with mental handicaps and with other impairments, as well as of children with various disabilities, orphans and abandoned children.

There is considerable diversity in the range of services offered within the special education systems and generalizations are hazardous. Pre-school provision can be generous, partly no doubt through its link to employment policy. Provision of therapeutic and other support services to schools, and of vocational training possibilities, varies greatly. Where there is general agreement is over the difficulty which young people with physical disabilities find in entering universities, whose facilities are typically inaccessible.

Problems of a quite different order concern resources. Most often observed is the widespread shortage of wheelchairs, for adults and even more critically for children. The deficiencies extend to daily living aids and prostheses generally, and in some cases to the maintenance and equipment of institutions. The closure in Poland and the Laender of the former German Democratic Republic of many of the sheltered workshops which have played such a large part in the social and economic integration of people with disabilities there, implies a serious reduction in the prospects of special needs children leaving school. The mere size of this problem is daunting: in 1990 some 250,000 people with disabilities were employed in special cooperatives in Poland. Moreover a general shortage of material resources (including technical aids) has been compounded by the relatively small contribution made by the voluntary sector, the creation of associations of disabled people or their families having been actually illegal until recently in some countries.

Positive factors

Against these constraints must be set many positive factors, both general and particular. Above all at the higher levels, professional training and commitment are probably as high as anywhere in the world. In some countries, in-service training is also well developed, and indeed compulsory for teachers in special needs education. It would be quite wrong to suppose any general distaste for innovation, still more a disinterest in quality of performance.

Already, voluntary associations are being established and flourishing. Examples are the new associations for physically disabled people in Romania (32 branches) and Russia; the group of young disabled people known as Caritas Humanitas in Hungary, planning now to form a 'Budapest Coalition of Disabled People'; the programme of integrated vacations for young people with disabilities organized by Auxilia in Czechoslovakia; and the rapid extension of the work of Lebenshilfe in the New Laender of Germany. A newly formed organization known as 'The Rebirth of the Disabled' in Moscow is a cooperative offering training as well as jobs in workshops and leisure and cultural facilities. The Federation of Disabled People in Czechoslovakia includes among many activities the publication of special magazines for people with hearing impairments and for physically disabled readers. The Landesarbeitsgemeinschaft Hilfe für Behinderte Sachsen has the affiliation of 18 of the 30 relevant associations so far formed in Saxony and has links with the other 12. Already too, voluntary bodies are active in organizing exchange programmes with the West; the programme of Mobility International, launched before the events of 1989, is particularly impressive. Underlying this is a widespread openness to Western contacts which possesses enormous promise for the future.

Though the same levels of participation do not apply throughout the region, the involvement of parents in assessment processes is widely provided for. In Czechoslovakia, parents are involved in the discussions leading to assessment, although their consent to placement is not required and an allocation to special education once decided on is mandatory. In Poland and in Yugoslavia, on the other hand, it is stated that a child may not be assigned to special education without the parents' consent. For reasons already apparent, it is too early to speak of 'parent power' in the sense of an established political influence exerted in a consistent way by parents united in associations.

In many cases the quality of provision on offer, albeit segregated, is high and founded on rigorous programmes for the training of specialist teachers. Special teachers in Czechoslovakia are trained only in universities (one in each of the three regions, Bohemia, Moravia and Slovakia); courses last for five years (six for part-time students) and are followed by an induction year in school. Professional standards are also generally high in Hungary, where students are often trained in both educational and therapeutic disciplines. The results can be seen (for example) in the primary school for some 190 children with physical disabilities (150 resident) in Budapest and in the Bratislava secondary school which provides examination opportunities to over 120 children in wheelchairs. Both these schools offer the normal school curriculum.

Other examples of relatively high aspiration are the two rehabilitation centres for children with cerebral palsy in Romania and the ten vocational training colleges for disabled students in Poland. The experiment in Moscow for the training of students with physical disabilities as foreign language translators is an excellent instance of well targeted innovation, as are the project in Czechoslovakia for the joint training of children with profound mental handicaps and their parents, and the creation there of an information system for the benefit of institutions, professionals and individual disabled people, one of the databases of which will cover special and integrated education.

Integration itself is a policy on which, in spite of the strength of the segregated tradition, the foundations for development have usually been laid. Before 1989 there existed an official policy to promote mainstreaming in Hungary, Poland and Romania. Integration is official policy in Croatia and said to be widely practised in Slovenia. In Bulgaria too, a number of special classes have already been established in regular schools. Even in two countries which were reported by UNESCO in 1988 as having no policy for integration, there are signs of change. In Czechoslovakia the Education Act of 1989 opened up the possibility of the integration of pupils with special needs, and there is evidence of a positive interest in integration within the newly emerging parents' organizations in the former German Democratic Republic.

Hungary has been the source of a prominent example of innovation transfer from East to West in recent years: conductive education. Launched by Andras Peto in 1945, conductive education was officially recognized by the Hungarian government in 1963; a new Peto Institute in Budapest was opened in 1984, and there is now also an Institute in southern Hungary at Kiskunhalas; an international Institute is due to open in Budapest. The system has been developed particularly for children with cerebral palsy, but is applicable to other motor impairments including Parkinson's Disease. The aim is to develop auto-functioning over all activities relevant to independent living. All skills are taught by a 'conductor', a new class of four-year trained professional who replaces nurse, teacher and therapist. A continuous range and series of activities is carefully planned and executed for each child by the conductor, motor and linguistic elements being linked, while the children work always in groups and in a specially disposed and furnished environment. Parental involvement is also stressed.

A very special interest in conductive education has been shown in the United Kingdom, and over a number of years British parents of children with cerebral palsy have gone with them to Budapest for education. A Foundation and Institute have now been established in Birmingham, and conductors trained there will be recognized by the Peto Institute. Other centres have sprung up in Britain, for example at Hornsey in London and Craigalbert in Scotland. Much is hoped for from these initiatives, although they are the subject of some controversy in professional circles.

The approach to cooperative and supportive action

There is already abundant evidence of enthusiasm in Western countries to bring help to those in the new democracies who see an opportunity which has not existed in the recent past for advancing the quality and range of education offered to children and young people with special needs. There is every reason to believe that the West can and should be a source of collaboration and support which is relevant, applicable and welcome. Yet there are evidently important issues to address concerning the priorities which should be identified, the legal and financial frameworks in which such cooperation might be best undertaken, the means for coordination (avoidance both of 'double emploi' and of crucial gaps), the identification of the best Western partners and – most important, perhaps, of all – the spirit and style in which assistance is offered and delivered.

Gargiulo and Cerna (1991), discussing the impact of the theory of defectology, quote Sovak (1984) to the effect that 'the focus is on the impact of the defect on the integrity of the personality of the individual', and Obuchova (1987) for the view that the idea behind special education is

to develop through the application of particular methods and forms of work the undisturbed components of personality of handicapped children and young people; to remove, or to compensate for, the consequences of the defect and to bring them as close as possible to healthy individuals.

For those who have worked in a Western European context, what is missing here is something already enshrined in the World Health Organization's definition of handicap as not simply a defect in the individual but rather the negative consequence of the interaction between the functional limitations resulting from an impairment and an environment which has not been adapted so as to minimize or annul this. The notion that the living, learning and working environment can be adapted so as to come (as it were) half-way or more to meet the disabled person, and the conviction that this approach, while facilitating the promotion of equal opportunity, is actually demanded by a philosophy of equal value – these are the fundamental ideas which Western professionals, disabled people and family members cannot fail to bring with them in the contacts and cooperations they develop with partners in the new democracies.

This, however, raises at once what is now already a classic question, familiar from many experiences acquired within the relations between developing and developed countries in the educational field as well as in many others: how can those organizing and involved in collaborative and supportive activities avoid the imposition of inappropriate solutions which misinterpret or even ignore the economic and, perhaps even more importantly, social and cultural realities of the country they are trying to help? How will it be possible to get beyond the affirmation of concepts such as 'normalization' on the one side, and 'recuperation' on the other, at risk of becoming little more than an exchange of slogans? Western experts would do well to recognize that in the new democracies they will encounter highly qualified professionals who do not look forward to the degrading of their expertise as one of the consequences of liberation from a totalitarian regime.

A tentative answer to this question will require four elements: a statement of the spirit which must guide all supporting iniatives; an identification of the frameworks in which collaborative actions may be launched, and of the principal partners likely to be involved; a consideration of the means for coordinating what will certainly be a diverse endeavour; and, finally, some practical suggestions of specific actions which could be undertaken.

Evidently, western experts will need to be cautious about promoting specific strategies, however successful these may have proved in their own situations. Even such a fundamental policy component as integration may need careful and sensitive discussion before methods and timescales for its realization can even begin to be outlined. In particular, proposals which ignore professional realities are more likely to be unhelpful than productive.

There are two clear implications of this need to avoid ineptitude. The first is that assistance programmes should allow plenty of initial time for discussion and preparation before any project is actually detailed and set in motion; this means that preparation needs to be funded and therefore specifically included as an eligible – better still, obligatory – activity in any funding body's regulation. A second implication is that, wherever possible, assistance programmes should be negotiated on the Western side not by individuals but by teams representing different Western cultures; the participation of disabled people and family members as well as experts – involving most likely cooperation between institutes and NGOs – could be especially rewarding, as a means not only of avoiding errors but for brainstorming creative solutions and therefore eliciting vigorous responses of a much higher quality than could be achieved by means of a more narrowly based approach.

As to frameworks, there will no doubt be many useful initiatives undertaken by national non-governmental or semi-governmental agencies, and by international and European NGOs, including the federations of associations of and for disabled people. Among the international organizations, both UNESCO and UNICEF are, as would be expected, already active, and the International Labour Organization will have a valuable contribution to make in the field of vocational training. The report of the secretariat of the Council of Europe, presented in November 1991 to a conference of the Ministers responsible for policies for people with disabilities, included a section on education; the conference was attended by Czechoslovakia and Hungary as members and by representatives of the other new democracies as observers.

Considerable help may be available from the European Community, above all through carefully targeted participation in the TEMPUS programme which offers financial support to collaborations between universities in EC countries and the new democracies, aimed at supporting development of the latter. TEMPUS support for the development of newly devised higher level professional training courses for key multipliers and change agents (such as inspectors, educational psychologists, teacher trainers, head teachers) could make a uniquely valuable contribution to model or pilot actions for the implementation of new policies for the education of children with special needs. The capacity of TEMPUS to offer financial aid for administrative and travel costs (including those incurred at the phase of preparation), as well as costs of new equipment and curriculum development, suggests that it is exceptionally well designed to meet the requirements of cooperative development in the special education field.

If the best use of these and other resources is to be achieved, there will be the need for a mechanism both for coordination and for the exchange of information. Ideally, this would involve setting up a steering group in which the UN agencies, the Council of Europe and the Commission of the European Community would participate, in order to ensure that the programmes operated under their auspices were complementary, duplication and conflict avoided, and the overall pattern of support moulded so as to meet as directly as possible the needs expressed by the new democracies themselves. The same group could act as a clearing house of information about programmes to which application could be made and projects actually under way, for the benefit of governments, official agencies and voluntary bodies in all the countries concerned, as well as for the European NGOs, the autonomous action of all these none the less being respected.

Finally, a comprehensive effort to support positive development of the educational provision for all children and young people with special needs in the new democracies, operated in this spirit and within these frameworks and coordinated by these means, could be composed of these elements:

- Information, especially through the direct exchange of experience, about how problems can and have been addressed and solved; there will be a particularly important role here for voluntary associations of professionals, families and disabled people.
- Training programmes at all professional levels, but particularly targeting selected multipliers; the focus should be on practical approaches, inter-professional cooperation and innovation.
- Advice on policy development, especially for the establishment of coherent but flexible national integration plans; such strategies as the stopping of admissions to large institutions and the planned replacement of these by small units would also come in here.
- Financial support for pilot projects in implementation of the new policies once established.
- Substantial earmarked financial support for the provision of material resources, including wheelchairs and other technical, educational and communication aids.

There will be a need here for a powerful political initiative in order to find the finances necessary for an endeavour of this kind to have a significant impact and, in particular, to overcome the bias of the European Community against supporting basic education. It must not be forgotten that the greater appreciation of need, with extreme financial constraints in all the countries constitutes a crisis which it is impossible to ignore.

To underline the value of a coherent strategy of support such as this does not of course imply that there will not be many useful lessons which the Western countries can learn from the experience and achievements of the special needs education systems in the new democracies.

Reference

Gargiulo, M and Cerna, M (1991) *Special Education in Czechoslovakia: characteristics and issues*, Prague: Charles University.

9. Education of youths with disabilities in the United States of America

Edwin W Martin

Historical background

Under the Constitution of the United States of America, education is one of the areas of governing left as a responsibility of local communities and states, not the national government. The federal government's efforts in education have generally been based on the assumption that a compelling national interest was involved. For example, in the late 1950s, the federal National Defense Education Act was passed by Congress as a response to the first 'Sputnik' being sent into space by the Soviet Union. The rationale was that increased support for mathematics and science education was critical to national defence, which was a federal responsibility under the Constitution, even if education was not. Members of Congress who had wished to provide federal aid to education welcomed this opportunity and gradually expanded federal aid over the following years to less defence-related educational areas, such as the humanities.

In the 1960s Congress again passed major education legislation providing aid for improving schools serving low-income and minority-group children and, similarly, expanding programmes of assistance for youth wishing to attend colleges and universities. The federal rationale in these instances was that the Constitution required equal treatment under the law, and that historic patterns of racism and segregation had not provided such equal treatment. Federal aid to education was seen as part of a civil rights movement to overcome the effects of discrimination and poverty. Again, the rationale for federal education aid was tied to a Constitutional role of the federal government.

It is instructive to note that despite Congress' interest in aiding economically disadvantaged and minority-group children, passing major legislative programmes in 1965 to improve education and create access to post-secondary education, no programmes specially designated for children with disabilities were included. The classic position, 'out of sight–out of mind', seemed to be demonstrated. Within a year, Congress began to consider special education problems and legislation.

Despite the importance, philosophically and financially, of the new federal programmes to improve education for the disadvantaged, they still represented a small share of educational expenditures in the USA – approximately 10 per cent – with the remainder being raised by local and state governments.

Programmes for the education of children with disabilities followed a similar pattern. In the period before 1966, parents petitioned the local school authorities to offer programmes for their children with disabilities. Many local authorities, citing costs, lack of trained personnel, etc, declined to provide school programmes, or provided only a few such opportunities, not fully meeting the needs.

It was a period of great frustration and parents organized their own programmes and also banded together to try to influence the legislators. In every state, one or more parents, often a mother, emerged as a key persuader. Parents turned to the legislatures and asked for laws which would provide extra funds to local school districts for such programmes. Even with this assistance, many school districts did not offer sufficient programmes, and many children either attended school without appropriate services or remained at home. Some children, primarily children who were blind or deaf, were enrolled in special schools operated by the states, often requiring that they live away from home. Similarly, states operated residential institutions for children who were mentally retarded or mentally ill. Most of these institutions did not offer appropriate educational programmes, providing humane residential services at best, and frequently not even that.

In the 1950–75 period, when parents determined that these programmes of state financial incentives were not going to be fully successful, they once again petitioned the state legislatures, this time for what became known as 'mandatory' laws. These *required* local school districts to educate children with disabilities and provided state financial assistance. Many states passed such laws, but, unfortunately, they often were not enforced, or had provisions exempting children with severe disabilities from their protections.

To the extent these laws were successful, a pattern of special education services did develop in many communities. By the mid-1960s, many communities offered one or more special classes for children who were identified as mentally retarded; some also had a special class for children with orthopaedic disabilities. Children with speech problems were offered the services of a speech pathologist in addition to their regular classroom work. Generally, only the largest cities or most affluent suburbs had extensive programmes which might offer services to children with each of the different kinds of sensory, physical or mental disabilities.

Federal assistance

In 1967, federal efforts on behalf of children with disabilities began to take on new significance. For the first time, Congress began to provide assistance to the states to 'initiate, expand or improve' programmes and services for education of 'handicapped children'. A new Education for the Handicapped Act authorized these grants and also established a new federal agency, the Bureau of Education for the Handicapped, in the US Office of Education. The amount of funding to help the states was very small by national standards, only $14 million in the first full year, and about $29 million by the third year. With an estimated four to five million children requiring special education, and less than half those children then being served, the amount per child was small. More important, however, was that this programme and the new federal bureau represented the beginning of a national policy to recognize the needs of children with disabilities, and such programmes were sure to grow.

In addition to the new programme of grants to states for services, the federal government also supported an important programme of grants to colleges and universities for teacher education and research and demonstration. Most major university special education programmes were developed or strengthened significantly by federal aid.

Planned programmes supported demonstrations in many sites throughout the nation, thereby focusing attention on such topics as early childhood education, education for children with specific learning disabilities and on children with severe and multiple problems, including children who were deaf–blind. Still other programmes supported the development of new technology and media. While there has been some scepticism in the USA about the value of government-supported demonstration projects, (eg, 'Do they continue after federal funds end?', or 'Are they conducted in realistic environments?'), there is little doubt that those programmes in special education have been very effective. From the early childhood demonstration projects which began in 1969, a major service programme, a professional literature, trained specialists, carefully evaluated programmes and other benefits have accrued. Some of the early projects, the Portage Project, for example, which delivered services to homes of children with severe disabilities, using persons with little or no formal training as teachers, have been translated into other languages and used around the world.

In 1971 and 1972 national policy affecting education for children with disabilities took another major step forward when, for the first time, the federal judicial system affirmed that children with disabilities must be educated. First in Pennsylvania and then in the District of Columbia, the courts required states and local school districts to educate children with disabilities and refused to allow them to argue that there were not sufficient funds. The courts said existing funds must be spread fairly across all children, and the disabled could not be singled out for less services.

PL 94-142: The Education of All Handicapped Children's Act

The federal law that formally established the public policy of the USA in relation to education of children with disabilities followed in 1975. It was known as Public Law 94-142, The Education of All Handicapped Children's Act, (retitled in 1991 as The Individuals with Disabilities Education Act – IDEA) (Levine and Wexler, 1981; Martin, 1976). This law, which now provides more than $2 billion each year to the local school districts and states, also established many policies affecting educational programmes. Each state had a choice whether to submit a state plan to the federal government under the Act. If they did not, they could not receive the associated federal funds, and they might have to provide essentially the same services under the provisions of another new federal law, Section 504 of the Rehabilitation Act, which prohibited discrimination against people with handicaps in any federally-funded programme.

In the period just prior to PL 94-142's approval by Congress, while it was being considered and most people felt it would pass, many state legislatures strengthened their laws to be similar to the proposed federal law. After the federal law was passed, additional changes in state law were widespread and common policies were developed. At the same time, the courts in many states ruled that education for children with disabilities was required, spelling out policies they felt were necessary. Through this process, Public Law 94-142 and the accompanying federal regulations issued by the Bureau of Education for the Handicapped basically set the overall policies under which each state and local school district operated special education programmes. The choice of actual curricular material taught in the schools was a local responsibility, as was the choice of texts and materials, the certification of teachers and the standards for graduation. The federal law required a series of procedures designed to protect the child and the family, but primary responsibility remained at the local level.

Public Law 94-142 had a historic importance in the United States beyond its impact on children with disabilities and the schools which serve them. It was a statement affirming the civil rights of children with disabilities, and it was much more detailed in its prescriptions than earlier federal education law. As such, it was somewhat controversial, and state and local administrators and public officials sometimes expressed resentment that it was 'telling them what to do'. Each state had to develop a state plan according to the law's requirements if the state wished to receive the federal funds. A number of states discussed the possibility of not participating because of concerns about 'federal control', particularly, it seemed, over problems that might occur in including children with disabilities in regular school programmes. All but one state submitted a plan, and that state, New Mexico, later lost a federal court suit which held that they were violating a separate federal law, Sections 503–4 of The Rehabilitation Act which prohibited discrimination against persons with handicaps. Ultimately, as political winds changed, New Mexico filed its state plan.

Characteristics of the national law

School districts have to seek out and identify children with disabilities. They must offer appropriate testing for each child, and notify the parents in advance so that they may be aware of the test procedures. If use of languages other than English is necessary to communicate with parent or child, the school district has to adapt its communications accordingly.

An individual plan

Each child suspected of having a disability is entitled to appropriate diagnosis. A team of teachers, school psychologists, administrators, etc, identifies the child as needing special education and develops an individual education programme (IEP) for each child. The IEP should include short-term and long-term goals and proposed means of evaluating progress. A recent amendment to the law requires that older school children be provided with a 'transition plan' which spells out the goals for post-school activities, eg, higher education or employment.

The child's parents are entitled to discuss this IEP with the school officials and help in its development. The law provides that if the parents and the school officials do not agree in the diagnosis or plan, an impartial hearing examiner will review the decisions and make a determination. Should there again be disagreement, a hearing examiner at the level of the state education agency will have a second hearing, and that person's decision will be binding on the school district or parent. Ultimately, a disagreement can be settled in a federal court. To strengthen the parents' role in such disagreements, Congress later decided that if the parents had to take a school district or state to federal court, and if the court upheld their position, the expenses for that whole process would have to be paid by the school district.

A continuum of services

School districts and states are expected to offer a range of educational opportunities to children with disabilities. This set of choices is seen as a continuum of services with one end including the opportunity to be educated in a regular classroom. A second alternative might be to receive supplemental special education services on a part-time basis and spend some time in a regular classroom. Other services along the continuum might include enrolment in special resource rooms or in special classes. Special schools for day attendance or special residential schools are other variations in service delivery. In some instances, programmes might be available in special hospitals. In essence, this 'continuum of services' is designed to try to assure that children with very unique abilities and needs will all have the opportunity to receive the 'free, appropriate, public education' that the law requires. The law also requires that children should be placed in an education programme with non-disabled children to the extent that it is 'appropriate'; that provision of the law has become known as the 'least restrictive environment' provision and has become the centre of considerable debate and professional disagreement. The law and its regulations assume that children will not be separated from the regular school unless a team of educators, psychologists, etc, and the child's parents, through the IEP process, decide a more specialized setting is appropriate.

While there is little disagreement with the philosophy of mainstreaming and its goals, there are divisions between those who feel most children can be educated in the regular classroom and that all special schools should be abolished, and those who feel that some special class and special school programmes have been very successful. Compounding this debate have been suggestions that many handicapped children have 'mild' disabilities and that these children would be better assisted in the regular classroom. This view has become known as the 'Regular Education Initiative', and it has evoked a lively, passionate and, occasionally, bitter debate (Bryan and Bryan, 1988); Hocutt et al., 1991; Lloyd and Gambatese, 1991).

Brief statistical overview

Each year the federal government, through its Office of Special Education Programs, which is the successor to the original Bureau of Education for the Handicapped, issues a report on the implementation of PL 94-142. The 14th Annual Report was issued in 1992 (US Department of Education, 1992) and some of the highlights of that report may help illustrate the scope and structure of special education services in the USA.

- In the 1990–91 school year 4,367,630 children between the ages of six and 21 were enrolled in special education programmese, about 10 per cent of all school-aged children. In addition, children aged 3–5 numbered 321,360 (1989–90 school year) and this population has been increasing quite rapidly.
- Of school-aged children with disabilities enrolled in special education, 94.4 per cent are identified as having one of four disabilities: children with specific learning disabilities (50.5 per cent); children with speech problems (23.4 per cent); children identified as mentally retarded (12 per cent); and children identified as emotionally disturbed (8.5 per cent). In recent years, the most rapid growth has been in the numbers of children identified as having specific learning disabilities, although that is now levelling out.
- Regarding the primary placement of children in special education, the report lists the largest number, 37.6 per cent, as in resource rooms and the second largest number, 31.5 per cent, in regular classrooms (the number of children placed in regular classrooms has been rising gradually in recent years); 24.9 per cent of children enrolled were in special classrooms. In general, all of these placements are in regular school buildings. Only 4.6 per cent of children are placed in separate school facilities, 0.9 per cent in home or hospital settings, and 0.6 per cent in separate residential facilities. In sum, 93.9 per cent of school children enrolled in special education programmes in the USA are located in local school buildings.
- Almost 600,000 teachers and related specialists and aides are employed in special education programmes, and a sense of the variety of services is provided by Tables 9.1 and 9.2. In writing Public Law 94-142, it was recognized that providing 'appropriate' education meant, for many children, providing additional services. These related services must be identified in the IEP and then provided by the school district or under its auspices.

Table 9.1 *Special education teachers employed to serve students with disabilities age 6–21: number and percentage change, school years 1988–9 and 1989–90*

	Teachers Employed		Change from 1988–89 to 1989–90 (%)	Total Employed 1989–90 (%)
Disability	1989–89	1989–90		
Specific learning disabilities	88,032	87,504	−0.6	30.1
Speech or language impairments	37,139	38,273	3.1	13.2
Mental retardation	44,668	43,113	−3.5	14.8
Serious emotional disturbance	27,547	27,779	0.8	9.6
Hearing impairments	7,062	6,468	−8.4	2.2
Multiple disabilities	7,575	7,491	−1.1	2.6
Orthopedic impairments	3,143	3,225	2.6	1.1
Other health impairments	2,763	2,674	−3.2	0.9
Visual impairments	2,892	2,719	−6.0	0.9
Deaf-blindness	221	143	−35.3	0.0
Cross-categorical	65,504	71,050	8.5	24.5
Total	286,546	290,439	1.4	100.0

Source: US Department of Education, Office of Special Education Programs, Data Analysis System (DANS).

Table 9.2 *Special education personnel other than teachers employed to serve students with disabilities age 6–21: Number and percentage change, school years 1988–9 and 1989–90*

Type of Personnel	1988–89	1989–90	Change from 1988–89 to 1989–90 (%)	Total Employed 1989–90 (%)
Psychologists	17,853	18,777	5.2	6.9
School social workers	8,559	8,761	2.4	3.2
Occupational therapists	4,207	4,612	9.6	1.7
Audiologists	1,323	838	−36.7	0.3
Paraprofessionals	144,907	154,738	6.8	56.7
Vocational education teachers	4,913	4,628	−5.8	1.7
Work-study coordinators	1,313	1,333	1.5	0.5
Physical education coordinators	5,957	5,871	−1.4	2.2
Recreational therapists	284	325	14.4	0.1
Diagnostic staff	8,994	9,822	9.2	3.6
Supervisors	15,707	15,581	−0.8	5.7
Physical therapists	3,003	3,177	5.8	1.2
Counselors	6,995	6,870	−1.8	2.5
SEA supervisors	1,209	1,125	−6.9	0.4
Other non-instructional staff[a]	30,681	22,653	−26.2	8.3
Non-professional staff[b]		13,759		5.0
Total	255,904	272,870	6.6	100.0

[a] Includes staff involved in health services (nurses, psychiatrists, etc), food services, maintenance, pupil transportation, etc.
[b] Data first collected in the 1989–90 school year.

Source: US Department of Education, Office of Special Education Programs, Data Analysis System (DANS).

Summary of programming in the USA

More than 4.5 million children were enrolled in special education in the USA in 1990. Most of these children were identified as having specific learning disabilities or speech disorders. Ninety-four per cent of children in special education are educated in local school buildings in resource rooms, special classes and the regular classrooms.

There is considerable variation from school district to school district and state to state in how children are classified and in the settings in which they are educated. Curricular materials and standards for graduation, etc, are the responsibility of state rather than federal officials. Public policy in the USA requires all children between the ages of three and 21 to have available a 'free, appropriate, public education'. A new federal law encourages interdisciplinary programmes for infants 0–2 years of age and provides the states with some funding to plan and organize programmes. There is a similar emphasis on older youth and on encouraging the transition from school to college and work. New legislation requires transitional planning for each high school student and provides federal support for demonstration programmes and state planning activities. Utilization of technology to assist in the education and rehabilitation of persons with disabilities is also receiving some federal stimulus through a programme of grants to states for planning.

Special education in the United States is based on policies developed by national, state and local governments and is provided by approximately 10,000 school districts and each of the education departments of the 50 states and the associated territories such as Puerto Rico and Guam.

Approximately 300,000 teachers are employed as well as an almost equal number of special personnel such as speech pathologists, psychologists, physical and occupational therapists, social workers, etc. These professionals, working together, provide the services called for in each child's individual education plan which should include not only basic educational skills but also such activities as physical education, art and vocational planning.

In the broadest policy sense, the objectives of Public Law 94-142 and its later extensions to pre-school and infant programmes, are being met (National Council on Disabilities, 1989). Children are no longer excluded from schooling. Most programmes are offered in the local community school, and each child has an IEP, at least on paper. On the other hand, there has been insufficient attention to the long-term outcomes of special education. It may be asked, for example, 'How many children go on to college and vocational training? How many are employed? How many would describe their lives as satisfactory, and their schooling as appropriate?' An interest in studying these outcomes is growing and should become a significant factor in special education planning in the 1990s (Fairweather and Shaver, 1990; Martin, in press).

Some observations on special education in Canada and the USA

Special education programmes in Canada and the USA share many similarities in policy and practice. Special education leaders and teachers from both countries, for example, participate in the activities of the Council for Exceptional Children, a professional organization. Through journals, conferences, etc, a common set of assumptions is developing among North American professionals.

Education policy in both nations is strongly influenced at the state (US) or provincial (Canada) level and local and provincial governments support special education in both nations. While the mechanisms are not identical, fiscal support and correlated policy development is more localized rather than nationalized in each nation. National policies in the USA, eg, the Individual Education Plan, are more prescriptive than in Canada – where there is, essentially, no national policy role.

In each nation the drive toward 'normalization' (Canada) or 'least restrictive environment/mainstreaming' (US) is a major policy objective, and in each nation this philosophically attractive goal has created some ambiguities and conflict among professionals. There are many advocates for educating as many children as possible in regular school classrooms with children who are not disabled. The assumptions driving this movement include beliefs that *any* separation is not in the interest of a child with a disability, and that existing special education programmes are not successful enough to justify separateness. Interacting with these arguments has been a belief that many children in special education are 'mildly' handicapped and have common learning needs although they may be identified as having mild mental retardation, mild emotional disorders, or learning disabilities.

A number of special educators, however, do not support this position, at least in absolute terms, although almost all agree that the goal of special education is to assist the individual to function in everyday society to the fullest extent possible. Concerns are raised that the effectiveness of integrated programmes in terms of long-term outcomes such as completing schooling, post-secondary schooling, employment, positive self-regard, etc, have not been measured, for the most part, by educators, and so final decisions on preferred models of service delivery are premature. Some arguments are made that outcomes from current programmes, many relatively more integrated, are not very successful, while isolated studies of special school populations sometimes demonstrate positive outcomes. In general, holders of these views feel some children may benefit from separate programmes for at least some periods of time.

None of these arguments has the benefit of high quality, long-term research, and so the debate is really one based on deeply-held beliefs. The history of education, both regular and special, seems to indicate that much change over the years has been based on similarly strong beliefs without much scientific basis, and the result has been a series of short-term fads that quickly fade as the pendulum of thought swings to the other side.

In addition to the professional/philosophical arguments, there are concerns expressed that not all the motives for integrating children with disabilities into regular education settings are pure – that politicians and administrators are letting budget shortages drive policies based on finances rather than the lofty philosophical goals which are expressed.

A positive result of these arguments is that there is a growing interest in measuring the outcomes of special education, and the national government in the USA is supporting research efforts to develop appropriate outcome measures and to track the progress of a sample of students now in schools.

Canada and the USA share several other significant challenges in providing special education based on the diversity within their nations. Providing special education services to children in rural, sparsely-populated areas creates problems with resource allocation, availability of specialists and specialized services. Conversely, large urban areas present discrete problems, including developing multilingual resources, working with persons who may recently have immigrated, etc. Reliance on local and provincial or state governments for financial resources also has a tendency to result in variations of services between wealthier and poorer communities.

In both nations, the overall pattern of services in the last two decades has been toward expanded and improved services, more sophisticated teacher education, more 'normalization' and, most recently, more concern for post-school employment and related outcomes.

Acknowledgement

Appreciation is expressed to a valued colleague, Harry Dahl, past president of the Council for Exceptional Children, and Regional Coordinator of Special Education in Saskatchewan, Canada, for his sharing, through personal communication, some perspectives on special education in Canada.

References

Bryan, J H and Bryan, T H (1988) 'Where's the beer? A review of published research on the Adaptive Learning Environment Model', *Learning Disabilities Focus*, **4**, 1, 9–14.

Fairweather, J S and Shaver, D M (1991) 'Making the transition to postsecondary education and training', *Exceptional Children*, **57**, 3, 264–70.

Hocutt, A M, Martin, E W and McKinney, J D (1991) 'Historical and legal context of mainstreaming' in Lloyd, J W, Singh, N H and Repp, A C (eds) *The Regular Education Initiative: Alternative Perspectives on Concepts, Issues and Models* (pp. 17–28), Sycamore, IL: Sycamore Press.

Levine, E L and Wexler, E M (1981) *P.L. 94–142: An Act of Congress*, New York: Macmillan.

Lloyd, J W and Gambatese, C (1991) 'Reforming the relationship between regular and special education: background and issues', in Lloyd, J W, Singh, N H and Repp, A C (eds) *The Regular Education Initiative: Alternative Perspectives on Concepts, Issues and Models* (pp. 3–16), Sycamore, IL: Sycamore Press.

Martin, E W (1976) 'A national commitment to the rights of the individual – 1776–1976, *Exceptional Children*, **43**, 3, 132–4 (see also other authors in this journal issue).

Martin, E W (1992) 'Learning disabilities and public policy: myths and outcomes', In Lyon, G R, Kevenagh, J and Krasnegor, N (eds) *Better Understanding Learning Disabilities: new views from research and their implications for public policy*, Baltimore, Ma.: Paul H Brookes.

National Council on Disability (1989) *The Education of Students with Disabilities – Where do we stand?: a report to the President and the Congress of the United States*, Washington, DC: NCD.

US Department of Education (1992) *To Assure the Free, Public Education of All Handicapped Children: Fourteenth annual report to Congress on the implementation of the education of the handicapped act*, Washington, DC: USDE.

10. Special education in Asia

Tehal Kohli

Introduction

The declaration of the UN International Year and International Decade of Disabled Persons (1981 and 1983–92 respectively) contains action plans to sensitize people to renew their global commitment to provide quality services to an expanded number of individuals with disabilities. The new focus is on those who have been denied their legitimate rights of respectable living for centuries.

The present review of the situation of special education in Asia with a population of more than 2.2 billion indicates that the region has a distance to travel in the directions prescribed by the UN agencies. These universal goals require translation at national level for the fuller development of persons with special needs.

Demographic profile

There are very few national sample surveys on the prevalence and incidence of different types of disabilities in different countries in Asia, though there are a few studies that throw light on the magnitude of the problem. Two of these studies are described below.

During the International Year of the Child (1979), a study was conducted to find out the situation of handicapped children in Bangladesh (Zaman and Munir, 1990). The study indicated that the incidence rate of handicapped children was 78.8 per 1000 children below 15 years of age. The Bangladesh child population in 1979 was 34.37 million, giving a total of 285,460 handicapped children in the country, of which 266,240 lived in rural areas and 20,060 in urban.

Table 10.1 summarizes the estimated total number of disabled people in India, according to the National Sample Survey conducted by the Government of India on 5,409 villages and 3,652 urban blocks in which 81,858 households in the rural areas and 56,452 households in the urban areas were contacted. Communication, visual and loco-motor disabilities were investigated.

Table 10.1 shows that the prevalence of disability was higher in the rural areas (about 80 per cent) than in urban areas (about 20 per cent) and that it was higher

Table 10.1 *Number of persons with disabilities in India, in 000s and (%)*

Type of disability	Total	Rural	Urban	Male	Female
Loco-motor	5,427	4,342 (80)	1,085 (20)	3,493 (64)	1,934 (36)
Visual	3,474	2,908 (84)	566 (16)	1,442 (42)	2,032 (58)
Hearing	3,019	2,477 (82)	542 (18)	1,654 (54)	1,365 (46)

among males (56.5 per cent) than among females (43.5 per cent). The total of those with disabilities comprised a modest estimate of 18 per cent of the population as compared to the expected UN estimates of 10 per cent, ie, 90 million disabled in India (including the category of mental retardation). But whether one follows the former or the latter estimates, the disabled in India are equal to the total population of some of the countries in the world. The prevalence and incidence of disabilities is quite similar in many other countries of Asia. In fact, it is a challenge of numbers.

Legislation

Legislation for special education is not clear-cut in most of the countries of Asia, in contrast to most of the countries of the West. There are a few countries in Asia such as Bangladesh, China, India, Indonesia, Japan, Jordan, Korea, Philippines and Thailand which have legislative support for declaring 'compulsory education for all' (eg, in Korea a special promotion law was put into effect in December 1977). But this does not mean that every child with special needs benefits, as enforcement is not strict and there are other problems for people with disabilities in attending the schools, such as distance involved, transport, etc. Some countries exclude certain categories of disabled from compulsory education for children. Syria excludes children who are multiply and severely handicapped; Iraq deprives handicapped children of special education, particularly if there is no special school in the vicinity.

On the whole, there has been a phenomenal expansion of special education and training and rehabilitation during the past two decades. A definite trend towards loosely knit policies or definite legislation for the handicapped is visible. For example, Articles 41, 46 and 47 of the constitution of India enjoin the states of India to provide assistance to those who are disabled. This support by the state can be in the form of education, economic welfare and employment. Even Articles 14 and 15 of the constitution of India can be exploited by an imaginative and informed judiciary for providing equality of educational opportunity to the handicapped with regard to mentally retarded individuals. The Lunacy Acts of 1912 and 1977 in India treated mentally ill and mentally retarded as belonging to the same category. However, these Acts have been repealed by the Provisions of section 98 of the Mental Health Act 1987 (THPI, 1987) which does not regard mentally retarded people as mentally ill. The Islam Committee of India, in their

report in 1989, stressed the need for compulsory rehabilitation services for all
the handicapped.

Thailand, under section 2, Article 15, states that,

> The state shall endeavour to make education accessible to the poor, the
> physically, mentally and socially handicapped as well as the educationally
> disadvantaged.

Section 3, Article 38 of the constitution states that,

> Special education is provided for those who have special character traits or
> who are physically, intellectually or mentally abnormal. It may be given in
> special schools or in ordinary schools as appropriate.

There are quite a few countries which are in the process of introducing new
legislation with regard to special education in general or for specific categories of
handicaps.

Existing provisions

Administration

In the majority of Asian countries, administrative responsibilities fall within the
purview of education ministries eg, China, Indonesia, Iraq, Israel, Kuwait,
Philippines, Saudi Arabia, Sri Lanka and Thailand (UNESCO, 1988). In India,
Jordan, Syria and Pakistan, major responsibilities lie with the department of
social welfare. In many countries, the responsibilities are shared by other
departments; for example, Philippines distribute the responsibilities to the
department of culture and sports, health and social welfare and Saudi Arabia
involves departments of social affairs and labour. In India, the Ministry of
Human Resources Development includes five departments: women and child
development, youth welfare and sports, culture, arts and education. Special
education is under the Ministry of Welfare, though it does collaborate with
various other departments such as those of women and child development and
education which are quite active for early intervention programmes in the
country.

Institutional facilities

Institutional facilities are quite inadequate in all the countries of Asia. In
most cases, they are serving less than 1 per cent of the population with
special education needs. India's special schools are: orthopaedic (60), visual
(243), speech and hearing (352), mental handicaps (322) and more than one
handicap (53). In all, there are only 1,035 special schools (RCI, 1990) for 12
million disabled, comprising 9.7 million rural and 2.3 million urban disabled in
the country.

The Government of India has established four national institutions, one each
for the visually handicapped, hearing, orthopaedically and mentally handicapped
at Dehradun, Bombay, Calcutta and Secunderabad, respectively. Major objectives of these institutions are service and research in the specific areas and the
training of personnel. There are two other organizations, the Institute for the

Physically Handicapped and the National Institute of Rehabilitation, Training and Research (Orissa State) which are service centres for people with physical handicaps, with facilities for training physiotherapists, occupational therapists and prosthetics technicians. In order to serve the disabled in the rural areas, the Union Ministry of Welfare has set up 12 District Rehabilitation Centres spread all over the country. Yet these efforts are too little compared to the magnitude of the problem in the country.

Special education provision

There is a great variety of special education provisions in different countries of Asia, depending on the policy and legislation of the country, manpower and physical facilities, resources available, etc, for different types of disabilities.

For the 11 countries for which data were available (UNESCO, 1988), enrolment for school-going children in special educational institutions in China, Indonesia, Jordan and Thailand was far less than 0.1 per cent of the needy; population school enrolment for Iraq, Kuwait, Saudi Arabia and Syrian Arab Republic ranged between 0.1 to 0.5 per cent; Philippines and Sri Lanka had enrolment figures between 0.5 to 1 per cent. The highest, ie, 50 per cent, was reported by Israel. Wide variations in provision for different kinds of handicaps exist in Asian countries. Maximum provision is available for persons with mental handicaps, followed by persons with visual, physical and hearing handicaps. Minimum provision exists for persons with emotional disturbances, learning difficulties and language difficulties. Maximum provision for the handicapped is available in boarding special schools and day special schools; support teaching in regular schools and special classes in regular schools come next. The least preferred mode of provision in all countries are schools in other institutions and schools in hospitals. Post-school provision is comparatively higher than pre-school. Provision for higher education is almost negligible, except for physical handicaps and, in some cases, hearing and visual impairments. Except for Iraq, Philippines and Thailand, voluntary agencies play equally active and effective roles in providing finance for special services. In some countries such as China and Indonesia, parents pay quite a lot to meet the expenses of fees, books, transport, etc.

There are great advances in Japan and Korea for early detection, identification and assessment. In most of the countries such as China, Jordan, Kuwait, Philippines and Thailand, this is primarily done in hospitals and health centres. In Iraq, Handicap Diagnosis Centres provide all these functions. In countries such as Saudi Arabia, Bangladesh and Nepal, there are no specific provisions, except for the efforts of the voluntary organizations in certain cases. Support services are also inadequate in most of the Asian countries. These are primarily available in special schools, but with the integrated education of the disabled, these services would also be available in normal schools.

Training

Out of the 17 countries reported here, 13 have opportunities for in-service training of short duration. In China, where special classes are attached to regular schools, in-service training programmes are available. In Iraq in-service and even pre-service training is provided by Handicap Diagnosis Centres. However, most of the countries reported very limited in-service training programmes; Thailand (Ministry of Education, 1991) did not report any.

Pre-service training for special education centres also greatly differs from country to country and within a country. Most of the countries reported basic teacher training programmes alongside special education training, either on-the-job or for six months to two years. In countries like Israel and Sri Lanka, there is an inbuilt system of special education curriculum during the teacher training course. In Israel, there are 200 to 250 hours of instruction in special education during the regular teacher training courses. In India, training is available for different duration for senior diploma, junior diploma, certificate course, Bachelor of Special Education and Master of Special Education. For training courses in mental retardation, there are 11 institutions in the whole of the country (Menon, 1989). Except for Jai Vakeel School for children in Bombay, which has been offering a diploma in mental retardation since 1952, the rest of the ten institutions had their inception between 1971 and 1988. To meet the target of the Government of India, ie, rehabilitation for all by the year 2000, institutions for manpower development for different categories of disabilities are on the increase and will continue to be so during the next decade. The Rehabilitation Council of India is an autonomous body which enforces uniform standards in the training of professionals in the field. So far, it has finalized the standardization of 35 courses (Ministry of Welfare, 1991).

Constraints

Meeting special needs is beset with many barriers, some of which are common to almost all the countries of Asia, some of which are specific to particular countries of the region. Obstacles include: economic constraints; endemic poverty; poor health standards; malnutrition; lack of support services; ignorance of the rights of the handicapped; little rural out-reach and little retention of teachers in these areas; ecological barriers (Baine, 1988; Mallory, 1990); lack of mass awareness and knowledge about special education; low salaries of grass-roots-level workers; shortage of schools; lack of trained manpower or on-the-job short-term training, especially through the use of published literature and tests which are often Western and inappropriate to the culture; lack of preventive measures; no proper curriculum for different categories of handicaps; lack of coordination of public and private efforts; lack of mobilization of public opinion; lack of knowledge about local services; unemployment among persons with handicaps; less open discussion about child's disabilities; and guilt feelings by parents and siblings.

Another common problem is that once certain programmes and projects are set up with the help of 'seed money' from national or international organiza-tions, there is a lack of 'feed money' to continue and stabilize those programmes or innovations. Some countries have stressed additional problems; for example, in Bangladesh, (Zaman and Munir, 1990) more acute problems are sheltered workshops and lack of mass awareness. In Pakistan, myths, social taboos and the genetic implications of consanguineous marriages common among Muslims complicate the scene. Wang (1991), in China, felt the major concerns were a lack of coordination of different bodies, a greater need for attention to all levels of handicaps, a need of overall reforms in the educational system and services, compounded by traditional beliefs and child-rearing practices.

Trends

Integrated education

The declaration on 'Education for All' (UNESCO, 1989) and the celebration of 1983–92 as the Decade of Disabled Persons led to the formulation of the 'World Programme of Action' for persons with disabilities. According to UNICEF reports, about 90 per cent of the disabled children can be educated in common with others and about 70 per cent of disabilities are preventable. The UNESCO Special Education Programme attempts to link and associate its activities with regular educational provision (UNESCO, 1991). One of the major action plans has been to propagate integrated education of the disabled as far as possible. Western countries picked up the momentum quickly. Asian countries (UNESCO, 1988) are also conceding the idea, though not with the same fervour and enthusiasm; Bangladesh, Indonesia, Nepal and Saudi Arabia are still cold about the idea. Trends towards integrated education are visible in Iraq, Israel, Jordan and Syria. In China, though mainstreaming does exist there is no special encouragement and backing of legislation for it. Pakistan (Miles, 1985; 1991) has introduced mainstreaming recently. In the Philippines, integration is mainly for visual and hearing handicaps. India, Singapore, Sri Lanka and Thailand are the countries which have planned policies and legislative backing for implementing integrated education on a mass scale. In Singapore, some special education is provided within the regular school system. In Sri Lanka, there is a policy to encourage integration for persons with visual, hearing and physical impairments from four years onwards. Section 3, Article 38 of the Constitution of Thailand supports integration for all categories. The Government of India launched a centrally sponsored scheme of 'Integrated Education of Disabled Children' in 1974 under the department of social welfare. The scheme was transferred to the Department of Education in 1982, then the National Policy of Education (NPE, 1986) envisaged that 'whenever it is feasible, the education of children with motor handicaps and other mild handicaps will be common with that of others'. It stressed that education of the handicapped in special schools is very costly,

> it will be ensured that only those children whose needs cannot be met in common schools are enrolled in these schools. As soon as the disabled children enrolled in special schools acquire the communication skills and study skills, they will be integrated in common schools.

Its further targets are that the group of disabled children who do not have learning problems (ie, orthopaedic handicaps) and children with mild handicaps should be covered by universal primary education goals along with other children by 1990, and elementary education by 1995.

Project Integrated Education of the Disabled (PIED) was launched in India in

1987 with inputs from the Ministry of Human Resources Development, UNICEF and the National Council of Educational Research and Training (NCERT, 1989). At present, it is functioning in rural areas of the states of Madhya Pradesh, Maharashtra, Nagaland, Orissa, Rajasthan, Tamil Nadu, Haryana and Mizoram along with two urban slum areas of Delhi and Baroda. It caters to the special needs of the blind and the partially sighted, the deaf and the partially hearing, those with orthopaedic, neurological and multiple handicaps. Manpower training follows a four-level training approach (Jangira, 1989; 1990), ie, five-day orientation courses for all teachers in regular schools, six-week training courses for 10 per cent of the teachers, one-year multi-category training for eight to ten general teachers in a project area, and level-four teacher education programmes for single disabilities. During 1987–90, a total of 5,386 teachers were trained; 5,890 parent contact programmes and 10,797 community programmes were held; 8,586 children with disabilities were identified; and 3,439 children with disabilities were assessed. In addition, 14 handbooks and other materials for circulation, along with seven non-print materials were made ready (NCERT, 1991) for supply to project states. Indigenous toys and slides were also made available.

Pre-school programmes

Early detection, diagnosis and pre-school early intervention programmes are a part of the current wave of concern so as to develop the optimum potential of all the young children with impairments or disabilities. Pre-school or early intervention services aimed at the development of the 'whole child' are stressed as being very important. These involve a combination of extended informal and non-formal education programmes including convergence of early stimulations. Health and nutritional activities directed to infants and young children have provided evidence in support of their developmental gains and the efficacy of such programmes and practices in varied localities and diverse settings (Bijou, 1989; Bronfenbrenner, 1974; Casto and Mastropieri, 1986; Mittler et al., 1986; Wang, 1991). Kohli (1982; 1988; 1989; 1990a; 1990b) also conducted action-oriented research to study the effectiveness of such programmes even under adverse conditions. Yet most of the Asian countries have very limited pre-schooling provision (UNESCO, 1988); Iran, Saudi Arabia and Nepal have none. Bangladesh, China, Indonesia, Israel, Jordan, Philippines, Syria and Pakistan have limited provision. India, Kuwait, Sri Lanka and Thailand are exemplary in this regard. The literature shows that before 1970, pre-primary/pre-school education and early intervention programmes were almost non-existent or were provided by the private sector in most of the countries of Asia. But now the slogan of 'First Call for Children' of the 1990 world summit for children 'should become an accepted ethic of a new world order' (UNICEF, 1992) for the next decades.

Community-based rehabilitation

Out of the 500 million of world's population with disabilities, 400 million live in the countries of the Third World. Over 80 per cent of these live in remote and isolated rural areas. Out of the less than 1 per cent existing services, hardly any of those reach these villagers. They must be provided with community-based rehabilitative services in their own surroundings instead of shifting them to prohibitive urbanized services. Though this service delivery model began in the late 1960s in the USA and Europe, it was delineated and popularized by the World Health Organization in 1974 and became more forceful during the International Year of the Disabled Persons. Since then, pilot projects and trials have been reported with encouraging results in Bangladesh, India, Indonesia, Nepal, Philippines, Sri Lanka and Thailand (Bleck, 1991; Desai and Patel, 1987; Dhar, 1990; Mallory, 1990; O'Toole, 1991; UNICEF, 1986). These are rural, family- and community-based, cost-effective, programmed within their cultural context and in their natural environment, focusing more on rehabilitative and curative approaches. In India, a UNICEF sponsored study was conducted to establish the rehabilitation potentials of rural India (BRA, 1984). At the national level, a pilot programme was also launched by the Government of India in collaboration with the National Institute of Disability and Rehabilitation Research in the United States in 1985, with the major objective of providing a package of model, comprehensive rehabilitation services to people with disabil-ities in the rural areas. 'This scheme caters to the medical, emotional, social, educational and economic needs of the people with disabilities in rural areas through a trained and dedicated team. Manpower training follows a four-level training approach and UNICEF joins hands in the scheme which covers 12 District Rehabilitation Centres. The revised scheme (Ministry of Welfare, 1991; NIPCCD, 1985) envisages linkages with the national scheme of Integrated Child Development Services (ICDS) which is a single major national scheme covering 170,393 anganwadis (ie, centres of pre-school education, with an average attendance of 33 children between three and six years old per anganwadi [NIPCCD, 1990]. Projected targets are that there would be one and two million anganwadis all over the country by 1995 and 2000, respectively. Their grass-roots-level functionaries such as anganwadi workers and supervisors would be given training in rehabilitation programmes.

In addition, other individual rural projects for specific categories of handicaps are being implemented successfully. For example, more than 13 such projects (Desai and Patel, 1987) are underway for the social and economic rehabilitation of the rural blind; the Dholka project in Gujarat state is well known in the country. Well trained 'mobile touring teams' are also helping the blind.

For children with developmental delays, Portage home-centre-based training programmes with active involvement of parents are helping in more than 60 countries of the world including many of the Asian countries such as Bangladesh, China, India, Japan, Korea, Thailand, etc. In India, the Portage package was originally adapted, translated and successfully tried under different models by Kohli (1982; 1990a; 1990b; 1990c) and Kohli and Dutta (1985). A lot of 'low-cost' or 'no-cost' toys, slides and training materials were developed during these studies and many more by Kohli and her team of research workers. Now it is being used all over the country. Here, in most cases, professionals, para- and non-professionals work together as a team for the benefit of the young children 'at risk' or with evident mental retardation or sometimes other types of disabilities and handicaps. These are known as 'family-intensive approaches', with more deprofessionalization and deinstitutionalization of services (see Brouillette, J et al., this volume).

Special education services through 'self-help groups' is another community-based rehabilitation strategy which is being used in some of the countries such as India and Bangladesh, since 1981 and 1984 respectively, with satisfactory results. Services are provided through mutual aid of the parents for the benefit of their mentally retarded children. Parents share their problems and experiences for the benefit of one another under active supervision of a professional during weekly or fortnightly meetings held at one of the residences of the parents.

Use of media

Another trend is greater use of mass media to transmit information, knowledge and training through broadcasts, print material, cinema (even temporary and touring ones), unconventional media (used during fairs and festivals), etc, which work as potential partners in promoting special education. Kolucki (1989) has extended thoughtful discussions of her own experiences to draw more upon social marketing techniques and systematic approaches to special education through media and introduced subjects on disability into television programming. Miles (1986) wrote radio scripts in 1984 for broadcasting special education messages to Pakhtun villages in Pakistan. Media appeals to the common people and, at the same time, tends to be congruent with the resource constraints.

Research and development

A review of the present situation of special education (UNESCO, 1988) and various other reports from Asian countries have shown that there are no separate funds for research in Iraq, Israel, Kuwait, Philippines, Saudi Arabia, Sri Lanka or Thailand. China, India, Indonesia, Pakistan and Syria have separate funds from the government for conducting research in different areas of special education. Major areas of research are the impact of integration, pre-school and early intervention programmes, transition from pre-school to school to adult life, community-based rehabilitation models, use of media and use of advanced technological facilities, toy libraries, vocational training and employability, development of print material such as sign and Braille language, development, etc. In some countries, such as India, various special awards are instituted by different National Institutes like NCERT and DRCs for research innovations in the field. Many innovative ideas, eg, school clusters, are being tried in the developing countries of Asia (Bray, 1987).

Issues

Two major issues concerning the future development of special education in Asia are integration and vocational preparation/job placement (UNESCO, 1988). India, Iraq, Israel, Pakistan, Saudi Arabia, Syria and Thailand have expressed great concern for mainstreaming children with special needs. Bangladesh, India, Jordan, Saudi Arabia, Singapore and Sri Lanka have, in one way or the other, expressed greater need for speeding up pre-vocational and vocational training in sheltered workshops or in the open market. Japan and Korea are very much ahead in this area.

In fact, a changing trend is observable towards more concessions and reservations and increased employment of persons with disabilities in almost all Asian countries. Earlier, there were inept, irrational and discriminatory views that employability for such persons would mean higher costs, inflated medical bills and poor production. Experience has proved that if 'the right man is given the right job' after skill assessment, proper training, judicious and correct placement, he would rarely make mistakes and that this would lead to increased productivity.

Now there is a sea change in the attitudes of the public and the government and there are various schemes for training, rehabilitation and suitable employment of these persons. In India, there are about 1,000 voluntary organizations working for various categories of disabilities. These organizations are being aided and supported by the Ministry of Welfare. Various concessions given to them are in the form of scholarships, stipends, travel, communication, customs, conveyance allowance, purchase of aids and appliances, income tax, etc (NIVH, 1990). There are 23 special employment exchanges. The Government of India has reserved a further 3 per cent of vacancies in central government/public sector undertakings ie, 1 per cent each for persons with visual, hearing and orthopaedic handicaps. In fact, these people are an economic discovery and a great human resource of the country.

Many issues that have not been given much priority (UNESCO, 1988) include community-based rehabilitation services, more involvement of parents, siblings, grandparents and para-professionals in delivering services, curriculum and programme developments within cultural diversities, legislative details, involvement of institutions of higher learning in preventing disabilities (Diggs, 1983) and the application of micro-computers, etc. There is an urgent need of information exchange and a common forum with proper global-local-global linkages for sharing innovative ideas, experiences and existing programmes and practices.

References

Baine, D (1988) *Handicapped Children in Developing Countries: Assessment, Curriculum and Instruction*, Edmonton, Canada: University of Alberta.

Bijou, S W (1989) 'An overview of early intervention for developmentally delayed children', in Yamaguchi, K (ed) *A Challenge to Potentiality: the vision of early intervention for developmentally delayed children*, Proceedings of the 1988 International Portage Conference, Tokyo.

Bleck, E (1991) 'A study of mobility of disabled persons in rural villages of Karnataka State, India', *Action-Aid*, Newsletter, Disability Division, Bangalore, **2**, 1, 10.

BRA (1984) *Study of Family Based Rehabilitation Potential of the Disabled in Rural Areas*, Delhi: The Blind Relief Association.

Bray, M (1987) 'School clusters in the third world: Making them work', *Digest 23*, Paris: UNESCO-UNICEF Cooperative Programme.

Bronfenbrenner, U (1974) 'Is early intervention effective?', in Guttentag, M and Struening, E (eds) *Handbook of Education and Research*, Beverly Hills, CA: Sage.

Casto, G and Mastropieri, M A (1986) 'The efficacy of early intervention programs: a meta analysis', *Exceptional Children*, **52**, 417–24.

Desai, H J M and Patel, J K (1987) *Guidelines for Social and Economic Rehabilitation of the Rural Blind*, Bombay: Rural Activities Committee, National Association of the Blind.

Dhar, R S (1990) 'Community-based rehabilitation: the District Rehabilitation (DRC) Scheme. A rehabilitation strategy in rural areas of India', *Interchange*, Newsletter of World Rehabilitation Fund, New York, spring, 7–10.

Diggs, R W (1983) 'The role of institutions of higher learning in preventing or minimizing mental retardation', *Monograph of the President's Committee on Mental Retardation*, Washington, DC.

Jangira, N K (1989) 'Education of the disabled: implications for teacher education', *Bull of National Council for Teacher Education*, (NCERT, Delhi) 1, 1.

Jangira, N K (1990) 'Education without colouring children: design model to meet special needs in general education', paper presented at the International Special Education Congress, Cardiff, August.

Kohli, T (1982) 'Appraising innovative helping strategies for the education and training of mentally retarded', *Indian Journal of Mental Retardation*, 15, 1, 10–18.

Kohli, T (1988) 'Effectiveness of Portage in India', in White, M and Cameron, R J (eds) *Portage: progress, problems and possibilities*, Windsor: NFER-Nelson, pp. 64–8.

Kohli, T (1989) 'Emerging trends in early intervention services for childhood disability', *Indian Journal of Disability and Rehabilitation*, 3, 1, 71–3.

Kohli, T (1990a) 'Comparison of effectiveness of Portage training by professionals, para and non-professionals', in *Innovative Thoughts and Experiments in Teacher Education*, Delhi: NCERT. Also pub. (1991) in Rani, P U (ed) *Prevention and Management of Down's Syndrome*, pp. 95–112, Hyderabad.

Kohli, T (1990b) 'A Decade of strides of Portage in India', paper presented at the Third International Portage Conference, Wisconsin, USA, August.

Kohli, T (1990c) 'Impact of home-centre based training programme in reducing developmental deficiencies of disadvantaged young children', abridged paper (based on UNICEF sponsored project), *Indian Journal of Disability and Rehabilitation*, 4, 2, 65–74.

Kohli, T and Dutta, R (1985) 'Portage service: an international programme for pre-school mentally retarded children with motor handicaps', *Journal of Practical Approaches to Developmental Handicap*, 1, 1, 12–19.

Kolucki, B (1989) 'Developing strategies for communication, about disability; experiences in the US, Hong Kong, India and Pakistan', New York: *Monograph 47, World Rehabilitation Fund*.

Mallory, B L (1990) 'Community–based services in Malaysia. An example from the State of Sabah', *Interchange*, Newsletter of World Rehabilitation Fund, New York.

Menon, D K (1989) 'Planning human resource development of special teachers for persons with mental handicap', paper presented at the Second Annual Seminar, national Institute for Mentally Handicap, Secunderabad.

Miles, M (1985) *Children with Disabilities in Ordinary Schools*, Peshawar: Mental Health Centre.

Miles, M (1986) 'Rehabilitation broadcasts for rural areas', background paper presented during the workshop on Media Strategy, District Rehabilitation Centre, Delhi.

Miles, M (1991) 'Using action-oriented disability studies in Pakistan', *Interchange*, Newsletter of World Rehabilitation Fund, New York, November-December.

Ministry of Education (1991) *Special Education in Thailand*, Report of Special Education Division of Department of General Education, Ministry of Education, Thailand.

Ministry of Welfare (1982) *A Summary of the Report on Survey of Disabled Persons*, Ministry of Welfare, Government of India.

Ministry of Welfare (1991) *Annual Report, 1990–91*, Department of Welfare, Ministry of Welfare, Government of India.

Mittler, P, Mittler, H and McConachie, H (1986) *Working Together; Guidelines for Partnership Between Professionals and Parents of Children and Young People with Disabilities*, Guides for Special Education, 2, Pairs.

NCERT (1987) *Scheme of Integrated Education of Disabled*, Delhi: National Council of Educational Research and Training.

NCERT (1989) *Orientation Course on Emerging Trends in Special Education for University Faculty*, Delhi: Report of National Council of Educational Research and Training.

NCERT (1991) *Project Integrated Education for Disabled*, Progress Report, 1987–90, Delhi: National Council of Educational Research and Training.

NIPCCD (1985) *Prevention and Early Detection of Childhood Disability. Role of Anganwadi workers*, Delhi: National Institute of Public Cooperation and Child Development.

NIPCCD (1990) *Statistics on Children In India: pocket book*, Delhi: National Institute of Public Cooperation and Child Development.

NIVH (1990) *Programmes and Concessions for the Disabled*, The National Institute for the Visually Handicapped, Ministry of Welfare, Government of India.

NPE (1986) *National Policy on Education*, Ministry of Human Resources Development, Government of India.

O'Toole, B (1991) *Guide to Community-based Rehabilitation Services*, Guides for Special Education No. 8, Paris: UNESCO.

RCI (1990) *Statement Showing Number of Special Schools in India*, Rehabilitation Council of India, Ministry of Welfare, Government of India.

THPI (1987) *Report on National Policy on Mental Retardation*. Hyderabad: Thakur Hari Prasad Institute of Rehabilitation for the Mentally Handicapped Children.

UNESCO (1988) *Review of the Present Situation of Special Education*, Paris: UNESCO.

UNESCO (1989) *Education for All*, Bulletin of the UNESCO Principal Officer for Asia and Pacific, Bangkok.

UNESCO (1991) *Special Education, Summary of Activities 1990–91*, Paris: UNESCO.

UNICEF (1986) *Community Based Rehabilitation for the Disabled Persons. An evaluative study of CBR projects in Katchi Abadis of Lahore and rural areas of Jhelum*, University of the Punjab, Lahore: Research and Publication Unit, Department of Social Work.

UNICEF (1992) *The State of the World's Children 1992*, United Nations Children Fund.

Wang, T M (1991) 'Quality of life? The promise of early intervention programs for handicapped youngsters and their families in Asia', paper presented at the 10th Asian Conference on Mental Retardation, Karachi.

Zaman, S S and Munir, S Z (1990) 'Development of early intervention programme for the handicapped in Bangladesh', in Zaman, S S (ed) *Research on Mental Retardation*, pp. 65–83, Bangladesh: Bangladesh Protibandhi Foundation.

11. Special education in Australia and New Zealand
James Ward

Introduction

Australia and New Zealand share a common heritage in that each has grown up within the same broad legal and political traditions and has English as its dominant language. The two countries share a number of significant geophysical features, not the least of which is their isolation from Europe and North America, even in an age of rapid communications and transport. In terms of population, both Australia and New Zealand have received considerable numbers of migrants since World War II, often coming from non-English speaking countries. An important social and educational set of issues surrounds what has historically been an uneasy relationship with the indigenous peoples. Inevitably, such factors have had a profound effect upon the development of both general and special education.

However, there are many differences and for this reason it is proposed to deal with each country separately. This account will not attempt to deal with detailed practices within each of the Australian states and territories. Likewise, developments in aboriginal education and the education of the gifted are taken as being outside the scope of the chapter.

Australia

Geopolitical influences

Australia is a very large island subcontinent which, with its associated islands and territories, covers about 7,686,856 square kilometres. Its current population is approximately 17 million, over 50 per cent of which represents mainly European migration since World War II. There remain substantial numbers of the indigenous peoples who presently own about one-seventh of the area as tribal lands. Despite its size, Australia is one of the most heavily urbanized of the developed countries, the vast majority of its inhabitants living in cities or large towns on the eastern seaboard.

Australia is a federation which consists of six states and the Northern Territory, each with its own parliament and responsibilities for delivering basic services. The Commonwealth Government levies the vast majority of taxes from which it discharges its responsibilities for national budgetary policy and for providing finances to the states. However, until it started to fund the universities in the late 1960s, the Commonwealth Government did not directly involve itself in education. Since then there have been a number of important changes in the organization of education, among which has been a movement towards greater administrative and financial control by central government. The result has been a somewhat complex pattern of services with both Commonwealth and state agencies operating within the states. The areas of special education and rehabilitation have figured prominently in government initiatives. A further complication arises in the very large numbers of students who are educated in denominational (mostly Catholic) and private schools (between 25-30 per cent in some states).

Historical developments

The first special facilities were set up by charities and voluntary organizations in order to cater for blind and deaf children. These included the Institution for Deaf, Dumb and Blind established in Sydney, New South Wales in 1860; a number of similar ventures occurred in Victoria and South Australia over the next 20 years. After World War I a growing interest in the problems of physically handicapped children led to the establishment of several important special schools and clinic facilities. This process was further stimulated by the outbreaks of poliomyelitis which occurred in the period immediately following World War II. Further substantial developments were to take place in provisions for children with cerebral palsy, multiple handicap and, somewhat later, autism.

However, in terms of the numbers served, the major effort was probably made in the area of intellectual disability. Here the main impetus came from parent and community organizations: indeed, the involvement of non-government agencies has been a noteworthy feature of Australian special education and rehabilitation. However, by the late 1960s it was clear that neither the non-state system nor the regular state schools were able to meet the demand for high quality services for children with special needs: in particular there was a shortage of trained personnel of all types. The result was that special education became a significant issue at state and Commonwealth level. Following the establishment of the Commonwealth Schools Commission in 1972, funds were released for teacher training and in New South Wales new research and training centres were set up at Macquarie University in 1975 and Newcastle College of Advanced Education in 1976. These joined the well-established Fred and Eleanor Schonell Centre for Educational Research at the University of Queensland. A Select Committee of the House of Representatives issued a report in 1976 which identified a number of major problem areas and stimulated the formulation of policy in several states (at the same time as the publication of the Warnock Committee Report in the UK and the enactment of Public Law 94-142 in the USA). Thus, by 1981 (the International Year of Disabled Persons) Australian developments paralleled those taking place in other countries, although often on a more limited scale.

The Commonwealth Schools Commission had played an important developmental role. For instance, attention was focused upon significant target areas such as the problems of children from disadvantaged schools, children in residential institutions and other forms of substitute care, early intervention and integration. To contribute to the database for these initiatives, several major policy studies were commissioned (see for example, Andrews *et al.*, 1979). After 1983, however, a new pattern of Commonwealth educational funding and organization was implemented. The Commission was dissolved and its core functions taken over by the new Department of Employment, Education and Training.

Service organization

It is perhaps not surprising that the states, settled at different times and geographically remote from each other, developed distinctive characteristics which were to influence the organization of general and special education. Thus the survey by Andrews *et al.* (1979) and a later study commissioned by the Commonwealth Schools Commission on behalf of the Organization for Economic Cooperation and Development (Gow *et al.*, 1987) found enormous diversity in the organization and quality of services.

Developmental disability (mental retardation, autism, epilepsy, severe multiple disabilities)

The majority of children are identified at birth, steps then being taken to ensure that appropriate therapies are given and the parents are adequately informed. Usually, contact is made with a parent support group and/or early intervention programme. A particular target for home-based early intervention programmes has been children with Down Syndrome. Here, evidence that they could be successfully taught led to the demise of much routine institutionalization, a practice which was common in some states until the mid-1970s (Clunies-Ross, 1988; Pieterse, 1988).

Early intervention, combined with attendance at integrated nurseries and preschools has created favourable conditions for integrating or mainstreaming children with moderate-mild degrees of intellectual disability. Thus many are now being retained within regular classrooms, at least until the later years of primary school when the formal demands of the curriculum tend to create difficulties for them. Children with low-incidence conditions such as autism still tend to be placed in special schools, classes and units where they can obtain a high degree of support. There are still large numbers of special day schools in Australia, but they are becoming progressively more rare as a result of the drive towards integration; for many DD children the special class is now seen as the placement of choice.

At the secondary or high school level, those in the regular schools are usually placed in small special classes in the care of specialist teachers. The extent to which they participate in the regular curriculum and are integrated into the life of the school varies considerably. An additional form of facility exists for the less-disabled students who may be placed in larger classes containing students with a wide range of learning and/or behavioural difficulties. The basic approach is to provide programmes in functional literacy and numeracy, training for competences which will be relevant to the work force and independent living. Indeed, confidence in the future employability of most of the DD group is now reflected in a range of work preparation and transitional education programmes. Experience of employment is routinely available in the later years of the high school and may lead to job opportunities at a later stage.

The provision of education and other services is a dynamic field, its main challenge being to combine the benefits of normal curricula and participant experiences with the necessary degree of technically sophisticated instruction.

Physical disability

In Australia as elsewhere, the physically disabled or medically fragile represent an increasingly diverse group, the traditional categories of cerebral palsy and post-traumatic disability being augmented by the various forms of physical and psychological risk caused through prematurity, low birth weight, maternal substance abuse and sexually transmitted diseases. Early intervention represents a natural continuation of medical services and support. It has always been recognized that the provision of adequate therapy services at this stage is crucial.

The main impetus for change has inevitably derived from integration but there has also been a strong drive towards decentralization in the form of regional out-patient services, clinics and other community-based facilities. The result has been that a high proportion of special schools have been closed down to be replaced by special classes or integration programmes, exceptions being the cases in which concentrated medical and therapy services are required but which cannot be supplied by other means.

A high proportion of the physically disabled are now successfully main-streamed, both at primary and high school levels but others would be considered integrated as a result of placement in a special class attached to the regular school. This would particularly apply to those with severe neurological impairments such as spasticity.

Visual and auditory disabilities

The provision of services for children of this type has followed upon the same lines as other developed countries. The general policy is to place children with severe visual impairments in regular classes, the teachers being assisted by visiting specialists who provide assistance over adapting the curriculum, supply Brailled materials as necessary and give advice. The field is gradually coming to terms with the complex technologies available to the visually impaired who now have a much greater range of career options through higher education and training.

By contrast, the numbers of children with varying degrees of auditory impairment are very much higher, although their precise incidence is difficult to establish. The education of the deaf in Australia was very much influenced by the Ewings, teachers at the University of Manchester, who visited the country in the 1940s and promoted an oralist approach which is still the subject of controversy. Most workers in fact now appear to prefer a Total Communication approach, reflecting trends in other countries.

As in the case of the visually impaired, most children with auditory impairments are mainstreamed with the help of visiting teachers. Both groups enjoy the traditional support of well-established societies and associations. The small numbers of children with a combination of severe visual and auditory disabilities tend to be placed in schools for the multiply handicapped.

Psycho-educational problems

Children in this broad category comprise by far the most numerous and diverse target for special educational services, ranging from the gifted with severe learning problems to the mildly intellectually disabled. There are reasons to believe that the numbers at risk would be comparable to those identified in Europe and North America, ie, 8–12 per cent at least. The influences of poverty and social disadvantage are significant and are often compounded by family breakdown and linguistic problems.

Australian practice represents the full range of school-based and other services, ranging from retention in the regular class to placement in special schools for those with the most severe learning problems. However, the sheer magnitude of the problem dictates that the most common approach is retention with the child's age peers in the regular class together with help from visiting or school-based resource personnel. There is some dispute over whether such additional help should be given on a withdrawal basis or whether the resource professional should work in the classroom along with the regular teacher.

Problems in literacy and numeracy are a challenge to the whole educational and general community, thereby receiving considerable attention and advocacy from all sides. Underachievement in basic skills has generated a host of preventive and remedial approaches with virtually every form of intervention being applied: peer tutoring, parent and other volunteer teaching along with withdrawal, individualized teaching, visiting teacher support. One of the preventive schemes being tried out is the 'Reading Recovery' approach devised by Clay and her co-workers in New Zealand.

Specific learning disabilities such as dyslexia have recently become prominent and the range of approaches is similar to those found in other developed countries. This is demonstrated by the adoption of the term 'Attention Deficit Hyperactivity Disorder' (ADHD) and its consequent treatment by pharmacological means.

Another aspect of the problem is that issues of curriculum and teaching methods have been brought into sharp focus, ie, data-based instruction, direct instruction and precision teaching and those who advocate current child-centred methods such as the so-called 'whole language' approach to reading. More recently, work in the field of cognitive training has been commenced and this might generate significant new methods for this perennially difficult teaching area (Ashman and Conway, 1989).

The need for remediation in the primary school continues in the high school and beyond, since basic education courses are required in technical and further education and other community programmes.

Behavioural and emotional difficulties

A high proportion of children and young people who exhibit learning difficulties also have associated behavioural problems of varying degrees of severity. These tend to be transitory in nature, stemming from temporary stress within families and peer groups: they are now so common as to account for much of the world-wide demand for special educational services. A sub-group of such children, however, represent a much more important problem in that the level of deviant behaviour may be both long-standing and clinically significant. Their numbers are probably at least as large as those with developmental disability but, thus far, the services available to them and their families lag far behind what is necessary. This would apply to all the Australian states.

Behavioural and emotional problems tend to be approached through pastoral care systems within the school, involving the use of treatment by school counsellors and visiting clinical/school psychologists. Usually this requires the collaboration of professionals from the health and social work services in organizing an approach to the child and his or her family. However, the extreme nature of some of the behaviour concerned may lead to removal to a special class or withdrawal group: often such services are both rare and over-subscribed.

Overview

The Australian states have typically represented a bewildering diversity of philosophies and practices in special education. However, all now face the common challenge of how to provide effective instruction in surroundings which are socially and physically as close to normal as possible. The study by Gow and her associates (1987) identified progress in this area, as recently as the mid-1980s at least. Here it is to be noted that, other than in the area of discrimination, Australia does not possess over-arching legislation which establishes rights over and above the common law, mandates standards of provision, and guarantees adequate financial commitment to the disabled. It could be argued, however, that progress occurs in a somewhat less strident and adversarial manner than is the case, for example, in the USA.

As Australian general and special education have moved gradually towards a merging of services for children with disabilities within the regular school, the experiences of the two largest states, Victoria and New South Wales, may be of interest. Both these states have a long history of involvement in special education and with it a commitment to providing comprehensive facilities, mostly of the segregated type. However, in 1984, the Victorian Government received a report into special education which called for wholesale changes and the adoption of a so-called human rights policy which gave parents of children with disabilities the right to insist that their children be educated in their neighbourhood school with support. As Tarr (1988) observed, the extensive special school system was maintained, and the costs of maintaining the dual systems rapidly became excessive. There were, however, a number of other serious problems, such as lack of appropriately trained personnel and inadequate preparations being made in the regular schools. Some of the issues are discussed by Sykes (1989) in an interesting paper which examines the implementation of the policy. Despite initial problems, there appears to be a gradual acceptance of the approach, at least as measured by attitude scales (Harvey, 1992).

A rather more cautious approach was taken by New South Wales, despite the fact that it had dismantled much of its special education and guidance infrastructure in the late 1980s. Funds for integration were earmarked on a regional basis and a specialist advisory service set up to monitor and advise on their disposal and use. Along with this, a research project was commissioned with a view to identifying the factors which seemed to be influential in the success or failure of integration (mainstreaming) programmes (Center *et al.*, 1991). The results, which were mainly positive, suggested that the outcomes of a mainstreaming policy might differ according to disability group but probably the most significant factors were school-based school ethos, resource availability and appropriate instructional techniques.

Training and research

Training

The Report of the House of Representatives Select Committee and the 1978 survey by the Andrews group indicated a severe shortage of trained personnel at all levels of special education and rehabilitation. Most regular classroom teachers had received little if any relevant training and a high proportion of teachers in special schools were not qualified for the work. Since then there have been remarkable changes in both the numbers of appropriately trained personnel and their level of training. At the pre-service stage, most early childhood and primary teachers will have had at least one course on children with special needs, sometimes with associated practicum experiences. However, this would not be a mandatory element of training. Along with this, opportunities for postgraduate teacher training have markedly increased as a result of the expansion of the tertiary education sector. There is a heavy emphasis upon the application of contemporary learning theory to classroom problems.

The more advanced courses have occupied a dual role of training for consultancy/leadership and also providing a pool of potential researchers. A thriving special education subculture in professional activities and research attests to the success of special education training (c.f. recent monographs by Ashman and Elkins, 1990; Butler, 1991; Pieterse *et al.*, 1988; Ward *et al.*, 1987). The movement towards integration has provided strength to classroom-based resource roles and has changed some of the routine work of other professionals such as school psychologists and counsellors. De-institutionalization and integration have also created needs for change in the training and practice of therapists of all types since their practices tend to be community-rather than clinic-based. As part of this, provision for specialized postgraduate courses in developmental disability has been made, particularly in occupational therapy. Interest in preparation for work and independent living has led to a demand for rehabilitation counselling and adult trainers.

Research

The presence of four internationally recognized research journals in the field gives an indication of a wide-ranging research effort in special education and its related problem areas. Among the more longstanding work has been research into various aspects of early intervention (Pieterse *et al.*, 1988) and in particular Down's Syndrome (Foreman, 1988). The issue of integration has preoccupied researchers at several tertiary institutions (eg, Center and Ward, 1987); Ashman, 1988; 1991) and has led to several large-scale policy-oriented researches. In the area of developmental disability, a number of researches have focused upon technical applications such as computer-assisted learning (Lally, 1981; Williams, 1986). Transitional education and rehabilitation are also subjects which are attracting current research interest. A particular issue which has attracted considerable international interest is the quality of life which the disabled will achieve (Parmenter, 1988; 1992).

Among the research into what might be thought of as preventive classroom practice, two recent approaches have emerged through the application of strategy-based instruction (Ashman and Conway, 1989) and social behaviourism (Wheldall, 1991). It must be stressed that the work cited above is not intended to be representative or exemplary: but there can be no doubt that Australian research in these fields has grown in scale, quality and diversity.

Future developments

Australian special education is likely to expand in such areas as early identification and intervention, the prevention of learning difficulties in the basic subject areas through computer-assisted learning and strategy training, social learning and the containment at least of delinquency, integration of children with severe to moderate intellectual disability, preparation for work and independent living. The major challenge will be how to develop more effective schools as the bulk of the above problems will have to be faced by the regular education systems. To what extent such developments will receive financial support from government or will be the subject of legislation is unpredictable at the present time.

New Zealand

At the time of writing, New Zealand is committed to far-reaching changes in both regular and special education systems. At least seven examinations of the special education area have been undertaken since 1987, culminating in a major 'Statement of Intent' issued by the Ministry of Education in 1991. The following will lean heavily upon this document and also commentaries by Mitchell (1991) and Ballard (1990).

Geopolitical factors

New Zealand is made up of a group of Pacific islands, covering in all about 268,000 square kilometres. The majority of the population lives in the North Island which also contains Auckland, the only significant urban centre, by international standards, with a population approaching one million out of a total population of 3.4 million. Of these, over 400,000 represent the indigenous people: the Maoris. A further 100,000 or so are fairly recent migrants, mainly from Polynesia. Unlike Australia, the administration of education is organized centrally and much of the ferment in this area derives from the need to decentralize education and make it responsive to consumer and community needs.

Historical developments

As in other developed countries, early provision focused upon the visually impaired, the auditorily impaired and the slow learning, in this case in residential special schools. In the early years of this century the principle of special classes for the backward was adopted and by 1944 there were 48 such classes as part of a range of services which included day special schools and correspondence school classes. Private, denominational and charitable agencies featured prominently in these services. However, there was considerable dissatisfaction with a system which had evolved in 'a piecemeal fashion' as a result of historical accident and which represented a number of important deficiencies and inequities. Among these were: an unfair allocation of resources by which rural areas were seen to be disadvantaged; a lack of coordination among the various private and state agencies; excessive preoccupation with administrative and assessment procedures; and a failure to cater properly for Maori students.

With a view to improving the situation, the Special Education Act in 1989 provided for the special education of persons under the age of 21 in what might be described as a spectrum of services. Subsequent to this, the right of all students with disabilities to be educated in the state system was achieved the following year. An important feature of the 1989 legislation was the creation of a Special Education Service which amalgamated existing psychological, speech therapy and visiting teacher services with advisory services for the deaf and early intervention programmes.

Service organization

As described by the Ministry statement in 1991, special education provision for children of school age is largely concentrated in urban areas. There are eight residential schools, presumably catering for students from outlying rural areas, and a wide range of day special schools and classes.

Developmental disability

Provision for the intellectually disabled is made through a system currently composed of 29 day schools and 214 special classes. Substantial numbers of ID children remain in regular classes but the system is predominantly segregated at the present time.

Physical disability

Other than placement at two special schools and two area health board facilities, the vast majority of PD children either attend one of the 42 units attached to regular schools or are mainstreamed. Area health boards are responsible for another 36 facilities (health camp school, hospital schools and classes) which serve the needs of PD and medically fragile children.

Visual and auditory disabilities

A small number of visually disabled students attend a residential school in Auckland but most of the approximately 1,000 students receiving services attend regular schools or special classes attached to regular schools and are supported by itinerant teachers.

Those with auditory disabilities are similarly catered for through a mixture of large residential schools (of which there are two), units in regular schools and placement in the regular class with itinerant support.

Psycho-educational problems

The approximately 4,000 students described as having educational and social difficulties may be taught in special units or regular classes through a system of Resource Teachers (Special Needs), of which there were 328 at the time of the Ministry statement.

Additional issues

Through various early childhood services and inter-departmental cooperation, a strong emphasis has traditionally been placed upon early intervention programmes for children with special needs. This involves the provision of early childhood centres, staffed by teachers who, in addition to providing appropriate teaching, instruct and support parents. Wherever possible, Maori and Pacific Islander staff are employed in areas with high concentrations of these groups. As a consequence of current policy, these provisions are now being desegregated in favour of other forms of support services.

At the post-school level, the principle of equal opportunity has led to a limited allocation of funding for persons with special needs in further education, this being a recent initiative although persons with auditory and visual disabilities have always been able to attend universities and polytechnics.

Provision of services

The proposals for reform of the New Zealand education system are based upon principles which would be familiar to most governments, service delivery and community organizations at the present time: equity, quality, efficiency, effectiveness and economy. Implementation of such principles should, if effective, reduce the costs of central government in educational interventions and, at the same time, lead to socially desirable outcomes. As Mitchell (1991) points out, this represents a minimalist approach aimed at reducing costs and increasing benefits at a time of scarce financial resources. As is the case in similar reforms, the procedures are devolutionary, giving considerable power to schools and the local communities in financial and educational decision-making. The 'Statement of Intent' represents, therefore, policies to align special education practices with those of a reformed education system. Some of its principles are quite interesting in the light of practices elsewhere.

The primary focus is upon the student's learning needs, efforts being made to identify problems as early as possible; along with this there will be a greater

degree of informed parental choice and participation in programme development. In general, the statement favours integration within regular education
settings but what might eventually become controversial is the retention of
special schools and units as long as they are supported by enrolments. The
principles acknowledge the student's culture, provide for targeted and tagged
(accountable) special resources, call for better coordination between agencies
and re-affirm the primary responsibility of early childhood centres, schools and
tertiary institutions in providing an appropriate education for all students. As a
consequence of these policies, the new structure for special education is
anticipated as having such characteristics as simplicity, fairness, accessibility,
removal of labels, local decision-making and accountability.

Training and research

New Zealand has developed a substantial capacity for training teachers and
resource professionals of all types. It is inevitable, however, that the adoption of
the new system will demand changes in roles and functions and modifications to
training. For these reasons a range of in-service programme procedures are
envisaged. There is also evidence of a sustained research effort in such fields as
developmental disability (Wilton, 1988) and classroom practices (Wheldall and
Glynn, 1989).

Future developments

The policy to be implemented in special education incorporates much of that
contemporary thinking which relates to local control of schools, increased
parental choice and participation, cost-effectiveness and social relevance. The
changes in philosophy and practice being advocated are similar to those in other
developed countries which are faced with the demand for high quality services
at a time of financial constraint. However, what may be of most significance is
the notion of 'contestability' which is founded upon the premise that services are
more efficient and cost-effective when they operate within a climate of
competition. Thus it is proposed that by 1994 schools will have discretion to buy
the special education services they require on the open market rather than
obtaining them from the Special Education Service.

   A number of significant reservations about this policy have been made by
Mitchell (1991) in a closely argued analysis. These include the possibilities of
fragmented service delivery, diversion of special education funds, a move into
private practice by professional staffs, etc. In essence they represent disquiet
that the high quality elements of present services might not be guaranteed and
indeed may be lost permanently.

Final comments

Australia and New Zealand are in a transitional period as they move towards the
delivery of special education services within the regular school system rather
than in segregated or partially segregated schools and units. Both face the same
organizational and technical challenges in the context of demands for greater

efficiency in times of extreme financial constraint. However, regional diversities will ensure that over the next decade or so the implementation of policies will provide some interesting and instructive case studies. For instance, emphasis upon outcomes rather than human rights issues may lead to a reappraisal of current policies and practices. Moreover, future complexities in the social matrix within which schools and other service agencies operate may have unpredictable effects – including demands for a return to traditional policies for selection, segregation and parent choice.

References

Andrews, R J, Elkins, J, Berry, P B and Burge, J (1979) *A Survey of Special Education in Australia: provisions, needs and priorities in the education of children with handicaps and learning difficulties*, St Lucia: Fred and Eleanor Schonell Special Education Research Centre.

Ashman, A F (1988) (ed.) 'Integration twenty five years on', *The Exceptional Child, Monograph Number One*, Brisbane: Schonnell Educational Research Centre.

Ashman, A F (1991) (ed.) 'Current themes in integration', *The Exceptional Child, Monograph Number Two*, Brisbane: Schonnell Educational Research Centre.

Ashman, A F and Conway, R N F (1989) *Cognitive Strategies for Special Education*, London: Routledge.

Ashman, A F and Elkins, J (1990) *Educating Children with Special Needs*, Sydney: Prentice.

Ballard, K D (1990) 'Special education in New Zealand: disability, politics and improvement', *International Journal of Special Education*, 5, 3, 311–21.

Butler, S (1990) (ed.) *The Exceptional Child: an introduction to special education*, Sydney: Harcourt Brace Jovanovich.

Center, Y and Ward, J (1987) 'Teachers' attitudes towards the integration of disabled children into regular schools', *The Exceptional Child*, 34, 149–61.

Center, Y, Ward, J, Ferguson, C, Conway, R N F and Linfoot, K (1991) 'Towards an index to evaluate the integration of children with disabilities in regular classes', *Educational Psychology II*, 1, 77–96.

Clunies-Ross, R (1988) 'Early education and integration for children with intellectual disabilities: some results of a 10 year EPIC', in Pieterse, M, Bochner, S and Bettison, S (eds) *Early Intervention for Children with Disabilities: the Australian experience*, (pp 97–104), Sydney: Special Education Centre, Macquarie University.

Elkins, J and Atkinson, J K (1985) *Comparative Study of Three School Programs: OECD/CERI project on the transition of handicapped youth*, St Lucia: Fred and Eleanor Schonell, Special Education Research Centre.

Foreman, P J (1988) 'Alternative and controversial treatments in Down's Syndrome: are they effective and why are they popular?', in Pieterse, M, Bochner, S and Bettison, S (eds) *Early Intervention for Children with Disabilities: the Australian experience*, Sydney: Special Education Centre, Macquarie University.

Glynn, T and Wheldall, K (eds) (1988) 'Changing Academic Behaviour', special issue of *Educational Psychology*, 8, 1 and 2.

Gow, L, Snow, D, Balla, J and Hall, J (1987). *Report to the Commonwealth Schools Commission on Integration in Australia* (5 Vols) Canberra: Commonwealth Schools Commission.

Harvey, D H P (1992) 'Integration in Victoria: teachers' attitudes after six years of a no-choice policy', *International Journal of Disability, Development and Education*, 39, 1, 33–45.

Lally, M (1981) 'Computer assisted teaching: two applications in special education', *The Australian Journal of Special Education*, 51, 17–20.

Mitchell, D (1991) 'Special education: whose responsibility?', keynote address to 1st National Conference of the New Zealand Association for Research in Education, Dunedin, November 28 – December 1.

Parmenter, T R (1988) 'An analysis of the quality of life for people with disabilities', in Brown, R I (ed.) *Quality of Life for Handicapped People*, Beckenham: Croom Helm.

Parmenter, T R (1992) 'Quality of life of people with disabilities', in Bray, N (ed.) *International Review of Research in Mental Retardation*, New York: Academic Press.

Pieterse, M (1988) 'The Down Syndrome program at Macquarie University: a model early intervention program', in Pieterse, M, Bochner, S and Bettison, S (eds) *Early Intervention for*

Children with Disabilities: the Australian experience, (pp 81–96), Sydney: Special Education Centre, Macquarie University.

Pieterse, M, Bochner, S and Bettison, S (eds) (1988) *Early Intervention for Children with Disabilities: the Australian experience*, Sydney: Special Education Centre, Macquarie University.

Sykes, S (1989) 'Integration in Victorian schools: a review of policy and progress (1984–89), *International Journal of Disability, Development and Education*, **36**, 85–106.

Tarr, P (1988) 'Integration policy and practice in Victoria: an examination of the Victorian Government's educational provision for students with impairments, disabilities and problems in schooling since 1984', in Ashman, A F (ed.) 'Integration twenty five years on', *The Exceptional Child Monograph Number One*, (pp 63–67).

Ward, J, Bochner, S, Center, Y, Outhred, L and Pieterse, M (1987) (eds) *Educating Children with Special Needs in Regular Classrooms: an Australian perspective*, Sydney: Special Education Centre, Macquarie University.

Wheldall, K (1991) 'Managing troublesome classroom behaviour in regular schools', *International Journal of Disability, Development and Education*, **38** 1, 99–116.

Wheldall, K and Glynn, T (1988) 'Contingencies in context: a behavioural interactionist perspective in education', *Educational Psychology*, **8**, 5–19.

Wheldall, K and Glynn, T (1989). *Effective Classroom Learning: a behavioural interactionist approach to teaching and learning*, Oxford: Basil Blackwell.

Williams, A E (1986) 'A rationale for the use of micro-computers in special education', *The Australian Journal of Special Education*, **10**, 2, 30–34.

Wilton, K (1988) 'Research on integration of children with mild intellectual disabilities: issues and problems', in Ashman, A F (ed.) 'Integration twenty five years on', *The Exceptional Child. Monograph Number One*.

12. Special education in Ibero-American countries: current situation and tendencies

María del Carmen Malbrán and María Isabel Mac Donagh

If we have been able to survive and to fight against so many obstacles, why don't you call us 'plusvalid' instead of 'minusvalid'?

Words of a Mexican disabled person

Introduction

The authors wonder whether they have been able to reliably depict the state of special education in Ibero-American (IA) countries. It is difficult to be sure about the extent to which this chapter does justice to the many persons who are doing their best, fighting against difficulties in a creative way in order to improve and develop special education in IA countries.

Both authors are Argentineans, a fact that may have given a rather local emphasis to the chapter. Besides, they both have a professional career mainly with mentally retarded people, so their information may not cover all kinds of disability in the same depth. Contextual reasons relate to the difficult access to complete and up-to-date information on the many countries included, and therefore the collection of data was complemented with personal communications, informal publications and mimeographed material, thus trying to fill the gap produced by the insufficiency of formal publications. The authors have no specific information about special education in some countries of the area.

Bearing in mind the above mentioned reasons, this chapter must be considered as a sampling of the state of special education in our area, in the hope that it may help to increase the world community's interest in the problems of people with special needs in IA and to arouse general awareness about the potential contribution everyone can make to improve this situation.

Some general data

This chapter refers to IA countries, ie, the North, Central and South American countries that were colonized by Spain and Portugal. In alphabetical order, they are Argentina, Bolivia, Brazil, Chile, Colombia, Costa Rica, Cuba, Dominican Republic, Ecuador, El Salvador, Guatemala, Honduras, Mexico, Nicaragua, Panama, Paraguay, Peru, Puerto Rico, Uruguay and Venezuela. The Pacific Ocean on the west, and on the east, the Caribbean Sea and the Atlantic Ocean surround the IA region along the three subcontinents. The region's long extension from north to south, from the Tropic of Capricorn to near the Antarctic Circle, and the width from east to west determine a vast surface of

19,937,148 sq.km, where a tropical climate prevails, followed by temperate climate zones. Only a comparatively small portion is cold, at the southern end. The main geographical features such as the Amazonian jungle and the Cordillera de los Andes are obstacles to communication between regions and areas.

History has left two strong imprints that help to define regional identity and facilitate interchange: language and religion. Spanish is the official language in all countries, with the exception of Portuguese in Brazil. In spite of regional variations and several linguistic styles, the predominance of these two similar languages is basic for a certain homogeneity in the region. Fifteen countries present 90 per cent or more of Iberic languages speakers, but in two countries, Paraguay and Bolivia, the predominant language is aboriginal. As for religion, Roman Catholicism is predominant, ranging from 95 per cent of the population in Colombia to 66 per cent in Uruguay. Cuba is the only country where this religion amounts to 40 per cent, with 55 per cent of the population non-religious.

Diversity is remarkable in the ethnic composition of the population, estimated at 445 million people. IA countries join, in very different proportions, a heterogeneous population, resulting from the mingling of European and Asian immigrants, African descendants and aboriginal people. Proportions also vary within the same country, according to different zones. The combination of these ethnic groups justifies the expression 'América mestiza' used by poets and writers and has produced many interesting cases of cultural synthesis.

It is difficult to assess the number of children requiring special education, since IA countries have not generally collected epidemiologic data. They use the UNESCO and WHO estimations: 7 to 10 per cent of the general population have some kind of disability, 3 per cent require some kind of special provision and support, with only 1 to 5 per cent receiving this support. Nevertheless, it is not fair to automatically apply these percentages to every country, because there are remarkable differences within the region, and also between states or provinces in one and the same country. As an alternative, the rates of infant mortality and literacy may be analysed, considering them as general indicators of levels of health and education that correlate with unsatisfied basic needs in a given country.

Infant mortality ranges from 16 per thousand in Cuba and Puerto Rico to 69 per thousand in Peru, and rises abruptly to 123 per thousand in Bolivia. Literacy rates are between 96 per cent and 86 per cent in eleven countries (Cuba, Argentina, Uruguay, Chile, Costa Rica, Mexico, Venezuela, Puerto Rico, Panama, Peru and Paraguay), while in nine countries the figures gradually descend from 79 per cent to 55 per cent (Brazil, Dominican Republic, Nicaragua, Ecuador, Colombia, El Salvador, Bolivia, Honduras and Guatemala). School repetition and the high proportion of school dropouts are endemic in spite of social and educational policies. Teaching is not considered as a prestigious social position, is generally underpaid and is usually performed by women.

Emigration from rural to urban places has been common. As a result, surrounding the main IA cities are poverty belts of overcrowded slums and poor suburbs. Urban poverty is associated with social abandonment, theft, abuse, begging, mainly by children and young people, the so called 'children of the street'. Thus, groups of children coming from the socially marginal sectors of big cities are subject to rejection, exploitation and abandonment. In these cases prostitution and drug consumption are not exceptional. These socially deprived sectors, considered as social high-risk groups, share some features in the different countries: mother and child malnutrition, illnesses such as tuberculosis, venereal diseases, alcoholism, parent abandonment and promiscuity. In some places, sex discrimination against women, and paternalism are evident and particularly acute for disabled women.

Women are usually the ones who take care of the disabled person in the family without receiving enough support from their husbands – provided they exist. In some areas, women perform mother and father roles. In certain cases, the values and beliefs of mothers can be barriers to the improvement of child nutrition, diet changes, vaccination and the use of medicines. Problems of child nutrition are also associated with inadequate diet practices, lack of information on the nutritional value of food ingredients, ways of cooking, and mistaken selection of food influenced by models coming from others contexts disseminated by TV.

Negative influences of precarious health conditions, inadequate labour and transportation conditions and urban violence are contributing factors. The occurrence of illnesses already eliminated in developed countries is another factor to be considered.

Public health services have to solve the problems of eliminating garbage, provision of drinkable water and elements for environmental and personal hygiene. Lack of drinkable water is also responsible for children's diarrhoea. Premature and low-weight newborns are a potential target of disability. Traffic accidents in some crowded cities are responsible for large number of disabilities.

In striking contrast with these socially deprived sectors, highly developed and wealthy social groups coexist in some countries, while in others a solid middle class contributes to a more balanced social composition.

An overview of special education

Educational provisions for people with special needs usually include services for the blind and visually impaired, the deaf, people with motor disability and mental handicap. In some countries there also exist provisions for people with severe behavioural difficulties (Argentina, Chile and Brazil). School learning difficulties are sometimes considered within special education. Brazil has provisions for the gifted. In Venezuela there have also been systematic programmes for gifted children. In other countries, this group has not received particular consideration.

Socio-cultural disadvantages and scant resources must be taken into account in explaining the presence of some groups of children with special educational needs in the most marginal social sectors. Services take different forms according to existing facilities and to the state of development. As a general overview, the following services for children can be mentioned:

- early stimulation plans and services;
- special schools and pre-school groups for children with similar kinds or degrees of handicap;
- special schools or special groups in hospitals and institutions for socially abandoned children;
- special schools for children with different kinds and degrees of disability;

- special groups in the ordinary schools;
- special children or groups integrated in ordinary schools groups;
- centres and services for psycho-educational support.

Other services assist adolescents and adults:

- centres for work training and vocational habilitation;
- sheltered workshops;
- day centres.

Programmes for training personnel, mainly educators, exist in most countries, some of them at university level, as in-service programmes or as specific courses, varying in length according to demand and available resources. Their contents usually focus on one kind of disability. Training for health personnel such as doctors and nurses also exists to a lesser degree. There are also some programmes for parent assistance. Voluntary and parent associations are organized in most countries. Some of them were founded more than 20 years ago and have national influence, particularly in Argentina and Brazil.

Protective legislation exists unevenly in different countries, but legal requirements are not fully observed or are not translated into action, for instance in employment quotas for disabled employees, pensions, credits, loans, medical and social benefits, etc.

The overall diversity is also reflected in special education. Thus, while some developments and services can match the most advanced provision in the world, other situations that recall unfortunate ancient times are still found.

A retrospective glance

It is difficult to search historical data because information is dispersed or only briefly mentioned in available documents, with the exception of Brazil where an attempt has been made to bring out a historical account. Some common themes may be identified.

The first services for special education were organized in Argentina, Brazil and Mexico in the second half of the 19th century and in Uruguay at the beginning of this century. They were devoted to the education of blind and deaf people. Educative services for the physically and mentally disabled were developed during the 1940s and 1950s.

The influence of foreign educators who emigrated to IA countries was remarkable. They were responsible for initiatives in the creation of services, for the training of special educators and for spreading information. This fact is associated, for instance, with the names of the French E Hudet, and the Russian H Antipoff in Brazil and with the Italian L Morzone in Argentina and Uruguay.

The first books on special education were published during the first half of this century in Argentina, Brazil and Uruguay, as well as books written in Braille. Systematic courses for training special education teachers began in the late 1930s and 1940s. Development of ideas and derived practices followed similar patterns in the different countries:

- Interest in providing a kind of education useful to prepare disabled people for living in society, an idea that was not always reflected in actual educational practice. Thus, an emphasis on literacy according to the model of ordinary school was the rule, without being encompassed with a similar stress on social habilitation.

• Prevalence of a medical model without a corresponding balance in social and educational trends. The adherence to a medical model is evident in the use of terminology, for instance in conceptualizing the phases of special education as diagnosis, prognosis and therapy. Consideration of disability as a kind of illness is another example of the central role ascribed to doctors. The role of special education was more one of assistance than one of education. Expressions such as 'people who suffer from . . .' were common. Mentally handicapped people were usually labelled as 'educable', 'trainable' and 'custodiable', and treated as such.

• Educational practice was usually irrespective of age, as can be seen in school curricula and planning implementation. Emphasis was given to disability more than to existing functional capabilities, as illustrated by statements such as 'education according to limitations and handicaps', 'irreversible conditions', etc.

Although expansion and improvement of special education were slow during the initial period, in the last three decades a rapid development occurred in ideas and attitudes, mainly due to the participation of the disabled persons and their families.

In spite of the recognition in early writings of the personhood and dignity of disabled people, attitudes were not always congruent with these values. From plain survival, superstition, charity, and consideration of disability as a biological and fixed inherited condition, they slowly changed to an educational approach, to the recognition of rights and of the need of disabled people and their families to participate in the search for solutions to their own problems.

The evolution in terminology is a useful indicator of the attitudinal change: from words like 'abnormal', 'exceptional', 'different', 'patients', through expressions like 'mentally handicapped people', 'people with impaired hearing', etc, to 'people with special needs'.

The focus on special education also reflects the shift from restricted models, medical ideas, and concentration on individual liabilities to new paradigms centred on integrated education and to a culture of normalization where environment plays a crucial role. In the near past, creation of new special schools and services were seen as a sign of progress. Today, progress is appreciated in terms of the development of services and support integrated in the community.

Some critical points

While all publications and declarations related to people with special needs highlight the relevance of education, shortcomings in the curricular area derive from:

• lack of ecological validity resulting from the adoption of models, methods and materials produced in developed countries;
• non-functional learning, that is learning not directly applicable to common daily task demands in the natural and social environment;
• training in unsuitable skills, not based on an analysis of the cultural context and projected future needs;

- little balance between academic, recreational, socio-cultural and vocational skill training.

These inadequacies affect motivation and expectations about the validity of special education. The philosophy of social education, normalization and integration has resulted in some curricular plans which take into account these ideas and developments from the psychology of learning. There is still a need to promote a wider acceptance as well as training of parents and teachers to implement them.

School integration is largely limited to blind, deaf and motor-impaired people. Slow learners and mildly retarded people sometimes go to ordinary schools but they are not really integrated because they are assimilated to special groups or included within the regular class without special supports. People who present lower levels of ability go to special schools – provided they exist in the community. With few exceptions, there are no global plans for school integration but only individual or family initiatives. Architectural and transportation barriers also impede school integration of people who have a motor disability.

It has been noted that special schools have poor long-term results as regards rehabilitation and social integration. Many students remain for long periods in the services, becoming dependent on them, a fact that impedes their social integration afterwards.

Illiteracy, usual among disabled people, reduces their chances of working. The actual proportion of people with disability who work in the open market is very small, they are often underpaid or their jobs are not under social security regulations. Besides the negative influence of illiteracy and low levels of schooling, there are other barriers inherent in disabled people themselves, such as poor working habits and abilities. Absence in potential employers of valid knowledge about the abilities of disabled people, failures in defence of their rights, lack of facilities, scarcity in legislation, etc, are cumulative obstacles that hinder rehabilitation. There are no work placement services for the disabled, a task done unsystematically by NGOs.

Poor quality institutions are still a remnant. Large institutions which mix people of all ages, types and degrees of handicap have not been eradicated yet. Overcrowded wards for mentally retarded people in hospitals for mentally ill persons can be found in several countries. Abuses which take place in these institutions have been reported in the mass media and in publications on special education in various IA countries. Initiatives for deinstitutionalization and the creation of smaller institutions have not received enough support yet. This situation affects mainly mentally handicapped people who come from socially deprived sectors. There are institutions financed and run by parents that offer services of remarkable quality, but they are usually confined to wealthy social sectors, or require from the families excessive efforts that endanger their continuity.

The majority of IA countries confront common difficulties which hinder progress in special education in several ways:

1. Difficulties in collecting up-to-date information due to:
   - incomplete or non-existent directories of services;
   - slow, inefficient postal delivery;

- high cost of posting, fax, telex, etc.
2. Difficulties for implementation of policies due to:
   - bureaucratic obstacles;
   - institutional and political instability;
   - centralized policies resulting in poor development of local organizations and inadequacy in relation to socio-cultural peculiarities and rural contexts.
3. Shortage of data due to:
   - inadequacy of financial resources for making surveys and epidemiologic studies;
   - fragmentary or unreliable information;
   - difficulties over coverage of long distances;
   - limited availability of trained people for collecting data, mainly in the regions located far from the urban centres.
4. Difficult access to valid information due to:
   - length of time elapsed before information on new procedures and resources, planning techniques, technical aids, etc, currently in use in developed centres, are available in the less-developed areas;
   - unsystematic or limited contacts with international agencies and experts, sometimes confined to selected academic or research groups;
   - difficulties with attending international meetings;
   - delay in translations to local languages (the great majority of people cannot read languages other than Spanish or Portuguese even in academic centres);
   - high cost of technical and bibliographical materials.
5. Lack of coordinated action between organizations and also between government and private initiatives. Parent and voluntary institutions face difficulties in gaining a national influence and coverage in geographically-extended countries such as Brazil, Argentina and Mexico. Also, effective cooperative action between countries has not yet been achieved. Promising developments are the Latin American Group of Professional Rehabilitation (GLARP); the Inter American Confederation (CILPEDIM) created in 1991 by the ILSMH, and the Latin American Union of Blind Persons (ULAC).
6. Local organizations and voluntary groups usually fail to generate financial resources. Thus, training of potential and current organization leaders is necessary. The Inter American Child's Institute, a specialized branch of OAS, is planning a seminar on innovative models for service delivery in cooperation with the Marian Beach Institute of Kansas University.
7. Few policies for adapting the physical and cultural environment to people with special needs.
8. The use of mass media to inform seriously about disabilities is notoriously insufficient.
9. Research work has not only been insufficient, but medically focused. Social and educational matters have not received similar attention.

Innovations, initiatives and examples of good practice

This section intends to provide information on some advances that are taking place in different IA countries. They have been grouped according to the three main headings of the *World Programme of Action Concerning Disabled Persons* adopted by the United Nations.

Prevention

- Courses on disability are being introduced in schools of medicine, nursery and social work.
- The Andean Institute for Studies of Population and Development in Lima, Peru, implemented screening in Villa El Salvador, an impoverished community, to diagnose and prevent acute diarrhoea and acute respiratory disease in children under two years old.
- In Argentina, prevention programmes to control congenital rubella and to detect congenital hypothyroidism and phenylketonuria are being developed. In Mexico and Brazil there are also plans to detect and prevent congenital hypothyroidism, phenylketonuria and toxoplasmosis.
- An odontology programme, set up in 1979, for people with special needs is giving specialized assistance to disabled people and is training parents and handicapped people to prevent problems in odontology through hygiene and dental care in Argentina.

Rehabilitation and support

- A Central American Seminar on Functional Writing for Women took place in El Salvador in 1991. It brought together women from countries like El Salvador, Nicaragua, Guatemala, Panama, Honduras and Costa Rica.
- A special section for blind and visually impaired people was recently created in the Zoo of La Plata, Argentina. It has various embalmed animals to provide tactile experience, accompanied by a tape in which the sound made by the animal can be heard. A Braille card depicts the shape and name of the animal and skeletal and anatomical pieces illustrate further differences. The training is completed with touching and feeding harmless live animals. The experience will be extended to people with severe motor difficulties.
- The Cabeceira de Basto Project in Brazil is an attempt at implementing a global model confined to a well-defined geographical area in the interior of the country. It is a rural district concentrated on agricultural activities and with poor economic resources. The project covers all age groups and various degrees of disability and involves official and non-official agencies. The activities comprise nursing at home, home help, integration into ordinary schools, work training, protected employment and occupational support.
- An augmentative communication code has been developed in Argentina for moderately retarded and multiple handicapped people who have difficulties with oral language. The system is an attempt at adapting the existing pictographic systems to lower levels of cognitive functioning
- The UNED (State University for Distance Education) in Costa Rica offers

a course to train educators for people with special needs who live in rural areas. The course combines distance and ordinary methodology and provides tutorial help for students

• The Province of Rio Negro, Argentina, is implementing the inclusion of all disabled students in the general educational system, offering courses to school teachers as a first step towards total implementation.

• Colombia is engaged in inter-institutional rehabilitation activities which join efforts from public and private agencies, including the Colombian Association of Disabled People (ACOPIM).

• Specific solutions for blind people in rural areas are approached, among other programmes, by a blind veterinarian doctor who travels along his country, Argentina, training professors and students in agrotechnical schools in order to facilitate the integration of blind students to learn rural tasks.

• Lekotek ludoteca assists children aged up to 12 with special needs and their families. Play sessions are led by a trained professional who shows parents how to play with their handicapped child in Buenos Aires, Argentina.

• A Masters Degree course on neurological rehabilitation is taking place at the Autonomous University of Mexico (UAM). It focuses on prevention from a social interdisciplinary perspective. The curriculum includes a programme to give basic information to families in the community.

• The Mexican Confederation of Associations for Mentally Handicapped People (Comfe) has an information centre whose library is considered the most complete source of information on the subject all over the country. The Comfe also has a computerized service of registration for mentally handicapped people coordinated with other non-profit social organizations to give information, assistance and other social benefits. The programme is supplemented with a localization service for mentally handicapped persons who are lost in the city in order to help them come back home. This programme has proved very useful for people who cannot speak or communicate effectively and get lost in crowded places such as Mexico City.

• The Ministry of Social Affairs in the Province of Buenos Aires, Argentina, has courses for blind persons who wish to improve their Braille skills and obtain certificates as Braille technicians that will allow them to work as Braille librarians and editors.

• Private initiatives have greatly increased in the region in recent years. Day centres, substitute homes, services for people severely and profoundly retarded were born as a result of private effort.

Equality of opportunities and social integration

• A group called 'Arts without barriers' has been set up in Costa Rica to assist disabled people in the enjoyment and performance of artistic activities such as music, painting and drama. Similar groups work in other countries.

• A school for training dogs for the blind and the visually impaired satisfies an acute need in a crowded city like Mexico.

• A factory producing alpaca wool garments integrates disabled and non-disabled people in Bolivia. Fine pieces of hand-made clothing are then distributed all over the country and abroad. The threading is also hand-made, a time-consuming task which results in high-quality texture.

- In Nicaragua and Honduras, local production of wheelchairs is being developed in order to lower prices and to avoid delays in obtaining prostheses.
- The Group of Siblings of Persons with Mental Handicap in Sao Paulo, Brazil, aims at improving the quality of life in mentally handicapped people through transmitting their life experiences and feelings connected with their role as siblings to other people in the same condition. The group is specially concerned with children and younger siblings.
- The last revision of the Brazilian Constitution in 1988 included preparatory meetings and public audiences in which disabled people and representatives of associations discussed their expectations, needs and claims about the law, which now includes special provisions for people with disabilities.
- The San Juan de los Chillos Capacitation, Production and Service Center in Ecuador is a place where labour, craft, art, sport and social training is given to mentally handicapped young people.
- A programme for training parents of disabled children in Chile, called 'Parents to Children', includes capacitation and monitoring. It uses trained parents as teachers of other parents who cannot attend the training sessions.
- Legislation on the defence of rights of disabled people has made remarkable progress in Argentina both on the federal and provincial levels.
- National Advisory Boards have been created in some countries (eg, Argentina, Brazil and Chile) to give advice on decision-making to government authorities at the highest level.
- Special Olympics have taken place in many IA countries.
- The Center for Independent Living in Rio de Janeiro orients and informs disabled people on how to apply their personal resources for a full, independent and productive life in the best possible way. Activities such as dance, work-readiness courses, sports and leisure and fishing, are organized and performed.
- Home farms located in suburban or rural areas exist in some countries. They usually house mentally handicapped people and people with behavioural difficulties. Training in agricultural labour, poultry activities and related tasks is given. Products are sold to neighbours, shops and institutions.
- The University Association of Disabled People in Mexico is an organization directed to obtain opportunities to show the possibilities of disabled people contributing to the progress of society.
- Participation Committees and the nomination of mentally handicapped people as members of regional and local institutions as well as participants in meetings and congresses are becoming common practice.
- Many journals and publications include declarations and expressions of disabled people about their expectations, needs, feelings, opinions and claims.

Conclusions

A review of sources from different countries reflects some shared beliefs and aims: principles of normalization, social integration and participation are common to all. The struggle for human rights of people with special needs is also a shared concern.

The idea of disability changes according to the new conceptions in terms of barriers, expectations, needs, support and acknowledgement of the potential value of suitable action to reduce or even remove disability, changing the emphasis from the person to the environment and from beliefs on static, irreversible conditions, to more dynamic and modifiable ones. There is a need to construct a new image of disabled persons, to abandon irrational fears and the apprehension of failure, and to take risks.

Terminology related to disabilities is being re-examined in order to eliminate words that do not contribute to social acceptance and call for pity, commiseration or discrimination, such as 'invalid', 'incapable', 'feeble', 'deficient', etc, and to control their use in the mass media, replacing them with expressions indicative of the social responsibility towards 'persons with special needs'.

The family is considered the key to success in every programme of prevention and/or rehabilitation. In the area of prevention, plans for nutrition and for early stimulation use parents as aids and teachers. However, long-term studies and evaluation of the relative efficacy of these initiatives are necessary. This task would be helpful in facilitating later integration into the ordinary school system of children with cognitive special needs and to reduce school failure.

The need for support for families and the role of parents and disabled people as the consumers of services, is also great. National organizations should play the role of schools for the defence and exercise of the rights of disabled people, as a means of creating awareness in society and in people with special needs, and also controlling the observance of world agreements in their respective countries.

School integration and deinstitutionalization are also on the way. Integration of children with special needs into the ordinary school system and plans for promoting cultural and educational enrichment are being introduced. There are also plans for community-based rehabilitation and itinerant teams for giving support in rural and isolated areas.

Initiatives and projects to bring about changes in natural and social contexts to make them more suitable for people with special needs are receiving careful attention. They include accessibility to public benefits, leisure and sports, pensions and fellowships, transportation and architectural facilities, and availability of technological aids. As social benefits are not only scarce but unevenly distributed, it is necessary to widen the scope of social security so as to cover non-employment insurance, provision of prostheses, emergency assistance, and payment for mothers during the first months of the baby's life. Movements to social integration include claims to the rights of disabled people to have a normalized life.

Two particular groups that deserve attention in the near future are older disabled persons and those who present severe behavioural difficulties. Both are the most neglected groups of people with special needs, with few qualified services to meet their needs in IA.

There is an urgent need to introduce appropriate technology that can satisfy local demands and be used and maintained with the available local means. As legislation about rights and duties has become a must, it would be useful to have a reference directory comprising legal regulations existing in IA countries at a national, provincial and local level. Ethical issues related to biomedical means of prevention and the humane use of technological devices are receiving renewed consideration.

Actions tending to change the status of disabled people are not fully into practice yet. Advocacy and efforts to promote self-advocacy are remarkable tendencies. Campaigns should be developed by organizations and disabled persons in the near future. Awareness amongst the public is very important: some people do not know how to behave when they meet a disabled person, because they lack reliable information and are not familiar with disability. The role of the mass media is vital.

Epilogue

In spite of its present limitations, education is considered the promise of progress in the area. The school is currently a physical and human environment where children are being considered as such, and for many children it provides a way of escaping from the adverse social conditions existing outside. The school continues to be the means for fighting illiteracy and cultural disadvantage in IA.

Last but not least is the effort to turn principles into action, to bridge the gap between ideas and practice, but the critical situation that many IA countries are confronting nowadays is a barrier to reach such a desired aim. Consequently, the aid of world organizations is necessary to overcome this situation. A programme of priorities must be prepared by the eventual beneficiaries to guide this action. This programme should be based on a careful analysis of the current situation and needs.

Bibliography

American Association on Mental Retardation (1991) *Definition and Classification in Mental Retardation*, 9th edn, Draft.
American Psychiatric Association (1980) *Diagnostic and Statistical Manual of Mental Disorders*, third edn. Washington, DC.
Araneda, P and Ahumada, H (1990) *¿Integración o segregación. Guía para integrar niños discapacitados a la educación regular*, Chile: Interamericana.
Archambault, C (1989) 'Las endebles "favelas" de Rio', *Informa el CIID*, **18**, 2, 18–19.
Ardore, M *et al*. (1988) *Eu Tenho um Irmão Deficiente*, Sao Paulo, Brazil: APAE.
Asociación Boliviana para el Estudio Científico de la Deficiencia Mental (1989) *La Discapacidad Mental en Bolivia*, Cochabamba, Bolivia, mimeograph.
Athayde Figueiredo, M and Prado, D (1989) 'Mujeres de Arembepe', *El Correo de la UNESCO*, July, 38–41.
AVEPANE, *Futuro del niño latinoamericano: prevencion del retardo en el desarrollo psico-social*, Caracas, Venezuela, mimeograph.
Baine, D (1988) *Handicapped Children in Developing Countries: assessment, curriculum and instruction*, Edmonton: University of Alberta.
Bralic, S *et al* (1979) *Estimulación Temprana*, Santiago, Chile: UNICEF.
Braslavsky, B (1962) *La querella de los métodos en la enseñanza de la lectura*, Buenos Aires, Argentina: Kapelusz.
Buenos Aires, Provincia, Direccion de Educación Especial (1983) *Plan Curricular para Alumnos con Retardo Mental de Grado Leve* (1981) *Retardo Mental de Grado Severo. Plan Curricular*, La Plata, Argentina, mimeograph.
Buenos Aires, Provincia, Direccion de Educación Especial (1988) *Rehabilitación Basada en la Comunidad: Programa Provincial para la Integración y Rehabilitación de las Personas con Discapacidad*, La Plata, Argentina, mimeograph.
Carbonell de Grompone, M (1984) 'Dislexia Escolar y Dislexia Experimental', in Ferreiro, E and Gomez Palacio, M (eds) *Nuevas Perspectivas sobre los Procesos de Lectura y Escritura*, Mexico: Siglo XXI Editores.
Charbonneau, R (1988) 'Punto ciego de la medicina chilena', *Informa el CIID*, **17**, 3, 22.

Chaves, N (1975) 'En el noroeste del Brasil: Una experiencia prometedora de lucha contra el hambre', *El Correo de la UNESCO*, May, 28–32.

COANIL (1992) *Programa de Acciones*, Chile Comision Mixta sobre Aspectos Internacionales del Retraso Mental (1985) *Retraso Mental: respuesta a un reto*, Publicación en Offset No 86, Ginebra, Suiza: OMS.

Confederacion Mexicana de Asociaciones en Beneficio de la Persona con Deficiencia Mental (1989) *Informe presentado al Encuentro Latinoamericano sobre Deficiencia Mental*, Buenos Aires, Argentina.

Congreso de la IASSMD, octavo (1990) *Temas Clave en Inves tigacion del Retardo Mental*, Madrid, Spain: SIIS.

Dybwad, R (1990) *International Directory of Mental Retardation Resources*, Washington, DC: President's Committee on Mental Retardation.

Edgerton, R (1980) *Retraso Mental*, Madrid, Spain: Morata.

Eisemon, T O (1988) *The Consequences of Schooling: A review of research on the outcomes of primary schooling in developing countries*, Paper No. 3, Centre for Cognitive and Ethnographic Studies, McGill University, Montreal, Canada.

Encuentro Latino-Iberoamericano sobre Deficiencia Mental (1989) ILSMH, FENDIM, *Reports presented by Argentina, Bolivia, Brazil, Chile, Ecuador and Mexico*, Buenos Aires, Argentina: Actas.

Federacion Ecuatoriana Pro Atencion a la Persona con Deficiencia Mental (FEPAPDEM) *Personal Communication*.

Ferreiro, E and Teberosky, A (1985) *Los Sistemas de Escritura en el Desarrollo del Niño*, Mexico: Siglo XXI Editores.

Fourcade de Alvarez, M (1982) El aspecto social de la problemática de la rehabilitacion, *AACEDEM*, **XVI**, 1, 16–-4.

Fundacion Navarro Viola (1989) *ABC de la Familia del Discapacitado Mental*, Buenos Aires, Argentina.

Fundaçao Getulio Vargas, Instituto de Estudios Avançados em Educaçao (1988) *Educaçâo Especial No Brasil, Sintese Historica*.

Goetz, L V and Rojo Vivot, A (1986) *La educación especial en la República Argentina*, Montevideo, Uruguay: INN.

Guthrie, D (1986) *Who can Best Help? A paper on services for disabled children in the Third World – particularly in child-to-child programmes*, Montevideo, Uruguay: Inter-American Children's Institute.

Helander, E et al. (1989) *Training in the Community for People with Disabilities*, Geneva: WHO.

ICYT (1987), 9, 129. *Por una cultura de la minusvalia*, Consejo Nacional de Ciencia y Tecnologia, Mexico.

ILSMH, Comité de Asuntos Americanos (1991) *Reports presented by delegates from Uruguay, Chile, Mexico, Argentina, Ecuador, Nicaragua and Brazil*, Santiago, Chile: Actas, mimeograph.

ILSMH, Comité de Asuntos Latino Iberoamericanos (1990) Paris: Actas.

ILSMH and The National Association for Retarded Citizens (1977) *Improving the Quality of Life: A Symposium on Normalization and Integration*, Airlie House, Airlie, VA, USA.

Independence 92, *Book of Abstracts*, Vancouver, Canada.

Inness, R (1989) 'El regreso de la quinua', *Informa el CIID*, **18**, 2, 22–3.

Instituto Interamericano del Niño (1987 and 1988) *Seminario Latinoamericano de Capacitacion de Líderes de Organizaciones de Personas con Discapacidad*, Montevideo, Uruguay, mimeograph.

International Development Research Centre (1989) *Teaching Children of the Poor: an ethnographic study in Latin America*, Ottawa, Canada: IDRC.

Inter-American Children's Institute (1986) *Declaration of Cuenca*, Montevideo, Uruguay: OAS.

Jurado Garcia, E (1982) *Frecuencia é impacto de la prematurez e hipotrofia al nacimiento*, Asociacion Argentina para el Estudio Cientifico de la Deficiencia Mental (AACEDEM), pp. 30–41.

Kadlec, V P S and Glat, R (1984) *A Criança e suas Deficiências*, Rio de Janeiro, Brazil: Livraria AGIR Editora.

La Mujer 2000 (1991) No 1, Centro Internacional de Viena, Austria.

Liberoff, M (1992) *Comunicacion Aumentativa. Programa de Comunicacion Pictografica*, Buenos Aires, Argentina: Ediciones Marymar.

Lira, M I and Folch, S (1979) *Manuales de estimulación 1 y 2*, Buenos Aires, Argentina: Galdoc.

Lorenzo, E E (1984) *Resource Centres. Reflections on an increasing service*, Montevideo, Uruguay: Inter-American Children's Institute.

Lorenzo, E E (1985) *Bonding and Attachment. A call of attention for intervention and early stimulation strategies*, Montevideo, Uruguay: Inter-American Children's Institute.

'Los caminos de la participacion', (1981) *El Correo de la UNESCO*, June.

'Los disminuidos: una humanidad al margen', (1981) *El Correo de la UNESCO*, January.

Mac Donagh, M I (1991) 'Improving the quality of life of persons with mental handicap in Argentina', paper submitted to the 1st International Congress of ESEEPA, Athens, Greece.

Mac Donagh, M I (1992) 'Informe sobre la Educacion Integrada de los Alumnos con Discapacidad Intelectual en la Argentina', paper submitted to the ILSMH Committee on Integrated Education, Vancouver, Canada.

Malbrán, M and Feoli, I (1981) *La Educación de los Deficientes Mentales en la Provincia de Buenos Aires*, La Plata, Argentina, mimeograph.

Malbrán, M (1992) 'Argentine report on new bioethical issues', paper submitted to the ILSMH Seminar, Vancouver, Canada.

Mercer, J *Conceptos pluralísticos del Retardo Mental en Sociedades Culturalmente Complejas*, Mexico.

Ministerio Da Açâo Social, Coordenadoria Nacional Para Integraçâo Da Pessoa Portadora De Deficiencia, *Relaçâo de Entidades e Instituçoes*, Brasilia, Brazil.

Ministerio de Educación de Chile (1990) *Normas Legales sobre Educación Especial*, Santiago, Chile.

Mittler, P (1991) 'Assessing people with mental handicap: an overview', draft paper on assessment prepared for WHO by Joint Commission on International Aspects of Mental Retardation.

Morzone, L (1934) *La Infancia Anormal*, Buenos Aires, Argentina: Libreria del Colegio.

Pantano, L (1987) *La Discapacidad como Problema Social*, Buenos Aires, Argentina: EUDEBA.

PC Globe, Inc (1990) *PC Globe 4.0*, Tempe, AZ, diskette.

Piacente, T, Talou, C and Rodrigo, M A (1990) *Piden pan . . . y algo más: un estudio sobre crecimiento y desarrollo infantil*, Buenos Aires, Argentina: UNICEF, Siglo XXI.

Portocarrero, J (1988) 'Promoción de la artesanía y la pequeña industria en el Perú', *Informa el CIID*, **17**, 2, 14–15.

República Argentina, Instituto Nacional de Estadística y Censos (1985) *La pobreza en la Argentina*, Buenos Aires: INDEC.

República Argentina, Dirección Nacional de Educación Especial (1989) *Esto es DINEES*, Buenos Aires, Argentina.

Río Negro, Provincia, Consejo Provincial de Educación, (1990) *Integracion: un abordaje teórico práctico que facilite su implementación*, Viedma, Argentina, mimeograph.

Río Negro, Provincia, Consejo Provincial de Educación (1991) *Curso de capacitación en educación especial para docentes en ejericio* General Roca, R N Argentina, mimeograph.

Rivera Pizarro, J (1991) *Investigación sobre Educación en Algunos Países de America Latina*, International Development Research Centre, Canada.

Rodriguez, S and Haeussler, I M (1985) *Manual de estimulación del niño preescolar. Guía para padres y edu cadores*, Galdoc, Chile.

Ruiz, W (1988) 'Niños de la pobreza', *Informa el CIID*, **17**, 4, 4–5.

Rutter, M *et al* (1970) *Education, Health and Behaviour*, London: Longman.

Serpell, R (1981) *Influencia de la Cultura en el Comportamiento*, Barcelona, Spain: Ediciones CEAC.

Situaçâo Da Educaçâo Especial No Brasil, Minuta.

UNESCO (1977) *La educación especial. Situación actual y tendencias en la investigación*, Salamanca, Spain: Ediciones Sígueme.

United Nations Decade of Disabled Persons (1983) *World Programme of Action Concerning Disabled Persons*, New York: United Nations.

Werner, D (1977) *Donde no hay doctor*, Palo Alto, CA: Hesperian Foundation.

Werner, D (1978) *Disabled Village Children*, Palo Alto, CA: Hesperian Foundation.

Wilson, J (1986) *Impact against Disability*, Sussex: IMPACT Foundation.

WHO (1978) *International classification of diseases*, ninth revision, New York: WHO.

WHO (1980) *International classification of impairments, disabilities and handicaps*, Geneva: WHO.

World Congress of the IASSMD, (1988) *Book of Abstracts*, Dublin, Ireland, mimeograph.

World Congress of the ILSMH, (1986) *Papers and Reports*, Rio de Janeiro, Brazil.

Periodicals

Asociación Argentina de Logopedia, Foniatría y Audiología. *Fonoaudiológica*, Buenos Aires, Argentina.

Asociación Argentina para el Estudio Científico de la Deficiencia Mental, *Revista AACEDEM*, Buenos Aires, Argentina.

Asociación Síndrome de Down República Argentina, *Boletín ASDRA*, Buenos Aires, Argentina.

Boletin de la Region Latinoamericana de Personas Discapacitadas, (1992) año 1, 1, Panama.

Centro de Par lisis Cerebral, *Revista CPC*, Buenos Aires, Argentina.

Disabled People International, *Vox Nostra*, Winnipeg, Canada.

Elite Ediciones, *Rehabilitación: enfoque integral de la discapacidad*, Buenos Aires, Argentina.

Federación Argentina de Asociaciones Pro Atención al Discapacitado Mental, *Revista FENDIM – Circulares.*

Federación Ecuatoriana pro Atención a la Persona con Deficiencia Mental, *Revista FEPAPDEM,* Quito, Ecuador.

Grupo Latinoamericano de Rehabilitación Profesional, *Boletín GLARP-CEDIR,* Bogotá, Colombia.

Instituto Interamericano del Niño, *Publicaciones sobre retardo mental – Boletines,* Montevideo, Uruguay.

International League of Societies for Persons with Mental Handicap, *ILSMH News; Bulletins; Publications,* Brussels, Belgium.

Tiempo de Integración, Newspaper, Buenos Aires, Argentina.

Union Mundial de Ciegos, *Los ciegos en el mundo,* Madrid, Spain.

13. Special education in Africa

Joseph Kisanji

Introduction

Several attempts have been made to describe special education in Africa at national, sub-regional and regional level (Marfo *et al.*, 1983; Ross, 1988). However, an analysis of those factors accounting for the low profile that special education occupies in national planning and development requires further elaboration. This chapter, while considering the level of provision, attempts to situate special education within the African region's socio-cultural dynamics, the existing face-lifting education policies and the current international advocacy for people with disabilities towards their right to education, to equality of opportunity and to participation in the life of the community.

Africa is a vast continent with a population of 539 million (UNESCO, 1985) residing in 54 nation states. As would be expected, there are great cultural differences within the region, from one sub-region to another, within a given sub-region and within a given country. This overview covers Africa south of the Sahara including the Republic of South Africa.

Socio-cultural background

Development of services for persons with disabilities may be hindered or accelerated by the perceptions and conceptions a community holds concerning the target group. Groce (1990) posits that a rehabilitation project can be most effective if it takes into account and capitalizes upon folk belief systems existing in the community. Several examples exist to illustrate Groce's contention. The medical rehabilitation project in East Kasai, Zaire, in which foreign orthopaedic surgeons carried out operations to correct physical defects resulted in a significant proportion of the disabled children not gaining the independence expected by the project planners due to underlying attitudes about physically disabled persons (Devlieger, 1989). Examples of frustrated development efforts attributable to folk belief systems can be found all over Africa. It is all too common that a child with a disability is taken to several traditional healers, herbalists or fetish priests before conventional medical help and educational placement are sought (Okeahialam, 1974; Walker, 1986). This practice not only

Table 13.1 *Range of folk beliefs in Africa*

Disability	Stated causes	Family/Community Action	Child rearing practice	Education/training	Vocational options	Participation in community life and acceptance	
						Social Events	Economic Activities
Visual Impairment	Witchcraft; Curse from God/Gods; Anger of ancestral spirits, Diseases/Accidents	Let live	Over-protection, hiding, rejection, sent to grandparents	Traditional informal education. School too dangerous	Weaving, basketry playing musical instruments	Active	Slightly
Hearing Impairment	Curse from God/Gods; Anger of ancestral spirits, Witchcraft; Genetic	Let live	Over-protection, hiding, normal, rough work because strong	Difficult to teach but primary school only, training in local activities	Mechanical and physical labour	Passive	Active
Severe Physical Disability	Curse from God/Gods Bad omen Anger of ancestors Witchcraft Reincarnation	Kill/let live	Ambiguous status, Custodial care, God appeasing rituals, with application of talismans, over-protection, rejection	No education	None	Passive	Passive
	Supernatural being	Let live	Ceremonies for the supernatural being	Traditional/oral informal education	None	Passive	Passive
Lepers	Curse from God Witchcraft Infections Disease	Isolated	Witch-hunting, hiding	None	None	N/A	N/A
Mental handicap	Curse from God/Gods; Bad omen Witchcraft Reincarnation	Kill/let live	Custodial care, over-protection, rejection, sent to grandparents	No formal education (Mildly handicapped go to school before being noticed)	None	Passive	Passive
Albinos	Bad omen, Reincarnation Witchcraft; Curse from God/Gods, ancestral spirits	Let live; Avoided to be seen by pregnant women	Over-protection, rejection, sent to grandparents	Informal education	Menial jobs	Passive	Passive

postpones onset of intervention, but also allows an erstwhile impairment to develop into a significant disability and handicap.

There are six main focal points around which the folk belief systems evolve. These are:

1. causes of disability;
2. decision on whether the individual should live or die;
3. family reaction to the living child;
4. educability and trainability of the child;
5. range of vocational options within the community;
6. participation in community life and acceptance.

The literature is replete with examples in each of these areas; Chowo (1978), Devlieger (1989), Kisanji (1991), Possi (1988) and Walker (1986) cover one or more of them. The major attitude components under each of the six belief system areas are shown in Table 13.1.

The most frequently stated cause of disability is witchcraft. Others include a curse or punishment from God, anger of ancestral spirits, bad omen, reincarnation and heredity, in that order. Reincarnation, whereby an individual who was notorious for evil deeds is reborn in the form of a disabled person, has been related to severe physical disability in Zaire (Devlieger, 1989) and to the stigmatism associated with albinos in East, Central and West Africa (Possi, 1988; Walker, 1986). Attitudes towards the causes of disability may sometimes be interpreted to represent a low level of understanding of the characteristic features of persons with given disabilities. However, as indicated by Sechrest et al. (1973), all cultures show a clear and sharp distinction of disabilities except where mild intellectual and behavioural malfunctioning are involved.

The foregoing discussion does not assume that socio-cultural factors are static. Studies have shown that the level of economic status, demographic factors (age and sex) and amount of contact determine the kind and nature of attitudes portrayed (Sechrest et al., 1973; Mba 1978; Bickford and Wickham, 1986). The influence of these factors can be gauged against levels of special education provision in African states as described in this chapter.

The concept of 'Education For All'

The Jomtien Conference set the stage for the universalization of education as the world prepares for the 21st century. Although the concept of education for all includes people with disabilities, countries which have adopted Universal Primary Education (UPE) such as Botswana (Government of Botswana, 1990), Nigeria (Federal Ministry of Education, 1976), Tanzania (Ministry of Education, 1978) and Zambia (Ministry of Education and Culture, 1977) have net enrolment ratios at primary school level below 100 per cent. Zimbabwe boasts the highest net enrolment figures, of 100 per cent at primary and 95 per cent when primary and secondary enrolments are combined (UNDP, 1991).

Nigeria, Tanzania and Zambia adopted UPE during the latter part of the 1970s. Yet nearly 20 years later, the number of school-age children actually in school is below 70 per cent. Drop-out rates are high, being 37 per cent, 29 per cent and 20 per cent for Nigeria, Tanzania and Zambia respectively (UNDP,

1991). Botswana and Zimbabwe also have drop-outs at the rate of 11 and 26 per cent respectively. Dery (1991) and Marfo (1986) argue that a large proportion of children who drop out are those with disabilities.

Among the French-speaking countries, the following are reported to have compulsory education: Gabon, Congo, Madagascar, Cameroon, Ivory Coast, Zaire, Togo, Rwanda, Senegal, Equatorial Guinea, Burundi, Central African Republic, Benin, Guinea Bissau, Chad, Burkina Faso, Niger, Mali and Guinea. Their net enrolment rates range from 18 (Mali) to 64 per cent (Rwanda). Similarly, Portuguese-speaking countries which also have compulsory education policies and low net enrolment ratios.

The above situation suggests that, with all the good intentions for universal and compulsory education, the policies have not been implemented to the full, even where there is the capability to do so. Botswana, for instance, concerned about the 15 per cent of the children who are not in school, commissioned a study to find out who comprised the missing 15 per cent (Kann *et al.*, 1989). The study revealed that disabled children were part of the 15 per cent. Studies in Ghana and Nigeria further suggest that the drop-outs in school are some of the disabled children for whom the curriculum and the school social environment are inappropriate (Dery, 1991; Obiakor and Maltby, 1992).

UPE and compulsory education have, therefore, not yielded the intended results. Certainly, for disabled young people, the promises enshrined in these policies are far from being fulfilled. New strategies have to be developed to ensure that these promises are realised.

Policy and legislation

Specific policies for special education development

Policies provide vision and direction for any human endeavour. They are reviewed regularly to incorporate new trends, knowledge and skills and to correct irregularities. African countries, despite their stated educational policies, have in the main left special education to 'follow the wind' of their external pioneers. This is evidenced by the reluctance or hesitation of some countries to include sign language in the education of hearing impaired persons, the imposition of Braille reading and writing to children and adults with low vision and the 'basket weaving and singing' type of pre-vocational curriculum for visually impaired children and youth (Ross, 1988). Lack of a specific national policy on special education has resulted in the relegation of this sub-sector to the bottom of the list of priorities in budgetary and other resource allocations and planning (Obiakor and Maltby, 1992).

Nigeria is the only country in sub-Saharan Africa with a comprehensive special education policy incorporated in the national education policy package (UNESCO, 1988). However, evaluation of the implementation of that policy carried out in 1984 and 1986 revealed that the established mechanisms for policy implementation were not consistently enforced (Obiakor and Maltby, 1992). As a result, student enrolment was not commensurate with teacher preparation and there was a lack of specialized consultants and qualified educational planners in strategic areas. None the less, the number of qualified teachers had increased and their quality had been improved relative to the 1976 position when the policy came into force.

Special education in some countries is directed by adopted recommendations of Education Commissions which are established from time to time to review education practices. The Education Reform in Zambia (Ministry of Education and Culture, 1977) stipulated that there would be positive discrimination in favour of disabled persons and that integration would guide future special education. Though not comprehensive, this reform paper is regarded in Zambia as a statement of policy. The Botswana National Commission on Education of 1977 recommended that more emphasis should be placed on basic education, providing for universal access to education and reducing inequalities (Government of Botswana, 1990). These recommendations were reflected in the education policy and influenced the Ministry of Education draft special education policy of 1984. The influence of Education Commissions can be similarly traced in Kenya, Tanzania and other countries.

Several countries are in the process of, or contemplating, developing national special education policies. Recent consultancies in Botswana (Kisanji, 1991) and Tanzania (Mkaali et al., 1992) were aimed at providing guidelines for such policies. Informal requests for assistance were received by the UNESCO Sub-regional Project for Special Education in Eastern and Southern Africa, terminated in June 1989, from Ethiopia and Malawi (UNESCO, 1989).

Legislation

Some countries have policy documents designated as 'government white papers'. These were the object of the preceding section. This section describes parliamentary legislation which lays down procedures for implementing or carrying out government objectives and plans. Legislation, therefore, assumes the functions of a policy in specific areas and terms. With this distinction in mind,

Table 13.2 *Special education policies and legislation in selected African countries*

	Absence of Policy Paper and Legislation	Policy, No Legislation	Legislation, No Policy Statement	Presence of Policy and Legislation
Botswana	x			
Cameroon			x	
Congo	x			
Ethiopia	x			
Ghana	x			
Madagascar	x			
Malawi			x	
Mali		x		
Nigeria				x
Senegal	x			
Uganda			x	
Zaire			x	
Zambia				x

some countries have neither policy documents nor legislation, some have policy and no legislation, others have legislation without policy statements, while still others have both policy guidelines and legislation (UNESCO, 1988). Table 13.2 gives examples of countries in each of these situations.

Legislation covers a wide range of areas. It defines the various categories of disabled persons and prescribes provision in the family and community, the school and vocational rehabilitation centre in terms of age range, disability, curriculum content, assessment, personnel, equipment and material and referral procedures (UNESCO, 1988). It is worth noting that in some countries such as Malawi, legislation was not initiated by ministries of education. However, irrespective of the source of initiatives, amendments are required to accommodate current trends and new thinking as well as to take advantage of sociocultural changes brought about by rising literacy and disability-awareness initiatives of the world community.

Special education services

Services for children and young people with disabilities can be considered as early childhood and pre-school, primary, secondary and higher education programmes. They are described below in that order.

Early childhood and pre-school programmes

Children with disabilities aged 0–6 years are the least catered for educationally. A few exemplary programmes exist in West, Eastern and Southern Africa, but they reach very few children indeed. The actual programmes include assessment and resource services (Kenya and Tanzania), community-based early intervention programmes involving children and their parents in Kenya, Mauritius and Zimbabwe and pre-schools attached to special schools and teacher training institutions in Ethiopia, Ghana, Kenya, Mauritius, Tanzania, Zambia and Zimbabwe (Dery, 1981; McConkey and Templer, 1986; UNESCO, 1987). Assessment and resource centres based at special and ordinary schools in Kenya and Tanzania, started in 1984 and 1987 respectively, carry out several activities. They include assessment (so far using simple screening tests and case-history questionnaires); guidance of parents of handicapped children; organization of parents' courses and groups; preparation of educational and rehabilitative/mobility aids; provision of support to children integrated in ordinary schools (peripatetic/itinerant service); referral to special schools and medical services; and collection of information on disability and disabled persons. Until December 1987 over 20,000 and 2,500 were screened in Kenya and Tanzania respectively (UNESCO, 1989). However, very few of those confirmed to have special education needs have been placed in any recognized intervention programme.

Community-based early intervention programmes which existed in 1987 in Kenya and Zimbabwe were initiated by non-government organisations (NGOs). In Kenya, for instance, the projects consist of fieldworkers who:

a. identify children with disabilities, work with parents, siblings and relatives training them to train their children using individualized programmes, mainly the Portage or other material developed by the fieldworkers themselves;

b. organize playgroups for early stimulation and pre-school activities; and
c. organize meetings and workshops for parents.

The field workers selected from the community are trained on-the-job (AMREF, 1987). The projects are run by management committees, but rely heavily on external funding. ActionAid (Kenya), AMREF and UNICEF are the major donors in Kenya. In Zimbabwe, the ZIMCARE Trust has, since 1984, set up community-based rural programmes in which parents and relatives of special needs children are helped to train their own children after an initial assessment by ZIMCARE (McConkey, 1986). Mauritius has developed a unique pro-gramme in which parents are trained to work with their special needs children and they, in turn, train other parents. This programme is based at APEIM, one of the two special schools for mentally handicapped children. Over 1,800 children were registered for services and over 218 children under the age of seven have been served through this scheme. Over 44 per cent of these were under the age of two (Brouillette, 1992).

Pre-schools for special needs children are not a common feature in West, Eastern and Southern Africa. Most pre-schools found in the region form a section of an existing special primary school (Anson-Yevu, 1988; Kisanji, 1992; UNESCO, 1987). Pre-schools and day care centres for non-disabled children exist and their members are growing fast in Botswana, Lesotho, Malawi, Mauritius, Seychelles, Tanzania (both Zanzibar and the mainland), Uganda, Zambia, and Zimbabwe (Otaala et al., 1988; UNESCO, 1989) as well as in West Africa (UNESCO, 1988).

Enrolment figures in these programmes are not easily available. However, an estimate based on available figures shows that children in early childhood and pre-school programmes number far less than 1,000 in the 15 countries which were associated with the UNESCO Project for Special Education in Eastern and Southern Africa.

Primary education

According to the UNESCO Sub-regional Project data (UNESCO, 1987), special education provision at the first level takes the form of special schools, resource centres, special classes, units or annexes in ordinary schools, as well as ordinary classes with specialist support from resource or peripatetic (itinerant) teachers, and ordinary classes without specialist support. The last type of provision is generally not, except for a few instances, recognized as a special education placement. However, universalization of primary education in Botswana, Ethiopia, Mauritius, Seychelles, Tanzania, Uganda, Zambia and Zimbabwe has meant that many children with moderate to severe learning difficulties are now expected to be in school.

Children with motor disabilities have enjoyed ordinary school placement for many years. Those who are fitted with orthopaedic aids may or may not attend hospital schools before some are placed in ordinary schools. Children with crutches may also go to ordinary schools.

Ordinary school and class provision with specialist support in the English-using countries in Eastern and Southern Africa, for example, are very few and represent, except for children with motor disabilities, a new development. In 1987 Malawi had four peripatetic teachers catering for 20 blind children and Kenya had one such teacher supporting 20 visually impaired children in Nairobi. In Kenya and Tanzania, peripatetic services for deaf children existed during the 1970s but was later abandoned. Kenya, Malawi and Tanzania have some hearing impaired children placed in ordinary classes in neighbourhood schools with special education teachers visiting them from time to time, on an irregular basis.

Provision in special classes, units or resource centres began in the late 1960s, especially in Malawi and Tanzania; Ghana established such units in 1976. Three types of special classes and units exist. There are those located on the ordinary school premises with very little interaction, socially or otherwise, with the rest of the school. The special education staff may be involved in all the non-classroom activities of the school. Sometimes the special unit is a 'school-within-a-school' with a unilaterally declared independence. In the second type of special unit there is social interaction between special needs and 'normal' children in all non-classroom activities. The third category includes special classes in which special needs children are taught separately and those that attain skill levels equivalent to ordinary classes are accordingly transferred to, or attend some lessons in, the latter.

Resource centres may be special education units at ordinary schools which provide assistance to special needs children in a resource room while the children attend ordinary classes in the same or other schools. The special education staff at the centre prepare materials required by the children with special education needs as well as repair their equipment. Such centres for visually impaired children exist mainly in Malawi, Kenya and Tanzania.

The number of special classes and units for mentally handicapped children in English-using countries in Eastern and Southern Africa grew by about 60 per cent from 103 in 1985 to 164 in 1987. This growth has helped to increase the number of this group of children at school, albeit only slightly due to the relatively small sizes of the units, ranging from two to fifteen. However, the number of units, classes and resource centres for visually, hearing and physically handicapped children is shown to have increased very slightly. This is explained by the fact that an increasing number of physically handicapped children are finding their way into ordinary classes, whereas in some countries, such as

Table 13.3 *Number of primary school special classes, units or resource centres in 1987*

Country	Visual Impairment	Hearing Impairment	Physical Impairment	Mental Handicap	Speech/ Language Problem	Emotional Behavioural Problem	Multi-Handicapped	Total
Kenya	5	4	5	40	0	0	0	54
Malawi	18	1	2	0	0	0	0	21
Mauritius	1	5	5	7	0	0	0	18
Tanzania	19	2	3	4	0	0	0	28
Zambia	3	16	2	18	1	0	0	40
Zimbabwe	18	0	0	149	0	0	1	168
Total	64	28	17	218	1	0	1	329

NB Namibia (SWAPO) has its disabled children included in the figures for Zambia. Some children are catered for in Angola. The number of special classes is less than 10 in Botswana, Ethiopia, Lesotho, Somalia, Sudan, Swaziland and Uganda.

Tanzania, some units for the blind were closed down due to unsupportive beliefs and attitudes and lack of appropriate support facilities. Integration of deaf children is considered to be difficult due to communication problems created by that deafness; there is, however, a steady increase in the number of units for hearing impaired children.

Number of special schools

The resource centres and units for children with special needs began in the late 1960s with Malawi taking the lead in the area of the visually handicapped. Since its beginning in the mid-1940s, special education has been characterized by special schools. In 1983, all English-using countries in Eastern and Southern Africa, except Somalia, had at least one special school. In 1983 the hearing impaired were leading in the number of special schools (40), although their enrolment was not significantly higher than those of the mentally handicapped (30), visually handicapped (29) and the physically handicapped (24). There has been a steady growth in the number of special schools since 1983.

Enrolment

The increase in the number of physical facilities is only one indicator of service growth and development. However, for an area which has been well-nigh neglected, the more important indicator is the number of persons the facilities are at any one time catering for. Although there has been a definite growth in the number of special needs children attending recognized special education facilities, in both special units/classes and special schools, as indicated in Table 13.4, the rapid population increase in the region means the percentage of children served has stagnated at less than 1 per cent.

A large number of special needs children are functionally integrated in the ordinary classes. This is related to the fact that universalization of primary education has made it possible for many children with mild to moderate learning difficulties to attend ordinary classes without any proper support. Several countries have made deliberate moves to functionally integrate special needs children. Botswana made this move in 1984, Ethiopia in 1981, Uganda in 1984 and Zimbabwe in 1987.

Table 13.4 *Special needs children at school 1983–87*

| | | Enrolment | | |
Year	Blind	Deaf	Physically Handicapped	Mentally Handicapped	Total
1983	3464	3898	3428	2315	13105
1985	4274	4274	3822	4228	16598
1987	5509	6293	4551	6589	22942
Increase 1983–1987	2045 (59%)	2395 (61%)	1123 (33%)	4274 (185%)	9837 (75%)

Staffing

Staffing of schools and units poses a serious problem in Africa. There is a serious shortage of specially trained teachers. This situation has led many countries to make use of teachers with no special education training. For instance, in Ethiopia, 19 per cent of teachers in special schools and units in 1987 did not have special education training; in the Seychelles 94 per cent; in Zimbabwe 72 per cent; and in Uganda 81 per cent. The problem is compounded by the fact that these countries do not have elements of special education in their regular pre-service and in-service teacher training programmes. Botswana, which did not report the presence of untrained teachers in its special schools and units in 1987, is the only country which can boast of a special education curriculum in all its teacher training colleges.

Post-primary education

Secondary and tertiary education for persons with disabilities is not well developed in Africa. Visually handicapped persons are more privileged in this respect because many countries such as Ethiopia, Kenya, Tanzania and Zambia have admitted them into secondary, teacher training colleges and universities since the 1970s. Botswana and Zimbabwe followed suit in the 1980s. In 1987 Ethiopia had 75 blind students in its universities and colleges. Integration of hearing impaired children at post-primary level is a development of the 1980s, while physically disabled persons have received their education in integrated settings for many years. Zimbabwe was the only country which reported in 1987 that mentally handicapped persons were being integrated at 23 secondary schools. Enrolment figures at the post-primary level are unreliable and have, therefore, not been given; however, there is a need to stimulate development of provision for persons with disabilities beyond primary school level.

New trends in special education in Africa

Despite the development pattern of being jolted and of dependence that was described earlier, there are several positive strands which can be isolated from observed special education practices in Africa. Some of these are general while others are specific to the education of traditional groups of children with special needs. The positive general features in the development of special education in Africa include the following:

  • There is a definite move from special to integrated educational provision. Special classes for visually, mentally and hearing impaired children have mushroomed over the past five years and, although individual enrolments are small, they have made total enrolments swell. This is particularly the case in Kenya, Tanzania and Zimbabwe (Kisanji, 1992; Ministry of Education, 1991; UNESCO, 1987).

  • Assessment is now recognized as a basic requirement for special education provision. Screening and diagnostic tools are being adapted and developed for educational assessment as a multi-disciplinary activity. Botswana, Ghana,

Kenya, Tanzania, Uganda and Zimbabwe provide examples for this trend (Anson-Yevu, 1988; Kisanji 1991; 1992).

• Itinerant or peripatetic programmes for assessment, consultancy and teaching services for homes, schools and employment centres are fast expanding as a form of out-reach services. These programmes have increased special education enrolments. Itinerant programmes are now established in Kenya, Ghana, Malawi, Tanzania and Zambia for sensory impairments (Anson-Yevu, 1988; Dery, 1991; Kisanji, 1992).

• There is increased regional and sub-regional cooperation in teacher training as well as strengthening of national staff training capabilities and capacities. Some examples of intra-regional cooperation include the following: Ghana has brought together training programmes under one roof, the Special Education College. The Federal College of Education (Special) at Oyo in Oyo State in Nigeria is being strengthened under the UNDP-funded Staff Development Project. Kenya has established an enviable Kenya Institute of Special Education with assistance from the Danish International Development Authority (DANIDA), while Uganda and Botswana are in the process of strengthening their training capabilities. While these developments are under way, the Ghana Special Education College, the Zambia College of Teachers of the Handicapped and Monfort College in Malawi have international students on their roll (Anson-Yevu, 1988; Croll and Kisanji, 1988; Jonsson, 1992; Kisanji, 1991; Kristensen et al., 1991; Ross, 1988). This development has resulted in an increase in the number of teachers in training.

• The search for more appropriate curricula has resulted in curriculum development centres, units or departments. In addition, national governments are responding to the needs for appropriate teaching/learning as well as rehabilitative low-cost aids. The establishment of Braille printing presses in Ethiopia, Ghana, Kenya, Nigeria, Tanzania, Zambia and Zimbabwe, a materials laboratory at the Kenya Institute of Special Education and a Central Resource Centre for Special Education in Botswana, as well as the mounting of regular low-cost aids workshops in Kenya, Tanzania and Zimbabwe are but a few examples in this area (Anson-Yevu, 1988; CBR News, 1991; Eklindh and Nchimbi, 1989).

• There is positive thinking in favour of the teaching of special education in all teacher training programmes at certificate, diploma and degree levels. Planning is under way in Nigeria and Tanzania, while Botswana has taken the lead in implementing this idea in all its four primary teacher training colleges. University special education courses are currently being offered in Botswana, Ghana, Kenya, Nigeria, South Africa, Tanzania and Zimbabwe (Anson-Yevu, 1988; Kisanji, 1991, 1992; Skuy and Partington, 1990).

In addition to these general trends, there are also positive strands related to the education of visually, hearing, mentally and physically handicapped young people.

• Integration in special classes and in itinerant programmes has called for more appropriate training for children and youth with low vision, without being required to use Braille in academic and daily life. Low-vision training in varying degrees of sophistication is practised, for example, in Botswana, Kenya, Malawi and Tanzania.

• Technological development has made it possible for the Sight Savers, formerly the Royal Commonwealth Society for the Blind (RCSB/Sight Savers) to set up a computerized Braille production centre in Kenya for Eastern and Southern Africa. The African Braille Computer Development (ABCD) programme serves Botswana, Kenya, Lesotho, Malawi, Swaziland, Tanzania, Uganda, Zambia and Zimbabwe with expected tail ends in Malawi, Swaziland and Zimbabwe. Computerized Braille production also exists at universities in Botswana and South Africa.

● Managers of schools for the hearing impaired and their teachers are now more open and receptive to other modes of instruction and communication. The philosophy of Total Communication is progressively and increasingly being accepted and introduced; for instance, Botswana, Kenya and Tanzania, hitherto opposed to sign language, have now allowed this method in all or some of their schools.

● Suitable and ecologically viable school curricula for mentally handicapped children are now being developed and evaluated to respond to the absence or inappropriateness of existing programmes. Nigeria, Tanzania and Zimbabwe have attempted to develop curriculum guidelines. However, these materials need to be subjected to rigorous scientific evaluations and modifications before they can meet the criteria related to ecological relevance, usefulness and essentialness (Baine, 1988).

The emerging trends presented above reflect a number of dynamic forces which are catalytic to special education development. The most important catalysts have been the United Nations through the International Year for Disabled Persons (IYDP) and multilateral and bilateral cooperation and support. United Nations specialized agencies such as the World Health Organization (WHO), the United Nations Children's Fund (UNICEF), the International Labour Organization (ILO) and the United Nations Educational, Scientific and Cultural Organization (UNESCO) have provided support to individual and/or groups of member states. The project IMPACT, the African Rehabilitation Institute (ARI) and the Sub-regional Project for Special Education in Eastern and Southern Africa are associated with these agencies, jointly or individually. Internal pressure has also contributed significantly towards the development of special education. Associations for and of various groups of disabled persons have been formed and are active in providing education themselves or asking governments to act in their favour. In addition, international governmental and non-governmental organizations have increased their support to government and local voluntary organizations' activities. Furthermore, reductions in illiteracy and increases in health services have gone a long way to weaken the stronghold of unfavourable local folk belief systems and attitudes.

Development bottlenecks

Although the new development trends described in the previous section point to the existence of some exemplary programmes – such as the assessment and resource services in Kenya, community-based rehabilitation experiences in Zimbabwe, itinerant teaching programmes for visually impaired children and youth in Kenya, Malawi and Tanzania and for the hearing impaired in Ghana, specialist teacher training in Ghana, Kenya and Nigeria and special needs in ordinary teacher training in Botswana – several areas of weakness can be identified. These factors are responsible for the slow development of special education in Africa.

- Although there are many factors which have made national governments slow to respond to the needs of disabled persons, the sad feature in Africa is that, even ten years after the International Year of Disabled Persons (IYDP) and after signing the Convention on the Rights of the Child (1990), the apparent situation in African UN member states is that governments assist voluntary efforts instead of the reverse. National governments have not assumed the desired leadership in the development of special education.

- Special education in some countries falls under ministries other than education. In some French-speaking countries, special education is mandated to the ministry or department of social welfare, whose emphasis rests on out-of-school service provision.

- Special education is conceived, through the influence of its pioneers and through existing categorical teacher training models as well as special school placement, as a field for the specialists to engage in (Jonsson, 1992). This position, also held by specialist teachers and other professionals, scares away non-specialists and militates against integration.

- There is too much reliance on heavy external funding and other resources such as equipment and materials, while by-passing or ignoring the existence of facilities such as under-utilized schools and other buildings (availability of space), interested teachers, community development, medical and paramedical staff, local artisans, the fast developing educational resource centres and the few existing special schools and units as resource bases. These locally available resources could be judiciously used to advantage.

- Existing special education facilities and services are concentrated in urban areas, although the majority of special needs children, up to 90 per cent, live in rural areas. This has forced some parents to migrate to towns, to send their child to live with a relative in urban areas or to favour special placement, in search of services for their disabled child. In the majority of cases, the children in rural areas, where there is no special education provision, remain at home without services.

- Disabled young people go through their education without learning skills relevant to their village or home conditions, and without attaining a reasonable level of communication and social skills. Curricula for visually, hearing and mentally handicapped persons do not, in certain cases, reflect their actual needs.

- Attrition of trained special education teachers is high in most African countries. This compounds the problem of teacher shortage (Dery, 1991; Kristensen *et al.*, 1991).

- Rivalry and tension exists among and between voluntary agencies and international aid agencies at national level. These are detrimental to the effectiveness and overall development of special education services. Ostentation and policy differences may sometimes explain these vices related to competition.

Summary and conclusion

The author has observed first hand those factors influencing special education in various African countries. Special education can only make some headway if those negative influences are adequately addressed. The proclaimed commitment of governments, usually the result of external prompting, has been insignificantly manifested. This is evidenced by the fact that most countries provide for less than 1 per cent of their children and adults with special needs. Why is this so? The answer is partly related to folk belief systems and implementation bottlenecks. Solutions to problems confronting the development of services in Africa are inherent in the weaknesses outlined in this chapter. Their nature and manner depends on the special physical, socio-political and economic circumstances within each African country. None the less, positive developments can be observed in the region. These include the exemplary provisions in assessment, community-based rehabilitation, out-reach itinerant services and teacher training, both in specialist and regular teacher training colleges. These may be considered the beginning in placing special education closer to the top of government priorities in the 54 nations in Africa.

References

Abosi, O C and Ozoji, E D (1985) *Educating the Blind – a descriptive Approach*, Ibadan: Spectrum Books.

AMREF (1987) *The Nairobi Family Support Service*, (a participatory evaluation report) Nairobi: NFSS.

Anson-Yevu, V (1988) *A Case Study on Special Education in Ghana*, Paris: UNESCO.

Baine, D (1988) *Handicapped Children in Developing Countries: Assessment, Curriculum and Instruction*, Edmonton, Alberta: Vector Project, Department of Educational Psychology, University of Alberta.

Bickford, T and Wickham, E R (1986) 'Attitudes towards the mentally retarded – results from six countries', in Marfi, K, Walker, S and Charles, B (eds) *Childhood Disability in Developing Countries – Issues in Habilitation and Special Education*, pp. 251–62 New York: Praeger.

Brouillette, R (1992) *The Development of Special Education in Mauritius: a case study*, Ann Arbor, MI: University of Michigan Microfilms.

CBR News (1981) 8, 9.

Chowo, H T (1978) *Survey of Disabled Children in 29 Villages with Community Schools in Tanzania*, Dar es Salaam, mimeograph.

Croll, P and Kisanji, J (1988) *Staff Development for Special Education*, Oyo, Nigeria, Federal College of Education (Special).

Devlieger, P (1989) 'The cultural significance of physical disability in Africa', paper presented at the Annual Meeting of the Society for Applied Anthropology, Santa Fe, New Mexico, USA, April 5–9.

Dery, S E (1981) 'Childhood deafness and preschool education in Ghana', *Educafrica*, Special Issue.

Dery, S E (1991) 'The education of hearing handicapped children: an African perspective', *KISE Bulletin*, April, 16–19.

Eklindh, K and Nchimbi, J E (1989) *Teacher Training for Education Special in Tanzania*, Dar es Salaam.

Federal Ministry of Education (1976) *The National Policy on Education*, Lagos: FME.

Gerber, F (1992) 'CBR in Benin', *CBR News*, **11**, 6–7.

Government of Botswana (GOB) (1990) *Improving the Quality of Basic Education in Botswana*. Paper prepared for the 11th Conference of Commonwealth Ministers, Barbados October 29–November 2, 1990.

Grant, J P (1991) *The State of the World's Children 1991*, New York: UNICEF.

Groce, N (1990) 'Traditional folk belief systems and disabilities: an important factor in policy planning', *One in Ten*, **8**, 1–4, 9, 102, p 2–7.

Jonsson, T (1992) 'Special education training in developing countries', *The View Finder: Expanding Boundaries and Perspectives in Special Education*, DISES Council for Exceptional Children, **1**, 8–10.

Kann, U, Mapoleto, D and Nleya, P (1989) *The Missing Children: achieving universal basic education in Botswana – the barriers and some suggestions for overcoming them*, a study for the Ministry of Education National Institute for Development Research (NIR) University of Botswana, Gaborone.

Kisanji, J (1991) *A Review of Special Education in Botswana and Recommendations for a National Policy*, Gaborone.

Kisanji, J (ed) (1992) *Basic Facts About Special Education in Tanzania*, Dar es Salaam: Ministry of Education.

Kristensen, K, Nyaga, G, Kristensen, K and Kisanji, J (1991) *Training Special Education Teachers in Tanzania: Tabora Teacher Training College*, A Participatory Evaluation, June 9–12, Dar es Salaam.

Kristensen, K (1989) *A Proposal for the Principles and Structure for Special Education and Related Services in Uganda*, report on the mission undertaken in Uganda, February 6–11 and March 13–22, Nairobi.

Marfo, K (1986) 'Confronting Childhood Disability in the Developing Countries', in Marfo, K, Walker, S and Charles, B (eds) *Childhood Disability in Developing Countries: Issues in Habilitation and Special Education* (pp 3–26), New York: Praeger.

Marfo, K, Walker, S and Charles, B (eds) (1983) *Education and Rehabilitation of the Disabled in Africa Vol 1 Towards Improved Services*, Edmonton, Alberta: Centre for International Education and Development.

Marfo, K, Walker, S and Charles, B (eds) (1986) *Childhood Disability in Developing Countries: Issues in Habilitation and Special Education*, New York: Praeger.

Mba, P O (1978) 'Priority Needs of Special Education in Developing Countries', Nigeria, in Fink, A H (ed.) *International Perspective in Future Special Education* (pp 30–34) Reston: CEC.

McConkey, R and Templer, S (1986) *More than Care*, Harare: Zimcare Trust.

Ministry of Education (1984) *Basic Facts about Education in Tanzania*, Dar es Salaam: United Republic of Tanzania.

Ministry of Education (1991) *Educational Assessment and Resource Services in Kenya*, Nairobi: ME.

Ministry of Education and Culture (1977) *The Education Reform*, Lusaka: Government of Zambia.

Mkaali, C, Kulwa, B, Kisanji, J and Eklindh, K (1992) *Policy Guidelines for the Development of Special Education in Tanzania*, Dar es Salaam/Stockholm.

Obiakor, F E and Maltby, G P (1992) 'Cultural and socio-economic factors that affect section 8 of the national education policy on education in Nigeria', in Michael, R and Juul, K D (eds) *The View Finder – Expanding Boundaries and Perspectives in Special Education*, DISES, **1**, 37–40.

Okeahialam, T (1974) 'The handicapped child in the African environment', in *The Child in the African Environment: Growth, Development and Survival*, Proceedings of the 1974 Annual Scientific Conference of the E A Medical Research Council, Kampala.

Possi, M K (1988) 'Some aspects of the education of albino children in Tanzania', *The Tanzanian Teacher*, **1**, 15–20.

Ross, D H (1988) *Educating Handicapped Young People in Eastern and Southern Africa*, Paris: UNESCO.

Sechrest, L, Fey, T, Zaidi, H and Flores, L (1973) 'Attitudes Towards Mental Disorder Among College Students in the United States, Pakistan and the Philippines', *Journal of Cross-Cultural Psychology*, **4**, 3, 342–59.

Skuy, M and Partington, H (1990) 'Special education in South Africa', *International Journal of Disability, Development and Education*, **37**, 2, 149–57.

UNESCO (1985) *Statistical Yearbook*, Paris: Author.

UNESCO (1987) *Special Education Bulletin For Eastern and Southern Africa*, 4, 4.

UNESCO (1988) *Review of the Present Situation of Special Education*, Paris: UNESCO.

UNESCO (1989) *Sub-Regional Project for Special Education in Eastern and Southern Africa*, Project Findings and Recommendations, Paris: UNESCO.

UNDP (1991) *Human Development Report 1991*, New York: Oxford University Press.

Walker, S (1986) 'Attitudes towards the Disabled as Reflected in the Social Moves in Africa', in Marfo, K, Walker, S and Charles, B (eds) *Childhood Disability in Developing Countries: Issues in Habilitation and Special Education* (pp 239–50), New York: Praeger Publishers.

Part 4:   Transitions

14. Early childhood special education: an international perspective

Jane Brouillette, Marigold Thorburn and Kaoru Yamaguchi

Since the late 1960s there has been accumulating evidence that children with various types of disadvantage, whether due to biological or social/psychological factors, can benefit in many ways from early intervention programmes, especially when parents actively participate. Views on the goals, methods and outcomes have varied and evolved over the last 20 years. Generally speaking, there are various types of benefits that accrue, such as gains in developmental milestones, changes in attitudes towards the child, support to the family, prevention of frustration, increased ability to gain entrance and adapt to school, decreased desire for institutional placement and, more recently, prevention of antisocial behaviour and spin-off benefits for other children in the family.

Efficacy

There is an increasing amount of research evidence that points to the need to develop early intervention services. In early intervention programmes, children show substantial gains in intelligence quotients (IQ) and in other measures of development during the first year of services. These gains match or surpass the developmental level of non-handicapped children of similar age (Bronfenbrenner, 1974; Lazar and Darlington, 1979). In addition, longitudinal studies suggest that early intervention not only affects a person's educational level but also the quality of life (Skeels, 1966; Skeels and Dye, 1939). At one time intelligence quotients were considered to be static but Lazar *et al* (1975), in a 17-year longitudinal study, found that measured IQ points increase with stimulation and those gains remain constant until around the age of eight. IQ gains then reappear when the child is around 12 or 13 years of age. Ramey and Bryant (1982) replicated earlier studies to find that the experimental group after three years of early stimulation scored 16 IQ points or one standard deviation higher than the control group. Ramey isolated parent education as the greatest contributing factor to the developmental gains.

The age of start

A strong rationale exists for suggesting that the earlier intervention begins the more effective it will be. Several researchers have pointed to the possible existence of certain sensitive periods in the early development of the central nervous system that may result in long-term adverse consequences in the absence of specific experiences, as well as the greater neural plasticity of the nervous system in young children (Anastasiow, 1990). Attachment theories suggest that early experiences have lasting influence, though moderated by current circumstance (Bowlby, 1969; Sroufe, 1979). There are also arguments suggesting that the earlier the intervention begins, the fewer secondary complications will arise including disruptions between parent-child interaction patterns (Guralnick and Bennett, 1987).

Children with Down Syndrome represent one group that is readily identifiable at birth. Families in many countries can promptly be referred to an early intervention service if available. When intervention occurs at this early time and is maintained, an important result is that the decline in cognitive development that typically occurs during the first 12 to 18 months of life for these children appears to be prevented (Berry et al., 1984; Guralnick and Bricker, 1987; Reed et al., 1980). The effect-size associated with this prevention of decline is approximately one half to three quarters of a standard deviation which approximates seven to ten IQ points. Children with Down's Syndrome are also responsive to intervention initiated at a later time but tend not to achieve the same developmental levels as those children with an early start (Clunies-Ross, 1979).

Decline in development can be prevented or reduced by early and continuous intervention programmes (Guralnick, 1988). However, not only is there documentation on the cognitive development of children, especially children with Down's Syndrome, but similar outcomes have been observed within the area of motor development for children with cerebral palsy (Palmer et al., 1988). Similar support has been reported in a number of studies of children 'at risk' due to biological factors. The delays in development that are often experienced by low birth-weight and premature babies have been substantially minimized or prevented entirely through a variety of preventive intervention programmes (Rauh et al., 1988).

In North America and Europe, technical programmes have escalated over the past 15 years. These programmes have potential for children in general but the results are difficult to transfer to other countries. There are three short-term studies (Kohli 1987; O'Toole, 1989; Thorburn, 1986) of early intervention reported from Third World countries, apart from nutritional studies. These studies indicate that children with all types of disabilities of mainly organic origin, made significant improvements in development. Family attitudes were positively affected by home-based interventions (Mariga and McConkey, 1987; O'Toole, 1989; Thorburn, 1981, 1991).

In many projects, younger children are typically served once older children who have been on waiting lists have been provided a service. As the community service matures, children tend to be referred earlier and the families receive the service over a longer period of time. Referral is also based on the attitudes of influential people in the community and those who refer into the projects. Intensity and quality of the service are important factors in the referral of young children.

Activities undertaken by the United Nations and by international NGOs

Since the early 1970s international agencies have increasingly realized that Third World countries will not get services for disabled people unless low-cost approaches utilizing existing resources are used. The World Health Organization (WHO) has been advocating the integration of community-based rehabilitation (CBR), which should include home-based early intervention, into primary health care programmes and now over half of WHO member countries are or have been implementing CBR programmes in spite of the lack of supporting research reports (see O'Toole, Chapter 16, this volume).

UNICEF has targeted the year 2000 and has developed a ten-year strategy for the world's children. The primary focus is the need to find moral, economic and political commitment to place children first. UNICEF suggests that the world cannot rely on the work of governments alone but depends on worldwide mobilization to find innovative and effective ways of translating these goals into action. Goals have been formulated using an interdisciplinary approach involving WHO, UNICEF, the United Nations Population Fund (UNFPA), UNESCO, UNDP, the World Bank and a large number of NGOs. The overall goals to be attained by the year 2000 were adopted by the World Summit for Children on 30 September 1990.

Some administrators and ministries assume that early intervention services to families are expensive and/or a luxury. However, there have been several pieces of research that suggest that it can be cost-effective. Rehabilitation International (1979) found the lifetime earnings of a person who has a mild intellectual disability is six times what it had cost to educate him or her. However, the improvement in the quality and standard of life should not be compared to the monetary value, even though research is favourable. Improvement in the quality of life of the disabled child should be a major goal of services. Schweinhart and Weikert (1980) suggested that there was a cost-benefit saving of 263 per cent for children at risk.

Factors that seem to influence the success of an intervention project focused on early childhood services include:

- sustainability provided by trained persons who live and remain in the locality;
- design of the programme – complex or general services;
- cost of the project;
- involvement of the community and business in the local endeavour;
- linkage into other existing community resources;
- involvement by families;
- relationship between worker and family;
- flexibility of the curriculum to adapt to the local environment and to be sensitive to different cultural and religious groups.

One programme which has been influential, progressive and has continually been seen as an international exemplar is the Portage model (Shearer and Shearer, 1972).

The Portage model

The original Portage model was developed as a home-teaching scheme as a result of the Head Start Programme which was initiated by John F Kennedy in the USA. The Portage model is named after the town in which it was founded. The original model was developed for children up to six years of age.

Portage broke the traditional form of centre-based provision in the quest to provide a quality service for children in rural settings. Therefore, it was decided to take the service to the families. Twenty-three years ago the Wisconsin Portage team decided to exploit the unique opportunities offered by parental teaching.

The Portage model advocates that family members are partners with staff. Portage has developed readings for families and a monitoring tool to guide the workers to assist family members in acquiring skills in a systematic manner. Together they monitor skills that the child is learning. As family members acquire skills they will increasingly be involved in all decisions regarding their child. This empowerment is essential.

The Portage model is designed to assist parents and extended family members to teach their child at his or her developmental level. The primary objective is to develop the skills of a family member who then works with the child within their home. The home is the best environment for the following reasons:

- It is a more natural and comfortable place to work in for both the parent and the child;
- the Portage worker can use materials and other aspects of the home environment;
- young children spend most of their time in the home;
- what is learned in a clinic or centre does not always transfer to the home.

When the Portage worker comes to the home they have a system of work which is the foundation of Portage. This process is backed up by materials, including the checklist, teaching cards and activity charts (Boyd *et al.*, 1977).

The Portage checklist is a colour-coded developmentally sequenced checklist of 580 items for children from birth to six years of age. Each colour represents a different area of development. The skills can be observed by the family member and the Portage worker. The areas of development are activities of daily living, motor, language, social and cognitive skills as well as a special section on infant stimulation. When a child first enters a Portage programme, a baseline is taken by the family member and the Portage worker. Together they observe the skills the child has acquired, and these skills are noted on the checklist. When the child learns a new skill it is marked on the Portage checklist. The checklist is very positive and looks at what the child can do and gives family members ideas of activities that the child could learn next.

The Portage teaching cards directly correspond to items on the Portage checklist. The teaching cards have each skill item on the checklist written as a behavioural objective, along with ideas on ways to teach that skill. Many Portage workers actually note additional ideas that they have been successful on their Portage teaching cards. These are colour coded in direct relation to the Portage checklist.

The activity charts are written records regarding one activity that the family member is to work on in the home until the next visit by the Portage worker. This has been mutually agreed and written in partnership and the family member has been given the information to fill in the activity chart correctly. The activity chart gives the Portage worker the information when she or he returns on their next visit to the home. The Portage worker does the activity with the child at the beginning of the visit to assess if the child has the skills to move on to another goal or if changes should be made in this activity to strengthen the skills being taught.

A home visit usually lasts about one and a half hours. It tends to have five major components. These components change over time as the parent or family member who participates within the Portage model gains skills. The five major components are as follows.

1. *The Portage worker presents a new activity and records the baseline.* The Portage worker does an activity directly with the child to adjust the activity so that the family member and the child can be successful in acquiring the goal. When the Portage worker has identified the activity, the parent models the new activity.

2. *Parent models the new activity.* The major role of the Portage worker is to teach the activity to the family member and assist them in knowing why it is important and how to be successful in doing this with their child.

3. *The Portage worker and the family member go into partnership.* This is critical, as in this component the worker and/or family member give ideas on improving the activity, or how to integrate the skills into everyday activities. The Portage worker should have a positive relationship with the family so that they feel comfortable enough to ask questions or clarify. This part of the visit is intended to achieve equality between the partners and to make decisions. The Portage worker should strive to increase the family members' personal skills. In this section the Portage worker and the family member also discuss what they together feel the family should work on with the child until the next visit.

4. *The Family member works with the child and records the activity.* Until the next visit, the family member will spend a few minutes every day working with the child in doing the activity or working at integrating the activity into the daily routine. The family writes down how they are doing on the activity. If problems or any questions come up, the families should be encouraged to contact the Portage worker.

5. *The Portage worker returns to the house and does the activity with the child.* Visits to a home are best if they are at the same time and day of the week. Most visits are once a week but some are less frequent, according to the needs of the child or the family. The Portage worker will evaluate the activity decided upon in the last visit to see how the child has done and make adjustments for this visit. If the child meets the goal set during the previous visit, the Portage worker will move on to the next step in learning. If the Portage worker can not get the child to do the activity then they should ask the family member to show them how they did it. If the family member is not successful then the activity will be modified. The focus of Portage is on what the child can do so that both the family member and the child are experiencing success.

Portage as a modular system

Portage has grown over recent years and has been translated into 30 languages.

As Portage has developed there has been a consistent commitment to provide quality information which is educationally and psychologically sound yet demystified by keeping the information in every-day language for families.

The global expansion of Portage has demanded that the model alter itself and become flexible to accommodate a wide variety of cultures. Through this challenge, Portage workers have found new applications, possible developments and fresh approaches within the basic Portage framework. This flexibility within the Portage model is conceived as a modular system in which the system can be put together a series of different ways to accommodate the service needs. The needs of the service could be tailored to the needs of the service provider, the community, the family and most importantly, the individual child. Adaptations can be made to the sequence children acquire skills, to meet the training or academic levels of the Portage workers, to the location of the Portage visit and to the age and disability group served.

The modular system has given flexibility to Portage so that it can be tailored to meet local need. Therefore, a Portage model within a culture may be very different in design between rural and urban areas. In some countries, expectations and needs of city dwellers are different from those in the rural areas. There may also be differences between religious groups and regions within a country. This accommodation of need is necessary if the Portage model is to be acceptable by the local community. Two of the countries which have adapted the Portage model to meet their needs are Japan and Jamaica.

The Portage model in Japan

The Japan Portage Association has found that Portage materials work very well with minor modification to meet needs and cultural differences (Yamaguchi, 1985). The Portage materials were translated into Japanese in 1977. Three years later a Japanese edition was published which modified, eliminated and added new skills to the checklist, to meet the cultural, social and the linguistic differences of the Japanese lifestyle. There are currently 562 items on the Japanese checklist. In addition to the differences in the checklist, the teaching cards were modified and illustrations were added to the materials.

The Portage model in Japan found that to best meet the needs within their culture, some modifications in service provision were necessary. Special Portage centres were established in which family members work with their child using the components of a Portage visit. During this time, activities are identified which the family will then do at home on a daily basis. Some families attend the Portage centre on a weekly basis and others fortnightly. In some instances, the Portage model in Japan has been offering services for home-teaching through instruction by telephone or correspondence for families who live far away.

The Portage centres established by the Japanese model are specifically to train family members with their child for the allocated times. They are day-care centres or early intervention centres in which the children attend on a daily basis with their families. However, in Japan many day centres do use the Portage curriculum in either a one-to-one or group setting.

The Japan Portage Association has formed a national association which publishes a newsletter every four months. In addition, the association holds seminars and has an annual meeting with international guest speakers. The

Japan Portage Association has an agreement with a Japanese publisher and has established close cooperation with the Japan Educational Television network.

Starting in 1983, investigations into the effectiveness of the Japanese Portage model have been conducted by Yamaguchi (1988) who compared the difference between the first and the latest development quotients (DQ) scores of the children. Yamaguchi selected five sites throughout Tokyo involving 144 children. These children were administered the Tsumori-Inage Developmental Test (standardized in Japan) every four months. The boys and girls with Down Syndrome gained +1.39 and +8.31 respectively and the boys and girls who did not have Down Syndrome gained +3.39 and + 1.74 respectively. Most other research in this area suggests that the DQ would have a tendency to decrease as the children grew older. However, this research suggests that the measured intelligence of most of the children stayed in the level of moderate learning disability after they reached school age (Yamaguchi et al., 1988).

A follow up study by Yamaguchi (1991) has been initiated for children whose families were involved during their pre-school years. These children are now of compulsory school age. The study looked at achievements of school activities and the type of educational environment. Additionally, the study compared a group of young adults with Down's Syndrome in Japan to a group at Washington University (Dmitriev, 1981). The individuals in the follow-up studies were administered the Vineland Social Maturity Scale. The findings showed that 55 per cent of those with no early intervention had a social quotient (SQ) of less then 50 while more than half of children who received early intervention through the Japan Portage model showed an average SQ of more than 71. In relation to Washington University, the results were more scattered but a little higher.

The Portage model in Jamaica

The Portage Guide to Early Education was first used in Jamaica in 1975 and during the following five years early intervention projects using Portage were initiated in Curacao, Haiti and Barbados. Since 1986, the model has been used in Trinidad, Guyana, Belize and Grenada. The Portage materials were adapted in 1976 by illustrating the cards and preparing a Jamaican manual. In 1978, the Jamaica Portage Guide to Early Education was printed. Two parallel home-based services have developed over the past 17 years. Parent and family member involvement are an integral part of both programmes.

The urban-based programme in Kingston is known as The Early Stimulation Project and was initiated in 1975. The Portage workers are known as child development aides. The workers visit families at their homes weekly. The rural-based programme, known as 3 D Projects, was started in 1985. 3 D Projects uses CBR workers and integrates the Portage programme into the CBR model for disabled children of all ages.

In 1978 the Early Stimulation Project in Kingston assessed the progress of 36 children who had been receiving early intervention using the Portage programme for two years or more. The results show that children learned at an increased rate. Even those with profound disability learned more skills than would have been expected, based on their previous rate of development (Thorburn, 1981).

More recently, the use of Portage materials by CBR workers was assessed (Thorburn, 1988). It was found that record-keeping was inadequate and indicated that tighter supervision and monitoring was necessary to maintain quality.

The International Portage Association

In 1989 the International Portage Association was as a result of global demand. Portage International has taken up several global issues in which Dr Sidney Bijou suggests seven future directions (Brouillette and Brouillette, 1992):

1. Increasing the use of para-professional Portage workers, especially where there is a shortage of trained professionals.
2. Improving the Portage instrument by shortening the developmental intervals and delineating differences that exist between babies and children who are severely handicapped.
3. Using the model flexibly to address children with multiple disabilities, sensory impairments and severe communication disorders.
4. Using the model flexibly to accommodate a variety of sites. Portage is currently being used in family homes, a variety of centres and combinations of both. Dr Bijou suggests that as long as the Portage model is carried out as prescribed by the manual, a variety of sites should be encouraged.
5. The model should be encouraged to be sensitive and adapted to local conditions and cultural practices.
6. Mere translation in a country has not been found to be appropriate. For some countries a number of translations and adaptations may be required.
7. Rendering support services to the family structure, as families usually have other needs to be addressed.

Some timely changes within Portage could be a possible addition within the CBR model. Portage has the benefit of a monitoring system for families and children and offers a variety of information around the curriculum. It could be expanded horizontally to explore options and adapt the curriculum to better meet the needs of each child. Portage materials could be directly linked with the CBR World Health Organization (WHO) Manual (Helander *et al*, 1989) in some areas. This horizontal expansion of activities for monitoring could be included in purpose-written booklets for each area of specific exceptionality which could assist workers, professionals, families and the community in how to change and alter the existing checklists to meet the needs of individuals in their community.

Relevance of the Portage model to Third World countriess

As the experience of Portage in the Third World increases, more questions are being asked about its relevance and suitability to really low-cost early intervention. O'Toole has modified his approach in Guyana and has developed more simplified materials. Miles (1992) has suggested that Portage is too 'reporter orientated' requiring too much writing to be suitable for community workers with limited education. Other simplifications have been made in

Zimbabwe (Mariga and McConkey, 1987) and Nepal (Brouillette and Brouillette, 1988). The Portage project in Wisconsin and the Portage service in England are making extensive curriculum adaptations. Baine (Chapter 17, this volume) has stressed the need for more ecologically valid sets of tasks which are actually identified in the community by local practioners and service givers.

With the completion of the UN Decade for the Disabled and the WHO target of 'Health for All by the Year 2000', the next eight years offer an opportunity to evaluate existing approaches and explore new ones to early intervention in the Third World. Many projects have been started in many countries, some of which utilise the Portage system and, to a lesser extent, the model. We need to critically evaluate what we are doing. Most people agree that early intervention is necessary. The main question now is, how?

References

Anastasiow, N (1990) 'Implications of the neurobiological model for early intervention, in Meisels, S and Shonkoff, J (eds) *Handbook of Early Childhood Intervention*, pp. 196–216, Cambridge: Cambridge University Press.

Berry, P, Gunn, V and Andrews, R (1984) 'Development of Down's Syndrome children from birth to five years', in Berg, J (ed) *Perspectives and Progress in Mental Retardation, Vol. 1 Social, Psychological and Educational Aspects*, pp 167–77, Baltimore, MD: University Park Press.

Bowlby, J (1969) *Attachment and Loss, Vol.1 Attachment*, New York: Basic Books.

Boyd, R, Stauber, K and Bluma, S (1977) *Instructors Manual Portage Parent Program*, Madison, WI: CESA.

Bronfenbrenner, U (1974) *Is Early Childhood Intervention Effective?*, Washington, DC: Office of Human Development.

Brouillette, J and Brouillette, R (1988) 'Serving the unserved through parent to parent training: examples from Mauritius and Nepal', in Yamaguchi, K, Shimizu, N, Dobashi, T, Yoshikawa, M (eds) *A Challenge To Potentiality: the vision of early intervention for developmentally delayed children*, Proceedings of the International Portage Conference, Tokyo.

Brouillette, J and Brouillette, R (1992) 'The Portage system and CBR', *CBR News*, 10, January.

Clunies-Ross, G (1979) 'Accelerating the developmentof Down's Syndrome infants and young children', *Journal of Special Education*, **13**, 169–77.

Guralnick, M (1988) 'Efficacy research in early childhood intervention programs', in Odom, S and Karnes, M (eds), *Early Intervention for Infants and Children With Handicaps: an empirical base*, pp. 75–88, Baltimore, MD: Paul H Brookes.

Guralnick, M and Bennett, F (1987) *The Effectiveness of Early Intervention for At-Risk and Handicapped Children*, New York: Academic Press.

Guralnick, M and Bricker, D (1987) 'The effectiveness of early intervention for children with cognitive and general developmental delays', in Guralnick, M and Bennett, F (eds) *The Effectiveness of Early Intervention for At-Risk and Handicapped Children*, New York: Academic Press.

Helander, E, Mendis, P, Nelson, L and Goerdt, A (1988) *Training Disabled Persons in the Community*, Geneva: WHO.

Kohli, T (1987) *Portage: Home-centre based non-formal teaching to enhance development of pre-schoolers in India*, New Delhi: NCERT.

Lazar, I and Darlington, R (1979) *Summary Report, Lasting Effect After Preschool* DHEW (OHDS) 79-30179 Washington, DC: US Government Printing Office.

Lazar, I, Haydon, A, Dmitriev, V (1975) 'The Multidisciplinary Preschool for Down's Syndrome Children at the University of Washington, Model Preschool Centre', in Friedlander, B Storritts, G and Kirk, G (eds) *Exceptional Infants* Vol. 3, 24–5. New York: Brunner and Mazel.

Mariga, L and McConkey, R (1987) 'Learning programmes for mentally handicapped people in rural areas of Zimbabwe', *International Journal of Rehabilitation Research*, 10.

Miles, M (1992) Paper circulated to MORE Committee, ILSMH.

O'Toole, B (1989) 'The relevance of parent involvement programmes in developing countries', *Child Care, Health and Development*, **15**, 329–42.

O'Toole, B (1990) 'Community based rehabilitation: the Guyana experience', in Thorburn, M and Marfo, K (eds) *Practical Approaches to Childhood Disability In Developing Countries*, Spanish Town, Jamaica: 3 D Projects.

Palmer, F, Shapiro, B, Allen, M, Mosher, B, Bilker, S, Harryman, S, Meinert, C and Capute, A (1990) 'Infant stimulation curriculum for infants with cerebral palsy: effects on infant temperament, parent-infant interaction and home environment', *Pediatrics*, **85** 411–15.

Ramey, C and Bryant, D (1982) 'Evidence for prevention of developmental retardation during infancy', *Journal of the Division of Early Childhood*, Fall, 72–8.

Rauh, V, Achenbach, T, Nurcombe, B, Howell, C and Teto, D (1988) 'Minimizing adverse effects of low birthweight: four year results of an early intervention program', *Child Development*, **59**, 544–53.

Reed, R, Pueschel, S, Schnell, R and Cronk, C (1980) 'Interrelationships of biological, environmental and competency variables in young children with Down's Syndrome', *Applied Research In Mental Retardation*, **1**, 161–74.

Rehabiliation International (1979) *Childhood Disability: Its Prevention and Rehabilitation*, report to the Executive Board of UNICEF, E/ICEF/L1410, Paris: United Nations.

Schweinhart, S and Weikert, L (1980) *Young Children Grow Up*, Monograph 7, Michigan: Ypsilanti.

Shearer, M and Shearer, D (1972) 'The Portage project. A model for early childhood education', *Exceptional Children*, **36**, 210–17.

Shearer, D (1980) *Portage Report: A Report On the Portage Project 10 Years Later*, Madison, WI: CESA.

Skeels, H (1966) 'Adult status of children with contrasting early life experiences: a follow up study', *Monographs of the Society for Research in Child Development*, **31**, 3, Serial No. 105.

Skeels, H and Dye, H (1939) 'A study of the effects of differential stimulation on mentally retarded children', *Proceedings of the American Association on Mental Deficiency*, **44**, 114–36.

Sroufe, L (1979) 'The coherence of individual development: early care, attachment and subsequent developmental issues', *American Psychologist*, **34**, 834–41.

Thorburn, M (1986) 'Early intervention for disabled children in developing countries in the Caribbean', in Marfo, K, Walker, S and Charles, B (eds) *Childhood Disability In Habilitation and Special Education*, New York: Praeger.

Thorburn, M (1981) 'In Jamaica: community aides for preschool disabled children', *Assignment Children*, 53/54, Geneva: United Nations.

Thorburn, M (1988) 'Portage in the Caribbean; a 13 year experience', in Yamaguchi, K, Shimizu, N, Dobashi, T and Yoshikawa, M, *A Challenge To Potentiality: The Vision of Early Intervention for Developmentally Delayed Children*, Proceedings of the International Portage Conference, Tokyo.

Thorburn, M (1991) 'Parent evaluation of community based rehabilitation in Jamaica', *West Indian Medical Journal*, Supplement.

Yamaguchi, K (1985) 'The role of parents especially in early education for the developmentally delayed training of Level I manpower', *Proceeding of the 7th Asian Conference on Mental Retardation*, Taipei, Republic of China: Asian Federation for the Mentally Retarded.

Yamaguchi, K (1988) 'The Japanese adaptation of the Portage early intervention model and some results', in White, M and Cameron, R (eds) *Portage: Progress, Problems and Possibilities*, Windsor: NFER-Nelson.

Yamaguchi, K, Shimizu, N, Dobashi, T and Yoshikawa, M (1988) *A Challenge to Potentiality: the Vision of Early Intervention for Developmentally Delayed Children'*, Proceedings, 1988 International Portage Conference, Tokyo: JAMR.

Yamaguchi, K (1991) 'Follow-up study of children who received early intervention by Portage program', paper presented at the International Conference on Mental Retardation, Hong Kong.

15. The transition to employment of disabled people: work by the Organization for Economic Cooperation and Development

Peter Evans

Introduction

The transition to work for young people with disabilities has become an increasingly important issue in developed countries. There are several reasons for this relatively new interest. Humanitarian concerns for the integration of the disabled into society have grown substantially over the past 20 years as a consequence of pressure by parents and professionals, as well as disabled people themselves, in the context of conceptual developments in thinking about democracy. The UN International Year of the Disabled (1981) had clearly signalled a new path for this minority group. The decision of the European Community in 1987 to implement policies in favour of the disabled was another key event (Daunt, 1991). The 'Americans with Disabilities Act (ADA)' passed in 1990 is very far-reaching in giving protection to people with disabilities in many areas of life. All of these changes reflect growing awareness of the need to implement principles of equality more widely, while at the same time promoting individual choice.

In parallel, and in some cases as part of these decisions, developed countries also began to review general policies relating to the support not only of the disabled but of all citizens. Policy initiatives have switched from those based on welfare state ideals of passive support for the disabled to those that emphasize the active role that the disabled could fulfil. The goal of the active society stresses not only the important part that the disabled can play in a productive capacity in the work place but also incorporates the right for disabled people to achieve 'full adult status with the pleasures and the pain, the privileges and the responsibilities that that concept entails' (OECD, 1991). Gerry (1992) points out some of the financial implications in the USA for maintaining disabled people on passive life-long total dependency programmes. He estimates (conservatively) that the cost for the USA of maintaining this policy for a disabled population of about 900,000 is in excess of $1 trillion.

Demographic changes

Demographic trends have also been important. There are two components. First, there has been a substantial decrease in the birth rate in most developed countries, to the extent that other things being equal, there is likely, in the coming years, to be a shortage of labour to fill the predicted available positions. In addition, increasing numbers of older people will be reaching retirement age and the number of retired citizens is growing. The implications of these changes for social protection raise potential difficulties for economies which may find themselves in the position of being unable to sustain adequate dynamism and gross national product to maintain the current size of the community with the inherent rising costs of an ageing population.

Technology

Developments in technology have also had an important impact on employment prospects. Studies have shown that technology can provide access to new opportunities in education and employment and increased independence. In addition, they can help to motivate disabled people and assist them to integrate into mainstream activities, thus increasing choice and enhancing opportunity. The work also revealed some weaknesses. Effective support in the form of information advice and technical services as well as necessary training in the use of technology by teachers and students alike was not forthcoming. Furthermore, there was no evaluation of whether the technology matched student needs and although students could acquire new skills in this way, there was little evidence that opportunities existed for them to be practised in the work place. Many employers seemed unaware of the enabling potential of the new technology for those with disabilities.

Taken together, the issues raised above indicate that all human resources will be needed to maintain not only the economies but also societies themselves. The positive side of these developments suggests that towards the end of the 1990s there are reasons to anticipate the possibility of a return to full employment in many countries (OECD, 1990). Finally, the expected need for ever-more skilled workers and the growth of technology in the work place suggest that for well-motivated and educated disabled persons the future prospects are perhaps the best they have been for many years.

What is transition?

The change in policy from passive support to the active society emphasizes not only the significance of work for all individuals but also their social and psychological development and the achievement of adult status and independence. This carries the understanding that people with disabilities have frequently been denied the responsibilities and privileges of adulthood, including the right to a normal family life. It is with this in mind that the definition of transition which has emerged during the development of the work at the OECD is,

> the process by which an individual grows through adolescence to adulthood in the social, cultural, economic and legal contexts provided by families, communities and national policies (OECD, 1988).

Thus the purposes of effective transition arrangements that have been developed are to encourage personal autonomy, independence and adult status; work and economic self-sufficiency; social interaction; community participation; leisure and recreation; and roles within the family. These goals would of course apply to all people, regardless of disability. But the means of achieving them, their extent and the time taken will vary between individuals. They are discussed more fully below.

Personal autonomy

This is seen as a human right and is an aspect of transition where the expectations of parents and professionals exert a crucial influence on the young person. Thus the transition phase must develop positive attitudes in parents and professionals towards young people with disabilities, with the aim of developing independence, confidence and self-advocacy.

Work and economic self sufficiency

Earlier discussions had emphasized, through a period of high youth unemployment, the concept of 'significant living without work' – an approach that is now considered to be unacceptable. Furthermore, analyses are showing that sheltered workshops are rarely an effective preparation for integration into the labour market (OECD, 1992). Thus the present aim is open, paid employment for all. Transitional arrangements must now plan for employment on the open labour market for all young people.

Social interaction and community participation

Developments in integrated education and the experience gained by the non-disabled of the disabled allow for fuller participation in the community. The work place cannot be separated from the development of a social life since, for very many people, work is an extremely important source of friendship and other social activities.

Roles within the family

The continued challenge by human rights movements to the state of dependency of the disabled has led to the recognition that marriage and the rearing of a family and other group-living patterns are acceptable goals. This contrasts strongly with the present understanding of transition and the expectations of many professionals, parents and others that for those with severe disabilities a dependent state of 'permanent childhood' is the only viable scenario.

Thus transition should be seen as a unitary process by which disabled and non-disabled individuals grow through adolescence to adulthood and achieve the balance between dependence and independence. A framework for transition which incorporate the features outlined above can serve to plan services and determine necessary transition arrangements.

The development of effective transition arrangements

From the discussion above, it can readily be seen that developing effective transition programmes will involve the coordination and development of the various service systems and invidiuals that are involved with the young person across various levels of those systems. A number of countries have developed services to help disabled students with transition. Some examples are discussed in this section.

The Danish Kurator model

In Denmark, transition is aided by a 'Kurator'. A Kurator is a qualified comprehensive school teacher and, although being a Kurator is not a separate career, most Kurators have taken additional relevant in-service courses. Teachers in schools apply for these posts where they know the school and neighbourhood well. Kurators work at local authority level and may cover more than one school. The Kurator is a transition specialist and the work entails the development of an individual transition plan for each disabled student. This is arrived at via consultation with parents, pupils and teachers, within the context of knowledge of local possibilities. Kurators remain teachers but they teach fewer hours and use the freed time to support young people in work.

Students with disabilities can organize their timetables so that schooling and work are mixed. Considerable flexibility is allowed for in the arrangements made. The work of the Kurator is much appreciated by parents, although some parents would like to be much more involved in the decision-making process.

The case manager in the USA

Case management began in the disabilities field following deinstitutionalization and with a commitment to least intrusion and least restrictive services. It emphasizes changes in the environment that are needed to meet clients' needs rather than changing the client to fit the environment through, for instance, clinical services. Following deinstitutionalization, it was necessary to identify a single point of accountability for the lives of people with disabilities (the case manager) – a role which a single service institution could not fulfil. Thus case managers assist clients to gain access to needed medical, social, educational and other services. Case managers have a pivotal role which includes,

> diagnosing, or assessment of the individual's services needs, the development of an individual services plan and methods for providing, evaluating and monitoring the services identified in the plan (OECD, 1991).

Individual transition plans

Individual transition plans (ITPs) have been developed in several countries; in the USA they are a natural extension of the individual education programme (IEP). An ITP is the place where a start is made on matching student strengths, wishes and needs to the current local labour market and identifying the support that will be necessary; this will include the expectations of the family. As implied above, successful transition involves multi-agency planning and coordination. Several issues must be taken into account: employment options, residential choice, financial support and recreational options. In addition, communication needs, community access and transportation issues as well as continuing medical and para-medical needs must be considered.

Support also needs to be provided in the work place and two particular approaches are described next.

Support in the work place

The Genoa approach

The programme in Genoa, Italy, for the integration of the disabled into work has developed in the context of school integration in Italy. Those who have been integrated into the mainstram school do not want to be segregated in work. In Genoa, the transition to work for students with moderate to severe disabilities includes six basic themes:

1. During the compulsory school period, there is an emphasis on integration in the regular classroom and the development of age-appropriate social and communication skills.
2. There is a need for expanded and intensive services intended to assist young people with disabilities to acquire work skills and experience before gainful employment.
3. Employers and other co-workers must be involved in the development of the necessary work skills and in the continued support of the employee.
4. Experimental work experiences are developed to create the financial incentives for employers to take a chance in employing those with disabilities.
5. Families must be involved to help in identifying needed support.
6. There must be support from community leaders.

The Genoa approach is based on two assumptions. The first is psychological: that it is immaturity which makes integration difficult. The second is procedural: that is there is a need for mediation between the disabled and work which can form a bridge between the two and can support both the disabled person and the employer. Active learning is an important principle in the Genoa approach and individuals are trained through work to develop social skills and work methods rather than technical skills. This is because, in their view, it is not difficult to teach a person with disabilities a trade but it is difficult to make him or her 'feel a worker'. These problems are overcome through the use of a multi-disciplinary support team consisting of speech-, occupational- and physio-therapists, psychological and psychiatric services, recreation and social work services, school health services, parent training and transport.

Supported employment

This is an approach which has developed particularly strongly in the USA. It is work in an integrated setting for those with severe handicaps who are expected to need continuous support services and for whom competitive employment has traditionally not been possible.

In the supported employment model, extra supervision and assistance for often severely disabled people is provided to help them to perform a normal job in open employment. The support can be very intensive and is maintained at a level necessary to keep the disabled person in work. There is a guarantee that the job will be done with the help of job coaches who are employed by the placement agency and who train, assist and support the worker in the work environment. Thus, instead of compensating the employer for low productivity as with wage-subsidy schemes, the emphasis is on the job being done at the usual level of competitivity.

In the USA, supported employment must meet the following criteria:

1. The job must provide a minimum of 20 hours per week of work up to full-time employment, consistent with the individual's stamina.
2. The employee must be paid at or above the minimum wage or at a rate which is commensurate with the individual's productivity level and based on the prevailing wage rate for the job.
3. Fringe benefits should be similar to those provided for the non-disabled.
4. Employment must be community-based and afford the disabled person regular opportunities for integration with non-disabled workers.
5. No more than eight persons with disabilities should work together.

The US government has set up well-funded programmes to assist individual states in supporting this approach through the development of cooperative inter-agency services (ie, educational and vocational rehabilitation). As in Genoa, this approach has become a viable alternative for employment and rehabilitation training for those with severe disabilities.

Supported employment has proved to be very successful in the USA even with very disabled clients and it also looks to be cost-effective. It is estimated to be cheaper than traditional day centres and sheltered employment.

Both the Genoa and the supported environment approaches lead to disabled workers being absorbed into the regular labour force. They both operate with an up-to-date model of disability which emphasizes the interaction between the person and the environment in their conceptualization of disability, along with the importance of finding ways to modify the environment to meet the needs of the disabled person. At the same time, they stress people's abilities in the work environment and not their disabilities, as is so often the case.

Support for people with disabilities must be broadly defined and include financial and human aspects. Support must also be looked at from the point of view of employers and trade unions. Other important issues include the length of the job support, the type of support, eg, whether it comes from inside the firm or from outside. The potential intrusiveness of support for preventing integration of the disabled person into the work place must also be considered.

Evaluation

Evaluation has a key role to play in the development of all services provision, including that of transition. Assessments of disabled students leaving school should not be such as to limit choice by stating what they may or may not be able to do, and thus fulfil a predictive function. Instead, they should be an evaluation of what the student can do in real-life situations outside the school and form the basis of the individual transition plan.

Monitoring of services

The transition services themselves require monitoring along a number of major dimensions from which a number of criteria for good transition services may be identified. They are discussed below.

1. *Do services have integrative or segregative policies and practices?* Comprehensiveness, clarity and relevance of information is essential because of the fragmentary nature of services for, and responsibilities to, disabled young people in most countries. Thus the extent to which policies and practices themselves are integrative or segregative must be considered.

2. *Are services oriented towards care or dependence?* The transition programme must be broadly conceived, having an adequate balance between preparation for work, independence, participation and adult family life. It must not be narrowly conceived to reflect the interests of a single professional group.

3. *Are staff client-oriented and do they consider the whole person?* Professionals should work together to ensure coherence and progression in what is offered. How are consistencies and continuities in programmes monitored? Do the professionals who work with disabled young people extend their interest in that individual to involve parents and family concerns?

4. *Are services flexible and do they recognise individuality and choice?* Services need to be flexible to meet the needs of individuals and should avoid stereotyping their clients who are entitled to an individual transition plan. Do services recognize individuality and choice and do they initiate cooperation with other agencies, or are they inward looking?

5. *Does the programme emphasize participation?* At the end of transition an effective programme should result in young people who are capable of managing many areas of their lives. Does the programme emphasize choice, self-presentation and participation in decision-making?

6. *Do professionals help their clients to make decisions?* Are professionals changing to a role whereby they help clients to make decisions and not merely guide them into something they, the professionals, deem appropriate?

7. *Who has control of the resources?* Are resources channelled through professionals or does the programme help the young person to gain control over them and take responsibility for managing both their own time and available resources?

Future directions

Like many aspects of work relating to the disabled and other minorities, work in the field of transition points to the necessity for simultaneous reform at many levels. There is an urgent need for progress, as this is such a crucial stage in the lives of disabled people. Since successful transition to work is dependent on the actions of so many different agencies such as education, employment, health and social services, the difficulties must not be underestimated. In addition, this period is one of change for students and their families and is quite naturally charged with much anxiety and emotion about future life styles. Furthermore, there are other reasons for concern. Disabled people are discriminated against on the labour market (OECD, 1992). It is sometimes suggested that if young people are not in employment by the age of 25, they become increasingly less able to find work and will join the ranks of the long-term unemployed. Transition work is, for all of these reasons, a key period (if not *the* key period) and deserves greater attention by governments. This section will discuss some of the main issues that have arisen in the course of the work at the OECD which are in need of further consideration.

In the past, services have developed in the context of care, but now, because of pressures from parents, the disabled themselves and professionals, governments are looking more towards the development of conditions in which independent living is the main goal. To achieve this, it is necessary for all parties concerned to try to see the possibilities in a new light. This is needed not only because of the change of attitude towards the disabled themselves by many in society, but also because most of the developed countries need to change the balance between passivity and activity and involve disabled people fully in the 'active society', and by so doing give them the opportunity to contribute to their own and their country's economic and social growth. The work that the OECD has carried out has pointed up very clearly where many of the problems lie.

Definition of disability

After many years of discussion, there is still no internationally agreed definition in the field of disability that is acceptable across the span of a young person's life. Many countries have adopted the term 'special educational needs', but many retain categories of handicap. The problem is amplified in the transition phase where so many different agencies, operating under different sets of rules, are involved, as a recent OECD report points out (OECD, 1992). Ideas of handicap still persist in countries in the employment field even if the term has no currency within education, and even though it is now widely agreed that the only acceptable definition is one that sees the handicapping nature of disability as situationally determined. In some circumstances, disabled people may be able to function as well as any non-disabled person but in others they will not. What determines success or otherwise is largely a feature of the conditions, the environment and attitudes and expectations of others. Examples of successful open labour market transition services have been described which demonstrate that, given the necessary support, disabled people can live and work perfectly adequately in open employment.

There is, then, an urgent need for further discussion in this area of definition in order to begin to align thinking across services and between countries. The work described above in Genoa, Italy, and the supported employment model of the USA are both clear examples of what can be done, given the determination. However, a recent OECD enquiry into employment policies for people with disabilities (OECD, 1992), which sought information from its member countries about their policies and practices for the employment of disabled people, found that adult disability resulting from illness or trauma was the main interest. There was very little material on the entry of young disabled persons into employment or on the employment of young people still completing their education. This was almost always seen as the responsibility of education and rehabilitation agencies designed for disabled adults. Thus re-entry into employment and not initial transition was the major concern.

Another recent OECD report (OECD, 1991) has identified the coordination of services as one of the key issues in developing effective transition; the examples of the Danish Kurator and the case manager in the USA hae been cited above. But a number of barriers to the effective coordination of services have also been identified. These include the following.

1. The duplication of services which leads to inefficient use of resources and confusion in the minds of clients, for instance with regard to different assessment procedures. The process of working with disabled people is poorly developed in determining what they want, how much independence they want and where they see their futures lying. This means that the process of assessment must change from one which assesses the present state of the disabled person and which attempts to predict some sort of future path, to one that has several stages at which individual needs and directions are identified and is open to adjustment as the life path develops.

2. There is a need to develop common goals for different services that will almost inevitably work under differing legal and policy frameworks and financing structures. Separate bureaucracies spring up which spend their time protecting their own turf.

3. 'Political fadism' is also a difficulty and if services do not have agreed common goals, these can often change with different prevailing ideologies, thus making cooperation, coordination and continuity extremely difficult.

4. There is a lack of defined outcomes for those with disabilities, such as whether people actually find homes or jobs. Too often the goals of agencies are to provide the services that they define, although often there is a genuine conflict between meeting needs and maintaining the service. Accountability requirements can frequently determine why a service *cannot* be provided. The problem then becomes how to make the top-down control responsive to bottom-up pressures.

5. Turf-guarding is also an important issue in the maintenance of the various services and agencies. A move to generic provision or a unified but multi-professional or multi-agency service will too often mean a loss of resources and status for many highly skilled professionals whose talents cannot afford to be lost. Furthermore, it is essential to have the new arrangements in place before dismantling the older services.

6. There is a need for joint professional training right at the beginning of the relevant courses. This is essential in developing an understanding of other professions' thinking and constraints on action. This problem can frequently exacerbate the lack of communication which may occur between services, each of which has developed its own way of proceeding.

7. Finally, there are financial disincentives. Financial support is often provided to help disabled people to live but which also has the effect of keeping them out of the labour market, since the allowances will be cut once work has been found. To lose this support or have it replaced by rewards for working would be threatening to any person, but it can be especially so for disabled people. For these reasons, passive benefits of this kind may well encourage dependence.

Addressing barriers

Two types of solution to the problems posed above have been suggested. The first involves identifying or setting up models of service that are multi-disciplinary, multi-agency and client-centred. Their effects would then need to be assessed and evaluated. It is important that the evaluation framework is broadly conceived and draws not only on statutory services but also on other inputs, eg, business, foundations and voluntary organizations. Furthermore, it should cover the whole life-span from birth to death. The object of this exercise would be to determine a structure that was effective in managing the problems of disabled people.

The second type of solution involves empowering individuals and giving personal choice. Professionals would need to change their attitudes and see their role as assisting individuals to select the most appropriate service or set of services to meet client needs. At the moment, disabled people must accept what services offer, in the way they offer them. The future objective would be to give disabled people the option of choosing what they need, when they need it. This approach requires a comprehensive assessment of the disabled person, and of course what is included under the umbrella term 'comprehensive' must be identified. This approach of empowerment gives adult status to individuals and allows them to assume responsibility for their own lives.

It is clear that managing the rights of disabled people has major implications for social reform and service organization. In spite of much rhetoric and considerable change in social policy in many countries, change has been slow in coming about. Difficulties in making structural changes to statutory services have already been mentioned, but the involvement of business has also been less then enthusiastic. An OECD report (OECD, 1992) showed that the disabled were heavily discriminated against in employment opportunities and even if they were able to find work, career paths were often difficult to carve out. In order to encourage business to employ the disabled, many countries have legally enforceable quota systems and other incentives to encourage employers to take on the disabled. However, in many countries employers opt to pay fines rather than employ disabled workers. The success of supported employment schemes may depend to some degree on flexibility between support services and employers in terms of wage subsidy. For example, in Italy wage subsidies are used to support mentally retarded employees during their first year of work. During this time, employers are not expected to pay wages while the employee learns both the job and how to interact with other workers. Support is also provided to the disabled worker. After a year, support and wage subsidy are withdrawn and the employer is expected to pay real wages. In many cases, other workers continue to support the disabled employee.

Conclusion

There are many interesting examples of cost-effective ways in which disabled people can make a full contribution to society. changes in support structures must emphasize unity of approach and the coordination of services. Most of all, employers must be persuaded that disabled workers can contribute as fully as the non-disabled; a point that has been reinforced time and again in the research literature.

Finally, it is useful to quote the concluding message of an OECD report on transition:

> The key message of this report is that young people with disabilities need a continuity of support if they are to make a successful transition to adult life. It is essential that departments, agencies and professionals work to agreed ends to provide this continuity so that independence in working life can be achieved by all (OECD, 1991).

References

Daunt, P (1991) *Meeting Disability: a European response*, London: Cassell.

Gerry, M (1992) 'Economic consequences of the unemployment of persons with disabilities', in *Transition to Employment*, proceedings of the 1990 international symposium on the employment of persons with disabilities, Institute for the study of exceptional children and youth, University of Maryland at College Park.

OECD (1988) *Disabled Youth: the right to adult status*, Paris: OECD.

OECD (1990) *Labour Market Policies for the 1990s*, Paris: OECD.

OECD (1991) *Disabled Youth: from school to work*, Paris: OECD.

OECD (1992) *Employment Policies for People with Disabilities*, Labour market and social policy occasional papers No. 8, Paris: OECD.

Part 5: Current issues

16. Community-based rehabilitation

Brian O'Toole

Present challenge

A decade ago a series of international reports estimated the population of disabled persons to be as high as 10 per cent (Rehab International, 1981; UN, 1982; UNICEF, 1980). More recently, the figures quoted are more conservative (Jaffar, 1985, Mittler, this volume). However, it is debatable whether any reliable surveys have been carried out in developing countries to ascertain the precise magnitude of the problem. There has been widespread reluctance to cooperate with such surveys (Husbands, 1985). Surveys in Botswana and Mexico were stopped because of the perceived futility of counting heads when no services were available (Hindley-Smith, 1981; Sebina and Kgosidintsi, 1981).

While the precise numbers could be debated, the need is very clear. Disability often creates considerable social, economic and emotional cost to the disabled person, their family and the wider community. Without effective rehabilitation, disabled persons may lead unhappy, dependent lives and may become burdens to themselves and to society. The challenge falls disproportionately on those in the developing world where disabled persons often live without dignity, victimized by beliefs that they are possessed by evil spirits or proof of divine retribution (Gudalefsky, 1985). An estimated 75 per cent of the disabled population live in developing countries. The indicators are that as long as poverty, ignorance, superstition and fear continue, the figure may well rise significantly by the end of the century (Noble, 1981).

Inadequate response

Disability perpetuates underdevelopment, in both the North and South, by the failure of nations to harvest the productive capacities of all their citizens. No nation can morally or practically ignore a problem affecting such numbers. However, the present model of rehabilitation, based on institutional care, would absorb more than the total health and education budgets of most developing countries if serious attempts were made to meet the needs of all disabled persons. Governments have to respond. For practical reasons however, more economical approaches will need to be explored to meet the magnitude of the task.

It has been estimated that existing services may be meeting no more than 2 per cent of those in need (Mendis, 1988). Such an assessment is based on reports from Africa (Arnold, 1986; Nyathi, 1983; Serpell, 1983) and Asia (Berman and Sisler, 1984; Miles, 1991). Lest we make the mistake of feeling that the problem is only acute in the developing world, a recent report by the International League of Societies for Persons with Mental Handicap, *Education for All* (ILSMH, 1990) concludes that the regular school has denied participation to handicapped children throughout the world. Their conclusion is that handicapped children have been deprived of their right to belong and to contribute to their communities.

This bleak assessment is therefore based on reports from all corners of the world. Where rehabilitation services are available, they are concentrated predominantly in urban areas. The intention was to establish comprehensive services centrally, staffed by highly competent personnel with the hope of expanding them progressively as resources increased until the whole target population was covered. The reality has been very different. Services have become centred on urban areas accessible only to a small and privileged section of the community.

In light of the millions of persons in need, the prevailing institution-based model of rehabilitation has come under severe criticism (O'Toole, 1991). The undue concentration on an urban élite, the adoption of unnecessarily high standards of training, the narrowness of specializations and the isolation from normal life are some of the criticisms levelled at this approach to rehabilitation.

The problem is aggravated by a low take up of services in certain sections of the community as a result of dissonance between the cultural orientation, values and expectations of service providers and potential clients. McConkey (1986) observes that the very persons in need of services are the least likely to seek out help. Some method therefore needs to be found to make the services relevant and accessible to rural and minority peoples.

Search for an appropriate model of services

One reason for the lack of progress is that the professional roles which have been adopted in developing countries are inappropriate to the needs of those societies. Karey's (1984) comment that 'special education in Africa is profoundly European in origin, practice and prejudice, in spite of Africanisation', is relevant to much of the developing world.

Bolden's (1985) review of rehabilitation provision in the Caribbean notes that services are patterned on an inappropriate North American model, including intensive overseas training, which results in the therapist returning home with an expertise which is often too sophisticated to apply and which is unsupported by the technology to which they had grown accustomed.

We have been seduced by the modernization mirage which has fostered the illusion that Western skills, knowledge and attitudes should be diffused to developing peoples (Arbab, 1984). In some cases the mirage has become so vivid that many civil servants insist that Western-style institutions are the solution and anything else is humiliatingly second rate. In our blinkered desire to imitate the West, we have lost sight of the true magnitude of the problem. The justification for this focus is the need to 'maintain standards'. However, to the 98 per cent of families who are presently receiving little assistance, the argument concerning 'standards' has no relevance. For them the question becomes, quite simply, whether any significant service will reach them during their lifetime (Mittler and Serpell, 1985).

As we move towards a new century, there is a growing realization of the need for a new concept of development. A top-down model of service delivery is becoming increasingly discredited. The practice in the past was often for social service programmes to have been planned and implemented by bureaucratic institutions without the consultation and involvement of the intended consumers. However, there is increasing recognition that if those who are meant to be helped by innovations do not participate actively with those who would promote the development process, change will be impossible. The active participation of the subjects of development at all phases of the development process is therefore essential.

One of the basic questions now concerns how we can guide individuals who, for so long have been led by others, to take charge of their own affairs. We need to move away from regarding rehabilitation as a product to be dispensed, to offering rehabilitation as a process in which the villagers are intimately involved (O'Toole, 1990).

Emergence of community-based rehabilitation

The 1969 meeting in Dublin of the International Society of Rehabilitation (now Rehab International) voiced the first public misgivings concerning the institutional-based model of rehabilitation (Hindley-Smith, 1981). It was becoming increasingly recognized that the gap between needed services and available provision could not be closed by developing, or even expanding, conventional services. There was a need for a new pattern of services with fewer experts, less advanced forms of training and simplified methods of rehabilitation. The challenge was how to provide the most essential assistance to high numbers of persons utilizing the readily available resources.

The emergence of the concept of primary health care entailed the acceptance of two important principles which had been vigorously resisted earlier. First, that it is more important to bring about even small improvements amongst a large number of people rather than provide the highest standard of care to a privileged few. Second, that non-professionals, with limited training, could provide crucial services. The World Health Organization (WHO) has provided the stimulus for incorporating rehabilitation into primary health care with the publication of a manual, *Training the Disabled in the Community* (Helander *et al.*, 1989).

Because disabled persons live in rural communities, rehabilitation is best done in that environment, with the child's care givers as the primary training agents. The family therefore needs to learn what to do to help and requires a system of support and encouragement.

The goal of community-based rehabilitation (CBR) is to demystify the rehabilitation process and give responsibility back to the individual, family and community. In WHO parlance, a 'Local Supervisor' is recruited from the community and trained. The Local Supervisor could be a health worker, teacher, social worker or volunteer. The Local Supervisor shows a member of the family how to carry out the training programme. A simplified method of rehabilitation is therefore promoted which, in the WHO scheme, is described in a series of booklets. CBR attempts to use existing organizations and infrastructure for the provision of services. Simple tasks are delegated to auxiliaries or volunteers whose performance is monitored by an intermediate-level supervisor.

CBR attempts to involve the community in the planning, implementation and evaluation of the programmes. Links are established with higher referral services to cope with more specialized needs. CBR is an attempt to generate an exponential increase in appropriate skills, distributed to where the needs are by utilizing hitherto unexploited resources in the community. The goal is for rehabilitation to be perceived as part of community development whereby the community seeks to improve itself. Once the community takes on the responsibility for the rehabilitation of their disabled persons, then the process could truly be called community-based. In such a process, rehabilitation becomes one element of a broader community integration effort. CBR therefore emerged as an alternative to institutional-based rehabilitation. It was originally designed for developing countries where disability estimates were very high and the countries were under severe economic constraints.

One decade of experience with CBR

Momm and Konig (1989) observe that rarely in the history of services for disabled persons has an approach attracted as much unqualified support as has CBR. The approach has been adopted and co-sponsored by WHO, UNICEF, ILO, UNESCO and the UNHCR as part of their contribution towards the 'Decade of the Disabled' and is supported by a host of NGOs including Rehab International, World Rehabilitation Fund, Red Cross, SIDA and NORAD. By 1984, 40,000 copies of the WHO manual had been produced, translated into 20 languages (Krol, 1984). The past decade has seen some notable advances in terms of exploring new concepts of service delivery. In addition to the WHO initiatives, there have been a number of other attempts at exploring varieties of CBR programmes.

The Zimcare programme in Zimbabwe (Mariga, 1986) grew out of the recognition that the existing services were not meeting the present needs. The rural out-reach programme was organized by Zimcare Trust which was responsible for the education and training of mentally handicapped persons in the country. Their 15 centres, employing 300 staff, were catering for only 900 persons. Zimcare recognized that more centres were not the solution and therefore began an out-reach programme to help disabled persons in their own communities. An effective partnership was formed with agencies already working in the rural areas – Red Cross, Ministry of Health and the Cheshire Foundation. An effective infrastructure already existed and was well accepted in rural communities, thereby allowing the new programme to be speedily implemented and effectively integrated into the existing community work. The Zimbabwe programme has developed its own materials in the form of illustrated cards complemented by a series of video programmes. The programme offers a ready-made teaching package with a curriculum of activities for parents to use in their homes.

In Kenya, the Family Support Service grew out of a local self-help group which ran a small school in the capital and which realized the need to move into rural areas to meet the needs of disabled persons in the community (Arnold, 1986). The parents learnt methods of helping to facilitate the child's development.The approach was a major step out of isolation for the disabled persons and their families.

Project Projimo in Mexico (Werner, 1986) grew out of a local realization by the village health workers that the needs of disabled persons in the rural areas were not being met. The very name of the project, 'Projimo', means 'good friend' or 'neighbour' in Spanish. The leaders of the community were interviewed and all were found to be involved in some way in the programme (Villegas, 1985). A major objective of the programme was to give the disabled persons and their families the understanding and skill they needed to help disabled persons reach their full potential. Out of a decade of experience, an excellent manual, *Disabled Village Children* has been produced. The detailed and beautifully illustrated manual offers suggestions for working with disabled persons and their families in the areas of recognizing, helping with and preventing common disabilities.

In the Philippines (Valdez, 1991) a high degree of local involvement in the programme was achieved through a process of effective dialogue with the barangay leaders and extensive publicity. The programme expanded into a number of other areas including mini-olympics, leadership training programmes and cultural programmes.

The 3 D Project in Jamaica (Thorburn, 1990) provides integrated community-based services to 600 disabled children of all ages and aetiologies (see Brouillette, J *et al.*, this volume).

Quantitative and qualitative methods have been used to evaluate the Guyana CBR programme (O'Toole, 1991). Portage and Griffiths pre/post-test results showed significant improvements following the training programme. Noticeable changes in the attitudes of the parents towards the child, the community and towards themselves were observed. The effective involvement of the community was also a key feature of the programme. On the basis of the pilot study with 53 pre-school disabled children, a three-year project is now in train in three coastal and two interior areas of the country.

In the great majority of the above examples, if it were not for the CBR programmes, the disabled persons concerned would have received no help from any other source. A significant number of the disabled children responded to the simplified rehabilitation that CBR offered. People began to see what could be used within their immediate environment to help the child acquire the next development task.

Despite the very real achievements illustrated in the above programmes, there are as many other programmes where the limitations of the approach have been highlighted. Overwork, poverty, severe social tensions and sheer exhaustion make parental involvement a challenging proposition in developing countries (Miles, 1990; Thorburn, 1990). Amidst poverty the scarcest resource is time which is devoted to survival. Such practical limitations are not only apparent in developing countries; indeed, for the poor in the West, the progress of the handicapped child may be the least of the parents' worries (McConkey, 1986).

The parents most in need may have neither the resources nor the psychological energy necessary to participate in an intervention programme; for them, only fundamental ecological intervention may be appropriate. It may therefore be unrealistic and unreasonable to assume that all parents can adopt the role of teacher in relation to their child.

The overriding conclusion of the International Labour Organization (ILO) in reviewing a decade of experience in the area of CBR has been the realization of the difficulty of introducing effective CBR programmes which will endure beyond the time of external inputs (Momm and Konig, 1989). The ILO conclusion states that they have no experience with a really effective CBR programme which could demonstrate its ability to carry on solely with local resources once external support ends. Presenting CBR as a cheap alternative overlooks the significant needs for resources, supervision and follow-up which are essential to win the support of the community and the disabled persons. The main experience of the ILO has been a respect for the difficulties inherent in introducing CBR programmes.

While there have been some notable successes in the introduction of a simplified model of rehabilitation in the last decade, there is nevertheless a need to look beyond uniformity myths and to explore for whom the CBR approach is meaningful: which children, which families, what types of disabilities and what cadre of workers to use.

The real test of CBR has yet to come. Can CBR expand beyond a relatively small-scale, home-based teaching model into a nationwide community care programme? The logistics of organizing and effectively supporting a widely dispersed cadre of workers needs to be examined. What happens when the protected sub-culture disappears and the temporary system is absorbed into the government system using local officials not so committed to the approach?

Expanding CBR

What infrastructure to use?

A review of the first decade of experience with CBR reveals some fundamental differences in philosophy. In some examples, CBR has been conceived as an entirely non-institutional service, whilst in others it has developed as an out-reach of conventional services. In theory, the approach has been offered as inter-disciplinary, but in practice the majority of studies work within the traditional health system. The difficulty of superimposing rehabilitation tasks on to professional roles which are already clearly delineated is becoming increasingly apparent. The potential contribution of the most extensive rural service, the school system, has yet to be fully explored. The UNESCO (1988) 'Consultation on Special Education' reviewing data from 51 countries makes it clear that the challenge within the education system is no less than the challenge addressed within the health system. Just as the institutional response alone is inadequate within the health system, so too special schools alone could not meet the needs of disabled children.

Of the 51 countries responding to the UNESCO study, 34 acknowledged that they were providing for no more than 1 per cent of those in need. Just as there have been radical changes within the health service in the movement towards primary health care, so too there needs to be a fundamental change in special education.

As yet there is little experience to draw on in terms of CBR provision within an educational perspective. The Kenyan (Arnold, 1986) and Zimbabwe (Mariga, 1986) experience has been in terms of the special schools reaching out. Experience within the regular school system is far more limited. The element of the Guyana programme (O'Toole, 1991) that worked with regular nursery school teachers achieved only moderate success. The challenge is how to incorporate CBR into an existing government infrastructure to expand coverage at an economically viable manner.

Need for on-going training and support

The effective CBR programmes reviewed earlier (Arnold, 1986; O'Toole, 1991; Thorburn, 1990; Valdez, 1991; Werner, 1986) featured regular in-service training even once the initial training was completed. Each client was given a one-year follow-up and visits were gradually phased out once it was demonstrated that more intensive support was no longer necessary. The extensive and prolonged follow-up characteristic of these programmes shows the manner in which these projects do not underestimate the task at hand. The Guyana programme (O'Toole, 1991) illustrated the danger of thinking that the placement of a disabled child into the regular school was enough; it highlighted that this is only the beginning of a process and revealed the need for on-going support of the teachers and the other children in the school. The effective CBR programmes also encourage reflection as to what constitutes effective training. A significant element, no doubt, is influencing the attitudes and expectations of the parents and nurturing the belief that the child is capable of learning and worth helping. If attitude change proves to be a key variable, it will significantly influence the type of training programme offered to the home visitors.

Adequate and appropriate training is therefore a crucial first step. The need for support and supervision is equally essential. For integration to be a viable consideration, particularly in developing countries, we need to examine what support can be offered the regular class teacher in terms of personnel, training and special resources. These were key ingredients in the effective examples from Britain, Sweden and Norway highlighted in the UNESCO report (UNESCO, 1988). Throughout the world a basic need will be for smaller classes which can then allow the teacher the luxury of beginning to address the special needs of each of his or her pupils. The effectiveness of this simple intervention has been seen in Spain (UNESCO, 1988). The experience from Zimbabwe (Mariga, 1986) and from Gaza (Mashal, 1991) shows how Portage-style services can be offered to several hundred families with mentally handicapped children through mobile teams managed by professional staff from the special schools.

A key to improved services depends on a more innovative approach to manpower utilization and preparation. The Projimo experience (Werner, 1986) offers a very supportive model of supervision where the goal of the support appeared to be to promote the confidence of the home visitor and develop the respect of the family for the volunteer. The role of the supervisor was to help the volunteers, the disabled persons and the families to identify their own needs and then to assist in formulating creative responses to the challenges. It is crucial to know when to stand back and allow the participants to take the programme in the direction they choose.

What resources exist to draw from?

More research is needed concerning the qualities needed to be effective as a home visitor. In the Guyana study (O'Toole, 1991) there was no significant correlation between the educational background, income or occupation of the home visitors and their effectiveness on the task. Both the Guyana and the Philippine (Valdez, 1991) programmes show that volunteers can be highly effective in the role of home visitors. More imagination is now needed in terms of the deployment and recruitment of volunteers from the community with limited time commitments, linked on a person-to-person basis. Project Projimo (Werner, 1986) illustrates the impact such a programme can have on its principal players. The self-confidence and self-worth of the participants grew as they realized they could contribute something of value to others. Such people can become agents for change, awakening people to their potential and to their rights.

Of all the resources available, the other children in the school offer the greatest potential for real change in the lives of disabled children. A decade of experience with CHILD to CHILD activities has illustrated the value of simple and practical approaches for improving the lives of children. Careful thought needs to be given to see how to develop this rich potential for peer tutoring.

Work needs to be done to see how the whole staff of a school could be prepared for the task of integrating children with special needs into the regular school. We need to move beyond depending on the skill and initiative of individual teachers and see how the integration process could be regarded as part of a broad-based programme.

What role can family members play in the partnership with professionals?

Brouillette, J et al. (Chapter 14, this volume) stress the benefits of involving parents as partners when working with children with special needs. The challenge is not to add one more demand on an already overburdened family but to assist in improving the quality of the interaction between parents and children in the time which is available.

A challenge within the school system is to see how to establish an effective partnership between parents and teachers. A major problem to overcome is the parent's scepticism concerning the treatment their disabled child might receive from other children in the school.

Many of the social and emotional needs of parents may be met most effectively by participation in an informal voluntary association with other parents. CBR could, therefore, be supplemented by the establishment of a local network of families who could provide mutual support and assume an advocacy role.

How can community involvement be generated?

Community involvement is repeatedly exhorted in the literature and yet few effective examples are readily available of how it translates into practice. Coordinators of programmes are often highly qualified in technical skills but they also need organizational, social and political skills. The coordinators need to be nurtured for a wider role, helping the community examine their own problems and letting them realize that they have within themselves the capacity to meet many of their needs.

Relationship between CBR and more traditional forms of rehabilitation

In the early days of CBR, the approach was sometimes viewed as an alternative to the institutional model of rehabilitation. Now the two approaches are more wisely regarded as complementary. The institutions still possess an accumulation of experience, opportunities for in-service training, the possibilities for breakthroughs and much-needed family relief. Miles (1985) advocates the development of community-based centres with mid-level trained workers, run by the community, using local materials which could become valuable training bases for both parents and professionals. Such centres could provide a link between the community worker and the professionals and between the disciplines of health and education. The sustainability and technical quality of the programme may depend on this intermediate link.

For too long the literature surrounding CBR has been emotive. Those developing countries where services are only now being developed may offer the background for the emergence of a new pattern of rehabilitation, drawing on the strengths of both CBR and the merits of more traditional approaches. Within the school system, a major challenge is to see what can be done to modify the traditional academic curriculum of the regular school to make it meaningful to the child with special needs. In following the standard curriculum, the handicapped child may well be left at the back of the class to dream the day away.

How can the effectiveness of a programme be judged?

Does CBR work? If so, how? For whom is the approach most effective? How could CBR work better? What types of parents, with what types of children, benefit from which aspects of the programme? Such questions are not easy to answer at present, in part because of the lack of suitable methods for evaluating 'success'. In the evaluation of Project Projimo (Werner, 1986) 60 per cent were found to have clearly benefited from the programme, but many of the remaining 40 per cent had also progressed in more subtle ways. There is a danger in focusing only on what can be readily measured. Intangible feelings of increased hope, improved relationships with others and self-satisfaction are often overlooked. There are few measurement tools for social, affective and interpersonal change. We need to rethink the concept of 'success' and investigate better methods for assessing the quality of life of the child and the family. The 'process' of the intervention needs to be understood, not only the 'results'.

As McConkey (1986) observes, CBR is not one approach, but a philosophy of care which inevitably embraces a number of forms of services in the areas of health, education and social welfare. Each service may play a different role at various times in the person's life. Greatly improved communication is needed between these different partners in the rehabilitation process if meaningful progress is to be achieved in the remaining years of this century. The independent evaluation of the Zimcare programme (Madzima *et al.*, 1985) revealed that the home visitors spent a high proportion of their time on matters other than rehabilitation, such as counselling of family members and assisting the home economically. It is becoming increasingly clear, therefore, that CBR workers need to be skilled in more than the traditional clinical tasks of rehabilitation.

Conclusion

A clear government policy is needed concerning who does what and when, with clear commitments of resources and materials and dissemination of good practice. Few CBR projects have moved beyond small-scale projects to large-scale innovations. As yet few governments have made any significant commitments and investments to establish national CBR services. Most CBR programmes are regarded as 'additional programmes'. Moreover, the attempts that have been made to work within existing infrastructures have often become little more than a minor facet of an existing service provision to which no particular priority is given.

Despite these limitations, in its best examples CBR has demonstrated what can be achieved, at low cost, to create not only better opportunities for disabled children, but a sense of hope on the part of parents that they can play a significant role in the development process. Communities have become more aware of disabled persons in their midst and, at times, have played a major role in planning ways of meeting their needs. CBR offers a new approach to rehabilitation to policy-makers, professionals, planners and community leaders and to the disabled persons themselves.

Progress has been slow and uneven when one surveys the first decade of CBR. It is significant, however, that some of the most creative examples of parental-professional collaboration have come from some of the poorest nations. It may be a case of the developed world looking south for innovative approaches to meeting the challenge of working with disabled persons.

As we move closer to a new century it becomes evident that the challenge of disability has yet to be met. It is, however, quite clear now that traditional approaches can do no more than scratch the surface . A radical reappraisal of our respective roles in the rehabilitation and education of persons with disability is required. CBR offers such a role.

References

Arbab, F (1984) 'Development a challenge to Baha'i scholars', *Baha'i Studies Notebook*, **3**, 1–19.

Arnold, C (1986) 'Reaching families in rural areas', paper presented at the 9th International Conference of the International League of Societies for Persons with Mental Handicap, (ILSMH), Rio de Janeiro, Brazil, August 21–9.

Berman, P A and Sisler, D G (1984) *Rehabilitation of the rural blind: an economic assessment of a programme in the Philippines, 1978–1983*, New York: Helen Keller International.

Bolden, J (1985) 'The deficit of rehabilitation services in the Caribbean', *NEWS Cart*, **1**, Jan-Mar.

Gudelefsky, A (1985) 'Training programmes for persons who are working with the mentally handicapped', paper presented at the 7th Asian Conference on Mental Retardation, Taipei, Taiwan.

Helander, E, Mendis, P, Nelson, G and Goerdt, A (1989) *Training the Disabled in the Community*, Geneva: WHO.

Hindley-Smith, R (1981) 'Helping disabled people in the home; a new approach to rehabilitation', *PAHO Sci Pub*, No. 411.

Husbands, E (1985) 'CBR in St Lucia', paper presented at the First Joint Caribbean Congress on Disability and Rehabilitation, San Juan, Puerto Rico, August 18–23.

ILSMH (1990) *Education for All*, Brussels, Belgium: ILSMH.

Jaffar, R (1985) 'Report on the Community Based Rehabilitation in District Jhelum, Pakistan', prepared for UNICEF, Lahore, Pakistan.

Karey, K (1984) 'Who needs literacy?', *British Journal of Visual Impairment*, Spring, 111–13.

Krol, J (1984) 'Principles and implementation of CBR', paper presented at the 15th World Congress of Rehabilitation International, Lisbon.

McConkey, R (1986) *Working with Parents; a practical guide for teachers and therapists*, Beckenham: Croom Helm.

Madzima, S, Matambo, A R and Else, J F (1985) 'Report on the evaluation of Zimcare Trust's home-based education programme', (mimeo).

Mariga, L (1986) 'Promoting a better quality of life for persons with mental handicap', paper presented at the 9th ILSMH Conference, Brazil.

Mashal, T (1991) 'Caring for disabled children in the West Bank and the Gaza strip', *CBR News*, April, No. 8.

Mendis, P (1988) 'Evaluation of a Community Based Rehabilitation project in Tiang Giang and Ho Chi Minh', (mimeo).

Miles, M (1985) *Where there is no Rehab Plan; a critique of the WHO scheme and some suggestions for future directions*, Peshawar, Pakistan: Mental Health Centre.

Miles, M (1990) 'A resource centre developing information based rehabilitation', in Thorburn, M and Marfo, K (eds) *Practical Approaches to Childhood Disability in Developing Countries: insights from experience and research*, Memorial University of Newfoundland: Project SEREDEC.

Miles, M (1991) *Mental Handicap Services: development trends in Pakistan*, Peshawar, Pakistan: Mental Health Centre.

Mittler, P and Serpell, R (1985) 'Services for persons with intellectual disabilities: an international perspective, in Clarke, A M, Clarke, A B D and Berg, V (eds) *Mental Deficiency; the changing outlook*, 4th edn, London: Methuen.

Momm, W and Konig, A (1989) 'ILO conceptual paper on CBR', submitted at the 6th Inter Agency meeting of the UN Decade of Disabled Persons, Vienna, Austria, December 5–7.

Noble, J H (1981) 'Special inquiry in the prevalence of disability; projections for the year 2000', *Assignment Children*, **1**, 53/4, 23–32.

Nyathi, L (1983) 'The disabled in rural Zimbabwe', *African Rehabilitation Journal*, **1**, 11.

O'Toole, B (1990) 'Step by step, a community based rehabilitation programme with disabled children in Guyana', *Notes, Comments Series*, No. 189, Paris: UNESCO.

O'Toole, B (1991) *Guide to Community Based Rehabilitation Services*, UNESCO Guides for Special Education No. 8, Paris: UNESCO.

Rehab International (1981) 'Childhood disability its prevention and rehabilitation', *Assignment Children*, 53–4, 43–76.

Sebina, D and Kgosidintsi, A D (1981) 'Disability prevention and rehabilitation in Botswana', *Assignment Children*, 53–4, 135–52.

Serpell, R (1983) *Mobilising Local Resources in Africa for Persons with Learning Difficulties or Mental Handicap*, report of a workshop in Nairobi, November 1982, Belgium: ILSMH.

Thorburn, M (1990) 'Childhood disability in developing countries; in Thorburn, M and Marfo, K, *Practical Approaches to Childhood Disability in Developing Countries*, Memorial University of Newfoundland: Project SEREDEC.

United Nations (1982) *Vienna Affirmative Action Plan*, IYDP/SYMP/LR/Rev. 1, New York: UN.

UNESCO (1988) *Consultation on Special Education*, Paris: UNESCO.

UNICEF (1980) *Childhood Disability, its Prevention and Rehabilitation*, report of Rehab International to UNICEF, New York: UNICEF.

Valdez, J (1991) 'CBR in the Philippines', *CBR News*, 8, May, 6–7.

Villegas, J C H (1985) 'A study of a CBR programme in Mexico', dissertation for MSc in Maternal and Child Health, Institute of Child Health, University of London.

Werner, D (1986) *Project Projimo, a Village-run Rehabilitation Programme for Disabled Children in Mexico*, Palo Alto, CA: Hesperian Foundation.

Werner, D (1987) *Disabled Village Children*, Palo Alto, CA: Hesperian Foundation.

17. Special education in developing countries: instructional content and process

David Baine

Introduction

The following discussion reviews the nature of special education curricula, instrumental methods and instructional environments commonly found in developing countries. Various types of integrated and segregated instructional programmes are described. Also discussed are methods for deciding which types of instructional environments (integrated, segregated and/or community-based), curricula and programme (activity, pre-academic/academic, pre-vocational/vocational) may most effectively meet the needs of handicapped students. Although examples from particular developing countries are described, it is felt that the circumstances discussed are representative of developing countries in general.

Curricula

In India, the national government provides a broad framework of objectives and principles along with prototype texts and learning materials for the regular education curriculum (Kohli, this volume). The preparation of curricula and textbooks is the responsibility of each state where the curriculum has become highly centralized. In principle, some adaptation is possible at the local level; in practice, however, the pervasive emphasis on using elementary schooling as academic preparation for secondary schooling discourages local adaptations (Ahmed *et al.*, 1991). A number of special education curricula are available from places like the National Institute for the Mentally Handicapped in Hyderabad; the National Council for Educational Research and Training in Delhi, and the HJ College of Education in Bombay.

In China, there is a national curriculum and the same books are used across the country in both regular and special schools. Although current regulations permit 20 per cent of the primary curriculum to be locally developed, because resources are limited, there is essentially a uniform and standardized curriculum all over the country (Ahmed *et al.*, 1991). Handicapped children follow the regular curriculum but at a slower rate; there are no printed materials adapted to children with learning difficulties (Potts, 1989). The programme for deaf and blind students is basically the same as that for regular primary students. There are some Braille textbooks for blind children having the same content as textbooks for normal children, but there are no books about mobility and orientation, daily living and vocational skills (Bailun and Jinglin, 1991). Stevens *et al.* (1990), in a recent review of schools in China, found no evidence of curricular and instructional adaptation for students with mild learning problems in regular primary schools. Because of the highly competitive system of promotion by examination, children with handicaps are generally unable to gain entry to regular, junior high schools.

In Tanzania, the programme for students with handicaps lists three categories of instruction; a) ordinary subjects (taught in regular education), b) compensatory skills (such as orientation and mobility, and auditory training), and c) activities of daily living and self-help (see Kisanji, this volume). Currently, however, compensatory skills and activities of daily living are not on the timetable and are treated as extra-curricular subjects taught outside the regular school schedule. Furthermore, these subjects do not have syllabi and, as a result, they frequently go untaught (Msengi, 1990). Comprehensive special education curriculum development is currently under way at the Institute for Curriculum Development in Dar es Salaam (Msengi, 1990).

Instructional environments

In China, there are no classes in ordinary schools for students who are deaf or blind. At the Xian School for the Deaf, instruction is based on the textbooks of the national curriculum with all pupils doing the same thing at the same time (Potts, 1989).

Since the mid-1980s, priority has been given to the education of students having intellectual handicaps; mildly to moderately retarded students attend special classes or special schools. The needs of students having learning disabilities have not yet been addressed (Stevens *et al.*, 1990).

In India, most specialized programmes/schools for children with handicaps are located in urban areas (Narayan, 1992; NCERT, 1987). Special schools are not generally available in rural areas; non-government programmes, barring a few exceptions, do not operate extensively in rural areas (Narayan, 1992). Seva-in-Action is one of the exceptions. This programme, operating out of Bangalore, provides a comprehensive rural education programme.

Referring to students who are blind, Vlaardingerbroek and Tottemham (1991) reported that special schools are usually located in larger cities. Educational programmes are not offered to many rural areas in the Middle East, Latin America, the Philippines, Nigeria or India.

How common is integration?

In Tanzania, most units for special education students are self-contained classrooms within regular school compounds and are not integrated with the rest of the school. These units usually provide services for children having visual impairments or mental retardation. There is some integration of students having visual impairments, but no integration of students having mental retardation (Mboya, 1991). Referring to children with hearing impairments in Africa, Dery (1991) reported that educational provision centres on children with severe and profound losses; large numbers of students with mild and undetected cases are enrolled in ordinary schools, with no support.

In Zambia, the unit model is located in primary schools, where predominantly partially sighted children are taught separately by a specialist teacher; these students do not attend any lessons in the ordinary class of the main school (Kalabula, 1991). Referring to students who are blind, Vlaardingerbroek and Tottemham (1991) reported that the situation in developing countries continues to be dominated by special schools as the site of both disability-specific and general education. In India, all visually handicapped students are placed in residential schools; the students are segregated from home, neighbourhood and society (Sharma, 1988).

Although the philosophy of integration of students with hearing impairments may be popular in other parts of the world, Dery (1991) suggested that in Africa, considering the difficulties integration programmes would face resulting from large classes, inadequate teaching and learning aids, food shortages, transportation problems, illiteracy and the scattered nature of communities, it makes sense to have special schools. In these circumstances, special, residential schools tend to provide a more stimulating and enabling environment than do regular schools.

'Involuntary' rather than 'intentional' mainstreaming is the norm for schools for black students in South Africa. Students having moderate to mild physical or mental handicaps are frequently found in regular classrooms because no other option is available. Many severely handicapped children receive no education (Green, 1991).

Whether on the basis of a philosophy of education or simple economic necessity, some handicapped students in developing countries are placed into regular education classrooms. For example, Costa Rica has adopted a general policy of integration (Villarreal, 1989). In China, because the 124 blind children in one area were spread over 116 villages, because of problems involved in transportation and because it was not possible to provide a specialized school in each village, children having visual impairments were required to study in regular classrooms in their villages (Bailun and Jinglin, 1991).

Regular classrooms

In India, 41 per cent of all primary schools were housed in thatch huts, tents and similar improvised facilities, and 36 per cent had only one teacher (in the mid-1980s) while 20 per cent of rural habitations had no primary school at all (Ahmed et al., 1991). In China, in 1988, 5 per cent of all primary school facilities were classified as dangerous, 6 per cent of the schools had no desks or chairs (the proportion reached 25 per cent in some provinces) and under 10 per cent had the minimum prescribed learning aids and equipment. Over 25 per cent did not meet minimum state qualifications for teaching in 1990 (Ahmed et al., 1991). It is common practice in large parts of rural areas of both India and China for children to squat on mud floors in the absence of desks and benches (Ahmed et al., 1991).

Usually the number of students in regular classrooms in various developing countries is quite large. For example, in Lesotho, the ratio of teachers to students is from 1:65 to 1:100+ (Pachaka, 1990). Villarreal (1989) reported that in Costa Rica, with large numbers of students, inadequate numbers and types of instructional materials and a lack of adequately trained personnel, it is very difficult to provide individualized or even small-group instruction.

In the discussion that follows, practical suggestions are made for improving the instruction of students with special needs, integrated into large, regular classrooms in developing countries. These techniques are more fully described in Baine (1989/1991b).

Buddy system

A 'buddy' is a student assigned to help another less capable student. For example, a buddy may read printed materials to a student having visual impairments, aid movement of a student having physical handicaps, and assist recall of a set of instructions for a student having intellectual deficits.

Student tutoring

In student tutoring, one student offers one-to-one instruction to another student. The tutor may be older than the tutee (cross-age tutoring) or of the same age (peer tutoring). Usually, the tutor is of average or above average ability, but students with handicaps have also been successfully engaged as tutors (Osguthorpe and Scruggs, 1986). In ripple tutoring, a few students are trained to tutor each other, then the number of tutors is gradually increased as the tutors train additional students to act as tutors (Osguthorpe, 1984). In all cases, tutors and tutees must be properly matched, and tutors must be appropriately trained and supervised. In a well-designed tutoring programme, both the tutor and the tutee can benefit academically, socially and attitudinally.

Cooperative learning

In cooperative learning, students with various levels and types of abilities are organized into groups so that different students engage in different sub-tasks, according to their abilities, while working toward group goals. Each student contributes to achieving the common group goals. Cooperative learning has been used effectively in grades 2–12 in language arts, mathematics, social studies, science and foreign language learning (Salend, 1990; Slavin, 1987). (See Baine [1991a] and Johnson and Johnson [1980] for a description of the steps required to establish cooperative learning.)

Teacher aides

Teacher aides may include parents and/or people from the community with specialized skills, who are paid or unpaid. Teacher aides should be taught exactly what to do, how to do it, when, where and with whom.

Teaching tutoring scripts

Teaching scripts guide aides and tutors. The scripts describe what to say and do at each step of instruction, how to present materials, how to reward correct performance and how to correct error responses. Aides and tutors rehearse the script and, in advance of teaching, demonstrate their ability to use the scripts in the appropriate manner. Once trained to teach specific skills, aides or tutors, rather than staying in one classroom, can be shared by several teachers. Baine (1991a) provides examples of teaching scripts.

Resource teachers

Bailun and Chong (1990) describe the Golden Key Project under way in 50 counties in China. Because blind children are scattered over wide geographic rural areas where no specialized programmes exist, the children are integrated into regular classrooms. To assist each of these blind children, resource teachers are trained in Braille and instructional methodology for blind children. Each county has one or two itinerant teachers who assist the regular classroom teachers. The blind students also receive the assistance of 'juvenile vanguards' and the student's parents.

Small-group instruction

Lecturing to the hypothetical average student in a classroom may not suit the needs of individual students who deviate from average. Baine (1991a) and Salend (1990) describe a series of guidelines for delivering lectures. Alternatively, teaching students on a one-to-one basis may not be the most effective or efficient method of instruction. There are a variety of approaches to small group instruction (Baine, 1989/1991b).

In concurrent instruction, several closely grouped students are taught the same skills by a teacher, at the same time. All students in the group must be at the same general level of achievement and must be able to benefit equally from the same type of instruction.

In sequential group instruction, students may be at the same or different levels of achievement and may be taught the same or different skills, using various methods of instruction. A teacher works briefly with one student, then works briefly with another. During the total period of instruction, the teacher works several times with each student in the group. Sequential instruction involves massed instruction (rapidly repeated trials on the same task) and distributed practice (repeated trials on a task alternating with other activities). Massed and distributed practice enhance acquisition and maintenance of learning. In addition, sequential instruction may improve observational learning and behaviour management. Methods of individual and group instruction are discussed in Baine (1989/1991b).

Learning centres

A learning centre is a space in a classroom reserved for students to work on independent, guided learning. The centre provides a student with a) space to work, b) all the equipment and materials required, c) instructions describing what to do and how to do it, d) a checklist for evaluating work, e) answer sheets, f) forms for recording performance and g) a guide for correcting work. Learning centres may be used to provide students with individualized instruction, additional practice, alternate instructional activities, and/or enrichment activities. Learning centres are designed so that one or more students can be involved at the same or different times with little or no maintenance (Baine, 1991a).

Creative scheduling

Scheduling arrangements may make it possible for teachers to provide occasional individual or small-group instruction to students with special needs. For example, one teacher may take most of the students from two classrooms for an activity requiring little supervision, while the other teacher may provide special instruction to the remaining students. Alternatively, both teachers may be freed to provide more individualized instruction when relatively untrained aides, volunteers or students supervise activities that do not require teacher supervision.

Another scheduling strategy that may provide teachers with increased opportunities for individual or small-group instruction involves concurrent rather than sequential scheduling of instructional activities. For example, reading (in which some students may require individualized instruction) and arts and crafts (requiring less intensive instruction) may be scheduled for the same period of instruction. While some students are involved with the craft activities, the teacher may provide individual or small group instruction in reading. During the one-hour period, all students would have the opportunity to participate in both activities for various periods of time, depending upon their individual needs.

Transitional placements

Transitional placements in specialized programmes are sometimes used as preparation for placement in regular classrooms. Vlaardingerbroek and Tottemham (1991) describe brief transitional placements of students with limited vision in residential schools in Papua New Guinea. In these programmes, children are trained to master disability – specific skills such as mobility, reading and writing in Braille and social skills in preparation for integrated enrolment in primary schools in their home area. Teachers in the regular classrooms in which the students will be placed receive in-service preparation. In the regular classroom, integrated students sit at desks with Braille machines and take part in normal classroom activities such as discussion and questioning. A buddy is appointed to help them by reading aloud exercises written on the blackboard or in books. In addition, a specialist resource teacher prepares materials and assists regular classroom teachers.

The National Council for Educational Research and Training (NCERT, 1987) in India has published an excellent handbook on integrated education of persons with various types of disabilities. The handbook recommends integration of students having physical, intellectual or sensory handicaps, to the extent possible, in

a. regular schools/classrooms with regular education instruction; or
b. regular classrooms with curricular and instructional modifications and support from a special teacher; or
c. regular classrooms with modifications and part-time withdrawal to a resource room for special instruction; or
d. a special education classroom in a regular school.

The handbook recommends that to benefit from regular school/classroom, preliminary preparation may have to be done in homes and/or early childhood care and education programmes, and/or in pre-schools attached to regular schools, and/or in pre-school and parent counselling centres, or special schools. Narayan (1989) has prepared two booklets describing methods of organizing special schools and special classes in regular schools in India.

The National Council of Educational Research and Training discusses composite area planning for the sharing of resources within classrooms, schools or districts within a geographical area (particularly in rural areas with scattered populations). Based on a survey of needs and resources, composite area planning may involve establishing regional resource centres, itinerant resource personnel, and organizing sharing of personnel and material resources.

Integration?

In developing countries a very small percentage of children having disabilities are served in schools. For example, in India not more than 1 per cent of mentally retarded children and 5 per cent of deaf and blind children are estimated to be in schools (NCERT, 1987). In Zimbabwe, only 5 per cent of deaf children are in school (Dery, 1991). In Tanzania, only 1.4 per cent of children with handicaps are receiving an education (Msengi, 1990). In many parts of Africa, since education in general is neither free nor compulsory, there are few laws governing the provision of special education (Dery, 1991).

Should students with handicaps be integrated? During a recent tour of India, American disability experts (McWhorter, 1992) repeatedly discussed the dangers of creating segregated services, with audiences whose grandest visions for people with mental retardation were the luxury of special schools and even residential centres to save the children from the dearth of support available in villages.

The decision as to what instructional environment to choose must be made not simply on the basis of philosophy, but of student needs and where and how these needs can be best met. Students with special needs often require teachers and other personnel (eg, occupational, physical, sensory and speech therapists) with specialized skills, as well as specially adapted environmental conditions/ arrangements, curricula, instruction, equipment and instructional aids and materials. The decision is not simply one of choosing between an integrated or segregated environment. The essential question is that of determining what variety of environments are or could be available and which combination of environments, curricula, instructional methods, etc, will best fulfil a student's social, communication, academic, vocational, recreational and life skill needs. The selection of optimal instructional environments must be based on outcome measures; which combination of environments and instructional methods and materials will best prepare a student to perform as effectively as possible in the current and future environments in which he or she must ultimately perform? A series of considerations related to selecting instructional environments are listed below.

Environmental considerations

• The environments selected should be the least restrictive and most effective instructional environments depending on the particular students (current skills and type of instruction required), the skills to be taught and the stage of instruction (acquisition, maintenance and generalization). Thus, for a particular student, various skills may be taught at different times in a combination of integrated or segregated, normative or specially designed, school or community-based environments, depending on the student's needs, at the time.

• Because instruction in classrooms is often not directly related to common, daily task demands students face in natural environments, and because many handicapped students frequently have difficulty generalizing the skills they learn in classrooms to an improvement in performing functional tasks in the community, it is recommended that some instruction should be conducted in the community. For example, people in the community, having specialized skills and equipment, could be brought into the classroom to assist teachers to train specific skills to students. Students could be taught child-care at the local nursery, animal and plant care at a community farm, and carpentry and tinsmithing at village workshops. Construction of separate school facilities may be neither necessary nor desirable. (See Bergmann [1985] for an excellent discussion of how agriculture can be meaningfully taught at the primary level of school.)

• The least restrictive, most effective, instructional environments should be selected, based on the results of testing each student's actual performance in less restrictive environments. It cannot be assumed that an individual who behaves inappropriately in one environment will also behave inappropriately in another, less restrictive environment (Brown *et al.*, 1983).

• To the maximum extent possible, instruction should be provided in the environments (eg, markets, paddies, villages, streets, etc) where the skills being taught are ultimately expected to be performed.

• To the maximum extent possible (based on an evaluation of instructional effectiveness), a variety of activities (recreational, social, educational, home skills, vocational and community) should be conducted in the presence of a variety of non-handicapped persons (children, adolescents, adults, friends and strangers, playing a variety of roles). Wherever necessary and possible, well organized and structured interactions should be arranged between non-handicapped persons and students with handicaps (adapted from Baine, 1991c).

• In the past, a bottom-up approach was commonly used; students with handicaps were placed in segregated facilities and a rationale had to be given for moving up the instructional environments hierarchy to less restrictive, more normative environments. It is now considered more appropriate to take a top-down approach in which students are placed at the top of the instructional environment hierarchy and evidence has to be given for moving to a more restrictive environment.

• In the past, it was common to select one level of the instructional environment hierarchy at a time, for example, a residential care facility, a segregated classroom in a regular school, or a regular classroom placement. It may be of greater benefit to use a combination of instructional environments to answer the variety of instructional needs that may occur at any one time. Classrooms may not be the only or the best instructional option. Instruction in one or more natural environments in the community may enhance acquisition, maintenance and generalization of skills. For example, for one student it may be appropriate to conduct most of the instruction in community environments: recreational, vocational, residential and retail. The same student may receive some instruction in regular classrooms and in highly structured, segregated environments in which community-related skills can be repeatedly rehearsed under controlled conditions. At various times, students may require different combinations of segregated and integrated instruction; the proportionate combination of each type of instructional environment may change, depending on the skills being taught.

Instructional programme and curricula

Over the last decade, in spite of limited economic and personnel resources, there has been an heroic growth of programmes for handicapped students in developing countries. For example, two recent directories of services in India (Reddy and Narayan, 1988; 1989) list 348 special schools and training centres for persons who are mentally handicapped.

Many of the programmes in various developing countries are excellent. They have a clear and well determined sense of purpose. Programme goals and instructional methods are well suited to both the types of students being served and to local resources and circumstances. Other programmes appear to have difficulty selecting instructional goals and methods to best serve their students. The following discussion provides a review of various common types of instructional programmes.

Activity programmes

Some programmes focus primarily on providing activities such as simple cut-and-paste crafts, colouring pictures, assembling picture puzzles, etc. These programmes provide basic motor and sensory stimulation, teach students to identify some of the primary colours, teach simple counting, and train students in basic social and communication skills. For students who would not benefit from academic or vocational training, and for whom alternate types of programme are not available – frequently because of the absence of well trained teachers with specialized skills – these programmes provide a protective and entertaining environment. Considering the alternative of sitting at home, these programmes provide an essential service. Activity programmes, however, are not suitable for all handicapped students. Although it is necessary for all students to learn suitable recreational skills, the acquisition of *functional* home and community skills is also essential. There is substantial evidence to indicate that most handicapped students can learn a variety of functional skills that will enhance their ability to perform more effectively in a variety of environments in which they find themselves each day. These functional skills must be taught, directly. Frequently, it is apparent that some students in activity programmes have the capability of acquiring skills at a much higher level.

Pre-academic and academic programmes

Many programmes in developing countries teach readiness or pre-academic skills that have commonly been included in curricula developed in the West. Readiness tasks include activities such as: stacking blocks, putting rings on a peg in order of size, stringing beads, completing interlocking puzzles, and putting geometric shapes in a formboard. These tasks are taught, not because students will be required to perform any of these tasks in their daily lives, but because the skills required to perform these tasks, for example, eye–hand coordination and colour, size and shape discrimination are a part of many tasks. As such, these skills are sometimes considered to prepare learners to perform other, more functional tasks requiring the same skills. Unfortunately, students who improve their ability to perform readiness tasks may not experience a similar improvement in the performance of functional tasks requiring similar skills. The research literature strongly suggests that skills should be taught directly in the form in which they must ultimately be performed in the natural environment (see Baine, 1987; 1989/1991b).

Other programmes focus primarily on academic activities. Sometimes, the special education academic curriculum is merely a 'watered-down' version of the regular education curriculum. Some of the more difficult tasks have been replaced by simpler craft activities and/or a limited number and type of life skills (Baine, 1989/1991b). Often the expected academic achievement of the handicapped students in these programmes is extremely low and subsequently, instruction in academic skills is neither intensive nor enthusiastic. Thus, the prophecy of low achievement is fulfilled and the cycle repeats itself.

For students who can learn to read and/or write and/or compute well enough to use these skills in the natural environments in which they perform, academic programmes are essential, provided, of course, that these students also learn the variety of recreational, social, communication and vocational skills that are equally required in their current and future environments. It is apparent, however, that some of the students in programmes that focus primarily on academic skill training are unlikely ever to acquire a sufficient level of competency to use these skills in the natural environments they frequent. For students having moderate mental retardation, it should be clearly understood that academic achievements are relatively unimportant in comparison to social adaptation and vocational training (Narayan, 1992).

Pre-vocational and vocational programmes

What types of programmes are available and how should suitable programme options be selected? Some guidelines for selection follow.

General programme goals

What are the general goals that should direct the development/selection of suitable programmes, curricula and methods of instruction for all students with handicaps?

- To teach functional skills – those social, personal, emotional, communication, recreational, vocational, etc, skills required in each student's daily life.
- To teach the skills required in each student's contemporary and future life.
- To teach the skills that will permit each student to participate in as many least restrictive environments as possible: home, school, community and vocational.
- To teach the skills that will permit each student to perform as fully, as normatively, as independently and as chronologically age-appropriately as possible.

Goals for selecting instructional methods

- To teach the optimum number and type of skills in a cost-effective manner, requiring the least time, effort and resources expended by both students and teachers.
- To teach in a manner which will best enhance skill acquisition, maintenance and generalization; for example:
  - teach skills in the same form and in the variety of natural environments in which they must eventually be performed;
  - provide opportunities for massed trial training to assist the acquisition of difficult skills (those requiring more training trials for mastery) and distributed practice to enhance maintenance (see Baine, 1989/1991b);
  - teach combinations of various functional skills in the natural sequences in which they characteristically occur in the natural environment. For example, in combination, teach the social, language, motor and academic skills required to make a purchase in a market;
  - test for generalization and maintenance of skills in the environments in which they must eventually be performed; whether skills are initially taught in segregated or simulated conditions, ultimately, sufficient practice must be provided under the usual variation of naturally occurring conditions.
- Be cost-effective to both the teacher and student; that is, the amount of time and effort put into teaching and learning skills should be in proportion to the relative functional value of the skills to the particular learner involved.
- Teach skills in the least intrusive, most positive, most normative and most effective manner possible. (The foregoing suggestions are adapted from Baine [1991c].)

Goals for selecting curricula

- Academic skill training should be directly related to common, daily task demands students are or will be required to perform in their current or future daily lives.

- A suitable blend of academic and practical skill training should have the following goals:
  - acquisition of a sufficient number, level and type of academic skills for the student to attain the highest level of academic training of which she or he is able to achieve *competent, practical use;*
  - acquisition of basic life skills required to function effectively in home, school, community and vocational environments, now and in the future;
  - acquisition of a broad spectrum of social, communication, recreational and vocational skills required to function adequately as an adult;
  - acquisition of the skills required to adapt to environmental changes resulting from factors such as increased industrialization, technological change, and movement from rural to urban areas.
- Ahmed *et al.* (1991), writing about China and India, stated that an emphasis on life skills has to replace the emphasis on academic preparation for successive levels of instruction that overshadows the whole teaching and learning process. An environment has to be created for a learning process responsive to local conditions and learner's needs.
- A number of basic needs and non-formal education programme in existence for some time (eg, Botti *et al.*, 1978; Mbilinyi, 1977; Saunders and Vulliamy, 1983; Tietze, 1985; UNESCO–UNICEF, 1978) include the type of skills that should be taught in curricula for handicapped students in developing countries. Briefly, some of these skills include:
  - reading, writing and arithmetic related directly to real life situations in, for example, agriculture, health and home care;
  - communication related to common daily events;
  - individual and group recreation in the home and community;
  - agriculture, such as soil cultivation, fertilization and irrigation;
  - home management such as food selection, storage and preparation;
  - health care, such as identification, prevention and treatment of common diseases (Baine, 1989/1991b).
- The skills taught in a curriculum should fulfil the immediate and long-term needs for individuals, the family and the community. Although some basic skills may be common to curricula designed for various geographical areas, many specific skills and knowledge taught will vary according to the locality in which students live.

Building curricula

- Curricula should be built following a study of the economic, social, political and cultural characteristics of the particular environments within which students do or will live. Baine (1989/1991b) describes an ecological inventory method for developing special education curricula in rural and urban areas of developing countries.
- Vocational programmes should be offered following a careful assessment of current and projected community needs.
- Curriculum content should be selected on the basis of regional trends in areas such as, farming technology, industrialization and movement from rural to urban areas.
- Curricula should be developed following an analysis of the skills and

knowledge students will require to live and function adequately as adults (adapted from Baine, 1989/1991b).

Conclusions

In spite of limited economic, technical and personnel resources, there has been an heroic growth of programmes for students with handicaps in developing countries. Many of these programmes are excellent; some less so.

In developing countries, limited resources make successful programme development and implementation most difficult and most necessary. This chapter has attempted to describe some of the difficulties associated with the development and implementation of effective, culturally suitable, special education, institutional curricula, methods and environments. Also identified are some of the many considerations essential to effective programme development.

References

Ahmed, M, Ming, C K, Jalaluddin, A K and Ramachandran, K (1991) *Basic Education and National Development*, New York: UNICEF.

Bailun, X and Chong, C Y (1990) 'The Golden Key Project: the status of integrated education for blind children in China', *The ICEVH Educator*, **3**, 31-3.

Bailun, X and Jinglin, H (1991) 'Promoting development and popularization of integrated education for visually impaired children, *The ICEVH Educator*, **4**, 22-9.

Baine, D (1987) 'Testing and teaching functional versus generic skills in early childhood education in developing countries', *International Review of Education*, **33**, 147-58.

Baine, D (1989/1991b) *Handicapped Children in Developing Countries: assessment, curriculum and instruction*, Edmonton, Alberta: Vector Project, Department of Educational Psychology, University of Alberta.

Baine, D (1991a) 'Methods for instructing students with handicaps integrated into regular education classrooms in developing countries', *Psychology and Developing Societies*, **3**, 3, 157-69.

Baine, D (ed.) (1991c) *Instructional Environments for Learners Having Severe Handicaps*, Edmonton, Alberta: Vector Project, Department of Educational Psychology, University of Alberta.

Bergmann, H (1985) 'Agriculture as a subject in primary school', *International Review of Education*, **31**, 155-74.

Botti, M, Carelli, M D and Saliba, M (1978) *Basic Education in the Sahel Countries*, Hamburg: UNESCO Institute for Education.

Brown, L, Nisbet, J, Sweet, M, Donnellan, A and Gruenewald, L (1983) 'Opportunities available when severely handicapped students attend chronological, age-appropriate regular schools', *Journal of the Association for Persons with Severe Handicaps*, **8**, 3, 71-77.

Dery, S E (1991) 'The education of visually handicapped children: an African perspective', *Kenya Institute of Special Education (KISE) Bulletin*, **5**, 16-19.

Green, L (1991) 'Mainstreaming: the challenge for teachers in South Africa'. *Support for Learning*, **6**, 2, 84-9.

Johnson, D W and Johnson, R T (1980) 'Integrating handicapped students in the mainstream', *Exceptional Children*, **47**, 90-98.

Kalabula, D M (1991) 'Educating visually handicapped children in Zambia: a summary of provision and a look to the future', *The ICEVH Educator*, **9**, 2, 20-24.

Mbilinyi, M (1977) 'Primary school education: aims and objectives of primary education', in *The Young Child Study in Tanzania, Age 7-15*, Dar es Salaam: Tanzania National Scientific Research Council.

Mboya, R M (1991) 'Instructional methods for students with mental retardation in Tanzania', unpublished doctoral dissertation, University of Alberta, Edmonton, Alberta, Canada.

McWhorter, C (1992) 'Rehabilitation in India', *TASH Newsletter*, **18**, 2 and 3, 11.

Msengi, Z M (1990) *A Proposal for Special Education Curriculum Package in Tanzania*, Dar es Salaam: Institute of Curriculum Development.

Narayan, J (1989) *Organization of Special Classes in a Regular School and Organization of Special Schools for Mentally Retarded Children*, Secunderabad, India: National Institute for the Mentally Handicapped.

Narayan, J (1992) Personal communication with the National Institute for the Mentally Handicapped in Secunderabad, India regarding India's national policy on Education, Program of Action.

NCERT (1987) *Planning and Management of IED (Integrated Education of Disabled) Programme: a handbook*, New Delhi: National Council of Educational Research and Training.

Osguthorpe, R T (1984) 'Handicapped students as tutors for non-handicapped peers', *Academic Therapy*, **19**, 474–83.

Osguthorpe, R T and Scruggs, T (1986) 'Special education students as tutors: a review and analysis', *Remedial and Special Education (RASE)*, **7**, 15–25.

Pachaka, L (1990) 'Early childhood special education in Lesotho', *International Journal of Special Education*, **5**, 3, 370–73.

Potts, P (1989) 'Working report: educating children and young people with disabilities and difficulties in learning in the People's Republic of China', in Barton, L (ed.) *Integration: myth or reality?*, London: Falmer Press.

Reddy, S H K and Narayan, J (1988; 1989) *Directory of Institutions for the Mentally Handicapped Persons in India*, Secunderabad, India: National Institute for the Mentally Handicapped.

Salend, S P (1990) *Effective Mainstreaming*, New York: Macmillan.

Saunders, M and Vulliamy, G (1983) 'The implementation of curricular reform: Tanzania and Papua New Guinea', *Comparative Education Review*, **27**, 351–73.

Sharma, S (1988) 'Mainstreaming the visually handicapped', *Indian Educational Review*, **13**, 30–41

Slavin, R E (1987) 'Cooperative learning: where behavioral and humanistic approaches to classroom motivation meet', *The Elementary School Journal*, **18**, 29–37.

Stevens, R, Bowen, J, Dila, K and O'Shaughnessy, R (1990) 'Chinese priorities in special education', *International Journal of Special Education*, **5**, 3, 324–34.

Tietze, U (1985) 'Non-formal primary education of fisherfolk in Orissa: an experimental approach', *Journal of Indian Education*, **11**, 11–24.

UNESCO–UNICEF (1978) *Basic Services for Children: a continuing search for learning priorities*, Paris: UNESCO.

Villarreal, B (1989) 'An analysis of the special education services for children and youth in Costa Rica', unpublished doctoral dissertation, University of San Diego.

Vlaardingerbroek, B and Tottemham, A (1991) 'Integrated primary schooling of the blind in Goroka, Papua, New Guinea', *International Journal of Special Education*, **6**, 297–308.

18. Varieties of school integration

Klaus Wedell

Introduction

Concern to integrate pupils with special education needs (SENs) into ordinary schools is widespread within many countries in the world. However, the way in which this concern is being acted upon, and the significance of the arrangements for individual pupils and their families, varies widely. In this chapter, integration will be discussed primarily in relation to practice in the age range of compulsory school attendance. The aim is to examine those factors which determine how integration is approached and how these influence its impact on those involved. Experience and practice from different countries will be used to illustrate the points made.

The chapter starts with a brief resumé of the origins of concern for integration and a description of how it is conceived. Following on from this, the main part of the chapter is concerned with the way educational policy and provision determines how integration occurs in schools.

The origins of concern for integration

Concern for integration arises in most countries from two origins: first, the recognition of the rights of all members of the community to equal opportunity and second, the development of the concept of special educational need.

Rights

The assumption that the aims of education are the same for all is one which affects how a country organizes its education system as a whole, but the assumption has a particular import for pupils with disabilities and significant learning difficulties. In England, the assumption was made explicit in the report on special educational need produced in 1978 by the Warnock Committee set up by the government (Department of Education and Science, 1978). The Committee stated that:

> The purpose of education for all children is the same; the goals are the same.

But the help that individual children need in progressing towards them will be different.

This assumption has been the basis on which all children are now regarded as entitled to be educated regardless of the degree of their SENs.

As Daunt (1992a) has pointed out, countries differ in how they set about formulating legislation about integration. In Brazil, the 1989 law concerning integration makes it subject to practicality, but similarly to the UK, does not allocate funds for ensuring its implementation. The USA Public Law 94-142 was more specifically based on the principle that all children are entitled to be educated in the 'least restricted environment'. It thus starts out from the requirement that the ordinary forms of educational provision should apply to all children. The Danish official policy specifies the requirements of integration in more detail:

- the child should attend school as close to home as possible;
- the support to the child should differ as little as possible from ordinary education;
- the child's education should be offered in the most 'normal' setting possible;
- the child's education should follow the ordinary curriculum requirements as far as possible;
- the education offered should meet, as far as possible, the wishes of the parents and the teachers (Labregere, 1992).

These are just some examples of the ways in which the right of children with SENs to participation are formulated in different countries. In many countries, the concern for integration forms part of a general commitment to the rights of minorities, and in most it was parents who pressed for the principle to be applied to the education of their children. In more recent times, some groups of individuals with disability have come to assert their rights as minorities to be *different*, rather than to be aligned to the majority (Oliver, 1992). Among those with hearing impairment, for example, there are some who have asserted their right to communicate in sign language as any other minority group with its own language. Educationally, the implication has been drawn that children should initially be taught sign language, and would then learn to communicate orally as a second language. This line of argument challenges the view which promotes integration with the majority.

The concept of SENs

The other main determinant of moves towards integration derives from the changing concept of SEN. This is a term which was used in the title of a book by Gulliford (1971) and taken over by the Warnock Commission in the UK. It was chosen as an explicit rejection of the categorical view of disability and handicap. The Warnock Commission recognized that the main question to be answered was: what were the educational needs of the children and young people? These needs could not be directly inferred from a description of a child's disabilities, since educational needs were the outcome of the interaction between the disabilities of the child and the extent to which they were compensated by the environment - including the school. In the UK, and increasingly in other countries there has, as a consequence, been a move away from describing children in terms of the categories of their particular disabilities, towards a description of the SENs of the child. In general, this can be seen to represent a move from a 'disease' model of children's deficits, to an educational model. The relevance of physical disabilities or impairments is not denied in this argument, but it does point up the fact that, because of the compensatory interaction mentioned above, physical impairment and disability only partly determine the nature of SENs.

The concept of SEN is of significance for integration in a number of respects. Because SENs are seen to be the *outcome* of the interaction between factors within the child and factors within the environment, they occur across a range of degree from mild to severe. As a result, it is not possible to draw a hard and fast line between children with and without SENs. Similarly, because it is not possible to make direct inferences from disabilities and impairments to educational need, children with SENs cannot be distinguished in this way. On both counts, it is therefore apparent that the 'specialness' of a child's needs is determined by the extent to which the educational provision available in ordinary schools affords an effective compensatory resource. In other words, whether or not a child's educational needs are 'special' is defined by the nature of the education which is generally offered in schools. To this extent, special education comes to be defined in relation to ordinary education (Wedell, 1990).

If 'special' educational provision is only offered in a segregated form, this may primarily be due to the way in which provision is organized, rather than to the needs of the child. The question then arises whether a child is educated in segregated provision only because the necessary level of support is not available within the ordinary schools system. Any analysis of integration therefore has to start with an examination of the nature of the systems of 'ordinary' education.

Systems of ordinary education

Patterns of educational development

When compulsory education becomes univerally enforced, the state usually starts to set up special schools, to meet the larger representation of pupils with SENs. In most countries, this development is paralleled by health or welfare provision for those with the most severe or multiple needs who, at that point in the development of educational provision, are usually not regarded as requiring education. Gradually, provision becomes more specialized as the variety of children's special needs becomes recognized. With increasing demands on achievement in schools, the learning needs of pupils become more apparent, and so special needs support starts to be provided in ordinary schools. However, for as long as there is less than total take-up of schooling, there is likely to be a group of children and young people who have SENs among non-attenders and early drop-outs. A high proportion of these are likely to have more severe SENs than those in ordinary schools, but less than those in special schools. Take-up may also vary between age ranges, and in the course of the development of educational provision in countries, primary education is usually made compulsory before secondary. For example, most Asian countries are currently aiming to provide universal primary education by the year 2000, and the World Bank is currently studying the scope for integration which this offers for primary pupils with SENs.

The demands for integration are superimposed on this historical sequence in the development of countries' patterns of educational provision. Integration obviously has a different significance in educational systems where the take-up is less than total in all or some of the provision made. Integration is also determined, in different countries, by policies about providing education in a segregated form, and by the scale of special support offered in ordinary schools. As a result, statistics about the proportion of pupils with SENs who are 'integrated' in a country are hard to obtain and even if they are available, their meaning may be uncertain. An attempt has recently been made to establish the proportion of children who are integrated in about 20 countries which are currently taking part in a study carried out under the aegis of the Centre for Educational Research and Innovation of the OECD, but it has been found to be almost impossible to make comparisons across these countries because of all the variability mentioned above and, additionally, because of differences in the definition of SENs and of their degree.

Policies for integration

In some countries, such as Italy, policies for integration have been adopted through legislation by the central government, and this has been the starting point for change throughout the education system provided by the state. Other countries, such as Spain, have adopted similar legislation, but the introduction of integration in schools for which the central government is responsible has been based on an incremental system, whereby individual schools are invited to change to integrated provision and are then provided with resources for doing so. Another form of policy, such as that in the UK, has been to establish enabling legislation, which permits schools or decentralized educational authorities to develop integrated provision, but does not make it obligatory. Some countries, such as Austria, introduce integration through a limited system of experimental projects, in which a variety of different forms of provision are studied.

A major variation between countries lies in the extent to which funds are made available to achieve integration. It is generally agreed that integration provision for SENs tends, at least initially, to be more costly than segregated provision (Bowman *et al.*, 1985). Consequently, legislation which does not include financial support is less likely to lead to change. The UK is one example of a country which introduced legislation encouraging integration without providing dedicated funding. Unless the general level of educational funding in a country is realistic, such legislation may have little beyond an exhortatory effect.

Many countries are currently decentralizing responsibility for educational provision to regions or districts. Decision-making about the education of children with SENs is then correspondingly devolved, leading to local variations in the level of provision. Such devolution may put integrated provision for children who have rarer forms of SENs in jeopardy, since it may not be possible to offer the necessary specialized services locally on an economical basis.

Furthermore, in times of financial constraint, funding to meet children's SENs may in any case be threatened because it has low priority in policies.

What is meant by integration?

There has been considerable debate about whether integration should be regarded as an aim of education or as a means of achieving an individual's integration into society. The outcome has been that some prefer to apply the concept of 'participation' in the normal life of a society, both during and after schooling. As indicated by Hegarty (this volume), this may be regarded as achievable through locational, social or functional means. Daunt (1992b) recognizes that these educational arrangements may be regarded as distinct but cumulative aspects of participation, so that functional integration, for example, involves participation at all the three levels. The scope for participation will vary from one activity to another. For pupils with severe learning difficulty, for example, it may be easier to achieve functional integration for music than for algebra, but as soon as one makes such a comment, the interaction between the context and the activity become apparent. This point will be discussed in the context of practice in the next section.

A major factor in the consideration of integration is that segregation is normally associated with stigma. However, in many countries there is now a strong move to link special and ordinary schools more closely (see Hegarty, Best and McCall, this volume, for details on special/ordinary school links and unit provision).

Ultimately, it is as important to consider how the pupil and the parents perceive the education offered, as how effective the learning experience is for the pupil. Participation has subjective as well as objective components. This is one of the reasons why it has been so difficult to evaluate integration as a process. The main problem about evaluating the effects of integration has been the fact that ethical considerations have made it unacceptable to allocate pupils randomly to the groups to be compared. The selection of pupils in ordinary provision inevitably leads to doubts about whether they are really comparable in the relevant dimensions. This problem then interacts with the nature of pupils' SENs. Meta-analyses have been attempted, such as that of Carlberg and Kavale (1980), and surveys of the literature carried out for the OECD/CERI which are as yet unpublished. Few consistent indications of differences have been found, apart from a trend that integration appears to favour aspects of educational achievement more than self-perception. The methodological problems raise doubts about the meaningfulness of such findings.

The evaluation of outcome studies of integration also have to be considered in the light of different perceptions of the aims of education. Given that educational provision is always constrained by finite financial resources, choices have inevitably to be made between goals. For example, an emphasis on the goal of social integration would lead one to value social integration within ordinary classrooms. However, this is then likely to make it difficult to give pupils with physical disabilities physiotherapy as regularly as would be possible in a designated special school, and the pupils might not achieve optimal mobility. One is therefore left with having to choose to prioritize one or the other goal. A recent study of the preference of parents of children with special needs in the

UK (Audit Commission and Her Majesty's Inspectorate, 1992) showed that 89 per cent of parents whose children were in ordinary schools were happy with their education, compared with 64 per cent of parents whose children were in special schools. The evaluation of integrated provision can only be meaningfully carried out within specified parameters. Retrospective studies of the opinions of those who have received their education in different types of provision are subject to the same kinds of considerations.

Integrated provision and practice for children with SENs

The previous sections of this chapter have indicated that the degree to which children and young people with SENs participate in a country's ordinary education provision is determined by a large number of ideological, policy, financial and conceptual factors. A closer examination of practice shows that there are many aspects of a country's education system which also have determining effects. I will consider these in turn.

The organisation of the education system

As has already been mentioned, a country's system of general education by definition determines the scope for participation by children and young people with SENs. A number of relevant aspects of the system have already been mentioned, such as the age range of compulsory education, and the take-up at successive ages. Scope for participation is determined also by whether schools are given a responsibility to serve the generality of pupils, or whether they are designed to serve pupils in stratified or other groupings. In most countries, primary education is offered on a comprehensive basis, and schools are expected to serve all the children in a locality. In many countries, secondary education is offered on a stratified basis, which implies that participation is already limited by the criteria used to allocate pupils to schools.

As Labregere (1992) has pointed out, a basic consideration is whether schools are geared to modifying themselves to the needs of individual children, or whether it is expected that the children adapt themselves to the schools. For example, in a system which is stratified by achievement level and by type of curriculum, schools catering for pupils with higher achievement levels are likely to have difficulty in meeting the needs of pupils with learning difficulties. Within each level of schooling, it is then likely that teachers are expected to offer only limited degrees of differentiation of the teaching offered, and only to have experience of a limited range of pupils. Participation in this context occurs very much on condition that pupils with SENs adapt themselves to the school. For example, in one of the Länder in Germany, which had a highly stratified secondary education system, the author was told that there was no limit to participation for pupils with SENs, so long as the pupils met the educational requirements of the relevant school. Similarly, the author was asked about the learning problems of pupils in an English medium primary school in Calcutta, India, and this prompted the thought that the problem might be due, in the first place, to the expectation that the pupils were required to communicate in a second language. By contrast, in Denmark, the educational system aspires to provide 'schools for all' (Hansen, 1992). The comment is made that a school without pupils who have SENs is not an 'ordinary' school, reflecting the view that schools should mirror the societies they serve.

The curriculum

Another aspect of countries' educational systems which directly affects the extent to which differentiation can occur, is the nature of the curriculum offered. In countries where the curriculum is prescribed in a very detailed way across a wide range of content, teachers feel that the scope for differentiation is very limited. Where textbooks are also prescribed, teachers may feel a greater obligation to teach the correct page of a textbook on a particular day, than to ensure that all the pupils in a class are in fact learning the prescribed content (Bowman et al., 1985).

Another determining factor is the nature of assessment in the curriculum. Curricula which are prescribed in detail tend to have equally detailed prescriptions for assessment. Teachers may then find it difficult to use the assessment formatively to gain an accurate indication of what the pupil has and has not achieved, and so to respond to the pupil's particular learning needs. In many countries, curricular assessment is predominantly summative, and this leads to the practice of requiring pupils who fail an end-of-year exam to repeat the year's schooling. Such repetition normally takes the literal form of exposing the pupil to the curriculum offered in the previous year, without any modification to match particular learning needs. In Japan, most pupils are sent for private coaching, in the hope that this will enable them to avoid repetition. In some countries, there is an almost automatic procedure whereby pupils who have been required to repeat a year more than two or three times are transferred to special schools.

Pre-school education

The availability of pre-school education also determines pupils' capacity to perform within the range of compulsory education, and this applies even more to children with SENs. In many countries, pre-school education may only be offered on a priority non-fee paying basis to children with SENs or with other forms of individual need. While, on the one hand, this of course offers important support for the children and often also for their parents, on the other hand it also 'selects-out' these children, and so represents a form of segregated provision with the consequent educational drawbacks.

In other countries where there are programmes of welfare and health support for children in general before the age of compulsory schooling, opportunities for supporting the early education of pupils may not necessarily be taken up. By contrast, the Indian Spastics Society has out-reach programmes in rural and deprived urban areas for just this kind of support for parents of children with physical disabilities. In many countries, the Portage programme is used as a way of enabling the parents of children with SENs to support their development (Brouillette, J, et al., this volume).

Provision in sparsely populated areas

Meeting children's needs in school is also likely to be determined by the distribution of population in a country. In sparsely populated areas, schools are often small, serve a small number of children and are staffed by one teacher or only a few. This places greater demands on the teaching offered. However, it has also led to some creative responses to compensate for these difficulties. For example, in Mozambique (Tomo, personal communication), because of the shortage of teachers, it is common for teachers in rural schools to organize the children to help each other and, indeed, to share in the running of the school. Even in contexts where there is a less deficient teacher supply, this form of peer support can make a major contribution to effective learning. Two-way radio can also be used to overcome some of the problems of providing support in sparsely populated areas. In Australia and in parts of the USA, this form of communication is used to offer teachers expert support and even to provide direct help to pupils.

However, provision for pupils with more severe forms of SENs is usually only available in certain locations, and children will then have to leave their home area in order to have access to it. However, this may not entail totally segregated provision. For example, in Finland, children with visual impairment from the sparsely populated areas are offered short-term intensive help at the school for the visually-impaired at Yvaskyla. This type of help is offered in a number of countries, sometimes on a 'summer school' basis, but is provided mainly to pupils with sensory impairment rather than more severe learning difficulties.

Another approach to supporting children with SENs from sparsely populated areas is to provide residential hostels in towns or cities where more support is available in ordinary schools (Best and McCall, this volume).

The professional status of teachers

Since it has been argued that the scope for the participation of pupils with SENs is determined by the support which ordinary schools can offer, it follows that the status of teachers themselves is a major contributory factory. Are teachers expected to use their initiative to modify the curriculum to meet pupils' needs, and if so, are they given time to think out what modification is needed? Furthermore, are teachers provided with training which gives them the necessary knowledge, understanding and skills to meet pupils' individual needs effectively? Last, but by no means least, are teachers paid at a level which encourages them to use their initiative, and at least enables them to derive a sufficient livelihood from their teaching? These are all factors which influence the way in which teachers perceive their potential contribution to supporting pupils with SENs, and their motivation to do so.

The extent to which teachers are expected to take initiatives in responding to individual pupils' needs is very much related to perceptions of the curriculum. In countries where the curriculum, the textbooks and the timetable are highly prescribed, little scope is left for teachers to attend to the individual differences among pupils. Teachers will see themselves under pressure to maintain the pace of curriculum delivery.

School systems differ in the proportion of a teacher's working time which is free of pupil contact. Stevenson and Shin-Ying Lee (1990), reporting on the different levels of curricular achievement reached by pupils in China, Japan and the USA, showed that countries where achievement levels were high allowed teachers greater proportions of non-contact time. This enabled teachers to consider the learning needs of their pupils and also to support each other in the planning of their teaching. One of the main findings of a study of the education of pupils with moderate learning difficulties in England was that this 'thinking time' was crucial if teachers were to tackle the considerable intellectual challenge of responding to pupils' learning needs (Evans et al., 1989).

If more is expected of teachers in ordinary schools to meet pupils' SENs, then they are likely to require more training. Mittler (1992) has commented on the need to include a relevant component in the initial training of teachers, and that those responsible for the training must have the necessary competence themselves. Initial teacher training also has the important task of shaping teachers' attitudes to pupils. Is the training directed at enabling teachers to be sensitive to pupils' learning needs, or are the teachers led to consider themselves solely as specialists in curriculum subjects? In most countries, there is traditionally a difference in this respect between the training of primary teachers and secondary teachers. Primary training is directed more at the learning–teaching aspects, since most teachers at this level are expected to teach across a broad range of the curriculum. Training for teaching at the secondary level tends to be directed more at subject teaching, with less emphasis on effective pedagogy. The limitations of this form of training have often been masked in countries where secondary education is highly stratified, or where it is only available to a selected proportion of the age group of potential pupils.

As Bowman et al. (1985) point out, the training must not only be directed at providing teachers with greater pedagogical competence, but must also provide them with the necessary managerial skills for mobilizing the resources available to them, and to alert them to more effective collaboration with the support services in a country. However, it is clear that further in-service training is also required not only to enhance teachers' knowledge and skills, but also to keep these up-to-date with developments. A project is being developed under the auspices of UNESCO, which is intended to foster collaboration among teachers in a school, with the aim of increasing awareness of pupils' needs and of enhancing teachers' competence in meeting the needs. The project, which has been piloted in several of the UNESCO world regions, aims to produce in-service materials which teachers themselves can use on a group basis (Ainscow, Chapter 19, this volume).

The factors contributing to teachers' effectiveness which have so far been mentioned are unlikely to be of much use unless teachers are paid commensurately with the role expected of them. First, although there is no doubt that the best teachers are attracted to the work through genuine interest in helping pupils to learn, the profession is not likely to attract the best applicants unless the level of pay has a parity with relevant alternative employment. Second, if teachers are not paid at a sufficient level to support themselves and their families, they will have to find supplementary employment.

The organization of the school

Much has been written about 'whole-school policies' for pupils with SENs. There is no doubt that teachers' scope for responding to pupils' needs is very much determined by the school's policy. Does the school see itself as a 'school for all' as already described in Denmark? This will imply that the school's resources are appropriately allocated and that staff are given commensurate responsibilities. It also implies that the school's organization allows for teachers to support each other to achieve the higher levels of skill and understanding required, particularly in developing ways of effectively differentiating the curriculum to fit pupils' needs (Ireson *et al.*, 1992).

Such a school will need to mobilize all the resources available within the school and from outside. Within the school, much will depend on the flexible deployment of staff and the grouping of pupils. For example, a secondary school, reported by Evans *et al.* (1989), which was concerned about its pupils' literacy achievements, gave all its teachers training in how to teach literacy skills and organized the timetable so that at certain times, all staff were involved in small-group work with those pupils who needed help in this area. Schools also supplement their teaching resources by organizing peer support among the pupils. Much attention has recently been paid to the scope for collaborative learning among pupils (Slavin, 1989). Some schools have extended their collaboration to include parents. Parents have been helped, for example, to share in their children's achievement of literacy and in overcoming behaviour difficulties. One of the most extensive examples of extending a school's resources through collaboration was reported by Melaragno *et al.* (1968). This involved the entire community in a very deprived area of California in what was termed a 'tutorial community'. One has to recognize that such a level of collaboration may well exist in a more spontaneous form in the rural communities of some countries, where it is not reported as a deliberate 'project'.

Whole-school policies need also to be directed at the attitudes of the majority of pupils to those with SENs. If participation is to be achieved, the school must establish the attitudes underlying the recognition of rights mentioned in the earlier part of this chapter. Many schools are well on the way to achieving this. For example, in schools where pupils with hearing impairment are included, the hearing pupils may well spontaneously learn signing. Similarly, in ordinary schools attended by pupils with physical disabilities, other pupils will take responsibility for helping pupils in wheelchairs to get around the school. Where there are pupils with more severe learning difficulties, they may share playtime activities with their peers. However, one has to consider whether such interaction actually represents attitudes reflecting parity of esteem between the pupils, which is certainly more difficult to achieve than attitudes which are patronizing to the pupils with SENs.

The effect of types of disability

The content of this chapter so far has indicated that the impact of the nature of pupils' SENs on integration/participation is influenced by the same factors which determine the nature of the educational system in a country. It will have become apparent that the less a pupil's disability requires the prevailing education system to be modified, the greater the scope for participation. For example, a pupil who is able, and who has a hearing impairment, may well be able to lip-read the teacher and to use his or her ability to extrapolate the partially discerned aspects of what is being communicated. This puts minimal demands on those providing the teaching. An able pupil with physical disabilities who is equipped with the necessary microtechnology to respond in a class, may well require little more than structural alterations. The scope for participation in an ordinary school is immediately reduced as the need to modify the curriculum or make the school organization flexible increases.

Teachers' attitudes to the integration of pupils with different forms of SENs also varies in this way. Bowman *et al.* (1985) in their study of teachers to countries in the several world regions of UNESCO, found that teachers' attitudes reflected the practical demands which they felt pupils with different forms of SENs would make within the pattern of resources available to them. Other researchers, eg, Hegarty *et al.* (1981) have found that teachers who had taught pupils with SENs were less apprehensive of having them in their classes.

Support services

The earlier sections of this chapter have covered the extent to which ordinary schools may be able to mobilize their own staff and other resources to meet pupils' SENs. But, as has just been mentioned, the nature of pupils' SENs will also determine how far their effective participation can be achieved, and this also depends on the pattern of specialist support available to a school. Such support take take a variety of forms, including in-service training of school staff, consultation with school managers about ways of increasing a school's responsiveness, consultation with teachers who have direct responsibility for a pupil with SENs and direct work with individual pupils with SENs or with groups. Specialist personnel may be members of peripatetic services provided by a school authority; they may be staff of special schools who have taken on an out-reach role; or they may be specialist staff employed by a school itself. Specialist personnel from health or social services provided by statutory or voluntary bodies may also provide help and advice in a school.

From the point of view of the staff of the ordinary school and of the pupil, the designation of the support personnel is less important than the nature of the actual support they offer. Fish (1989) has suggested a helplful taxonomy for analysing the nature of support. The point underlying the taxonomy is the need to identify the actual effective component of the support contribution. In practice, this is often determined by the particular style and nature of the contribution an individual professional is able to make, rather than by their official service designation. Indeed, it is well known that the degree to which an individual professional can offer expertise may be ultimately determined by the inter-personal skills of sharing the expertise with the teacher or pupil concerned.

Allocation of special provision

In almost all countries there exists a procedure through which pupils are given access to resources which are not generally available within the ordinary school system and which involve additional expenditure, either by statutory services or by insurance funds (Wedell, 1991). The procedures involve a number of principles such as establishing a right to resources, securing commitment to maintaining the resources, and ensuring that the resources match the pupils' SENs. In the USA the procedure involves drawing up an 'Individual Education Plan' and in the UK, maintaining a 'Statement'. In many countries, the procedures are used mainly to allocate pupils to segregated provision, but this depends on the nature of the education systems. Where the procedures are used to provide resources for pupils in ordinary schools, they still have implications for integration. The procedures result in a paradox – while they serve the essential purpose of giving pupils access to resources, they also, by definition, 'label' them and so single them out from others.

Conclusion

The scope for the participation of pupils with SENs in ordinary schools is directly related to the nature of the educational systems of a country and the schools within them. This scope is related to the way in which general educational policy specifies that the systems and the schools should adapt to the pupils they serve, or whether the pupils are required to adapt. In this chapter, the issue of integration has therefore been treated as an extension of the issues surrounding the conception of the general education provided in countries. There is no doubt that the participation of pupils with SENs makes greater demands on educational systems and on the schools and the teachers within them. But this is only a further consideration of what schools are expected to offer pupils in general. The issue of integration/participation challenges countries' education systems to a wide reconsideration of the way in which they are organized and the way in which they function.

References

Audit Commission and Her Majesty's Inspectorate (1992) *Getting in on the Act*, London: HMSO.
Bowman, I, Wedell, K and Wedell, N (1985) *Helping Handicapped Pupils in Ordinary Schools: strategies for teacher training*, Paris: UNESCO.
Carlberg, C and Kavale, K (1980) 'The efficacy of special versus regular class placement for exceptional children: a meta-analysis, *Journal of Special Education*, **14**, 3, 295–309.
Daunt, P (1992a) *Meeting Disability*, London: Cassell.
Daunt, P (1992b) 'Social and curricular integration – models and realities', *European Journal of Special Needs Education*, **7**, 29–35.
Department of Education and Science (1978) *Special Educational Needs*, London: HMSO.
Evans, P, Ireson, J, Redmond, P and Wedell, K (1989) 'Curriculum research for pupils with moderate learning difficulties', report to the Department of Education and Science.
Fish, J (1989) *What is Special Education?*, Milton Keynes: Open University Press.
Hansen, J (1992) 'The development of the Danish Folkeskole, towards a school for all', *European Journal of Special Needs Education*, **7**, 38–46.
Gulliford, R (1971) *Special Educational Needs*, London: Routledge and Kegan Paul.
Hegarty, S, Pocklington, K and Lucas, D (1981) *Educating Pupils with Special Needs in the Ordinary School*, Windsor: NFER-Nelson.
Ireson, J, Evans, P, Redmond, P and Wedell, K (1992) 'Developing the curriculum for pupils experiencing difficulties in learning in ordinary schools: a systematic comparative analysis', *British Educational Research Journal*, **18**, 2, 155–73.

Labregère, A (1992) Unpublished report to the Centre for Educational Research and Innovation, OECD.

Melaragno, R J, Newmark, G, Placeres, V M, Rogers, M M and Williams, S A (1968) *Tutorial Community Project: progress report*, California: System Development Corporation.

Mittler, P (1992) 'Preparing all initial teacher training students to teach children with special educational needs: a case study from England', *European Journal of Special Needs Education*, **7**, 1–10.

Oliver, M (1992) 'Intellectual masturbation: a rejoinder to Soder and Booth', *European Journal of Special Needs Education*, **7**, 20–28.

Slavin, R E (1989) 'Cooperative learning and student achievement', in Slavin, R E (ed.) *School and Classroom Organisation*, Hove, Sussex: Erlbaum.

Stevenson, H W and Shin-Ying Lee (1990) *Contexts of Achievement: a study of American, Chinese and Japanese children*, Chicago, IL: University of Chicago Press, *Monographs of the Society for Research in Child Development* 55, 1 and 2, serial No. 221.

Wedell, K (1990) 'Children with special educational needs: past, present and future', in Evans, P and Varma, V (eds) *Special Education: past, present and future*, London: Falmer Press.

Wedell, K (1991) 'Special educational provision in the context of legislative changes', in Segal, S and Varma, V (eds) *Prospects for People with Learning Difficulties*, London: David Fulton.

19. Teacher development and special needs: some Lessons from the UNESCO project, 'Special Needs in the Classroom'

Mel Ainscow

Introduction

There is evidence from a number of sources that suggests that an emphasis on meeting special educational needs in ordinary schools in part of the educational policies of an increasing number of countries (eg, Pijl and Meijer, 1991; UNESCO, 1988). However, the same sources indicate a gap between intention and practice. Indeed, there is some evidence that despite the existence of legislation that is intended to encourage integration of pupils said to have special needs, the proportion of pupils being excluded from mainstream education in some Western countries is increasing (Ainscow, 1991a; Fulcher, 1989).

A survey commissioned by UNESCO suggested a need to upgrade teacher education in order to support moves towards integration in various countries (Bowman, 1986). The findings of this survey were used as the basis of a series of regional workshops. As a result of this process of international consultation, I was invited by UNESCO to direct a project that would develop and disseminate a resource pack of teacher education materials. Detailed accounts of the evolution and rationale of the project are provided in Ainscow (1990; 1991b; 1992).

This chapter reflects some of the findings of the research associated with the project in order to make some proposals as to how teachers in ordinary schools can be helped to respond and reflect the diversity of their pupils and argues for the reconceptualization of the special needs task. It will also provide some suggestions that have implications for teacher education. Before addressing these issues a brief account of the UNESCO project is provided.

The UNESCO teacher education project

The aim of the UNESCO teacher education project, 'Special Needs in the Classroom', is to develop and disseminate a resource pack of ideas and materials that can be used by teacher educators in different parts of the world to support teachers in mainstream schools as they seek to respond to pupil diversity. Clearly, the design of materials that can be relevant to and take account of such a wide range of national contexts, including those in developing countries, presents an enormous challenge. This being the case, a number of measures were taken during the formulation of the materials in order to achieve a level of flexibility that could take account of diverse settings. These were as follows:

- a pilot workshop for teachers and teacher educators from various African countries was held in Nairobi, Kenya in April 1989. This allowed various materials and approaches to be evaluated;
- further trials were carried out in Turkey during September 1989;
- a number of advisory teams consisting of teacher educators and teachers were created in different parts of the world. These teams provided comment on draft materials and contributed materials and ideas of their own for inclusion in the pack;
- a number of special educators and others involved in teacher development around the world read and commented upon draft materials.

The limited dissemination that has taken place so far has been carried out in order to field-test a pilot version of the resource pack consisting of four modules of working materials and, in so doing, to develop an international resource team that can be used to support the widening of the work of the project.

In April 1990 two coordinators from each of eight countries (ie, Canada, Chile, India, Jordan, Kenya, Malta, Spain and Zimbabwe) took part in a two-week workshop/seminar at the University of Zimbabwe. The group included university lecturers, educational administrators, teachers and one headteacher. The first week took the form of a demonstration workshop during which materials from the resource pack were used to conduct a series of course sessions for the coordinators and a further group of local teachers and student teachers. In the second week, the demonstrated workshop was evaluated during a seminar in which the international coordinators planned together the ways in which they would field-test the resource pack in their own countries.

This field-testing was completed by March 1991 and each team of coordinators prepared an evaluation report on their work. The main aim of the field-testing was to gather information that could be used to inform the further development of the resource pack and to plan its future dissemination. In this way, it has been possible to develop the 16 coordinators into an international resource team who are now collaborating in the design and promotion of the overall project. Dissemination initiatives are under way in a number of countries.

In terms of evaluation, the central question was, 'How can the resource pack be developed and disseminated in a way that will be appropriate for teachers in different countries?' With this in mind, the evaluation was based upon a multi-site case study approach (Miles and Huberman, 1984) in which individual reports attempted to explain what happened as the resource materials were used in a particular context. Reports included interpretations of these events from the points of view of *all* participants. A particular interest was the ways in which the materials and ideas related to the social, cultural and educational tradition of each participating country (Miles, 1989).

Whilst the emphasis was on providing accounts that made sense of what happened in each national context, there was also a need to make comparisons between the experience in different countries. Consequently, a common framework was agreed amongst the team of coordinators in order that evaluation reports would have a common pattern.

Data that could be used to address the evaluation question were collected using a range of procedures, including: journals, group reports, questionnaires, interviews, video recordings and observations. These data were collected both during and after the courses. Care was taken in establishing the trustworthiness of findings. In particular, coordinators were asked to collaborate with their colleagues, including participants, in order to verify their interpretations. The emphasis throughout was placed on recording and taking account of multiple perspectives. Interpretations of the data were also subject to 'triangulation', a process of using two or more sets of information to study and validate an account of one event (Lincoln and Guba, 1985).

In total, the 16 coordinators worked with 235 participants. The field-testing sites involved a diversity of national, cultural, linguistic and teacher education contexts (pre- and in-service). All involved the use of materials from each of the four modules in the resource pack in courses or workshops consisting of at least 30 hours of instructional contact. Some of these were intensive in style (eg, one-week workshops), whereas others involved sessions spread over a period of months. Most included opportunities for participants to carry out follow-up activities with pupils in schools.

The evaluation data indicate that in all of the field-testing sites the materials were used as intended and that course leaders worked in ways that were largely consistent with the rationale of the project. The reports reflect a sense of acceptance and optimism about the approaches that were used. This was apparent even when coordinators were working in very difficult and stressful conditions, not least in Jordan where the field-testing took place during the period just prior to the outbreak of war.

Particular contextual factors created difficulties in certain places. For example, a number of coordinators reported hostility from certain of their colleagues who were unhappy with the emphasis on group work used in the project. Some of the student teachers experienced negative reactions from experienced teachers when they attempted to re-organize classrooms in order to move away from more traditional organizational formats. Difficulties sometimes arose when the materials were used as part of school-based staff development programmes. Once again, negative reactions seemed to occur when approaches were introduced that appeared to challenge existing patterns of working.

It is also worth noting a significant trend that emerged with respect to the reactions of those teachers who had previously been exposed to specialized training in special education. There is some evidence in the evaluation data that members of this group experienced greater difficulty in accepting the value of the approaches used in the resource pack (Ainscow, 1992).

Overall, however, the evidence supports the view that the content of the materials in the resource pack is appropriate for teachers in each of these national contexts, focusing on issues that they find meaningful and relevant. Furthermore, it seems that the activities and processes used are successful in helping teacher educators and, in turn, teachers, to develop their thinking and practice (Ainscow, 1992).

What follows is an account of the conceptualization that informs the content of the resource pack, and a description of the approaches upon which the activities and processes are based.

Reconceptualizing the special needs task

The conceptualization of the special needs task adopted within the UNESCO project has emerged as a result of a critique of existing approaches and through the processes of collaborative planning and enquiry. This has led to the view that the dominant perspective on special needs in education works to the disadvantage of the children it is intended to serve and, furthermore, that the domination of this thinking on practice in the field has the effect of preventing overall improvements in schooling for all pupils.

The dominant perspective that guides the organization of responses to children who experience difficulties in school has been characterized as an 'individualised gaze' (Fulcher, 1989). Put simply, this involves constructing or interpreting problems without reference to the wider environmental, social and political contexts in which they occur.

This individualized perspective on educational difficulties arises, in part at least, from certain assumptions about the purposes of schooling, the nature of knowledge and the process of learning. In their most extreme form, these assumptions lead to a view of schooling as a process by which those who know (ie, the teachers) are employed to transmit their knowledge to those who need to know (ie, the pupils). With this in mind, schools are organized in ways that will facilitate this transmission process efficiently and are, therefore, assumed to be rational (Skrtic, 1991). Consequently, pupils who are perceived as being unable or, indeed, unwilling to take reasonable advantage of the opportunities that are provided are taken to be in some way deficient. Therefore, the focus is on them as individuals and those of their attributes that would seem to be preventing their progress.

Many approaches have been used to provide help to children experiencing difficulties in school. Differences exist with respect to how their difficulties are defined, the forms of treatment that should be used and the organizational formats that are preferred in order to provide additional help. Whatever the style, however, the dominant perspective is usually individualized, thus requiring a process of identification and assessment based upon a scrutiny of those attributes that are assumed to be interfering with the individual child's learning.

Why, then, does this individualized perspective work to the disadvantage of the pupils it is intended to help? Surely a focus on the problems of individual pupils is a basis for positive actions that can help overcome their difficulties? The case rests on the following five sets of arguments:

1. The impact of labels.
2. The framing of responses.
3. Limitations of opportunity.
4. The use of resources.
5. The maintenance of the status quo.

1. The impact of labels

The use of labels to describe individual pupils and summarize the nature of their educational difficulties has been widely critiqued in recent years (eg, Ainscow and Tweddle, 1988; Tomlinson, 1982). Consequently, many teachers are aware of the way that the process of labelling can lead to a lowering of the expectations they have of certain pupils. In some countries, legislation attempts to eliminate the risks associated with labels by abolishing the use of special education categories as the basis of decision-making. However, there is considerable evidence that the phenomena of labelling continues to have a strong influence on thinking and practice (eg, Fulcher, 1989).

It may well be that it is the domination of the individualized perspective that most of all encourages labelling in that it encourages teachers to characterize particular pupils in terms of selected attributes that are assumed to be inhibiting their learning. If this is so, it is necessary to find ways of widening this perspective in order that the problem can be alleviated.

2. The framing of responses

A second set of arguments with respect to the individualized perspective are to do with the way in which it influences the style of teaching responses that are provided. Focusing attention on particular children in an individualized way leads the school population to be divided into 'types' of children to be taught in different ways or even by different types of teachers. Furthermore, since certain pupils are perceived as being special, it seems common sense that they must require special forms of teaching.

I have to say that during my career I have spent considerable time and energy attempting to find special ways of teaching that will help special children to learn successfully (eg, Ainscow and Tweddle, 1979). My conclusion now is that no such specialized approaches are worthy of consideration. Whilst certain techniques can help particular children gain access to the process of schooling, these are not in themselves the means by which they will experience educational success. Furthermore, framing our responses in this way tends to distract attention away from much more important questions related to how schooling can be improved in order to help all children to learn successfully.

3. Limitations of opportunity

A third set of arguments about the influence of the individualized perspective is to do with limitations of opportunity. As a result of focusing on selected attributes of individual pupils, it is usual to provide some form of individualized intervention. This may include the presentation of tasks or materials designed on the basis of an analysis of the child's existing attainment; or it may involve additional adult help in order to facilitate their progress. Despite the potential value of these responses on some occasions, we need to recognize that they can also lead to situations where pupils spend large parts of the school day working alone. If this is so, it is surely to their disadvantage. Most of us learn most successfully when we are engaged in activities with other people. Apart from the intellectual stimulation that this can provide, there is also the confidence that comes from having other people to provide support and help as we work. If children said to have special needs are working alone for much of their time in school, none of these benefits can accrue.

It is worth adding that the presence of additional adults in a mainstream classroom to provide support for individual pupils can also limit opportunities. Too often the support teacher or classroom assistant becomes a barrier to integration, standing between a particular child and the rest of the class, rather than acting as a facilitator of learning opportunities. If, however, additional adults are seen as a means of increasing the flexibility of the teaching that is provided for all pupils, it is likely that educational difficulties will be reduced.

4. The use of resources

Issues to do with the use of resources are a fourth area of concern with respect to the way educational difficulties are defined using an individualized perspective. Defining educational difficulty in terms of the attributes of individual pupils and conceptualizing responses in terms of specialized teaching leads to an assumption that responses to special needs are dependent upon the provision of additional resources. Resources are undoubtedly important, of course, and schools in most countries, even in the developed world, would benefit from better buildings, more equipment and books, smaller classes and more skilful teachers with higher morale. However, attaching additional resources to specific children has a number of potential disadvantages. First of all, it can discourage effort and confidence amongst teachers, since there is an implication that certain pupils cannot be taught within existing resources. Second, it encourages a waste of time and energy in fighting battles for such resources, including the necessity for additional administrators to manage allocations. Third, there is increasing evidence from around the world that struggles to win additional resources for particular pupils lead to an increase in the proportion of children placed in categories of exclusion (eg, Crawford, 1990; Fulcher, 1989; Slee, 1991; Wang, 1991). Finally, additional resources are often diverted from the general school budget. If this is the case we are witnessing a ludicrous procedure by which the 'victims' of a school system are given extra help by transferring finance in such a way that it becomes likely that even more victims will be created.

5. The maintenance of the status quo

A final set of arguments with respect to the individualized perspective is to do with its role in the maintenance of the status quo within a school. This perspective not only works to the disadvantage of particular pupils but also acts as a barrier to overall school improvement.

The dominant approach to the special needs task assumes that the problem is the child's. As a result, it excludes from consideration other factors that lie in larger social, political and organizational processes that are external to the individual (Skrtic, 1991). Consequently, the organization and curriculum of schools remain largely unquestioned and are assumed to be appropriate for the majority of pupils. In this way, opportunities for improvement are missed.

As a result of these five sets of arguments, the UNESCO project, 'Special Needs in the Classroom' has been seeking to conceptualize the special needs task in a different way. The wider perspective we are wishing to encourage involves a recognition that individuals have to be viewed within a given context. In this way, the progress of individual pupils can be understood only in respect to particular contexts, tasks and sets of relationships. Furthermore, we have to remember that our outstanding of individuals is limited by our own personal resources and previous experience. We can, however, compensate for these limitations by considering the points of view of others who bring additional resources and experiences that can help to supplement our understanding.

This wider perspective, therefore, involves teachers becoming more skilled in interpreting events and circumstances, using the resources of other people around them as a source of support. Its focus is on the improvement of learning conditions as a result of a consideration of difficulties experienced by certain pupils in their classes. In this way, pupils who experience difficulties can be seen more positively as a source of feedback on existing classroom conditions, providing us with insights as to how these conditions can be improved. Furthermore, given the interconnections between individuals within a given context, it seems reasonable to assume that these improvements are likely to be to the advantage of others in the class. Thus, widening our perspective with respect to educational difficulty can be seen as a way of improving schooling for all. In other words, an emphasis on equity is a means of achieving excellence (Skrtic, 1991).

Teacher development

In the light of this reconceptualization of the special needs task, how can teachers be helped to adopt a wider perspective to educational difficulties? What approaches to teacher education can contribute to this shift in perspective? These are the issues that we have been addressing in the UNESCO project. The responses to these questions represent our current thinking; this may well change as our work proceeds. In the meantime, the outcomes of the project so far provide some useful pointers to colleagues involved in similar initiatives. Furthermore, they lead to a series of suggestions that may help more generally in the reform of teacher education.

First of all, it is important to recognize the deliberate adoption of the term 'teacher development' as opposed to the more familiar term 'in-service training', avoiding the mistake of using an individualized perspective, in this case with respect to the learning of teachers. So, in a real sense, there is an attempt to conceptualize an approach to teacher development that is analogous to the one outlined in connection with children's learning. Just as successful classrooms provide the conditions that support and encourage all children's learning, so a successful approach to teacher development must address contextual matters in order to create the conditions that facilitate the learning of adults.

The research evidence that is available on the effectiveness of teacher development initiatives is far from encouraging. Despite all the effort and resources that have been utilized, the impact of such programmes in terms of improvements in teaching and better learning outcomes for pupils is rather disappointing (Fullan, 1991; Joyce and Showers, 1988). What is the explanation for this sad state of affairs? What is the nature of the mistakes that have been made?

As a result of his review of available research evidence, Fullan (1991, p. 316) provides the following summary of the reasons for the failure of in-service education:

1. One-shot workshops are widespread but are ineffective.
2. Topics are frequently selected by people other than those for whom the in-service is provided.
3. Follow-up support for ideas and practices introduced during in-service programmes occurs in only a very small minority of cases.
4. Follow-up evaluation occurs infrequently.
5. In-service programmes rarely address the individual needs and concerns of participants.
6. The majority of programmes involve teachers from many different schools and/or school districts, but there is no recognition of the differential impact of positive and negative factors within the system to which they must return.
7. There is a profound lack of any conceptual basis in the planning and implementation of in-service programmes that would ensure their effectiveness.

From this analysis we have a picture of in-service initiatives that are poorly conceptualized, insensitive to the concerns of individual participants and, perhaps critically, make little effort to help participants relate their learning experiences to their usual workplace conditions. It is these limitations that we are trying to avoid within the UNESCO project.

The resource pack contains the following elements:

Study materials. These include an extensive range of readings, stimulus sheets and classroom activities for use during course or workshop sessions.

Course leaders' guide. This provides detailed guidance on how to organize courses and facilitate sessions based on the study materials. A series of case studies describing projects that have been carried out in a number of countries is also included.

Training videos. These include examples of the various recommended approaches in use during courses and film of follow-up activities in schools.

It is important to understand that the materials and activities in the pack encourage course leaders to model at the adult level strategies for teaching that take account of and, indeed, make positive use of student diversity. In this way the features of the pack that are seen as facilitating adult learning within course sessions are intended to be used as a basis for working with classes of children in school.

The content of the materials emphasizes two main strategies for helping teachers to consider alternative perspectives to educational difficulty as a means of improving classroom practice. These are:

- *Reflective enquiry* – influenced by the writings of Schon (1983; 1987), this is an approach to professional development that encourages practitioners to question taken-for-granted knowledge that is implicit in their actions.

- *Collaboration* – here, teachers are encouraged to use the resources of others around them (including colleagues and pupils) to support them as they reflect upon difficulties that arise in their classrooms.

Our attempts to introduce teacher educators and teachers to these two strategies are based upon five sets of approaches that have been developed and refined within the project. These are as follows:

1. *Active learning*, ie, approaches that encourage participants to engage with opportunities for learning.
2. *Negotiation of objectives*, ie, approaches that enable teacher development activities to take account of the concerns and interests of individual participants.
3. *Demonstration, practice and feedback*, ie, approaches that model examples of practice, encourage their use in the classroom and incorporate opportunities for supportive feedback.
4. *Continuous evaluation*, ie, approaches that encourage enquiry and reflection as ways of reviewing learning.
5. *Support*, ie, approaches that help individuals to take risks.

Together, these five sets of approaches are intended to help teachers to be reflective about their practice and support one another in the process of improvement. These approaches also provide the theoretical basis of the successful field-testing that occurred in the eight countries referred to earlier. They were used in working with the 16 coordinators who in turn used them with teachers and student teachers in their own countries. These approaches are now considered in more detail.

1. Active learning

Programmes of teacher development should be devised in ways that encourage those involved to engage actively with resources that can facilitate their learning. In this context, resources might include course activities, other people's ideas and perspectives and evidence from elsewhere. The important point to note is that these external resources are intended to be used by teachers to consider their own previous experience, their current ways of working and their existing beliefs and assumptions. They can also be used to reflect upon wider issues that impact upon the teacher's work.

The concept 'active', therefore, does not necessarily imply physical engagement in some activity (although this can often be helpful in encouraging active learning). More importantly, it means that the learner (in this case, the teacher) is being required to take responsibility for engaging with certain experiences whilst taking note of alternative perspectives. In so doing, it is anticipated that they will be helped in relating new ideas to their existing frames of reference.

Traditional approaches to teacher education, with a strong emphasis on lectures as the main teaching mode, tend to discourage participants from being active learners. Rather, they encourage the view that the course leader has the answers to problems faced by participants and that the process of development simply requires the transmission of this knowledge. This creates a sense of dependence between teacher and learner and, of course, implies that the solutions being offered are relevant and easily transferred to different class-rooms. As we have already noted, the evidence indicates that this lack of attention to linking in-service experiences is one of the mistakes of much existing practice.

Within the project, we have explored a range of approaches that seem to encourage active learning. Many of these involve various forms of cooperative group work within which participants engaged in problem-solving. They encourage participants to recognize the value of considering alternative points of view and the importance of collaboration. They can also help individuals overcome the fear of change. However, these approaches are not easy to use and, therefore, within the project we are placing considerable emphasis on developing the skills of group work by those wishing to use the resource pack.

2. Negotiation of objectives

The leader of a course or workshop session faces similar problems to those that are encountered by teachers in school. In particular, there is the issue of how to manage the class as a whole and at the same time engage with the interests and concerns of individual participants. Approaches that attempt to negotiate objectives are our attempt to address this key issue.

We assume that participants have agreed to take part in some form of teacher development process as a result of discussions about the general aims and content. What is then needed are procedures that help individuals to determine their own learning objectives within the overall programme. We also need ways by which course leaders can become aware of these objectives. In this way, activities can be designed to take account of those concerns and to utililze the particular interests of individual participants.

Clearly, discussion has to be a central approach for this process of negotiation. In addition, participants may be asked to draw pictures of their classrooms in order to consider aspects of their practice. The process of drawing, whilst initially somewhat unsettling for some participants, enables them to think more analytically about issues in their work place.

Similarly, the use of writing is a powerful means of helping teachers to define and review aspects of their practice with a view to determining their learning objectives. With this in mind, courses based upon the UNESCO resource pack encourage leaders and participants to keep journals in which they write about their classrooms, the experience of the course and the issues that they are trying to address.

3. Demonstration, practice and feedback

Possibly the most difficult issue facing those who try to work with teachers in developing classroom practice is how to incorporate new ways of working into existing repertoires. Teaching in schools is a very demanding business, leaving little time for experimenting with new approaches. Understandably, teachers' priorities tend to be to do with managing the classes they are expected to teach. Furthermore, the culture of many schools is highly individualized, providing little or none of the support that might enable and encourage teachers to explore alternative ways of work (Little, 1982).

Approaches based upon demonstration, practice and feedback are intended to help create the conditions that will give teachers confidence to take some calculated risks in order to develop their practice. Demonstrations provide opportunities to see alternative classroom approaches in practice. They may simply encourage teachers to reflect once again upon their own ways of working, or they may stimulate the trial of a different technique. Demonstration can take a variety of forms. For example, it may mean observing a colleague at work; visits to other schools; or the study of video recordings.

Within the UNESCO project, further demonstrations of practice are provided by course leaders during the sessions themselves. In this way, the teacher educator is expected to demonstrate a commitment to teaching for diversity through the ways in which the sessions are conducted. A powerful feature of this approach is that participants are at the receiving end of these ways of working and, therefore, have the opportunity to judge the impact upon their own learning.

Alongside demonstrations, the use of practice and feedback is intended to give specific help to participants as they attempt to explore new ways of working. Practice and feedback may be conducted initially in simulated contexts, possibly using other course participants as 'guinea pigs' as alternative teaching approaches are trialled. However, it is essential that this is extended into the teacher's usual work place if there is to be a real possibility of continued use of new ways of working. The most helpful approach here is the notion of partnership teaching or, as it is sometimes called, peer coaching (Joyce and Showers, 1988). This involves pairs of colleagues working in one another's classrooms as they attempt to review aspects of their practice and experiment with alternative ways of working. This form of partnership is a powerful strategy for developing classroom practice but it requires a high level of confidence and trust between participants. We have found that it is necessary to agree specific guidelines and ground rules that enable these conditions to be met.

4. Continuous evaluation

As a further strategy for encouraging teachers to take responsibility for their own learning, it is necessary to encourage processes of continuous evaluation. These involve an emphasis on enquiry and reflection through which teachers collect and review information as they attempt to develop their own thinking and practice.

The learning journals referred to earlier provide one important means of encouraging teachers to enquire into aspects of their work. Within the project we have found that once the initial reluctance to write in this way is overcome, the use of the journal is adopted with enthusiasm. Indeed, many participants in the field-testing of the resource pack reported that writing about their teaching had become an essential feature of their practice.

Within course sessions, a variety of structured activities can also be used to encourage evaluation of learning. For example, groups may be asked to summarize their work and give an account to the rest of the course members. Similarly, groups may be asked to present the outcomes of their activities in the form of a poster illustrating their main ideas. The central strategy here involves people helping one another to draw out implications and messages from shared experience in ways that encourage individuals to recognize their own learning.

All these reporting strategies can provide course leaders with further information about the individual perspectives of their participants. They also give feedback on how far activities are catering for the interests of course members and helping them to achieve their objectives.

5. Support

The approaches to teacher development summarized here can be extremely demanding and, at times, stressful for participants and course leaders. The emphasis placed on enquiry, questioning and the consideration of alternative perspectives cuts across the conventional boundaries between teachers and students. They can expose gaps in understanding and knowledge, areas of prejudice, and unthought-out assumptions. They may also lead to individuals becoming destabilized as a result of their perspectives and ways of working being challenged.

Consequently, it is essential to establish a strong infrastructure of support that will help participants to take some risks with respect to their thinking and practice. Some of the approaches already described, such as group work and partnership teaching, help to provide a supportive network. In addition, a more general supportive atmosphere should be encouraged through the establishment of friendly, warm relationships and an atmosphere of openness between participants and course leaders. This may not always be so easy to achieve, however, particularly within school-based initiatives where existing differences between teachers may surface during staff development activities.

Our experience of using the resource pack to set up teacher development initiatives suggests that success is more likely if care is taken in planning. The aim must be to ensure appropriate arrangements for the support of the initiative at the following three stages:

   (i) the *initiation* stage, in order to ensure that all involved are clear about the expectations and commitments that are involved;
   (ii) the *implementation* stage, so that necessasry arrangements are made to support all participants and leaders as they engage in development activities;
   (iii) the *follow-up* stage, where it is vital that agreement has been reached to provide support to participants as they explore new ways of working in their own classrooms.

In summary, therefore, these five sets of approaches are intended to provide:

   - a supportive context for reflective enquiry;
   - resources and experiences that stimulate this approach to teacher development;
   - methods of scrutinizing and recording the outcomes;
   - help as participants attempt to develop aspects of practice in their classrooms.

The experience of our project indicates that participation in teacher development initiatives based upon these ideas encourages teacher educators and teachers to widen their perspectives on the nature of educational difficulty and, in so doing, to develop their practice.

Conclusion

The experience of the project, 'Special Needs in the Classroom', has provided some important lessons for all of us who are committed to finding ways of helping teachers to respond to pupil diversity. Most importantly, it has reinforced the necessity for conceptual clarity with respect to the special needs task. Specifically, it has led to the idea of reconstructing special needs in terms of school improvement and teacher development. In this way it has moved the work of the project from the margins of the education agenda right into the centre. The struggle to achieve equity in schools must be seen as the way of creating effective schools for all (Ainscow, 1991a).

However, this reconceptualization is fraught with potential hazards, not least because it leads to questions that challenge the status quo of schooling with respect to existing policies for organization, curriculum and assessment. It also, of course, requires teachers and teacher educators to look to themselves and their colleagues in order to find solutions to the day-to-day problems they face in their classrooms. All of this has the potential to destabilize systems and individuals, particularly those who have spent their careers in the field of special education. This being the case, it is essential that developments based upon the perspectives outlined in this chapter be planned with considerable care.

Acknowledgement

I would like to acknowledge the contributions to the ideas in this chapter of colleagues in many countries, particularly the members of the international resource team associated with the project. Readers wishing to receive further information about the UNESCO resource pack should contact Lena Saleh, Special Education Programme, UNESCO, 7, Place de Fontenoy, 75700 Paris, France.

References

Ainscow, M (1990) 'Special needs in the classroom: the development of a teacher education resource pack', *International Journal of Special Education*, **5**, 1, 13–20.
Ainscow, M (ed.) (1991a) *Effective Schools for All*, London: David Fulton.
Ainscow, M (1991b) 'Towards effective schools for all: an account of the rationale of the UNESCO teacher education project, "Special Needs in the classroom"', in Upton, G (ed.), *Staff Training and Special Educational Needs*, London: David Fulton.
Ainscow, M (1992) 'Teacher education as a strategy for developing inclusive schools', in Slee, R (ed.) *The Politics of Integration*, London: Falmer Press.
Ainscow, M and Tweddle, D A (1979) *Preventing Classroom Failure*, London: David Fulton.
Ainscow, M and Tweddle, D A (1988) *Encouraging Classroom Success*, London: David Fulton.
Bowman, I (1986) 'Teacher training and the integration of handicapped pupils: some findings from a fourteen nation UNESCO study', *European Journal of Special Needs Education*, **1**, 29–38.

Crawford, N B (1990) 'Integration in Hong Kong: rhetoric to reality in the field of mental handicap', *European Journal of Special Needs Education*, **5**, 3, 199–209.

Fulcher, G (1989) *Disabling Policies? A comparative approach to education policy and disability*, London: Falmer Press.

Fullan, M G (1991) *The New Meaning of Educational Change*, London: Cassell.

Joyce, B and Showers, B (1988) *Student Achievement Through Staff Development*, London: Longman.

Lincoln, Y S and Guba, E G (1985) *Naturalistic Inquiry*, Beverly Hills, CA: Sage.

Little, J W (1982) 'Norms of collegiality and experimentation: workplace conditions of school success', *American Educational Research Journal*, **19**, 325–40.

Miles, M (1989) 'The role of special education in information based rehabilitation', *International Journal of Special Education*, **4**, 2, 111–18.

Miles, M B and Huberman, A M (1984) *Qualitative Data Analysis*, Beverly Hills, CA: Sage.

Pijl, S J and Meijer, C J W (1991) 'Does integration count for much? An analysis of the practices of integration in either countries', *European Journal of Special Needs Education*, **6**, 2, 100–11.

Schon, D A (1983) *The Reflective Practitioner*, New York: Basic Books.

Schon, D A (1987) *Educating the Reflective Practitioner*, San Francisco: Jossey-Bass.

Skrtic, T M (1991) 'Students with special educational needs: artifacts of the traditional curriculum', in Ainscow, M (ed.), *Effective Schools for All*, London: David Fulton.

Slee, R (1991) 'Learning initiatives to include all students in regular schools', in Ainscow, M (ed.) *Effective Schools for All*, London: David Fulton.

Tomlinson, S (1982) *A Sociology of Special Education*, London: Routledge.

UNESCO (1988) *Review of the Present Situation in Special Education*, Paris: UNESCO.

Wang, M C (1991) 'Adaptive instruction: an alternative approach to providing for student diversity', in Ainscow, M (ed) *Effective Schools for All*, London: David Fulton.

20. The future of special education: who will pay the bill?

Ron Brouillette

Introduction

Can, indeed, the 21st century be better for individuals with disabilities than the 20th has been, as Mittler (this volume) queries? If the answer is to be 'yes', what is required of responsible societies? This volume has presented a myriad review of the major influences on the development of special education services and the global 'state of the art'. If the past can be regarded as a mirror through which the present may be better understood and the future conjured, this chapter serves to reflect what we might expect during the early decades of the 21st century. The author in no way feigns prescience in this presentation, but rather has confidence that what goes around comes around.

To put the future into perspective, we may want to recall the earliest record of disability in a community context. According to Solecki (1971), an Iraqi archaeological dig in 1950 unearthed the remains of Shanidar who lived around 45,000 years ago. Shanidar, in spite of severe physical handicapping conditions, lived a relatively long life of 40 years. His burial place suggested honour and respect and alluded to a life led as a cook. Shanidar's community, though probably nomadic, had integrated this disabled man into their community, and most probably assisted him during the long treks in search of food. One can only assume that Shanidar's survival was related to a sufficiently high place of religious or functional importance ascribed or achieved within his tribe. This chapter looks at how modern society might evolve to effectively include individuals like Shanidar into its midst.

The framework for the chapter borrows from the United Nations' proposals for implementing the World Programme of Action Concerning Disabled Persons (WPACD) (UN, 1983). If these guidelines were to be followed, where would they lead public attitudes and services for individuals with disabilities in the year 2032, 40 years after the end of the United Nations Decade of Disabled Persons (1983–92)? In particular, how does social policy relate to human rights and to economic development?

The outline of this chapter parallels the structure of the World Programme document and includes a brief history of social development; a summary of the WPACD and a review of current technological and economic practices and trends; and future perspectives for the full potentiation for 'extraordinary' individuals who in the 1990s are labelled as 'disabled'.

A brief history of social development

To prognosticate how persons with disabilities will receive specialized services 40 years hence requires a forecast of changes in social value systems. The social foundations for providing special education have, in the past, and will continue in the future, to influence why and how services are delivered (Wolfensberger, 1975). The patterns of service delivery will naturally vary across cultures.

As discussed in Chapter 3 of this volume, the developmental stages theory in special education appears to be evidenced by a consistent evolutionary pattern through which most societies pass in their efforts to integrate disabled individuals into their communities. Some cultures are currently moving through the first stage of social metamorphosis while very few are entering into the third. If, in 2032, we were to retrospect social history, we might observe three distinct stages.

During the *first stage* of social development lasting to the mid-20th century (and later for some places), attempts to care for handicapped persons could be defined as charitable, flowing from religious instructions. Services during this period followed a 'sacred' model. The categorical term used during these early years was 'handicap', which is thought to be of British origin, describing the prevalent begging gesture with the hand to cap, the receptacle for the blessings sought. Provision during this period was usually institutional where handicapped individuals were 'colonized' by philanthropists.

The *second stage* of social development followed World War II from which hundreds of thousands of soldiers returned debilitated. Rehabilitation during this period followed a medical model wherein disability was thought of as a pathological phenomenon seeking a cure. The term 'disability' was used to describe dysfunction in normative society. Disabled individuals and their families were sometimes consulted about treatment, and services were locationally integrated with non-disabled persons. Disabled persons who organized themselves into Disabled Persons International clung to the term 'disabled persons', anticipating that society would realistically face and accept their condition (Stanton, 1990). Irrespective of the preferences of disabled people, the terms 'exceptional' and 'individuals with special needs' were used in some parts of the world. The attempt to mandate equal access to full participation in all activities of society as a civil right was the dominant theme during this period.

The *third stage* of social development emerging in the beginning of the 21st century could be characterized by a higher regard and tolerance for the rights of an individual to be different; to be disabled. During this era, the term 'extraordinary' is used to indicate abilities and areas of strength within disabled (and non-disabled) persons. The term is considered correct by normalization criteria established by Wolfensberger (1983) and others in the late 20th century. The conservatism corollary, one of Wolfensberger's seven recurring themes of 'Social Role Valorization' (the replacement term for the normalization principle), suggests that,

It is not enough for a service to devalued people to use service means and tools that are neutral in a culture; rather, it should pursue the use of means and tools that actually enhance the image of its clients (p. 26).

This might require going a little over the top.

The social foundation during the third period is well beyond charity and even, somewhat, beyond equal rights. It is characterized by societies' unconditional acceptance of persons who have exceptionalities and the fundamental right to be different, to live on the fringes of society by choice.

Within this context, services provided for *extraordinary individuals* who opt for change follow a holistic, community participation model to 'potentiate' abilities. Potentiation is realized through trans-disciplinary teaming amongst the expansive array of available social, biomedical, educational, vocational and engineering technology in the wealthier developing nations. For the most part, developed nations clung to the more expensive, isolated, departmental approach to potentiation. The least developed nations entered the higher technological state much later in the third stage. The coordinator of potentiation is the local abilities' facilitator or conductor. Potentiation is offered to members of all ages in the community.

Financing human potentiation

The costs associated with human potentiation in the developing nations in the South continued to be government-subsidized through funds generated from specific 'pleasure' tax revenues and income derived from the Northern Region Social Development Trust, established among the Western nations to provide interest-free loans and grants for social development projects.

In the higher technological/higher income nations, services are for the most part privatized. The local National Social Development Trust Funds are established with strong participation and monitoring by extraordinary individuals. The Social Funds are financed through government grants and lotteries in the early years, and then through the taxes and other income generated by individuals who have been fully potentiated. The annual interest from the Fund is channelled into services' vouchers provided by the government to people who want them to purchase services provided by private vendors only. The privatized services are strictly monitored by consumer-oriented organizations. An honest brokerage system ensures that available services render value for money. The privatization of services is found to be highly efficient and financially attractive, considering the cost-benefit ratio produced from holistic, total potentiation. The welfare payments saved and taxes paid by productive potentiated people now living in dignity have significantly exceeded the costs of the vouchers which are now available to everyone without proof of need.

A review of the World Programme of Action Concerning Disabled Persons and current trends

We would need to look back to the late 1900s to fully appreciate how we arrived at the third stage for human potentiation. As a consequence of the quite successful United Nations 1981 International Year of Disabled Persons, The World Programme of Action Concerning Disabled Persons (WPACD) was drafted by the United Nations as the document to guide the Decade of Disabled Persons (1983–92). The Decade was adopted by the General Assembly of the United Nations on December 3 1982. The purpose of the World Programme was to promote positive attitudes and actions which would lead to the equalization of opportunities for the then estimated 10 per cent or 500 million individuals in the world who are born with or acquire some debilitating impairment. Mittler (1990, p. 2), in drafting the plan of action for going beyond the Decade, announced:

> the WPACD has been translated into many languages and has been widely disseminated and quoted, and is likely to remain as the starting point for future programmes and activities at all levels.

The WPACD elaborated three objectives: prevention of disability, rehabilitation (including cost-benefit analyses), and equalization of opportunities. How these objectives might influence the future is briefly discussed.

Prevention

The number of those children who fall out of death's lap into disability in the 21st century could be halved. Halving the incidence of impairment assumes the reduction of diseases as a result of the following: increased medical technology and the transfer of effective health-care through community education, participation and infrastructure development; redistribution of the world food and medicine supply; control over inter- and intra-national aggression leading to armed conflicts; safer vehicles and roads; a cleaner environment, especially in the more industrialized parts of the world; and a radical reduction in substance abuse through social and economic restructuring.

The incidence of physical impairments which now accounts for around 1 per cent of all impairments could be more than halved by the total elimination of disease-related polio, rubella, measles, meningitis, encephalitis, multiple sclerosis, etc, and the reduction of complicated birthing through more hospital births and training of traditional birth attendants. Genetic disorders could also be reduced through genetic screening and engineering and parent education.

Rehabilitation

Rehabilitation is currently defined by the WPACD to mean a goal-oriented and time-limited process aimed at enabling an impaired person to reach optimum mental, physical and social functional level through the provision of social, nutritional, health and vocational services and the provision of appropriate aids and equipment. The term is not universally accepted, however, due to the association of rehabilitation with institutional and overly medical approaches. These traditional rehabilitation measures also represent costs that are well beyond the means of nations that have a multitude of priorities where issues of survival are in the balance. The full costs of rehabilitation services are little understood in many developing nations. Even less understood are the potential returns on rehabilitation investments.

Cost-benefit analysis of rehabilitation

As depicted by Brouillette (Chapter 3, this volume), there is a strong relationship between the wealth of a nation and the services provided to its citizens with impairments. Bolstered by this information, developing governments have successfully fended off the demands from advocates for increased government participation. Government arguments are frequently deferred to the ministries of finance on grounds of insufficient resources and numerous higher priority areas to fund.

The economic tradition

Educating pupils with disabilities is thought to cost more than educating other pupils. Hegarty (1990) suggests that exactly how much more is difficult to say because of the lack of precision in specifying what educational provision is optimally required and the lack of information about how much these services cost. Special education is traditionally more expensive than ordinary education in developed nations. The range in the USA is 1.18 to 3.64 times more expensive than regular education, depending on the specific special educational needs (Rehabilitation International, 1981). In Czechoslovakia, for example, the per-pupil cost at an institution for physically handicapped children is seven times more than at a school for mentally retarded children. The overall cost of special education in New Zealand is 1.65 times that for ordinary education (UNESCO, 1978).

In developing nations, however, the initial cost of special education may be far less than regular education. A ten-year longitudinal study in Mauritius (Brouillette, 1992), where nearly all special facilities are run by NGOs, revealed that special education was 1.6 times *less* expensive than ordinary education. Possible reasons to explain the discrepancy include the NGOs' lack of large bureaucratic (ministerial) overhead; a higher teacher–pupil ratio found in developed nations; the relatively lower salary paid to special education teachers; the absence of expensive equipment (except those donated from mostly foreign sources); and non-reliance on high technology. Certainly, integrated education in developing nations does not have to be significantly more expensive than segregated, residential education.

Most governments in developing nations are currently confronted with those decisions about financing special education which were made by more developed governments a couple of decades ago. Mba (1978) suggests the distribution of meagre resources to special education in Nigeria is indicative of Africa, where governments still perceive their belated involvement as a kind of surplus funds to charity. While as much as 40 per cent of annual income in Africa is channelled to education, 'The education of the handicapped in most of these countries consists of mere crumbs that fall from the national educational table' (p. 30). The handicapped person's right to an education is still considered a utopian dream by governments in Africa which argue that they must first provide for the able-bodied who are believed to be more productive than disabled people.

It appears that local non-governmental efforts continue as best they can in instigating special education during the early stages of development when governments are allocating only token gestures through small charity grants to these NGOs. The real problem arises when the development of special education appears on the list of national priorities. If nations subscribe to Putnam's (1979) resource hypothesis suggesting that wealthier nations will spend more on education, including costlier special education, the resultant fatalistic, benign resignation to the problem will mean that 98 per cent of children with impairments in developing nations will remain without an education for some decades to come.

In spite of the above arguments supporting the importance of the resource hypothesis in special education development, some contradictory evidence discounts the influence of resources alone. What is needed is a cogent argument in favour of investments in the education of children and adults with disabilities.

Cost-benefit analyses

An important, but rarely used incentive for special education development is its justification based on proven economic returns on investment, or the cost-benefit analysis. Cost-benefit analysis is

a basic tool of economic analysis in which the actual and potential costs (both public and private) of various economic decisions are weighed against actual and potential, private and social, benefits. Those decisions or projects yielding the highest benefit-cost ratio are usually thought to be most desirable (Todaro, 1981, p. 452).

Prior to documenting the cost-benefit of special education, a caveat on overemphasizing an economic rationale is offered by UNESCO in Hegarty (1990):

Education does, of course, make people more employable . . . and can enhance their capacity to contribute to the economic well-being of the community, but neither of these is the reason why they are entitled to education. At a time when public expenditure is increasingly governed by market forces and instrumental views of education prevail, it is easy to lose sight of the inherent nature of the right to education. This is particularly significant where people with disabilities are concerned. Education may not succeed in making some people employable or economically self-sufficient, but that in no way reduces their entitlement to the resources that their education requires.

In places where human rights are a current issue and debt servicing is high, the additional argument based on economic return may be useful. UNESCO (1974) suggested that cost-benefit figures form a useful addition to other motivation in that they lead us to consider the development of special education system not as a levy on the national product, made out of fellow feeling for the handicapped, but as an investment on which the return to the community can be calculated. The major economic benefits for providing rehabilitation services include:

- reduced costs for future care;
- production benefits;

- reduced administrative costs for transfer payments (Rehabilitation International, 1981);
- tax recoupment on the income earned through production (UNESCO, 1974; 1978).

The cost-benefit ratio applied to special education and rehabilitation is not without limitations. Among these are an amazingly wide variability in published cost-benefit ratios ranging between six and 35 – all favourable (Conley, 1975). Reasons for the variability include faulty methodological procedures that utilize crude, incomplete and speculative data. Few of the studies envisage what future earnings might be without rehabilitation. Another problem is applying cost-benefit methods to developing nations where the varied patterns of cultural and economic life in a subsistence economy would make such analyses meaningless. Amoako (1977) describes the situation in Ghana where high rates of unemployment, and lack of employment opportunities following training, undermine vocational rehabilitation. Under such conditions, effective rural rehabilitation need not involve paid employment, but rather contribution in the family fields or hut.

Examples of cost-benefits

It appears that the earlier special education begins, the greater the return on the investment:

> Early education programs benefit young handicapped children. Without early intervention the degree of handicap becomes more severe, compounding the problems and the cost of intervention (McCarthy, 1982).

Wood (1980) reports that the costs of schooling of a disabled child from birth to the age of 18 is $37,273 in the USA. If the intervention is delayed until the age of six, the costs of the rehabilitation rise to $53,340.

In Peru, where educating a child with moderate disability cost $255 per year, the educated person will earn at least $300 annually after six years in school (half of what a non-disabled person would make). The adjusted return on the initial educational investment is 10 per cent per year (Wood, 1978). Excluded from this calculation are any payments the government might make to support these individuals if they were unemployed and dependent on the state. By contrast, the return on infrastructure investments in South America are around 12 per cent with no corresponding social benefits or tax return potential (Langoni, 1970).

An example from England indicates that one year's specialist training for employment of someone with a severe sensory impairment costs between an equivalent of $21,000 and $26,000. The direct taxes paid during a lifetime's employment would be a minimum of around $70,000 at current rates. The payback period for return of training costs would be 15 years. There is also the dividend of an enhanced enjoyment of life and dignity of being a contributor to the national economy rather than a dependent on it (Royal National College of the Blind and Doncaster College for the Deaf, 1991).

In a centralized economy like Czechoslovakia, where all health and education costs were met by the government, a disabled worker after 20 years will contribute nine times the cost of their rehabilitation. The annual contribution to the national income is between $2,609 and $4,348. The conclusion of the study (UNESCO, 1978) stresses that,

> The above mentioned economic aspects are not the only or most important aspect of . . . handicapped children and adult citizens in a socialist state. The main purpose of this care is to integrate these citizens . . . into the process of creative social labour, to provide them with a feeling of social usefulness (p. 62).

In the USA, studies conclude that the additional costs of special education are reimbursed to the community 35 times over through output and taxes paid within ten years (UNESCO, 1978). The cost-benefit ratio range in the USA is between 1:1 and 1:12, with an average around 1:11. This means that for every dollar spent on special education, the disabled adult will earn 11 dollars. The overall return on rehabilitative measures including special education, amounts to nine times the costs of the rehabilitation provided after nine years of employment by the rehabilitated person.

A promising, cost-effective approach to providing appropriate services to disabled children and adults is community-based rehabilitation (CBR). While conclusive analyses on cost-benefit are yet to be reported, O'Toole (1987), working in Guyana, has calculated the yearly cost for CBR is around $50 per capita (see O'Toole, this volume). Mariga (1992, personal communication) reports that her CBR project in Zimbabwe cost Z$1 per month for each of the 500 children who are seen at least every other week by health care staff and education specialists. The comparative per-client cost for providing services to 100 students attending a residential facility is Z$10 per day.

An analysis of public expenditure in the USA for institutional and community services, as calculated by Braddock et al. (1987) and reported by Heal (1987), works out at $127 per head for institution-based rehabilitation, compared to $81 per head for community rehabilitation approaches. Deinstitutionalization and decentralization have been recent forces shaping current rehabilitation. Menolascino (1978) has emphasized that 'Normalisation rightly understood can help a community to solve a handicapped person's needs for growth and support on a local level'. A bottom-up approach, such as the CBR concept, is advocated by the World Health Organization (1989) and discussed by O'Toole (this volume). The strategy illustrates the trend to transfer the responsibility for remedial actions to the community level. Seven UN agencies have adopted CBR as part of their contributions to the Decade of Disabled Persons. The Portage home-based services approach exemplifies empowerment. Family members are taught practical skills for stimulating a child who has an impairment, in the family. The trained and motivated family members are then encouraged to train others. As shown above, the approach is meant to be cost-effective and is closer to the principles of normalization, albeit somewhat segregated in its delivery in the home-based model (J Brouillette et al., this volume).

Equalization of opportunities

'Equalization of Opportunities', according to the WPACD, means the process of adapting the general system of society to make it equally accessible to those who have an impairment. Additionally, persons who have an impairment are given the required skills and equipment to fully participate in ordinary life. Current measures leading toward what is termed 'normalization' (Wolfensberger, 1972) include opening all facets of society to the possibilities for mainstreaming.

The aim of integration or mainstreaming is to enable the individual to participate fully as an equal member of society, beginning with the ordinary forms of education available to normal children. Integration was the declared policy in three-quarters of the countries responding to the Review of Special Education (UNESCO, 1988). There are at least four types of educational integration models currently in use worldwide: The Resource Room Model (USA), The Educational Pairing Model (Denmark), The Consultant Teacher Model (Norway) and the Combined Services Model (Poland). Results from a meta-analysis of mainstreaming programmes (Wang and Baker, 1985) provide an empirical basis for drawing conclusions about the efficacy of mainstreaming in improving performance, attitudinal and process outcomes for handicapped students.

Predictions in the area of equalization of opportunities were made using the Delphi technique. Schipper and Kenowitz (1975) asked 121 school administrators in the USA to respond to 60 special education future events. The respondents predicted that between 1980 and 1995:

- all handicapped children will be receiving education, including those with severe handicap;
- there will be increasing progress towards deinstitutionalization;
- there will be an expansion of parental input in schools;
- there will be expanded uses of technology and instructional media services;
- there will be an acceptance and implementation of mainstreaming;
- there will be changes in pre- and in-service training of teachers.

The predictions of administrators match well with the priorities set by the 58 nations in UNESCO's (1988) study (see Hegarty, this volume). A review of the literature on future trends reveals the following predictions for future development.

● The increased use of microcomputers for extension and expansion of memory, which is often an employment deficit for some mentally retarded and learning disabled individuals (Yates, 1986). Also the use of cognitive enhancement drugs (nootropics) for improving memory and cognitive processing among people with learning difficulties.

● The increasing use of individualized learning aids like reading machines, the Possum (breath) typewriter and environmental controller, transcription systems, the Canon Communicator and interactive voice technologies in cognitive-related tasks by handicapped persons in the integrated classroom (Vitu, 1978).

● The increased development of computerized educational satellite technology to disseminate expert information (conferencing) for diagnosis, assessment, teaching, evaluation and guidance (Chaudhury, 1990). In addition, the establishment of a worldwide special education television system to produce and broadcast material designed specifically to train personnel and to heighten public awareness.

• The dissolution of boundaries between regular and special education as each special needs child will be maximally served in the least restrictive setting following the principles of normalization (Gall, 1986).

• The use of robots in the social life of handicapped individuals: medical, living, recreation, educational and welfare assistance; services of amusements; substitution of repair and inspection; working in bad environments (Yukio, 1978).

• The increased influence of organizations of disabled individuals on national policy formation and implementation (Stanton, 1990).

Future perspectives for 2032

Legislation

Legislation could mandate the broad policy and financial commitment to allow extraordinary individuals to receive access to all activities of their culture. Formal policy would also ensure their rights to be unique. Pressure to conform to international standards led by Scandinavian and American legislation could become a powerful change impetus. Here again, international advocacy and leadership training by extraordinary individuals would lead to greater numbers of disabled individuals being elected to local and national governments and having a tremendous influence. Additionally, the unfailing inter-governmental agencies' promotion of human rights, including the right to be different, would have profound world influence.

Physical environment

Freedom of choice to participate within society would necessitate total physical accessibility. All public buildings and later all private buildings could be required through legislation to be completely accessible to mobility vehicles used by the non-ambulatory persons. The few remaining stairs to challenge anything with wheels would be those relics from the 20th century.

Mobility and orientation for all world citizens would be made easier. Computer-assisted guides utilizing radar, sonar, infra-red, synthesized speech, vibrators, etc could aid the tactically sensitive but visually and hearing limited individuals to get about efficiently. Similarly, computer-assisted visual encoding and decoding devices could translate sound to images and print to add to the compensatory abilities of those aurally limited extraordinary individuals who are vision-orientated. Both types of equipment could assist those who may not read or write, but who are sensorily and physically responsive.

Income maintenance/social security

The minimum guaranteed income for all persons would certainly extend to extraordinary individuals. The dignity and meaning which employment (with or without tied income) provides could be even more important to those individuals who choose this option. Social security could revert to the extended family system which could re-emerge out of necessity in an over-populated and insensitive world. The media could play a powerful role in popularizing the need for the extended family. The family unit could be asked to assume greater supportive responsibility for their relative who has an impairment. Tax incentives, other financial advantages and public opinion would further encourage the reunification of families and the reintegration of extraordinary individuals within them.

Education and training

Every student, whether extraordinary or non-extraordinary, would have a curriculum individually designed for maximum potentiation. Legislation could require all local authorities to provide appropriate and comprehensive training at every stage of life to maximize the talents latent in each individual. The content of the instruction would be highly individualized and thus practical to meet the individual's, more than society's, immediate and future requirements specific to daily living.

It may not be surprising to find a return to more segregated placements as research and public opinion could indicate better social and educational results from this approach. Social integration through positive interactions and attitudes could become products of a total community effort, but not necessarily one coming exclusively from the integrated classroom on a full-time basis. The practice of 'main-dumping' could cease on grounds of ineffectiveness for all concerned. Practical instruction will be supplemented by academic and other mentally stimulating activities to push out those boundaries which were once thought to be limiting. The use of interactive video training schemes and adult education would be specifically designed.

Employment

As discussed above, employment could fulfil a higher need in most societies. Extraordinary individuals could be in greater demand in the higher technological nations where manual types of labour are required. The concept of work could be more for the sake of personal and societal evolution and development than for personal or financial gain. For those extraordinary individuals who choose a non-academic education, a work-related curriculum could be followed from the first day of early education. The freedom of choice in the workplace is of highest priority for this group. But the talents and interests which are found beneath the impairment could prove to have great value in the labour market. Work would be matched to existing skills which are finely tuned.

Since the word 'avocation' could replace the term 'work', however, employment is only one of several options for daily living. Laws could exist in all societies which not only prohibit discrimination on the basis of being extraordinary, but which offer incentives and encouragement based on high returns on employers' investment to create meaningful employment. The earlier trends towards cooperatives of disabled persons and quota systems for the employment of extraordinary individuals would be maintained in places where unemployment continues to be an issue. Technology will play an important role in employment by training handicapped individuals in job skills through interactive television and video instruction; individualized work at home through the use of computers; and robotic and vocational aids to assist individuals with upper limbs dysfunction (Engelhardt, 1978).

Recreation

Leisure-time activities would be important to everyone since the work day would have been reduced considerably. Extraordinary individuals would have even greater free time to pursue arts and hobbies. They could participate fully in all social activities, including marriage and raising a family. They could even be sought-after to blend within the full range of social functions due to their popularity as fascinating mixers.

Culture

A large number of extraordinary individuals could be found who have islands of genius in the performing arts, music, literature and other art forms. As these talents become known, a treasure hunt may ensue to discover other hidden talents. The public could begin to associate extraordinary individuals with quality art forms. As a result of the wealth found, potentiation could be extended equally to non-impaired individuals as well. Sign language, once the exclusive domain of the hearing impaired sub-culture, could become an international medium for communication.

Religion

Extraordinary individuals could take a more active part in religious activities, given full accessibility. Their former role as receptacles for religious generosity could be reversed as they are seen to provide blessings to others.

Sports

Sports held exclusively for extraordinary individuals could continue to provide specialized sports training to prepare athletes for competition within the regular sports institution. A number of highly gifted athletes could be identified and developed through the specialised sports networks.

Community action

Since the community would be the responsible agent to foster acceptance and the participation of extraordinary individuals, the community would also be committed to meeting individual training and social needs. The family could be considered a key resource in this endeavour, but legislation and civil hearings could deem that it is the community at large and specifically the district coordination agency for extraordinary individuals which has more of a responsibility than the immediate families.

Staff training

Specialists at various levels of expertise could receive training as close to the community level as possible. The area of potentiation could be demystified sufficiently by 2032 to allow skill-trained generalists rather than highly technical personnel to lead potentiation. These front-line community managers could receive training and support from higher level supervisors and technologists. Extraordinary individuals themselves could be in leadership roles in staff training.

There could be a greater emphasis on international borrowing of good practices as the globe progressively shrinks. Staff training at the pre-service level could be conducted at mega-universities as well as at smaller community centres where practicum work is regarded as being as important as the theoretical. More stress could be laid on in-service training as a more efficient means of topping-up through quality-oriented practical instruction.

Information and public education

Electronic transfer of information between continents could take full advantage of a centre for international disability information which the UN could establish (Mittler, 1990) and which regional associations could plug into for personnel training and individual potentiation. But the informational needs could pale into insignificance when compared to the necessity for a shift in public attitudes.

Few, if any, of the above possibilities for extraordinary individuals to have the right to equal access, let alone the right to be different, could ever take place without social reform and a change in public opinion. Historically, the attitudes held by the public towards extraordinary individuals has been more handicapping than the impairment. Social attitudes could change dramatically by 2032. They would be changed by the pervasive and relentless portrayal of successful extraordinary individuals throughout the media and through the increase in opportunities for more positive encounters between those who have an impairment and those who do not. The WPACD could accept the suggestion to have the United Nations' Secretary General persuade the giants of the mass-media advertising sector on Madison Avenue in New York to put together a cross-cultural media package which would run from 1994 to 1997. State-of-the-art commercials aimed at favourable attitudes and actions toward extraordinary individuals could be shown on television and in cinema halls around the world in every language. Radio and educational packages could be used in every nation. Popular songs and jingles could be composed by the image-makers who could transform a once-avoided topic to one of unconditional acceptance. The role of the media in the process of societal integration could have the most pronounced of all influences (Brouillette, 1990).

The right to be different also carries with it the right to be excluded from those harsher aspects of society: its fierce competition and aggressiveness. Not all extraordinary individuals will be stars, and the media could understand this as it features the more average of this population. But individuals with impairments are in the spotlight as sterling examples of what a tolerant society can produce, and what the media can make.

International action

The World Programme of Action Concerning Disabled Persons could be a major milestone in the development of world values and attitudes concerning extraordinary individuals. If the United Nations family of specialized agencies let the decade 1983–92 run its inevitable course and die, the situation in 2032 would look far different. But it will not, and the credit for this will go to the world community of non-governmental organizations and individuals which prompted and encouraged the United Nations to continue its promotion of equal rights for extraordinary individuals through the media and its member nations. The real stars, though, will be those hundreds of people both with and without impairments who, through their individual and collective energies and initiatives, will take on the struggle to change world opinion and practices through mostly non-governmental and inter-governmental efforts. The decade starting 2030 will owe much to the past and holds still greater promise for the future.

Conclusion

A retrospective journey from the future reveals a synergistic relationship between social development, policies, programme trends and the financial implications for special education. Leading is far better than trying to keep pace with the swiftly changing patterns of providing services to develop the potential within extraordinary people. The United Nations family of agencies and international non-governmental organizations can have a tremendous impact by promoting changes in values, providing information and helping transfer technology and resources in culturally-sensitive ways.

The Decade of Disabled Persons that has just ended is really the beginning of policies that could affect attitudes and practices among generations to come. It makes humanitarian and economic sense to maintain the momentum beyond 1993. As we hurtle towards the 21st century, our best measure of a society's evolution might easily be the well-being of its citizens who have an impairment.

References

Amoako, J (1977) 'Socio-economic implications of investments in rehabilitation services for the disabled in a developing country', paper presented to United Nations expert group meeting on Socio-economic Implications of Investments in Rehabilitation Services for the Disabled, Geneva: ILO.

Braddock, D, Hemp, R and Fujura, G (1987) 'National study of public spending for mental retardation and developmental disabilities', *American Journal of Mental Deficiency*, **92**, 121–33.

Brouillette, R (1990) 'Ideas for the WPADP and the end of the decade', unpublished paper 21 March, University of Manchester.

Brouillette, R (1992) *The Development of Special Education: A Case Study in Mauritius*, Ann Arbor, MI: University Microfilms.

Chaudhury, K (1990) 'Global trends in special needs: 1970 – 2000', unpublished manuscript, University of Manchester.

Conley, R (1975) 'Issues in benefit-cost analysis of the vocational program', *American Rehabilitation*, **10**, 3.

Engelhardt, K (1978) 'Health and human services robotics laboratory', in *International Perspectives on Future Special Education*, Reston, VA: CEC.

Gall, R (1986) 'Framework for policy and action in special education: an international perspective', in *The Future of Special Education*, Reston, VA: CEC.

Grant, J (1991) *State of the World's Children*, New York: Oxford University Press.

Heal, L (1987) 'Institutions cost more than community services', *American Journal of Mental Deficiency*, **92**, 2, 136–7.

Hegarty, S (1990) *The Education of Children and Young People with Disabilities: principles and practices*, Paris: UNESCO.

Langoni, C (1970) 'A study in economic growth: the Brazilian case', PhD Dissertation, University of Chicago.

Mariga, L (1992) Personal communication on CBR and Institutional Based Rehabilitation costs 20 July, Maseru, Lesotho.

Mba, P O (1978) 'Special Education in Nigeria', in Fink, A (ed.), *International Perspectives on Future Special Education*, Reston, VA: CEC.

McCarthy, J (1982) 'Special education: Pre-school Handicapped Children Senate Bill 1056', Tucson AZ: University of Arizona.

Menolascino, F (1978) 'The future of the handicapped person and his community', in *International Perspectives on Future Special Education*, Reston, VA: CEC.

Mittler, P (1990) *United Nations Decade of Disabled Persons (1983–1992) Towards 2000 – From Awareness to Action*, Expert Group Meeting on Alternative Ways to Mark the End of the United Nations Decade of Disabled Persons 7–11 May, Vienna: UND Centre for Social Development, Expert Group Meeting on the socio-economic implications of investments in rehabilitation of the disabled, Helsinki.

O'Toole, B (1987) 'Community based rehabilitation: problems and possibilities', *European Journal of Special Needs Education*, **2**, 3, 117–90.

Putnam, R (1979) 'Special education: some cross-national comparisons', *Comparative Education*, **15**, 1, 83–98.

Rehabilitation International (1981) *The Economics of Disability: International Perspectives*, New York: Rehabilitation International.

Royal National College for the Blind and Doncaster College for the Deaf (1991) 'Overcoming impairment: an exhibition of employment opportunities for people with sensory impairments', London: Central Hall, Westminster.

Scheerenberger, R C (1983) *A History of Mental Retardation*, Baltimore, MD: Paul Brookes.

Schipper, W and Kenowitz, L (1975) 'Special education futures: A forecast of events affecting the education of exceptional children: 1975-2000', Washington, DC: National Association of Special Education.

Solecki, R (1971) *Shanidar*, New York: Alfred Knopf.

Stanton, I (1990) Personal Communication, Information Officer, Manchester Disability Forum, May.

Todaro, M (1981) *Economic Development in the Third World*, New York: Longman.

UNESCO (1974) *Case Studies In Special Education*, Paris: UNESCO.

UNESCO (1978) *Economic Aspects of Special Education*, Paris: UNESCO.

UNESCO (1985) *Regional Workshop on Teacher Training and Integration of Handicapped Pupils into Ordinary Schools*, Paris: UNESCO.

UNESCO (1988) *Review of the Present Situation in Special Education*, Paris: UNESCO.

United Nations (1983) *World Programme of Action Concerning Disabled Persons*, Vienna: United Nations Centre for Social Development and Humanitarian Affairs.

Vitu, E (1978) 'New opportunities for visually handicapped people through applying today's technology', in *International Perspectives on Future Special Education*, Reston, VA: CEC.

Wang, M and Baker, E (1985) 'Mainstreaming programs: design, features and effects', *Journal of Special Education*, **19**, 4, 503–21.

Wolfensberger, W (1972) *The Principle of Normalisation in Human Services*, Toronto: National Institute on Mental Retardation.

Wolfensberger, W (1975) *The Origin and Nature of Our Institutional Models*, Syracuse, NY: Human Policy Center.

Wolfensberger, W (1983) *PASSING: normalization criteria and ratings manual*, 2nd edition, Toronto: National Institute on Mental Retardation.

Wood, P (1980) 'Cost of services', in Garland, C, Stone, N, Swanson, J and Woodruff, G (eds) *Early Intervention for Children with Special Needs and Their Families: Findings and Recommendations*, Phoenix, AZ: Interact.

Wood, M (1978) 'The Economics of Special Education in a Develping Country', in *International Perspectives in the Future of World Special Education*, Reston, VA: CEC.

World Health Organization (1989) *A Manual on Training the Disabled in the Community: community based rehabilitation for developing countries*, Geneva: WHO.

Yates, JR (1986) 'Current and emerging forces impacting special education', in *The Future of Special Education*, Reston, VA: CEC.

Yukio, S (1978) 'The contribution of advanced technology in the field of rehabilitation and welfare', in *International Perspectives on Future Special Education*, Reston, VA: CEC.

Biographical notes on contributors

Mel Ainscow is a tutor in special educational needs at Cambridge Institute of Education and the Consultant for the UNESCO teacher education project 'Special Needs in the Classroom'.

David Baine is Professor of Educational Psychology at the University of Alberta, Canada. His book *Handicapped children in Developing Countries: Assessment, Curriculum and Instruction* is based on his extensive international work.

Tony Best is a tutor in the area of visual impairment at the University of Birmingham. He was formerly a teacher of deaf–blind children and has worked extensively overseas.

Jane Brouillette has worked for more than a decade in developing nations as a specialist in early childhood special education and portage. She is currently working for AHRTAG in London.

Ron Brouillette has worked in special education in developing nations for the past two decades. He has been a lecturer in Special Education (International) at the University of Manchester and is currently a freelance consultant.

Patrick Daunt has been Director of the Bureau of Action in Favour of Disabled Persons in the European Community in Brussels. Previously he was a secondary school headteacher in the UK.

Peter Evans is with the Office of Economic Cooperation and Development (OECD), Paris, in the area of special education. He is a Senior Lecturer in Education at University of London.

Seamus Hegarty is Deputy Director of the National Foundation for Educational Research (NFER) in England and Wales. He is editor of EJSNE and director of several major research programmes. He has served as a consultant to UNESCO and OECD among others.

Stan Herr is Associate Professor of Law at the University of Maryland in the USA. He has been a visiting scholar at leading universities focusing on law and developmental disabilities.

Marjo Joutselainen is a programme officer for the Finnish Red Cross with a focus on international development issues. She has been a research consultant to the World Federation of the Deaf.

Khalfan H Khalfan is a teacher in Zanzibar, Tanzania and the Head of Educational Affairs within Disabled People's International. He is active in the development of CBR projects in Tanzania.

Joseph Kisanji is a lecturer and coordinator of the MEd Special Education (International) at Manchester University. He was formerly a lecturer in Tanzania and managed the UNESCO Subregional Special Education Project in eastern and southern Africa for six years.

Tehal Kohli is Associate Professor at Punjab University, India. She has published several books and articles based on her research in areas of special education.

Steve McCall is a tutor in visual impairment at the University of Birmingham. He has been a peripatetic teacher supporting blind and partially sighted children in mainstream schools.

María Isabel Mac Donagh is a special education teacher trainer and government advisor in Buenos Aires, Argentina with a primary focus on mental retardation.

María del Carmen Malbrán is a lecturer at the National Universities of Buenos Aires and La Plata, Argentina. She serves on several international advisory committees on mental retardation.

Ed Martin is President of the National Center for Disability Services in the USA. He formerly served as Director of the US government's Bureau of Education for the Handicapped.

Christine Miles works in UK as a home–school liaison teacher for multilingual families that have a child with learning difficulties. She formerly developed a school in Peshawar, Pakistan.

Mike Miles is a writer and advisor on disability services in developing nations. He worked for 14 years in Pakistan as an administrator and planner of special education.

Peter Mittler is Professor of Special Education and Director and Dean of the School of Education, University of Manchester. He has served as Past President of the International League of Societies for Persons with Mental Handicap and is a UN consultant.

Brian O'Toole has worked for the past five years as a community-based rehabilitation (CBR) project director in Georgetown, Guyana. He has written widely on CBR and its effectiveness.

Marigold Thorburn is a physician residing in Jamaica. She has published widely on epidemiology of disabilities and early intervention systems such as Portage and community-based approaches.

James Ward is an adjunct professor at Bond University in Gold Coast Australia. He was formerly a child psychologist and Professor of Education at Macquarie University, Australia.

Klaus Wedell is Professor at the Department of Educational Psychology and Special Educational Needs at the University of London, Institute of Education and is an OECD consultant.

Kaoru Yamaguchi is a retired professor of special education at Tokyo University and is Past President of the International Portage Association.

An annotated bibliography on comparative education and rehabilitation for individuals with special needs

Ron Brouillette

Books and periodicals

African Rehabilitation Institute (1986) 'Report on the Regional (Vocational and Social Rehabilitation) Workshop on Mental Retardation in Africa: November 29–December 19', Geneva: ILO. (Chapter on developing vocational training and industries in Africa.)

AHRTAG (1984) *Personal Transport for Disabled People. Design and Manufacture*, London: AHRTAG.

Asian Federation for the Mentally Retarded (1975–1992) *Proceedings of AFMR Conferences.* (Overviews of programmes and research in Asia.)

Baine, D (1988) *Handicapped Children in Developing Countries: assessment, curriculum and instruction*, Edmonton: University of Alberta.

Braslavsky, B (1976) *Venezuela: democratization and modernization of special education*, Paris: UNESCO.

Braslavsky, B (1978) 'Human rights and special education in developing countries', in Fink, A (ed.) *International Perspectives on Future Special Education*, Reston, VA: CEC.

Brouillette, R (1983) *A Teachers' Handbook on Disabilities*, Reduit, Mauritius: MIE.

Brouillette, R (1985) *An Annotated Bibliography (and Resources) for Special Education Relevant to Africa (and Developing Nations)*, Nairobi/Paris: UNESCO.

Brouillette, R (1987) *The Future of Network Africa (for Mentally Retarded Persons): a report of the regional workshop*, Oslo/Brussels: NFPU and ILSMH. (A review of services provided to persons with mental handicap in 13 African nations with comparative statistics from 1982 to 1986.)

Brouillette, R (1992) *The Development of Special Education in Mauritius: a case study*, Ann Arbor, MI: University Microfilms.

Brouillette, R and Chaudhury, K (1990) 'Beyond the Decade of Disabled Persons: special education in 2032', Budapest: World Futures Studies Congress (WFSF), May 28.

Carrier, J (1984) 'Comparative special education: ideology, differentiation and allocation in England and the United States', in Barton, L and Tomlinson, S (eds) *Special Education and Social Interests*, Beckenham: Croom Helm.

CEC (1978) *International Perspectives on Future Special Education*, Reston, VA: CEC (Proceedings from the First World Congress on Future Special Education: Scotland. Contains articles on special education topics from over 30 nations.)

Commission of the European Communities (1980) *Studies: Special Education in the European Community*, Brussels: EEC. (Comparative overview of Italy, Netherlands, UK, Belgium, France, Denmark, Germany, Luxembourg and Ireland.)

Daunt, P (1991) *Meeting Disability: a European response*, London: Cassell.

Dixon, G (1982) *Peace Corps in Special Education*, Washington DC: Peace Corps, Information Office.

Dybwad, R (1989) *International Directory of Mental Retardation Resources*, Washington, DC: US Department of Health and Human Services. (Details the provisions in 70 countries.)

Epstein, I (1988) 'Special education provision in the People's Republic of China', *Comparative Education*, 24, 3.

Fujimoto, M (1984) 'Special education in Japan: present state and problems', Tokyo: unpublished manuscript.

Gallaudet College (1980) *International Directory of Services for the Deaf*, Danville: Interstate Press.

Gartner, A, Lipsky, D and Turnbull, A (1989) 'Supports for families with a disabled child: collected papers from an international cross-cultural conference', New York: City University of New York. (Describes family support systems in Australia, Canada, Israel, Japan, Kenya, Sweden, the United States, the United Kingdom and Uruguay.)

Helander, E (1989) 'Global statistics of disability', Geneva: WHO, unpublished manuscript.

Helander, E, Mendis, P, Nelson, G and Goerdt, A (1989) *Training in the Community for People with Disabilities*, Geneva: WHO.

Howlowinsky, I Z (1980) 'Special education in Eastern Europe', in Mann, L and Sabatino, D (eds) *The First Review of Special Education*, Philadelphia, PA: JSE Press:

International League of Societies for Persons with Mental Handicap (1989) *International Directory of Mental Retardation Resources*, Dybwad, R (ed.) Washington, DC: US Department of Education, President's Committee on Mental Retardation.

International League of Societies for Persons with Mental Handicap (1979) *International Directory of Mental Retardation Resources*, Dybwad, R (ed.) OHDS, 79-21019, Washington DC: US Department of Health, Education and Welfare, President's Committee on Mental Retardation.

International Portage Association *Newsletter* (free) c/o Sean Cameron, University College, Psychology Dept, London.

Japan Portage Association (1989) *Proceedings* Tokyo: International Portage Conference, July 1988. (Articles from 12 countries mostly in Asia which have initiated Portage programmes).

Japan League for the Mentally Retarded (1989) *Rehabilitation Services for People with Mental Retardation in Japan*, Tokyo: JLMR. (Very comprehensive survey of prevalence and services.)

Juul, K (1980) 'Special education in Europe', in Mann, L and Sabatino, D (eds) *The Fourth Review of Special Education*, Philadelphia PA: JSE Press.

Marfo, K, Walker, S and Charles, B (eds) (1986) *Childhood Disabilities in Developing Countries*, New York: Praeger. (Detection, early intervention, curriculum and attitudes.)

Mathis, S (ed) (1980) *International Directory of Services for the Deaf*, Washington, DC: Gallaudet College.

Mba, P O (1978) 'Special education in Nigeria', in Fink, A (ed.) *International Perspectives on Future Special Education*, Reston VA: CEC.

Miles, C (1990) *Special Education for Mentally Handicapped Pupils*, Peshawar: Mental Health Centre.

Miles, M (1982) 'Why Asia rejects Western disability advice', *International Rehabilitation Review*, New York: Rehabilitation International.

Mittler, P (1988) 'Special education in Britain', paper presented to Japanese Teachers' Association, Tokyo.

Mittler, P (1990) 'United Nations Decade of Disabled Persons (1983–1992) Towards 2000 – from awareness to action', background paper for UN Expert Group Meeting on Alternative Ways to End the Decade: UN ECOSOC.

Mittler, P and Serpell, R (1985) 'Services: an international perspective', in Clarke, A, Clarke, A D B and Berg, J (eds) *Mental Deficiency: the changing outlook*, 4th edn, London: Methuen.

Nobel, J (1981) *Special Education in the Twenty-First Century*, a reader in special education, University of Manchester (mimeo).

Organization for Economic Cooperation and Development (OECD) (1981; 1983) *Education of the Handicapped Adolescent: 1 Integration in School 2 Transition to Work*, Paris: OECD.

O'Toole, B (1991) *Guide to Community-Based Rehabilitation Services*, Guides for Special Education No 8, Paris: UNESCO.

Philippines Ministry of Education (1987) *Policies and Guidelines for Special Education in the Philippines*, Manila: Ministry of Education, Culture and Sports. (Comprehensive policy.)

Putnam, R (1979) 'Special education: some cross-national comparisons', *Comparative Education*, **15**, 1, 83–97.

Rehabilitation International (1988) *Proceedings – 16th World Congress of Rehabilitation International*, Tokyo: Japanese Society for the Rehabilitation of the Disabled. (Compendium of papers presented to the Congress on the full array of special needs provisions, with 93 nations represented. See also the RI World Congress proceedings from 1984, Lisbon and 1980, Winnipeg.

Rehabilitation International (1981) *The Economics of Disability: international perspectives*, New York: Rehabilitation International. (Reviews cost-benefit analyses of rehabilitation services in 40 nations.)

Rehabilitation International (1981) *International Statements on Disability Policy*, New York: Rehabilitation International. (Contains UN documents about disability from 1971 to 1981.)

Ross, D H (1988) *Educating Handicapped Young People in Eastern and Southern Africa*, Paris: UNESCO.

Scheerenberger, R C (1983) *A History of Mental Retardation*, Baltimore: Paul Brookes. (Reviews the historical development of social thought and practices relating to people with mental retardation in Western Europe and the United States.)

Serpell, R (1982) 'Mobilizing local resources in Africa for persons with learning difficulties or mental handicap', report on ILSPMH Workshop, Nairobi: NFPU.

Sterner, R (1976) *Social and Economic Conditions of the Mentally Retarded in Selected Countries*, Brussels: ILSMH. (Review of the status of provisions in 58 countries – 36 developed and 12 developing nations – with a thoughtful analysis of the situation.)

Taylor, R W and Taylor, I (1970) *Services for the Handicapped in India*, New York: International Society for Rehabilitation of the Disabled.

Taylor, W and Taylor IW (1960) *Special Education of Physically Handicapped Children in Western Europe*, New York: International Society for the Welfare of Cripples. (Chronicles the development of services for physically and sensorily impaired pupils in 20 European nations as well as surveying general disability services development.)

Thompson, R (1982) *Policies and Programmes for Disabled People in the Commonwealth* London: Commonwealth Secretariat. (Reports on general disability services delivery systems and IYDP contributions within 25 Commonwealth nations.)

Thorburn, M and Marfo, K (1990) *Practical Approaches To Childhood Disability in Developing Countries: insights from experience and research*, Kent: Project SEREDEC; Kingston, Jamaica: 3 D Project. (An excellent reader covering topics concerning CBR related to young children.)

UN (1983) *World Programme of Action Concerning Disabled Persons*, Vienna: United Nations Centre for Social Development and Humanitarian Affairs. (Overview of world situation and terminology for the decade.)

UN (1985) *Disabled Persons Bulletin*, Vienna: Centre for Social Development and Humanitarian Affairs. (Describes the fund for the Decade of Disabled Persons.)

UN (1986) *Disability: situation, strategies and policies*, New York: UN.

UN (1986) *Manual on the Equalization of Opportunities for Disabled Persons*, New York: UN.

UNESCO (1960) *Statistics on Special Education: statistical reports and studies*, Paris: UNESCO.

UNESCO (1969) *International Directories of Education: special education*, Paris: UNESCO.

UNESCO (1970) *Study of the Present Situation of Special Education*, Paris: UNESCO.

UNESCO (1973) *The Present Situation and Trends of Research in the Field of Special Education*, Paris: UNESCO. (Studies regarding all education for disabled students in Scandinavia, USSR, USA and Uruguay.)

UNESCO (1974) *Case Studies in Special Education*, Paris: UNESCO. (Case studies in Cuba, Japan, Kenya and Sweden plus an excellent presentation on stages theories on special education development.)

UNESCO (1977) *Integration of Technical and Vocational Education into Special Education*, Paris: UNESCO. (Good introduction to rationale for vocational education by Labregere followed by case studies from Austria, Colombia, Iran and Tunisia.)

UNESCO (1978) *Economic Aspects of Special Education*, Paris: UNESCO. (Case studies in Czechoslovakia, New Zealand and the USA, focusing on cost and benefits of special education.)

UNESCO (1979–1980) *Handicapped Children: early detection, intervention and education*, Paris: UNESCO.

UNESCO (1981) *Sub-regional Report from the Seminar on Planning for Special Education*, Nairobi: July.

UNESCO (1981) *Final Report, World Conference on Actions and Strategies for Education Prevention and Integration*, (Torremolinos, Spain) Paris: UNESCO.

UNESCO (1981) *Legal Study on the Protection of the Rights Afforded under Various International Instruments*, Paris: UNESCO.

UNESCO (1981) *Report on Sub-regional Training Seminar for Teachers of the Visually Handicapped Children in Eastern and Southern Africa*, Nairobi/Paris: UNESCO. (Survey of services for visually handicapped persons in 13 Eastern and Southern African nations.)

UNESCO (1982) 'Sub-regional Training Seminar on the Education of Hearing Handicapped Children', Lusaka, Zambia: UNESCO.

UNESCO (1982) 'Sub-regional Training Seminar on the Education of Mentally Retarded Children', Harare, Zimbabwe: UNESCO.

UNESCO (1982–1986) 'Eastern and Southern Africa Sub-regional Bulletin on Special Education', Nairobi: UNESCO (Articles on all areas of special education for the sub-region.)

UNESCO (1983) *Terminology of Special Education*, Paris: UNESCO. (Gives a detailed definition for each disability category and translations of the technical terminology in four languages, including Russian.)

UNESCO (1985) 'Regional Workshop on Teacher Training and Integration of Handicapped Pupils into Ordinary Schools', Paris: UNESCO. (Review of teacher training practices toward integration in Egypt, Jordan, Colombia, Mexico, Venezuela, Botswana, Senegal, Zambia, Australia, Thailand, Czechoslovakia, Italy, Norway and Portugal.)

UNESCO (1986) *Directory of Special Education*, Paris: UNESCO. (Contains statistical information and national addresses on the provisions to special needs individuals in 136 nations up to 1985.)

UNESCO (1986) *Special Education in Africa: research abstracts*, Nairobi: UNESCO. (Reviews research and research-related publications concerning Africa on the following areas: diagnosis, social environment, assessment, intervention, training and provision.)

UNESCO (1988) *UNESCO Consultation on Special Education*, final report of the May 2–6 meeting, Paris: UNESCO.

UNESCO (1988) *Review of the Present Situation of Special Education*, Paris: UNESCO. (Important information from 58 nations: 15 African; 15 European; eight Arabian and six Asian countries. Categories of information include special education: policy, legislation; disability categories (labelling); administration; provision; parental involvement; integration; personnel training; finance; research and future priorities.)

UNESCO (1988) *A Case Study of Special Education in Sri Lanka*, Paris: UNESCO.

UNESCO (1988) *A Case Study of Special Education in Ghana*, Paris: UNESCO.

UNESCO (1988) *A Case Study of Special Education in Yugoslavia*, Paris: UNESCO.

UNESCO (1988) *A Case Study of Special Education in Ireland*, Paris: UNESCO.

UNESCO (1988) *A Case Study of Special Education in Norway*, Paris: UNESCO.

UNESCO (1988) *A Case Study of Special Education in New Zealand*, Paris: UNESCO.

UNESCO (1988) *A Case Study of Special Education in Philippines*, Paris: UNESCO.

UNESCO (1988) *A Case Study of Special Education in Japan*, Paris: UNESCO.

UNESCO (1989) *Educational Opportunities for Adult Disabled Persons*, Paris: UNESCO. (Review of current thought and examples from Germany, USA, Denmark, France and others.)

UNICEF (1979) *Childhood Disability: its prevention and rehabilitation*, New York: UNICEF/Rehabilitation International.

UNICEF (1981) *Assignment Children: the disabled child*, New York: UNICEF. (Articles on economics, policies, trends, innovative approaches, deaf education, pre-school education, personnel, training, etc, throughout selected, mostly African, nations.)

Werner, D (1988) *Disabled Village Children*, Palo Alto, CA: Hesperian Foundation. (Excellent guide to practical application of rehabilitation techniques in the field.)

Werner, D and Bower, B (1982) *Helping Health Workers Learn*, Palo Alto CA: Hesperian Foundation.

Williams, P (1991) *The Special Education Handbook*, Milton Keynes: Open University Press.

Wolfensberger, W (1972) *Normalization*, Toronto: NIMH.

World Health Organization (1985) *Mental Retardation: meeting the challenge, Offset. Series No 86*, Geneva: WHO.

World Health Organization (1988) *International Reference List of Resource and Research Centres in the Field of Mental Retardation*, Geneva: WHO. (Directory of who's who and what's where.)

World Health Organization (1989) *Training Disabled People in the Community*, Geneva: WHO. (Practical manual for field-based workers.)

Selected journals with country reports

The following national reports have been gleaned from scanning some of the current international journals related to special education rehabilitation. The listing is by no means exhaustive.

British Journal of Special Education (published by National Association for Special Educational Needs). Editor, M Peter.

Aubrey, C and Sutton, A (September, 1986) research supplement, 'Handwriting: one measure of orthofunction in conductive education', **13**, 3, 110–14.

Merry, R (June, 1991) 'Curriculum lessons From Europe', **18**, 2, 71–4.

CBR News (the international newsletter on community based rehabilitation and the concerns of disabled people, AHRTAG – Appropriate Health Resources and Technologies Action Group Ltd).

Country references covered in issues 1–11 (1988–92) include: Angola, Benin, Cameroon, Ethiopia, Guyana, India, Jamaica, Kenya, Lesotho, Malawi, Malaysia, Mexico, Nepal, Nicaragua, Pakistan, Philippines, Rwanda, Solomon Islands, South Africa, Southern Africa, Sri Lanka, Sudan, Swaziland, Tanzania, Thailand, West Bank and Gaza Strip, Zanzibar and Zimbabwe.

Disability, Handicap and Society (editor Len Barton, published by Carfax Publishing Co.).

Jongbloed, L and Crichton, A (1990) 'Difficulties in shifting from individualistic to socio-political policy regarding disability in Canada, **5**, 1, 25–36.
Mittler, P (1990) 'Prospects for disabled children and their families: an international perspective', **5**, 1, 53–64.

European Journal of Special Needs Education (editor Seamus Hegarty, published by NFER-Nelson).

Alston, J (March, 1989) 'Short report – special education in Hungary: patterns of professional development programmes for physically handicapped children and new directions of professional concern and research', **4**, 1, 55–8.
Bowman, I (October, 1986) 'Teacher training and the integration of handicapped pupils: some findings from a fourteen nation UNESCO study', **1**, 1, 29–38.
Cook, J M M (October, 1989) 'Rethinking the work and training of special education teachers', Colorado, USA, viewed from a Scottish perspective, **4** 3, 203–10.
Crawford, N B (October, 1990) 'Integration in Hong Kong: rhetoric to reality in the field of mental handicap', **5**, 3, 199–210.
Daniels, H and Hogg, B (June, 1992) 'Report on the "European Exchange of Experiences in School Integration": the intercultural comparison of the quality of life of children and youth with handicaps in Aarhus (Denmark), Arezzo (Italy) Greenwich (London – UK) and Reutlingen (Germany)', **7**, 2, 104–16.
Den Boer, K (June, 1990) 'Special education in The Netherlands', **5**, 2, 136–50.
Detraux, J J and Dens, A (March, 1992) *A country briefing: special education in Belgium*, **7**, 1, 63–79.
Dwyer, E and Swann, W (March, 1987) 'Educational services for mentally handicapped children in Northern Ireland: a survey of provision, **2**, 1, 25–44.
Florian, L and West, J (October, 1990) 'Beyond access: special education in America', **6**, 2, 124–32.
Gow, L (March, 1988) 'Integration in Australia', **3**, 1, 1–12.
Hansen, J (March, 1992) 'The development of the Danish Folkeskole. Towards a school for all', **7**, 1, 38–46.
Hegarty, S (June, 1991) 'Toward an agenda for research in special education', **6**, 2, 87–99.
Helgeland, I (June, 1992) 'Country briefing: special education in Norway', **7**, 2, 169–83.
Maki, O M (October, 1989) 'Hearing impaired children in primary schools in Finland', a survey on hearing impaired pupils in primary schools in Finland in 1982–3, to provide an information base for the development of hearing services and teaching in Primary schools, **4**, 3, 199–202.
Marchesi, A, Echelta, G, Martin, E, Bavio, M and Galan, M (October, 1991) 'Assessment of the integration project in Spain', **6**, 3, 185–200.
McGee, P (March, 1990) 'Special education in Ireland', **5**, 1, 48–64.
Mittler, P (March, 1992) 'Preparing all initial teacher training students to teach children with special educational needs: a case study from England', **7**, 1, 1–10.
Pijl, S J and Meijer, C J W (June, 1991) 'Does integration count for much?, an analysis of the practices of integration in eight countries'. The article focuses on eight Western countries: Italy, Denmark, Sweden, United States, Germany, England, Belgium and The Netherlands, **6**, 2, 100–111.
Rodbard, G (October, 1990) 'Going Dutch!', a perspective on the Dutch system of special education, **5**, 3, 221–30.
Schindele, R A (October, 1986) 'Special educational support for visually handicapped students in regular schools: an analysis of its development and present state in the Federal Republic of Germany', **1**, 1, 39–56.
Walton, W T (June, 1990) 'Normalization and integration of handicapped students into the regular education system: contrasts between Sweden and the United States of America', **5**, 2, 111–25.

Exceptional Children (Council for Exceptional Children).

Seo, G, Oakland, T, Han, H and Hu, S, 'Special education in Korea', **58**, 3, 213–18.

International Journal of Disability, Development and Education (University of Queensland Press. Special theme – an international view of special education).

Ballard, K (1990) Special education in New Zealand: disability, politics and empowerment, **34**, 2, 109–24.
Becker, K and Grosse, K (1990) Educational rehabilitation in the German Democratic Republic, **37**, 2, 99–108.
Befring, E (1990) 'Special education in Norway', **37**, 2, 125–36.
Hrnjica, S (1990) 'Special education in Yugoslavia', **37**, 2, 169–78.
Miles, M (1990) 'Special education in Pakistan', **37**, 2, 159–68.
Quah, M M (1990) 'Special education in Singapore', **37**, 2, 137–48.
Sassi, M J and Moberg, S J (1990) 'Special education in Finland', **37**, 2, 91–8.
Skuy, M and Partington, H (1990) 'Special education in South Africa', **37**, 2, 149–57.

International Journal of Rehabilitation Research (editor P Cornes, published by Chapman and Hall).

Angermann, B and Deschler, H (1991) 'Results of statutory rehabilitation measures in Germany', **14**, 3, 195–202.
Bowe, F G (1990) 'Review – disabled and elderly people in the First, Second and Third Worlds', **13** 1, 1–14.
Dossa, (1992) 'Ethnography as narrative discourse: community integration of people with developmental disabilities', **15**, 1, 1–14.
Thorburn, M, Dewsai, P and Paul, T (1992) 'Service needs of children with disabilities in Jamaica', **15**, 1, 15–29.

International League of Societies for Persons with Mental Handicap (ILSMH)

The ILSMH or 'The League', based in Brussels, produces topical publications for an international readership. The range of topics include: prevention, personnel training, education, profound mental handicap, media and mental handicap (think positive), living conditions, starting societies, work opportunities, parent involvement and information about the league.

Journal of Practical Approaches to Developmental Handicap (editor R Brown, Vocational and Rehabilitation Research Institute and Rehabilitation Studies Programme, University of Calgary).

Brouillette, R and Brouillette, J (1992) 'A model for rural inservice education for specialist teachers in developing nations', **16**, 1/2.
Thorburn, M (1992) 'Training community workers in a simplified approach to early detection, assessment and intervention', **16**, 1/2.

Special Children (Questions Publishing Co. Birmingham, England).

Kelly, C (October, 1988) 'Defending choice in Norway', an investigation on special education provision in Norway, **24**, 8–9.
Kelly, C (April, 1988) 'The Polish Road', a report on three institutions providing special education provision in Poland, **20**, 10–12.
Lambert, M (January, 1987) 'An achievement unmatched in the West', special report on deaf/blind in the USSR, **7**, 8–11.
Madden, P (June, 1987) 'Crossing the bridge to work', designing work-orientated curricula for handicapped children in America, **12** 6–7.
Madden, P (April, 1989) 'What Katy did', the use of parental power in educating children with special needs in America, 29, 10–11.
Steven, G (October, 1986) 'Preparing for work with new technology', a report on technical developments in America for getting the handicapped into work, **4**, 16–17.
Suddaby, A (February, 1987) 'A temporary phenomenon', a special report on mainstreaming children in Russia who have 'temporary' delay, **8**, 22–3.
Sutton, A (December, 1986) 'The Soviet experience', special report on special education in the Soviet Union, **6**, 18–21.
Sutton, A and Sharron, H (March, 1987) 'Two great educators', exploring the work of Dr Maria Hari from Hungary and Professor Reuven Feuerstein from Israel, **9**, 12–13.

Sutton, A (April, 1990) 'Back in the USSR', a report on special education in the Soviet Union, **38**, 10.
Wenman, S (April, 1988) 'Lessons from America', the pros and cons of integration, **20**, 15.

The View Finder: Expanding Boundaries and Perspectives In Special Education (R J Michael and K D Juul, DISES – Division of International Special Education and Services of The Council For Exceptional Children. Articles cover special education topics in Iran, Nigeria, Russia, Norway and in general).

Ali Afrooz, G (1992) 'Development of special education in the Islamic Republic of Iran', **1**, 29–32.
Armfield, A (1992) 'Special education in China', **1**, 33–6.
Elliott, B J (1992) 'Special education and "Pokazukha" in the (former) USSR', **1**, 45–9.
Jonietz, P L (1992) 'International advocacy to develop international school special education opportunities', **1**, 25–8.
Jonsson, T (1992) 'Special education training in developing countries', **1**, 8–10.
Novy, F A, De Souza Pan, M A G and Jose Arns, F (1992) 'Special education in Brazil: service delivery in profile', **1**, 41–4.
Obiakor, F E and Maltby, G P (1992) 'Cultural and socio-economic factors that affect section 8 of the national policy on education in Nigeria', **1**, 37–40.
Saleh, L (1992) 'UNESCO and special education', **1**, 4–7.
Soli, K (1992) 'Special education and teacher training in Norway', **1**, 20–24.

Index